Prest and Coppock's

The UK Economy

A Manual of Applied Economics

Thirteenth Edition

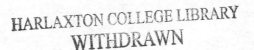
Edited by

M.J.Artis, B.A., F.B.A.
Professor of Economics, University of Manchester

Weidenfeld and Nicolson
London

© 1992 by M.J.Artis, M.C.Kennedy, R.L.Harrington, C.J.Green, M.C.Sawyer, G.Johnes, J.Taylor

First published 1966
Second impression 1967
Third impression 1968
Second edition 1968
Second impression 1969
Third edition 1970
Second impression 1971
Fourth edition 1972
Fifth edition 1974
Sixth edition 1976
Seventh edition 1978
Eighth edition 1980
Ninth edition 1982
Tenth edition 1984
Eleventh edition 1986
Reprinted 1987, 1988
Twelfth edition 1989
Thirteenth edition 1992

First published in Great Britain by
George Weidenfeld and Nicolson Limited
Orion House, 5 Upper St Martin's Lane, London WC2H 9EA

ISBN 0 297 82135 0 paperback

Printed in Great Britain at The Bath Press, Avon

Contents

1 THE ECONOMY AS A WHOLE
M. C. Kennedy

2   MONEY AND FINANCE: PUBLIC EXPENDITURE AND TAXATION
R. L. Harrington

5   LABOUR
Geraint Johnes and Jim Taylor

TABLES

Tables in the Statistical Appendix

FIGURES

ABBREVIATIONS

(1) Economic Terms

BOF	Balance for Official Financing
CAP	Common Agricultural Policy
CCFF	Compensatory and Contingency Financing Facility
CET	Common External Tariff
c.i.f.	Cost including Insurance and Freight
CPI	Consumer Price Index
EAP	Enlarged Access Policy
ECU	European Currency Unit
EER	Effective Exchange Rate
EFF	Extended Fund Facility
f.o.b.	Free on Board
GDP	Gross Domestic Product
GNP	Gross National Product
IPD	Interest Profits and Dividends
MCA	Monetary Compensation Amounts
MLH	Minimum List Headings
MTFS	Medium Term Financial Strategy
nie	Not included elsewhere
PAYE	Pay as you Earn
PDI	Personal Disposable Income
PPP	Purchasing Power Parity
PRT	Petroleum Revenue Tax
PSBR	Public Sector Borrowing Requirement
PSDR	Public Sector Debt Repayment
R&D	Research and Development
REX	Real Exchange Rate
RPM	Resale Price Maintenance
SDRs	Special Drawing Rights
SIC	Standard Industrial Classification
SITC	Standard Industrial Trade Classification
TFE	Total Final Expenditure at Market Prices
VAT	Value Added Tax

(2) Organizations, etc.

CBI	Confederation of British Industry
CSO	Central Statistical Office (UK)
DE	Department of Employment
DTI	Department of Trade and Industry
EC	European Community
EEC	European Economic Community
EFTA	European Free Trade Area
EMCF	European Monetary Co-operation Fund
EMS	European Monetary System
EMU	European Monetary Union

FAO   Food and Agriculture Organization
GATT   General Agreement on Tariffs and Trade
IMF   International Monetary Fund
MC   Monopolies and Mergers Commission
NEB   National Enterprise Board
NEDC(O)   National Economic Development Council (Office)
NIESR   National Institute of Economic and Social Research
OECD   Organization for Economic Cooperation and Development
OPEC   Organization of Petroleum Exporting Countries
OSA   Overseas Sterling Area
SEA   Single European Act
SEM   Single European Market
TUC   Trades Union Congress
UN   United Nations
UNCTAD   United Nations Commission for Trade and Development

(3) Journals, etc.

AAS   *Annual Abstract of Statistics* (HMSO)
AER   *American Economic Review*
BB   *National Accounts (Blue Book)* (HMSO)
BEQB   *Bank of England Quarterly Bulletin*
BJIR   *British Journal of Industrial Relations*
BOUIES   *Bulletin of the Oxford University Institute of Economics & Statistics*
CJE   *Cambridge Journal of Economics*
CSO   *Central Statistical Office*
EC   *Economica*
EG   *Department of Employment Gazette* (HMSO)
EJ   *Economic Journal*
ET   *Economic Trends*
ET(AS)   *Economic Trends* (Annual Supplement) (HMSO)
FD   *Finance and Development*
FES   *Family Expenditure Survey* (HMSO)
FRBSLR   *Federal Reserve Bank of St Louis Review*
FS   *Financial Statistics* (HMSO)
FSt   *Fiscal Studies*
FSBR   *Financial Statement and Budget Report* (HMSO)
GES   *Government Economic Service*
GHS   *General Household Survey*
HMSO   *Her Majesty's Stationery Office*
IFS   *International Financial Statistics*
IMFSP   *International Monetary Fund Staff Papers*
IRAE   *International Review of Applied Economics*
JET   *Journal of Economic Theory*
JIE   *Journal of Industrial Economics*
JPE   *Journal of Political Economy*
JRSS   *Journal of Royal Statistical Society*
LBR   *Lloyds Bank Review*
MBR   *Midland Bank Review*
MDS   *Monthly Digest of Statistics* (HMSO)

MS	*The Manchester School of Economic and Social Studies*
NIER	*National Institute Economic Review*
NWBQR	*National Westminster Bank Quarterly Review*
OEP	*Oxford Economic Papers*
OREP	*Oxford Review of Economic Policy*
QJE	*Quarterly Journal of Economics*
RBSR	*Royal Bank of Scotland Review*
REST	*Review of Economics and Statistics*
SJPE	*Scottish Journal of Political Economy*
ST	*Social Trends* (HMSO)
TBR	*Three Banks Review*
TI	*Trade and Industry* (HMSO)

Foreword to the Thirteenth Edition

This is the thirteenth edition of Prest and Coppock's *The UK Economy*. The objective of its present editor and authors has been to adhere as closely as possible to the approach the original editors set for the book, which has proved to be a durable and highly successful formula.

In the Foreword to the first edition that approach was set out as follows:

> The central idea behind this book is to give an account of the main features and problems of the UK economy today. The hope is that it will fulfil two functions simultaneously, in that it will be as up to date as possible and yet will not be simply a bare catalogue of facts and figures. There are many sources of information, official and otherwise, about the structure and progress of the UK economy. There are also many authors to whom one can turn for subtle analyses of the problems before us. Our effort here is based on the belief that there is both room and need for an attempt to combine the functions of chronicler and analyst in the confines of a single book.
>
> The contributors to these pages subscribe rather firmly to the belief that economists should practise, as well as preach, the principles of the division of labour. The complexity of a modern economy is such that, whether one likes it or not, it is no longer possible for any individual to be authoritative on all its aspects; so it is inevitable that the burden of producing work of this kind should be spread among a number of people, each a specialist in his or her particular field. Such a division carries with it obvious dangers of overlap and inconsistency. It is hoped that some of the worst pitfalls of this kind have been avoided and there is reasonable unity of purpose, treatment and layout. At the same time, it is wholly undesirable to impose a monolithic structure and it is just as apparent to the authors that there are differences in outlook and emphasis among them as it will be to the reader.
>
> The general intention was to base exposition on the assumption that the reader would have some elementary knowledge of economics – say a student in the latter part of a typical first-year course in economics in a British university. At the same time, it is hoped that most of the text will be intelligible to those without this degree of expertise. We may not have succeeded in this; if not, we shall try to do better in the future.

Chapter 1, 'The Economy as a Whole', is concerned with questions of applied macroeconomics: fluctuations in output and expenditure and the determinants and management of demand. Chapter 2, 'Money and Finance:

Public Expenditure and Taxation', begins with a description of the inter-relationship between fiscal and monetary policy and the background to each, which is provided on the one hand by the institutions of the financial system and on the other by the structure of the government's accounts. It describes the activities of the institutions making up the financial markets and the way in which the Bank of England influences and supervises them, emphasizing the global nature and international dimensions of financial activity. The discussion of the government's accounts covers all the main heads of expenditure and revenue and describes the many recent changes that have taken place. Chapter 3, 'The Balance of Payments', deals with the importance of foreign trade and payments to the UK economy and discusses the behaviour of, and policy towards, the exchange rate, including the implications of adherence to the exchange rate mechanism of the European Monetary System. It then looks at current problems and polices in this field, and ends with a discussion of recent developments in the field of inter-national economic policy co-ordination and of the world debt problem. Chapter 4, 'Industry', summarizes recent UK industrial performance and discusses competition and mergers policy, privatization, R&D and tech-nology policy and the performance of the nationalized industries. The clash of theoretical paradigms governing the approach of economists to these questions is made very clear. The last chapter, 'Labour', analyses employ-ment and unemployment among the UK workforce in considerable detail and then discusses problems of pay and income distribution. Each chapter is accompanied by a list of references and further reading. The Statistical Appendix includes tables dealing with different aspects of the UK economy. There is an index, as well as the detailed list of headings and sub-headings given in the Contents pages.

Certain themes, inevitably, crop up in more than one chapter. Much the most pervasive of these is Europe. Since the last edition of this book was prepared three years ago, the influence of the EC (and related institutions) over economic policy and events in Britain has tangibly increased. First and foremost, perhaps, the UK decided in October 1990 to participate fully in the operation of the European Monetary System. This decision has import-ant implications for the conduct of monetary and macroeconomic policy more generally, which are treated in Chapter 1 and Chapter 3. The ramifi-cations of the UK's decision to participate in the creation of the Single European Market (SEM) are scarcely less significant. Competition policy and the regulation of banks are particularly concerned, and these issues are discussed in Chapters 2 and 4. Regional policy issues have been highlighted by the perception that the SEM will unleash competitive forces which may result in large-scale restructuring; these issues are discussed in Chapter 5.

Finally, in the Maastricht Treaty, the countries of the European Com-munity set out conditions under which Community countries can move towards European Monetary Union (EMU). These 'entrance conditions' imply restrictions on monetary and fiscal policy in the transition to EMU (see the discussion in Chapter 3), whilst of course success in making the transition to the final stage of complete monetary union would by definition imply the total surrender of national monetary sovereignty. Included in the Maastricht Treaty was a 'Social Chapter', designed to set out some common features of legislation affecting labour markets; although the UK distanced itself from this aspect of the Treaty, the Social Chapter is nevertheless important for British labour market policies, as pointed out in Chapter 5. If the momentum towards the 'European solution' witnessed in the last three years is sustained over the next three, the fourteenth edition of this book will be produced on the very threshold of full economic and monetary union.

Acknowledgements

It is pleasant to acknowledge the great help given to this enterprise by those who have rendered secretarial assistance; in addition, acknowledgement is due to Nick Weaver who prepared the Figures for Chapters 1–4 and the index.

University of Manchester   M. J. ARTIS
May 1992

1

The economy as a whole

M.C.Kennedy

1 INTRODUCTION

1.1 Methodological Approach

This chapter is an introduction to applied macroeconomics. It begins with a brief description of the national income accounts, and goes on to discuss growth and fluctuations, aggregate demand, inflation and macroeconomic policy. It does not pretend to give all the answers to the questions raised, but aims to provide the reader with a basis for further and deeper study.

In principle there is no essential difference between applied economics and economic theory. The object of applied economics is to explain the way in which economic units work. It is just as much concerned with questions of causation (such as what determines total consumption or the level of prices) as the theory which is found in elementary textbooks. The difference between theoretical and applied economics is largely one of emphasis, with theory tending to stress logical connections between assumptions and conclusions, and applied economics the connections between theories and evidence. Applied economics does not seek description for its own sake, but it needs facts for the light they shed on the applicability of theory.

It is sometimes maintained that scientific theories are derived from factual information by a method of inference known as induction.[1] The supposition is that general laws about nature can be deduced from the knowledge of a limited number of facts. From a logical point of view, however, induction is invalid. If ten people are observed to save one-tenth of their income, it does not follow that the next person will do likewise. The conclusion may be true or false, but it cannot be said to rest validly on the assumptions. Inductive propositions of this kind simply have the status of conjectures and require further empirical investigation.

It is now recognized that scientific method is *hypothetico-deductive*. A hypothesis is proposed to explain a certain class of events. It will generally be

---

[1] For an introduction to the problems of scientific method the reader is referred to P.B.Medawar, *Induction and Intuition in Scientific Thought* (Methuen, 1969) and K.R.Popper, *The Logic of Scientific Discovery* (Hutchinson, 1959) and *Conjectures and Refutations* (Routledge and Kegan Paul, 1963). For a treatment of methodological problems in economics see M.Blaug, *The Methodology of Economics* (Cambridge University Press, 1980), B.J.Caldwell, *Beyond Positivism* (Allen and Unwin, 1982) and 'Clarifying Popper', *Journal of Economic Literature*, March 1991.

of the conditional form 'if *p* then *q*', from which the inference is that any particular instance of *p* must be accompanied by an instance of *q*. Thus the hypothesis is tested by all observations of *p*; corroborated when *p* and *q* are observed together; and falsified if *p* occurs in the absence of *q*.

It will be clear that this concept of scientific inference places the role of factual information in a different light from the inductive approach. Facts, instead of being the foundation on which to build economic or scientific theories, become the the basis for testing them. If a theory is able to survive a determined, yet unsuccessful attempt to refute it by factual evidence, it is regarded as well tested. But the discovery of evidence which is inconsistent with the theory will stimulate its modification or the development of a new theory altogether. One of the purposes of studying applied economics is to acquaint the theoretically equipped economist with the strengths and limitations of the theory he has studied. Applied economics is not an attempt to bolster up existing theory or, as its name implies, to demonstrate dogmatically that all the factual evidence is a neat application of textbook theory. Its aim is to understand the workings of the economy, and this means that it will sometimes expose the shortcomings of existing theory and go on to suggest improvements.

The discovery that a theory is falsified by factual observation need not mean that it must be rejected out of hand or relegated to total oblivion. Economists, as well as natural scientists, frequently have to work with theories that are inadequate in one way or another. Theories that explain part but not all the evidence may be retained until some new theory is found which fits a wider range of evidence. Frequently the theory will turn out to have been incomplete rather than just wrong, and when modified by the addition of some new variable (or a more careful specification of the *ceteris paribus* clause), the theory may regain its status. The reader who sees inconsistencies between theory and the facts need not take the line that the theory is total nonsense, for it may still hold enough grains of truth to become the basis of something better.

It is often argued that our ability to test economic theories by reference to evidence is sufficient to liberate economics from value judgements, i.e. to turn it into a *positive* subject. This position has more than an element of truth in it: when there is clear evidence against a theory it stands a fair chance of being dropped even by its most bigoted adherents. Nevertheless, it would be wrong to forget that a great deal of what passes for evidence in economics is infirm in character (e.g. the statistics of gross domestic product and personal saving), so that it is often possible for the 'facts' to be seen more sceptically by some than by others.

The discussion of economic policy which also figures in this chapter is partly normative in scope, and partly positive. The normative content involves the evaluation of goals and priorities. But the means for attaining such goals derive from the positive hypotheses of economics. They involve questions of cause and effect, to which the answers are hypothetical and testable by evidence. The combination of normative objectives and positive hypotheses leads to recommendations for policy. But in making such recommendations the economist treads on thin ice. This is partly because his positive knowledge is not inevitably correct, but also because it is seldom possible to foresee and properly appraise all the side-effects, some of which have implications for other policy goals. When economists differ in their advice on policy questions it is not always clear how much the difference is due to diagnostic disagreement, and how much to value judgements.

It is seldom possible for an economic adviser to reveal all the normative preferences which lie behind his or her policy recommendations. Policy judgements have to be scrutinized carefully for hidden normative assumptions, and the reader of this chapter should be on his guard against the author's personal value judgements.

1.2   Gross Domestic Product

Most of the topics in this chapter make some use of the national accounts statistics. A complete explanation of what these are and of how they are put together is available elsewhere.[1] It will be useful, however, in the next few pages to introduce the reader to the main national accounting categories in so far as they affect this chapter.

Gross domestic product (GDP) represents the output of the whole economy, i.e. the production of all enterprises resident in the UK. In principle, it can be assembled from three separate sets of data – from output, from income and from expenditure. The three totals should, in principle, be equal – a point which may seem surprising when it is recalled that spending and output are seldom equal for an individual firm. But the convention in national accounting is to include all unsold output in the change in stocks, and to regard this both as expenditure and as income (profits) in kind. Thus the three estimates are made equal to each other by the device of defining expenditure and income differently from their every-day meanings.

The two principal estimates of current-price GDP – the expenditure and income-based estimates – are shown in Table 1.1. The expenditure-based method classifies expenditure by four types of spending unit: persons, public authorities, firms, and foreign residents.[2] Purchases by persons are described as consumers' expenditure, but this excludes the purchase of new houses which are deemed to have been sold initially to 'firms'. Fixed investment represents purchases by firms of physical assets which add to or

---

[1]   See, for example, the introduction in CSO, *United Kingdom National Accounts* (*the CSO Blue Book*), *1991 Edition* (HMSO) and the CSO handbook, *United Kingdom National Accounts: Sources and Methods* (3rd edition, HMSO, 1985).
[2]   The distinctions between types of spending units are not always clear-cut, e.g. expenditure by self-employed persons is partly consumers' expenditure and partly investment.

TABLE 1.1
GDP at Current Prices, UK, 1990[1]

FROM EXPENDITURE

	£bn	% of TFE
Consumers' expenditure	349.4	50
General government final consumption	109.5	16
Gross domestic fixed investment	105.2	15
Change in stocks	−0.7	0
Exports of goods and services	134.1	19
Total final expenditure at market prices (TFE)	697.5	100
less Imports of goods and services	−147.6	
less Adjustment for factor cost	−72.9	
Gross domestic product at factor cost (from expenditure)	477.1	
Statistical discrepancy	0.6	
Gross domestic product at factor cost (average estimate)	477.7	

FROM INCOME

	£bn	% of domestic income
Income from employment	316.4	65
Income from self-employment	57.7	11
Income from rent	38.4	8
Gross trading profits of companies	62.9	13
Gross trading surpluses of public corporations & other public enterprises	4.3	1
Imputed charge for consumption of non-trading capital	4.3	1
Total domestic income	484.0	100
less Stock appreciation	−6.4	
Gross domestic product at factor cost (from income)	477.6	
Statistical discrepancy	0.1	
Gross domestic product at factor cost (average estimate)	477.7	

BY INDUSTRY (FROM INCOME)

	£bn	% of total
Agriculture, forestry and fishing	7.1	1
Energy and water supply	24.3	5
Construction	36.1	7
Manufacturing	107.0	21
Distribution, hotels and catering, repairs	70.2	14
Banking, finance, insurance, business services and leasing	87.3	17
Education and health	45.1	9
Other services	127.2	25
Total (after providing for stock appreciation)	504.3	100
Adjustment for financial services[2]	−26.7	
Gross domestic product at factor cost (from income)	477.6	

Source: BB, 1991, tables 1.2, 1.3, and 2.1.1
1 Details may not add to totals because of rounding.
2 Deduction of net receipts of interest by financial companies.

replace the nation's capital stock. The preface 'gross' warns us that a year's gross investment does not measure the change in the size of the capital stock during the year because it fails to allow for the erosion due to scrapping and wear and tear. The concept of gross capital formation is also carried through into the definition of domestic product itself, indicating that the value of *gross* domestic product makes no allowance for capital consumption. The other category of investment is the change in stocks, or, as the CSO puts it, the value of the physical increase in stocks. This makes no distinction between voluntary and involuntary stock changes.

The sum of exports, consumers' expenditure, government final consumption and gross investment is known as total final expenditure at market prices (TFE). This total, and the expenditures which comprise it, contains two elements which must be deducted before arriving at GDP at factor cost. The first is the import content, which is foreign, not domestically produced, output. The simplest way of removing imports is to take the global import total as given by the balance-of-payments accounts and to subtract it from TFE, and this is the usual method. Estimates do exist, however, for the import content of the separate components of final expenditure in the input-output tables – although these are drawn up much less frequently than the national accounts.

The second element of total final expenditure which must be deducted to obtain the factor cost value of GDP is the indirect-tax content (net of subsidies) of the various expenditures. This is present because the most readily available valuation of any commodity is the price at which it sells in the market. This valuation will overstate factor incomes earned from producing the commodity by the amount of indirect tax; it will understate factor income if the price is subsidized. The deduction of indirect taxes (net of subsidies) is known as the *factor cost adjustment*, and is most conveniently made globally since it can be found from the government's records of tax proceeds and subsidy payments. Annual estimates of its incidence on the individual components of TFE can be derived from the National Income *Blue Book*.[1]

The income-based estimate arrives at GDP by summing up the incomes of all residents of the UK earned in the production of goods and services in the UK during a stated period. It divides into income from employment, income from self-employment and profit, and income from rent. These are factor incomes earned in the process of production and are to be distinguished from *transfer incomes*, such as pensions and sickness benefits, which are not earned from production and which, therefore, are excluded from the total. The breakdown of factor incomes for 1990 is illustrated in Table 1.1.

The income breakdown of GDP contains two items which may need further explanation. The first is the imputed charge for consumption of

---

[1]   *BB, 1991*, Table 1.2.

non-trading capital. This represents the capital consumption of the non-trading activities of certain public and private non-profit-making bodies. It is added to the incomes which they generate so that they can be valued on the same basis – gross of depreciation – as the profit incomes of all other companies. A state school or hospital, for example, will generate employment income but no profits, but if gross income is to be recorded on the same gross-of-depreciation basis as in the trading sector, then a charge for capital depreciation must be added to its (zero) profits.

The other item, the adjustment for stock appreciation, is made in order to adjust changes in the book value of stocks for price increases which have occurred within the period for which output is being measured. The problem arises because the intention is to measure output, and it is only the *physical* rise in stocks which can be counted as production. The method is to find out how much of the book-value change in stocks is a volume change, and then to value this at the average price of the stocks during the period. Thus if the volume rises from, say, 100 units to 200 units between 1 January and 31 December, and the price from £1 to £1.10 per unit, the book value will be shown as a rise of £120: (£1.10 × 200) – (£1 × 100). With an average price during the year of, say, £1.05 per unit, the 'value of the physical increase in stocks' is put at £105, and the adjustment for stock appreciation is £15.

GDP by income can be rearranged in terms of the industries in which the incomes are earned. This breakdown is available annually and gives an up-to-date picture of the industrial composition of total output, showing, for example, that manufacturing output is now barely one-fifth of the value of GDP. The industry breakdown is shown in Table 1.1.

The expenditure and income estimates are derived from different and largely independent data. They never add up to exactly the same total, and the difference between them is known as the *residual error*.

An output-based estimate of GDP may, in principle, be compiled by adding up the *net output* or *value added* of all the firms and productive units in the economy. To obtain such a total it would be necessary to find the *gross output* of each firm in the economy and to subtract from it the value of *intermediate input*, i.e. goods and services purchased from other firms. In practice this very large task cannot be accomplished in the time-span of a single year. But the CSO has enough data on gross output to estimate changes in value added in real terms (i.e. at constant prices). The value of GDP by output is found directly by applying the deflator for expenditure-based GDP to the volume estimate – see section 1.3 below.

There are now four estimates for GDP in current prices: the expenditure, income, output and average estimates. The difference between the expenditure and income estimates is the residual error (and was 0.1% of GDP in 1990), and the differences between these two estimates and the average estimate are termed the 'statistical discrepancies'.

Gross domestic product is the most widely used of several national income aggregates, the others being GNP and National Income. The relationships between the various totals in 1990 were:

		£bn (current prices)
	GNP at market prices	554.6
less	Net property income from abroad	−4.0
equals	GDP at market prices	550.6
less	Factor cost adjustment	−72.9
equals	GDP at factor cost (from expenditure)	477.7
plus	Net property income from abroad	+4.1
equals	GNP at factor cost	481.8
less	Capital consumption	−61.2
equals	Net national product at factor cost ('national income')	420.6

GNP, like GDP, may be valued at market prices or factor cost. It differs from GDP by including net interest, profits and dividends earned by UK residents from productive enterprises owned overseas. The other concept, Net National Product, differs from GDP by the amount of capital consumption, this being the CSO's estimate of depreciation. It is also the figure which must be subtracted from gross investment to find net investment. GDP and the gross concept of investment are in much more frequent use than net product and net investment because they relate directly to employment. When a machine is being produced, it makes no difference to the number of workers employed whether it is to replace one already in use or whether it adds to the capital stock.

1.3   Gross Domestic Product at Constant Prices

One of the principal uses of the GDP accounts is to estimate changes between periods in output or expenditure in terms of *volume*. Such comparisons involve the use of the estimates of GDP at constant prices (see Statistical Appendix, Table A-1). These constant-price or real estimates show the value of GDP for each year in terms of the prices ruling in 1985. Similar estimates are available for the output-based total, together with its main industrial components. The components of both these GDP estimates are derived almost entirely from movements in volume, the various quantities for each year being added together by means of the value weights obtaining for 1985. With the income figures, however, the only way of obtaining a constant-price estimate is to take the value of GDP by income and deflate it by the implied price index (or 'deflator') for GDP. This index is simply the result of dividing GDP at current prices by GDP at constant prices (both on the expenditure basis). This means that for GDP as a whole three independent estimates of the constant-price total are published.

There are often sizeable discrepancies between the estimates. In 1990, for example, GDP in constant prices was put by the output estimate at 116.4% of the 1985 level, whereas the income and expenditure estimates were both 116.1. Since 1980 the largest spread between the three measures was 1.1% of GDP (in 1981) and the average difference was 0.5%. These discrepancies in the level of GDP also mean that changes between years are not known unambiguously. The decline in GDP from 1979 to 1981, for example, was put at 2.6% by the expenditure-based estimate, but at 4.2% by the output estimate. An inspection of annual changes in GDP since 1980 shows that, on average, the spread between the highest and lowest estimates of the change was 0.6% ; in 1983–4 the spread was 1.5%.

Gross domestic product is an important entity in its own right and changes in its real amount are the best estimates available of changes in total UK production. Even so, it must be remembered that it leaves a good deal out of the picture by excluding practically all productive work which is not sold for money. The national income statistics neglect activities like housework and 'do-it-yourself' as well as the so-called 'black economy', even though they must add millions of hours to UK production of goods and services.[1] It is also important to recognize that GDP stands for the production of UK residents, not for their expenditure. As an expenditure total it measures the spending of all persons, resident or foreign, on the goods and services produced by the residents of the UK. Thus if national welfare is conceived as spending by UK residents, it is incorrect to represent it by GDP. The total appropriate for this purpose is GDP *plus* imports *minus* exports. This total is referred to as total domestic expenditure, or 'absorption', and is equal to the UK's total use of resources. It is the sum of personal consumption, government consumption and gross investment.

2   ECONOMIC GROWTH AND FLUCTUATIONS

2.1   The Growth of the Economy

In 1937 the level of GDP at factor cost was £110 billion (at 1985 prices) ; by 1987 it had approximately trebled in size, to reach £332 billion – an average growth rate of 2.2% per annum. The population of the UK had grown from 47 million to 57 million, so that domestic output per head was about $2\frac{1}{2}$ times as high in 1987 as it had been 50 years earlier.

The growth of GDP over long periods of time must be contrasted with short-lived bursts of expansion due mainly to cyclical increases in the use of existing resources. Between 1972 and 1973, for example, real GDP 'grew' by over 7% in a single year. But this was only achieved by means of a sharp rise in employment which could not have been sustained for any length of time. Even the less dramatic rise in GDP between 1984 and 1989, when the average growth rate was 3.7% per annum, was achieved mainly through the reduction of excess capacity and a growing shortage of the required types of labour.

It is usual, therefore, to reserve the term 'economic growth' for long-term increases in the economy's ability to produce, or its *productive potential*. This, at any one time, depends on the quantity and quality of the economy's

---

[1] On 11 April 1989, the House of Commons gave a first reading to a private member's bill demanding the inclusion of unpaid work by women in the estimates of GDP.

TABLE 1.2

Economic Growth, UK, 1900–89 (percentage increase per annum)

	GDP (average estimate)	GDP per person employed	Employed labour force	Capital stock (excluding dwellings)
1900–13	1.5	0.6	0.9	1.7
1922–38	2.3	1.2	1.1	1.7
1950–60	2.7	2.2	0.4	2.8
1960–69	3.1	2.5	0.3	4.3
1969–78	2.2	1.8	0.1	3.6
1978–89	2.2	2.2	0.0	2.2

Sources: 1950–89: *BB*, 1991 and earlier; 1900–38: C. H. Feinstein, *National Income, Expenditure and Output, 1855–1965* (Cambridge University Press, 1972).

factors of production, and the skills with which they are combined. The traditional measure of productive potential is the level of output in a year when the economy is 'fully employed'. This could be when unemployment or job vacancies are at some standard rate. Unemployment, it is argued, represents the availability of unused resources, whilst the number of vacancies indicates the difficulty of obtaining labour. But over the last twenty years the numbers unemployed have been rising relative to vacancies – see section 4.3 below – whilst at the same time the economy has become increasingly inflationary at any given rate of unemployment. It seems preferable, therefore, to measure productive potential with reference to vacancies rather than to unemployment, and this is done in Table 1.2, where the standard vacancy rate for measuring the growth of potential is taken to be 0.77 or 0.78 – the rates which prevailed in the years 1969, 1979 and 1989. The table indicates that the growth of potential GDP fell between the 1960s and 1970s, and in the 1980s, when it was 2.2% per annum, was about the same as in the seventies. Growth in the 1970s was favourably affected by the development of North Sea oil, without which the decline from the 1960s would have been larger than the table indicates. Equally, if North Sea oil was excluded, the growth rate would be higher in the 1980s than in the 1970s, although still not as high as in the 1960s.[1]

The long-term rate of economic growth depends upon increases in the quantity and quality of the two main factors of production – labour and capital – and on the efficiency with which they are combined. Increases in the supply of labour come mainly from increases in the population of working age, including net migration, changes in the participation rate and in hours worked. The quality of labour depends upon the facilities available for education and training, and the degree to which they match changes in demand and technology. The mobility of labour from job to job and from area to area is a further factor.

---

[1] C. Feinstein and R. Matthews, 'The Growth of Output and Productivity in the UK: the 1980s as a Phase of the Post-war Period', *NIER*, August 1990. These authors estimate growth of GDP for 1973–9 to be 0.5 per cent less per annum if North Sea oil is removed from the figures.

A crucial influence on the growth of labour productivity is the rate of increase in the economy's stock of capital, both in quantity and in quality. Some indications of its growth are given in Table 1.2, where it can be seen that its rate of increase fell off in the 1970s and 1980s. It should be noted, however, that the capital stock is difficult to measure – partly because the figures for depreciation in the national accounts are based on data collected for tax purposes, and also because the type of capital equipment used changes as the result of technical innovation.

The quality of the capital stock depends partly on its age structure. Scientific and technical progress are embodied in the newest machines, so that the most recent equipment is likely to be most efficient. It is possible to see the capital stock as a series of vintages of gross investment, each vintage containing machines of higher quality than the previous one. Gross investment is, of course, affected by interest rates, so that countries, such as the UK, which tend to have higher rates of interest than elsewhere, are unlikely to invest as effectively in new technology as their competitors, and their growth rates will be lower.

The other influences on the rate of economic growth are the competitive climate, the facilities available for scientific and technological advance, and the propensity to save.[1]

2.2   Fluctuations Around the Growth Path

The long-term growth of the economy has been interrupted by periodic booms and cyclical collapses. During the nineteenth century these appeared to follow a uniform cycle, with a peak-to-peak duration of seven to ten years, and with a tendency for 'full employment' (roughly defined) to return at each cyclical peak. After the First World War this pattern ceased, and for nearly twenty years there were well over one million unemployed. Unemployment reached nearly 10% of the labour force in the downturn of 1926 and 17% (3.4 million) in 1932.

The period from the Second World War until the early 1970s was one of continuously high employment, with only the mildest fluctuations in GDP, employment and unemployment. The unemployment rate never exceeded an annual figure of 2.4% and, during peak periods of activity, was as low as 1 or $1\frac{1}{2}$% of the workforce. GDP never fell for more than a year at a time, and never by more than 1.0%. In most recessions GDP simply rose at a slower-than-average rate of increase.

Since 1970, business recessions have become much more severe than they were in the 1950s and sixties. The rapid boom of 1973 – when the vacancy rate was at a record level – was followed by a sharp downturn in GDP in

---

[1]   For a discussion of UK growth in comparison with that of other countries, see C.H. Feinstein, 'Economic Growth since 1870: Britain's Performance in International Perspective', *OREP*, Vol. 4, No. 1 (1988).

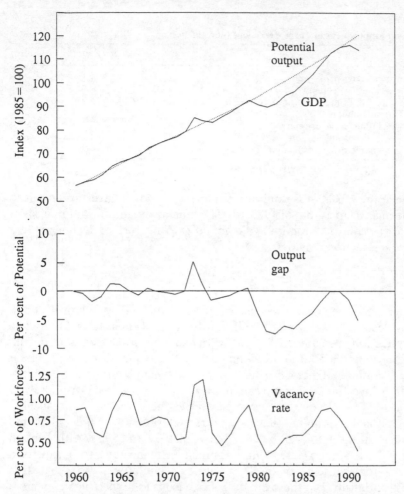

Figure 1.1   Actual and Potential Output, the Output Gap and the Vacancy Rate, UK, 1960–91
(*Sources: ET(AS)*, 1991; *ET*, October 1991; *FSBR*, 1992)

1973–5, and unemployment went on rising for two more years. It reached 4.4% of the workforce in 1977 and 1978, and in 1979, when the vacancy rate was at its peak, was still 4.1%.

The recession of 1979–81 was the sharpest since the 1930s, with GDP falling by 3.1% (average estimate) in two years. Unemployment went up to 8.0% in 1981, after which it continued to rise, despite rising output, for five years – reaching 11.2% (3.3 million) in 1986. During the next few years it fell, reaching 5.8% in 1990. By then, however, the economy was in recession again.

In the late 1980s the peak pressure of demand – as indicated by the vacancy rate – was in 1988. GDP, after rising at 3 or 4% per annum since 1985, rose much more slowly in 1989 and 1990, and fell in 1991 by an estimated 2.4%. Although this was said to be the largest decline in a single

TABLE 1.3

Output and Employment in Three Recessions (percentages)

	1973–5	1979–81	1990–91
Unemployment rate: peak year	2.1	4.1	5.8
trough year	3.0	8.0	8.0
highest year after trough	4.4 (1978)	11.2 (1986)	
Change in employment	0.0	−5.5	0.0
Change in GDP: average estimate	−2.3	−3.1	−2.4
output estimate	−3.4	−4.2	
Change in manufacturing production	−8.1	−14.2	−5.2

Sources: ET(AS), 1991; *BB*, 1991; *FSBR*, 1991; *ET, EG* (various issues).

year since the 1930s, it is doubtful if the recession will have turned out to have been as deep as that of 1979–81. The official and unofficial forecasts at the time of writing (March 1992) did not point to any further decline in GDP in 1992 (see section 6 below).

2.3 Expenditures in the Cycle

Business recessions occur because of declines in total spending. Capital-intensive economies devote a significant fraction of their annual output to the production of capital goods. The demand for such goods (fixed investment) is not a continuing demand like the demand for food, but is inherently satiable. Once a firm has equipped its plant with all the machinery it needs its investment demand can, in principle, fall to zero. Fortunately, it has not yet been known for aggregate investment to fall so drastically, although it is worth noting that in the Great Depression of the 1930s fixed investment in the USA fell by 70% between 1929 and 1933, with a fall in GNP of about 30%. Declines in investment demand tend to be reversed after a while because of the discovery of new technologies and a revival of business optimism. But there are no good reasons for expecting investment demand to remain stable.

Another source of instability in the modern economy is the change in stocks. When spending increases, stocks are initially run down. Producers then tend to restore stock levels to their 'normal' or desired relationship to sales, with the result that there is an essentially temporary increase in production for stocks – followed by a return to normal levels of output. The recorded change in stocks shows an initial fall (which is involuntary) followed by a rise (voluntary) and then no change.

The contribution of fixed investment and the change in stocks to the three most recent recessions in the UK can be seen from Table 1.4. Both in 1979–81 and 1990–91 fixed investment was the major component of the fall in GDP. The change in stocks fell most dramatically in 1973–5, when its absolute fall was three times as large as that of GDP, and in 1979–81 the change in stocks fell by about nine-tenths of the fall in GDP.

Recessions abroad or losses of competitiveness can lead to declines in exports, and these can also be a cause of cyclical decline in the home

TABLE 1.4

Expenditures in Three Recessions (£bn at 1985 prices)

	Level in 1973	Change 1973–5	Level in 1979	Change 1979–81	Level in 1990	Change 1990–1
Consumers' expenditure	180.8	−3.3	195.7	0.3	272.8	−4.6
Government expenditure	62.4	4.7	69.9	+1.3	79.6	1.9
Fixed investment	55.8	−2.4	56.5	−8.2	79.9	−8.1
Investment in stocks	6.6	−10.0	3.3	−6.5	−0.4	−2.4
Exports of goods and services	69.2	3.0	88.9	−0.6	123.8	1.1
TFE	376.0	−9.2	414.8	−14.8	555.7	−12.4
GDP (expenditure)	261.3	−3.3	284.5	−7.5	356.9	−8.5

Sources: ET(AS), 1991; *FSBR*, 1992.

economy. Thus the UK depression of 1929–32 was almost entirely due to a fall in exports. But, as Table 1.4 makes clear, exports were rising in 1973–5 and 1990–1, and although they fell in 1979–81, the fall was quite small.

Consumers' expenditure is more stable than fixed investment. It fell slightly in 1973–5, but rose in the recessions of 1979–81 and 1990–1.

Periods of recovery have not always been led by a revival of fixed investment. In 1975–9, the main stimuli came from exports and stockbuilding, and the same pattern was repeated between 1981 and 1983, with fixed investment not recovering until 1984. Real GDP regained its 1979 level in 1983, but the level of the workforce in employment did not recover until 1987. Unemployment continued to rise for five years after the output trough, and, although it was falling in 1989, was still very much higher than it had been ten years earlier.

3   DEMAND AND THE MULTIPLIER

The proximity of national output to its full-employment potential is determined by the level of total expenditure on goods and services, which, in the simplest terms, can be divided into two main categories: the 'autonomous' items, which are not affected by the current level of national income, and the 'dependent' items, which are related to current or to lagged income. In elementary accounts, the former category is represented as investment, and is said to be determined by business expectations of the rate of return, the rate of interest, and by the stock of unexploited technological potential. Consumption, on the other hand, is dependent on income itself, so that the line of causation runs from investment to income to consumption, with investment acting as the primary generator of movements in total output.

When this model is extended to the 'real world', it is necessary to add exports and government expenditure to the autonomous elements of demand, and to allow for imports and the factor cost adjustment as dependent items; the change in stocks is partly autonomous and partly dependent.

3.1   Consumers' Expenditure

Consumers' expenditure is the largest single item in aggregate demand. It accounts for one half of TFE (see Table 1.1) and, after the removal of its import and indirect-tax content, for about the same fraction of GDP at factor cost. Consumption is one of the more stable elements of demand. It fell only slightly in the recessions of 1973–5 and 1990–1, and held up well in 1979–81. Its total amount, however, is so large in relation to GDP that small percentage changes in its level can have important effects on output and employment. An understanding of consumption behaviour, therefore, and an ability to predict it, are important objectives for economic analysis.

The starting point for the early studies of consumer behaviour was the well-known statement by Keynes:[1] 'The fundamental law upon which we are entitled to depend with great confidence both *a priori* from our knowledge of human nature and from the detailed facts of experience, is that men are disposed, as a rule and on the average, to increase their consumption as their income increases, but not by as much as the increase in their income.' Keynes was suggesting that current income was the principal, although not the only, determinant of consumers' expenditure in the short run.

Keynes' statement can be taken to mean that the *marginal propensity to consume* (the ratio of additional consumption to additional income) is positive, fractional and reasonably stable over time. In point of fact the marginal propensity to consume (MPC) has not been as stable or as reliable as might have been hoped. The simplest way of estimating the MPC is to divide annual changes in consumption at constant prices by the corresponding changes in personal disposable income: but when this is done, the resulting MPC will be found to vary considerably from year to year, besides being negative in those years when income falls and consumption goes on rising. An alternative method is to take two- or three-year moving averages, and when this is done for the period since 1950 it shows the 3-year MPC as varying between 0.6 in 1974–7 and 1.5 in 1980–3. Even when the changes are taken for periods of as much as 10 years at a time, there is still an appreciable degree of variability:

	Change in consumption	Change in disposable income	Observed MPC
	(£m 1938 prices, £bn 1985 prices)		
1922–30	568	758	0.75
1930–38	570	647	0.88
1950–60	26.7	34.5	0.71
1960–70	33.3	39.1	0.85
1970–80	39.3	53.4	0.74
1980–90	77.5	75.5	1.03

Source: Feinstein, op. cit.; *ET(AS)*, 1991; *ET*, October 1991.

---

[1]   J.M.Keynes, *General Theory*, p. 96.

As these figures show, the observed MPC has varied quite considerably between decades; and in the 1980s the MPC was more than 1.0, which is contrary to expectations and all previous experience.

A shortcoming of this method for measuring the MPC is that it puts all the emphasis on the levels of consumption and income at the beginning and end of each period, whilst ignoring the years in between. A more formal method, which gets over this problem, is that of least squares regression analysis, in which an equation is fitted of the form:

$$C = a + bY$$

where a is an intercept and b is the estimated slope term or MPC. The line is fitted to a set of observations on a scatter diagram such that it minimizes the squared deviations between itself and the scatter points.[1] If this method is applied to the data for 1950–89, the estimated equation is:

$$C = £6.75bn + 0.877Y$$

where C is consumption and Y personal disposable income in 1985 prices.

Figure 1.2 shows the scatter of points from which the equation is estimated. The regression line may appear to fit reasonably well, but 7 of the 40 residuals (the deviations from the line) turn out to be more than 3% of consumption, which again confirms the impression of instability.[2] This view is reinforced, moreover, if regression equations are fitted to the four separate decades within the period:

1950–9	$C =$	$£10.5 + 0.86Y$
1960–9	$C =$	$£4.5 + 0.89Y$
1970–9	$C =$	$£29.0 + 0.75Y$
1980–9	$C =$	$-£62.2 + 1.16Y$

The estimated MPCs vary between decades, and the relationships estimated are also poor predictors outside the periods for which they are fitted. The equation for the 1970s, for example, can be shown to overpredict consumption in the 1950s by 9% and to underpredict the 1980s by about the same amount.

The conclusion must be that the MPC, however measured, is an elusive ratio. Even before the 1980s the MPC was highly variable from year to year and over decades, and the rise in the 1980s to a figure of more than one leaves much to be explained. It seems clear, therefore, that although income may be the predominant influence on consumer spending, other factors are also at work. These could be the ability to borrow, interest rates, inflation, expected future income, and personal wealth and indebtedness.

An important insight into both the MPC and APC (average propensity to consume) is provided by the *life-cycle hypothesis* which emphasizes expected

[1] For a non-technical account of the method of linear regression see R.G.Lipsey, *An Introduction to Positive Economics* (Weidenfeld and Nicolson, 7th edition, 1989, pp. 35–41).
[2] The value of r-squared is 0.992, standard error £4.1bn and the t-ratio on b is 70.5.

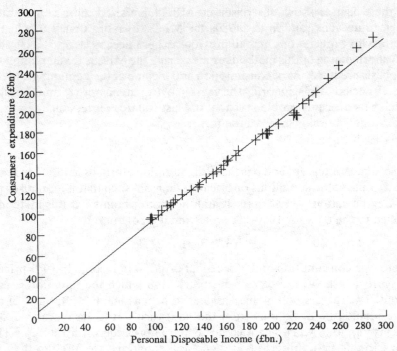

Figure 1.2   Consumption and Personal Disposable Income, UK, 1950–89
(*Source: ET(AS)*, 1991)

future income rather than current income as a determinant of consumer spending and saving. The central assumption of the life-cycle hypothesis is that the main motive for saving is the provision for old age. If the consumer expects to work for, say, 45 years, and to live for a further 15 years in retirement, then, assuming the same level of consumption in retirement as in work, he or she will be obliged to save 15/60ths of his income and to consume 45/60ths. In this way he will accumulate a stock of assets to pay for consumption during retirement. On this principle, consumers save whilst they are working and dissave in retirement. If all consumers behave in this way, and if the age distribution of the population is stable, the average propensity to consume for the economy as a whole will be 1.0 (or a bit less if consumers plan to leave bequests or if, perhaps, they save additional amounts as a precaution against living longer than expected). Advocates of the hypothesis can claim that the observed APC is not far from its expected value.

The hypothesis also implies that the MPC, at least for a representative rise in income, is likely to be less than the APC. An individual of representative age, say 40, will expect to live for 40 more years and to go on working for 25 years. If he receives an increase in income which is expected to be permanent – in the sense of lasting until retirement – then on the assumption that the additional consumption is to be spread evenly over his lifetime, the MPC will be given as 25/40, or 0.6. This would also be the MPC for the economy as a whole on the assumption that a rise in income is spread evenly across the age-groups. The important conclusion is that the MPC will be less than the APC, which (apart from the 1980s) is what the evidence seems to show.[1]

Turning to the APC itself, it is reasonable to expect that it will tend to decline as income rises. As real incomes rise over time, more people are in a position to save for their old age – thus putting the life-cycle hypothesis into effect – and to leave bequests to their children. Indeed this tendency for the APC to fall with income is an implication of all equations of the form $C = a + bY$ in which the intercept is positive and the slope less than unity. The evidence from long-term time series tends to support the view that the APC falls as income rises, although, as the following figures show, the decline has been quite gentle:

	APC (%)	Savings rate (%)	Durables spending (% of disposable income)
1920–9	98.5	1.5	
1930–9	95.2	4.8	
1950–9	96.0	4.0	6.9
1960–9	91.5	8.5	7.4
1970–9	89.9	10.1	8.6
1980–9	90.8	9.2	8.9

Source: Feinstein, op. cit.; *ET(AS)*, 1991.

This table also shows the savings rate (the average propensity to save expressed as a percentage of income) and expenditure on consumer durables. Spending on durables, which has also increased with the rise in income, can be regarded as a form of saving – since a new car or washing machine yields a flow of utility (or income in kind) over years to come. But the figures do not show a sharp rise in such spending in the 1980s, as might have been expected from the fall in the savings rate.

Year-to-year movements in the savings rate, which are shown in Figure 1.3, used to be correlated with the cycle, high savings rates appearing when the economy was at its cyclical peak, and when unemployment was high and vacancies low. This behaviour, which was evident in the 1950s and sixties, could be interpreted as support for the life-cycle hypothesis, which, as we have seen, stresses the dependence of saving and consumption on expected income, rather than on current income. The argument is that when the economy is at the peak of the cycle actual income will be above normal income, and the saving rate will, therefore, tend to be high relative to income: when the economy is in recession saving will, on this theory, be low. This pattern, however, is not visible in the data for the 1970s and eighties and there is now a negative correlation with vacancies. Indeed, it is now being suggested that in times of high and prolonged unemployment, such as we

---

[1] The classic reference is F. Modigliani and R. Brumberg, 'Utility Analysis and the Consumption Function' in K. Kurihara (ed.), *Post-Keynesian Economics* (Allen and Unwin, 1955).

have had since 1980, the fear of unemployment may tend to increase saving and reduce consumption.

During the 1970s the savings rate and the rate of inflation peaked together, and there has been a close correlation ever since.[1] The correlation was seen as causal, and the inference drawn was that inflation had eroded the purchasing power of liquid assets, with the consequence that people attempted to replenish their wealth by saving more. But the increased savings rate may also have arisen from the inclusion in personal income of the profits of unincorporated businesses. These profits are included gross of stock appreciation, which naturally tends to be high in periods of inflation. The effect is to raise personal-sector income without any effect on consumption, and although this may be a consequence of inflation, it is not a wealth effect of the kind envisaged.

An alternative explanation of the high savings rate in the 1970s may lie in the high level of nominal interest rates – which are also correlated with the savings rate. The causation may have gone from inflation to interest rates to saving, rather than directly from inflation. The interest rate is not only a pecuniary incentive to save, but high mortgage rates exert a critical squeeze on spendable incomes in much the same way as higher taxes. The reduced consumption of mortgage holders is unlikely to be offset by higher spending by lenders, since their MPCs are likely to be low.

Extensions of credit are partly cause and partly consequence of consumer buying, so that it is difficult to interpret the inverse correlation with the savings rate shown in Figure 1.3. But in the 1980s there was a major dismantling of the controls on lending and much aggressive selling of credit. Consumers had much more freedom to borrow than they had ever had before, and many were able to borrow on the basis of their income expectations whereas in earlier years they would have been constrained from doing so. A further factor was the windfall gain in wealth in the form of the very large rise in house prices in the mid-1980s, which consumers expected to be permanent. This gave consumers the impression that they were wealthier than they had been before and that they had, therefore, less need to save. It is probably these credit and wealth factors which were responsible for the fall in the savings rate from 13% in 1980 to 5% in 1988.[2] The fall in house prices since then may well tend to depress consumption into the 1990s.

---

[1] It should be noted that the figures for the savings ratio are prone to substantial revision: that for 1976 was put at 14.6% in 1980, but was revised in *ET(AS)* 1989 to 12.1%, and in *ET(AS)* 1991 to 10.7%.
[2] For a further discussion of the savings rate in the UK see K.A.Crystal, 'The Fall and Rise of Saving', *National Westminster Bank Review*, February 1992; J.R.Sargent, 'Deregulation, Debt and Downturn in the UK Economy', *NIER*, August 1991; and K.Cuthbertson, 'The Measurement and Behaviour of the UK Savings Ratio', *NIER*, February 1982. For more general discussions, see J.Thomas, 'The Early History of the Consumption Function' and A.Spanos, 'Early Empirical Findings on the Consumption Function, Stylized Facts or Fiction: A Retrospective View', *OEP*, January 1989, and R.L.Thomas, 'The Consumption Function', in D.Demery, N.W.Duck, M.T.Sumner, R.L.Thomas and W.N.Thompson, *Macroeconomics* (Longman, 1984).

Percentages

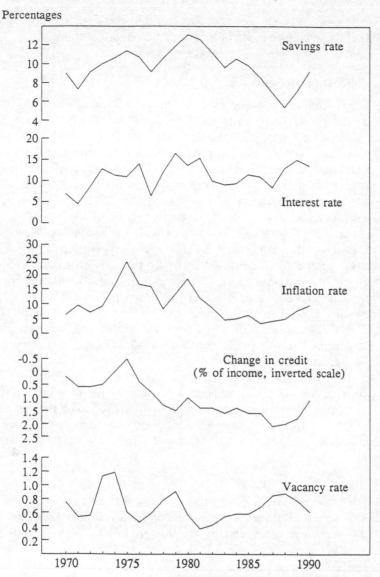

Figure 1.3 The Personal Savings Rate and Related Indicators, UK, 1970–90[1]
(*Sources: ET(AS)*, 1991; *ET*, October 1991)

To conclude: the salient influence on consumption and saving is probably current income, although expected future income and non-income factors such as the availability of credit, wealth windfalls, interest rates, and, perhaps, inflation may also have a role. It is possible that the MPC, which is

---

[1] The correlation coefficients (r) between the savings rate and the variables in Figure 1.3 are: interest rate (on Treasury bills) 0.38, inflation rate 0.58, vacancies as per cent of workforce −0.25, and change in consumer credit as per cent of disposable income 0.34.

the key variable when it comes to forecasting, would be found to be more reliable if these factors could be properly taken into account.

3.2 Fixed Investment

Fixed investment or gross domestic fixed capital formation consists of business investment in plant and machinery, and housebuilding in both the public and private sectors of the economy. Its breakdown by industry is shown in Table 1.5, where it can be seen that investment by the service industries is much larger than in manufacturing. Manufacturing investment, however, is the most volatile element in the total. In the recession of 1979–81, for example, manufacturing investment fell in real terms by 35% compared with a total decline in private fixed investment of 10%.

The explanation of investment is not without difficulties. New capital stock is purchased and old stock replaced in the expectation of profits in the future. It is not difficult to show formally that an investment project is profitable if its marginal efficiency exceeds the rate of interest, or if its present value exceeds zero. But these calculations have to be based upon *forecasts* of revenues and costs which extend for years, even decades, into the future. When so much depends upon vulnerable and uncertain guesses about the future it must be expected that investment expenditure will be less explicable than consumption.

Two of the models which are often advanced to explain investment behaviour make their own special assumptions about expected future income. The *acceleration principle* is sometimes justified on the assumption that the future growth of income will be equal to the past rate of growth, and on this basis it is suggested that investment is proportional to the change in income:

$$I = a\Delta Y$$

where I is investment, ΔY the change in income and a is a constant coefficient. A related model is the *capital stock adjustment principle*, which explains investment as an attempt to adjust the capital stock from its actual

TABLE 1.5
Gross Domestic Fixed Capital Formation, UK, 1989 (£bn)

	Private sector	Public sector	Total
Dwellings	16.2	3.8	20.1
Manufacturing	14.2	0.0	14.3
Energy and water supply	4.6	3.3	8.0
Distribution, hotels, catering repairs	9.5	0.0	9.5
Banking, finance, insurance, business services, leasing	18.4	1.1	19.5
Other	23.9	6.8	30.4
Total	86.8	15.0	101.8

Source: BB, 1991, p. 138: current prices. Detail may not add to totals because of rounding.

level to a desired level based on the expected level of output. It also assumes that there is a fixed relationship between output and the amount of capital equipment needed to produce it. The model can be expressed by the equation:

$$I = aY - K$$

where K is the actual level of the capital stock, and a is the assumed constant capital-output ratio.[1] Neither of these models says anything about costs or interest rates, and although they are right to focus on income expectations, they are still very crude. Another theory altogether is the view that investment can be predicted by the level of business profits, the idea being that firms simply spend what they can afford.

Whatever the theoretical merits of these models it is possible to assemble data that relate to them, and this is done in Figure 1.4, where the top graph is manufacturing investment in constant prices. The figure illustrates that manufacturing investment is indeed correlated with the change in income, where this is taken as the three-year change in real GDP at factor cost up to the previous year. (The three-year change in manufacturing output would have given a similarly good correlation.) Figure 1.4 also shows the relationship between investment and the level of manufacturers' real profits. What we have done here is to estimate a price deflator for profits by dividing manufacturing investment in current prices by manufacturing investment in constant (1985) prices. Profits are gross profits before adjustment for stock appreciation. A correlation also exists for the capital-output ratio, where the ratio shown on the graph is the capital stock at the end of the previous year divided by manufacturing output in that year (both at 1985 prices). Finally, the graph shows the long-term rate of interest on government securities, and for this there is a negative correlation.[2]

The question now arises as to whether we can interpret any of these correlations as causal. The high correlation with the change in income might seem to give a strong case for the acceleration principle. But the correlation may have more to do with the phasing of the business cycle than with the causation of investment. If peaks in the cycle occur every four or five years because of investment booms, then the fastest changes in GDP will occur in the two or three years between the trough and the peak of the cycle. Peaks in investment and the rate of change in GDP are bound to be correlated.

In the case of the profits hypothesis, a similar argument applies. Profits will be high when sales are high, and this will happen when autonomous

---

[1] Because K^*, the desired capital stock, is equal to aY^* where Y^* is expected income. Hence $I = K^* - K = aY^* - K$. And if Y^* is assumed to equal current income, Y, then $I = aY - K$. It is also possible to attach a coefficient to K on the assumption that investment demand in a single period is a constant fraction of $K^* - K$, i.e. $I = b(K^* - K) = abY^* - bK$. Replacement investment may also be allowed for on the assumption that it is proportional to income.

[2] The correlation coefficients (r) between investment and the variables in Figure 1.4 are: three-year change in GDP 0.91, profits 0.89, capital-output ratio -0.52, long-term interest rate -0.49.

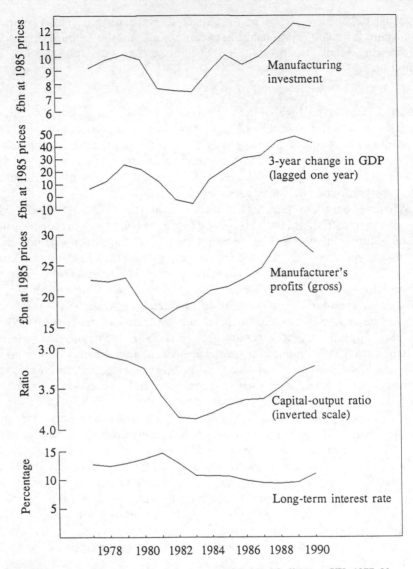

Figure 1.4   Manufacturing Investment and Related Indicators, UK, 1977–90
(*Sources: NIE*, 1991; *ETAS*, 1991)

spending is at its peak. Manufacturing investment is, of course, an important element in autonomous spending, and when it reaches a peak the level of income will tend to be high and so will profits. So we are now arguing that it is not profits which causes investment, but investment which causes a high level of sales, and hence high profits. But there *could* be causation in both directions.

The correlation with the lagged capital-output ratio is also quite good, but it could be simply a mechanical result of low investment leading to low economic activity and, therefore, to a high ratio of capital to output. The fact that we have incorporated a lag in the correlation does not completely remove this objection, since periods of low and high economic activity tend to occur for several years at a time. The hypothesis behind this correlation, the stock-adjustment principle, is open to the objection of naivety in assuming that next year's sales will be equal to this year's, and that a single year's sales are the crucial factor in buying plant and machinery designed to last for many years.

To the question of what actually caused manufacturing investment over the period shown, we can give only a tentative answer. We doubt whether the correlation with ΔY gives any real credence to the acceleration principle. We think that there is a bit of truth in both the profits and the capital-stock adjustment models, although it would not be surprising if the correlations overstated the importance of the variables. Finally, we believe on *a priori* grounds that interest rates are an influence even though there is not much correlation. The main econometric models of the UK have used both profits and interest variables to explain investment, besides making some use of the capital stock adjustment and acceleration principles. But at the end of the day it is still uncertain whether anybody has a robust and reliable model for explaining and forecasting manufacturing investment.

Housing investment needs to be divided between the public and private sectors and examined in relation to demand and supply influences in both sectors. The demand for public-sector building comes indirectly from population characteristics (family formation and size) and directly from the political and financial position of the public authorities. The demand for private-sector building depends upon population factors, the costs of mortgage credit, expected income and the prices of new houses and substitute accommodation. High interest rates also affect the supply of housing by adding to the cost of building. The building industry has claimed that a 1% rise in mortgage interest rates reduces house construction by 6–7%.[1] The problem of forecasting housing investment is eased, however, by the statistics of new houses started, which, with an assumption about completion times, makes it possible to predict housing for at least a short period ahead.

3.3   Stocks and Stockbuilding

Stockbuilding or investment in stocks is a change in a level – the level of all stocks held at the beginning of the period. In any one year, stock investment can be positive or negative, whilst the change in stock investment between successive years can exert an important influence upon GDP. The swing from stock accumulation to a stock rundown in 1973–5, for example, was

---

[1]   *Financial Times*, 2 March 1989.

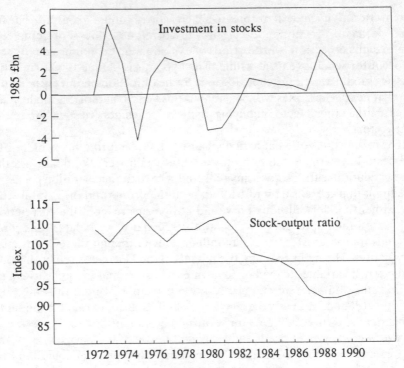

Figure 1.5   Investment in Stocks and the Stock–GDP Ratio, UK, 1972–91
(*Source: ET(AS)*, 1991)

equivalent to a fall of 5% in GDP, and the stock swing of 1979–81 to about
2½%.

At the end of 1990 the total value of stocks held in all industries was
approximately £124bn or 26% of the value of GDP in a year. Stocks held by
manufacturing industry accounted for nearly £53bn, and by wholesale and
retail business for £43bn.[1]

Stocks of work in progress are held because they are a technical necessity
of production, whilst stocks of materials and finished goods are held mainly
out of a precautionary motive. They are required as a 'buffer' between
deliveries and production; or, more precisely, because firms realize that
they cannot expect an exact correspondence between the amount of materials delivered each day and the amount taken into production, or between
completed production and deliveries to customers.

For these reasons it seems plausible to assume that firms carry in their
minds the notion of a certain optimum ratio between stocks and output.
If stocks fall below the optimum ratio, they will need to be replenished; if
they rise above it, they will be run down. The reasoning here is the same as
that of the stock-adjustment principle which we have already mentioned in

---

[1]   *BB*, 1991, Table 15.1.

connection with fixed investment. The principle holds quite well for some periods, and is illustrated in Figure 1.5. It can be seen that peaks in stock investment coincided with low levels of the stock-GDP ratio until about 1983, after which stock investment has been low despite a falling stock-output ratio.[1] This was partly due to the ending of stock relief in the budget of 1984.

The stock-adjustment principle is only the beginning of an explanation of investment in stocks. It makes no allowance for interest rates or price expectations, both of which are relevant to the preferred stock-output ratio. Nor can it account for unplanned movements in stocks, which for finished goods will occur when sales deviate from their expected levels.

3.4   Government Consumption, Exports, Imports and Indirect Taxes

Of the two remaining components of TFE, government consumption is primarily determined by the social and political priorities of the central and local authorities, and partly by macroeconomic and financial policy.

Exports of goods and services are determined by two principal sets of influence: the level of real income in overseas countries, and competitive factors such as price, quality and delivery dates. UK exports to particular countries are linked to national GNP. The influence of price is measured by the price elasticity of demand, which according to some econometric models is not too high: the range suggested by the National Institute, Bank of England and Treasury models is -0.6 to -0.8, but other estimates vary between -0.4 and -2.8.[2] The 3% drop in exports during 1980 was associated with a particularly sharp rise in the exchange rate and in UK export prices. Export trends are discussed in more detail in Chapter 3.

TFE is the sum total of exports of goods and services, government consumption, fixed investment, stockbuilding and personal consumption. These elements are normally measured at market prices and they all contain a substantial content of imported components and materials. To proceed from TFE to GDP at factor cost it is necessary, therefore, to remove the indirect-tax and import contents of the various expenditure items. The indirect-tax content (net of subsidies) is available annually for the various expenditure items, whereas the import content is known only for TFE. Estimates of the import content for individual expenditures can be obtained by input–output methods, and are shown, together with their indirect-tax contents, in Table 1.6 overleaf.

The main determinants of imports are the level of GDP and competitive factors, such as price and quality. It is probably these which have been

---

1   The correlation (r) is -0.64 for 1972–83, but almost zero for the period as a whole.
2   See S. Brooks, 'Systematic Econometric Comparisons: Exports of Manufactured Goods', *NIER*, August 1981, p. 70, and A. P. Thirlwall, *Balance of Payments Theory and the United Kingdom Experience* (London 1980), pp. 204, 210–11, 230–1, 237–8.

TABLE 1.6
Domestic Output Content of Total Final Expenditure at Market Prices, UK, 1990

	Percentages of market price totals:				
	Consumers' expenditure	*Government consumption*	*Gross domestic fixed investment*	*Exports of goods and services*	*Total final expenditure*
Indirect taxes (less subsidies)	15	6	8	5	10
Imports of goods and services	21	13	34	24	22
Domestic output content	64	81	58	71	68

Sources: BB, 1988, p. 29 and 1991, Table 1.2.

responsible for the strong upward trend (see Chapter 3) in the ratio of imports of goods and services at (constant 1985 prices) to TFE:

1950–4	14.0%
1955–9	14.7%
1960–4	15.6%
1965–9	16.6%
1970–4	18.8%
1975–9	19.2%
1980–4	20.5%
1985–9	23.2%
1990–1	24.9%

These are average relationships. The marginal import content of TFE is probably higher. Between 1984–86 and 1987–89, for example, imports rose by £85.7bn (in 1985 prices) compared with a rise in TFE of £205.5bn. This suggests a marginal propensity to import with respect to TFE of about 0.41. This, of course, is only a rough guide, and it presupposes that there were no other influences, such as price changes, at work during the period. But it is a better guide to the marginal response of imports to TFE than the average relationship.

3.5 Personal Income and the Multiplier

Any increase in GDP will normally give rise to a multiplier process. The initial rise in income leads to higher consumption, and thus to higher GDP. Successive rounds of higher income and consumption will lead to the eventual establishment of an 'equilibrium' level of GDP, this being the level which GDP finally settles at. The multiplier process is the succession of income changes, whilst the 'multiplier' itself is defined as the ratio of the total or cumulative increase in GDP to its initial or 'first round' increase.

In elementary models, the multiplier may be found quite simply because no distinctions are made between GDP and personal income, and because taxation, undistributed profits and the import content of expenditure are ignored. On these lines it can be seen that an initial increase in GDP of 100 units, combined with a marginal propensity to consume of, say, 0.5, will lead to an eventual increase in GDP of 200 units. This is because the initial rise in GDP will cause personal incomes to rise by the same amount, so that consumption will then increase (after a time-lag) by 50 units. This, in turn, raises personal incomes in the consumer-goods industries by 50 units so that consumption in the third round of the multiplier will increase by 25 units. Each increment of income leads to a rise in consumption half as large again, so that the sequence of period-to-period additions to GDP will be:

$$100, 50, 25, 12.5, 6.25, 3.125 \ldots \text{etc.}$$

It is not difficult to see that if all the terms are added together they sum to 200, which is the equilibrium rise in GDP. And since this is twice the original increase, the multiplier is 2, a value which may also be found from the formula:

$$\frac{\Delta Y}{\Delta I} = \frac{1}{1 - \text{MPC}} = \frac{1}{1 - 0.5} = 2$$

where ΔY is the final increase in GDP and ΔI the initial increase.[1]

The multiplier for the UK follows the same principles as the simple model. But its calculation is complicated by a number of factors, one of which is the distinction which must be drawn between GDP and personal income. This may be illustrated by a direct comparison for 1990:

GDP (£477.6bn)	equals	Income from employment and self-employment (£374.1bn)	plus	Rent, total profits and trading surpluses, and imputed charge for capital consumption (£109.9bn)	minus	Stock appreciation (£6.4bn)
Personal income (£493.1bn)	equals	Income from employment and self-employment (£374.1bn)	plus	Personal receipts of rent, dividends and interest (£54.4bn)	plus	Transfer incomes (£64.6bn)

Personal income and GDP are similar magnitudes, but differ in their composition. The element they have in common is employment income,

---

[1] The formula assumes that ΔI is a sustained increase in the level of investment expenditure. An unsustained or 'one shot' injection of new investment would lead only to a temporary rise in GDP.

which is included in both totals. Transfer incomes – mainly pensions and social security benefits – are included in personal income but excluded from GDP because they are not payments for production. A further difference is that the rent and profit element in personal income is only a small part of the rent and profits in GDP.

To arrive at an estimate of the multiplier for the UK, it is simplest to begin with an increase in expenditure, which when imports and indirect taxes are deducted gives rise to an increase in GDP of £100m. The coefficients in Table 1.6, for example, suggest that an increase in government expenditure of about £123m would be needed to generate a rise in GDP of £100m.

A series of assumptions must now be made as to the size of various 'withdrawals' or leakages between the first- and second-round increases in GDP. The first stage in the calculation concerns the likely increase in personal income, the size of which will depend on the way in which new GDP is divided between employment income and profits, on how much of the latter is distributed to the personal sector as dividend income, and also on how much transfer incomes decline as a result of lower unemployment and national social security benefits. It can be assumed that the increase in GDP is divided between employment income and profits in its usual ratio of about 4:1. Thus £80m will go directly into personal income in the form of income from employment and self-employment, and £20m will go to profits. Some of the rise in profits (about £7m), however, will find its way into business saving (undistributed profits) and will not generate any immediate rise in spending – at least for some time; some part will have to be paid in corporate taxes (£7m). So only about £6m finds its way into personal incomes in the form of dividends. There will also be some leakage from personal income on account of falling unemployment and unemployment benefits, and this, for a GDP rise of £100m, is likely to be of the order of £4m.[1]

Thus the total increase in personal income will be made up of £80m for employment incomes, plus £6m for dividends, but with £4m subtracted for the fall in transfer incomes – a total rise of £82 million. This is the marginal addition to personal income for a rise in GDP, and is the first in a series of coefficients needed to derive the multiplier (see Table 1.7).

The remaining stages of the calculation involve the marginal rate of direct taxation (including national insurance and pension contributions), the marginal propensity to consume, and the marginal indirect-tax and import contents of consumption. Once these are allowed for, it is possible to arrive at the second-round increase in GDP, which is the domestically produced element of the rise in consumption.

The marginal rate of taxation for standard-rate taxpayers is 25%, but national insurance contributions add a further 9% for most incomes, so that the total leakage can be put at about 33% for an across-the-board rise in

---

[1] Derived by assuming that every 1% rise in GDP leads to a 0.5% increase in employment, and from official estimates of the cost of unemployment benefit. See *Treasury Economic Progress Report*, February 1981.

TABLE 1.7

Stages in the Multiplier Estimate

	£m	Assumed marginal relationships
1st round increase in GDP	100	
Increase in personal income	82	$b_1 = 0.82$
Increase in personal disposable income	55	$b_2 = 0.67$
Increase (after a time-lag) in consumers' expenditure at market prices	50	$b_3 = 0.9$
Increase in consumers' expenditure at factor cost	41	$b_4 = 0.82$
Increase in domestically produced consumption at factor cost (equals second-round increase in GDP)	25	$b_5 = 0.61$

personal income. A good central estimate of the marginal propensity to consume is 0.9, although as we saw in section 3.1 there is no great certainty about this figure. The marginal rate of indirect tax on consumer goods and services can be taken as equal to the average rate of 0.18 – higher than in Table 1.6 to allow for the rise in VAT in 1991. Finally, the marginal import content of consumption (at market prices) has to be put well in excess of the average content. The figure is put at 0.32, although the rise in imports in relation to TFE discussed in section 3.4 may indicate that this is not high enough. There is some uncertainty about both the marginal propensity to consume and import content.

The upshot of the calculation is that the second-round increase in GDP – which is a rise in the domestic production of consumer goods – is only £25m, or 0.25 times the initial increase. It follows that the third, fourth and later increases will each be 0.25 times the previous rise, so that the sequence of period-to-period changes will be as follows:

$$£100, 25, 6.25, 1.6, 0.4, 0.1 \ldots 0 \text{ million.}$$

This series sums to a cumulative increase of £133m, so that the multiplier value is 1.33 – a figure which is also given by the expression:

$$\frac{1}{1 - 0.25} = 1.33$$

where 0.25 can be described as the marginal propensity to purchase new domestic output. It represents the five coefficients b_1, b_2, b_3, b_4 and b_5 all multiplied together.[1]

It should be noted that the multiplier is defined here as the ratio of the eventual increase in GDP to the initial increase in GDP, and not as the ratio of the GDP rise to the increase in market price expenditure. This is so as to keep the numerator and denominator both in terms of domestic output. The multiplier so defined applies much more directly to employment than the

---

[1] Thus $0.25 = \frac{82}{100} \cdot \frac{56}{82} \cdot \frac{50}{56} \cdot \frac{41}{50} \cdot \frac{25}{41} = b_1 b_2 b_3 b_4 b_5$ and the multiplier is $\frac{1}{1 - b_1 b_2 b_3 b_4 b_5}$.

ratio of the change in GDP at factor cost to a change in market price expenditure.[1]

This calculation of the multiplier is not meant to be a precise estimate, but is intended, rather, to suggest the key relationships and broad order of magnitude. Uncertainties about some of the coefficients suggest that the true multiplier could be anywhere in the range of 1.2 to 1.5. The estimate is based on the usual multiplier assumptions that there are unused resources of capital and labour, and that interest rates are held constant through a policy of monetary accommodation. There are, moreover, other effects of a rise in GDP, of which the most basic is the effect of higher sales on stocks. These will decline at the start of the process, but the decline is likely to be reversed later as production is stepped up to replenish stocks and to meet the higher level of demand.[2]

The multiplier calculation above can be used to estimate the effect on GDP of a £1bn increase in government expenditure, and the results compared with those given by large econometric models. On the reasoning given, a £1bn rise in government expenditure at market prices will involve an indirect-tax and import content of at least £0.19bn (see Table 1.6), with the consequence that the initial rise in GDP at factor cost will be £0.81bn. The multiplied effect will be this amount times 1.33, which is £1.08bn – or 0.17% of 1990 GDP at current prices. The main lag in the process is from the rise in personal incomes to consumption, and is likely to be fairly short. Thus most of the effect can be assumed to come through within six months of the initial rise in spending. Our estimates can be compared with the multiplier values embodied in various econometric models as follows:

Change in GDP, per cent, arising from a
£1bn increase in government expenditure:

	1st year	3rd year
Multiplier calculation in this chapter	0.17	0.17
Treasury model	0.21	0.25
London Business School	0.16	0.17
Bank of England	0.20	0.26
National Institute	0.31	0.24
Oxford Economic Forecasting	0.23	0.55
Liverpool model	0.44	0.23

Our estimate of the effect of a rise in government expenditure is very close to that of the London Business School, Treasury and Bank of England – although it should be remembered that these models attempt to allow for effects on stocks and fixed investment, so that the results are not entirely

---

[1] This discussion has followed an early estimate of the multiplier in W.A.Hopkin and W.A.H.Godley, 'An Analysis of Tax Changes', *NIER*, May 1965, the main difference being the estimate of the import content of consumption.
[2] In some cases there may be oscillations in GDP. On this the classic reference is L.A.Metzler, 'The Nature and Stability of Inventory Cycles', in R.A.Gordon and L.R.Klein (eds.), *Readings in Business Cycles* (Allen and Unwin, 1966).

comparable. But perhaps the main lesson of these figures is the enormous variation to be found between the main econometric models.[1]

3.6   The Effects of Tax and Interest Rate Changes

The multiplier calculation of the previous section may also be used to estimate the effects on the economy of changes in taxation. The effect of a change in income tax may be illustrated by reference to a reduction of 1p in the basic rate. This is estimated by the Treasury to reduce revenue by £2,175m.[2] Personal disposable income would be raised by an equal amount, so that the *initial*, or multiplicand, effect upon GDP can be found using the coefficients estimated in Table 1.7:

	£m
change in tax revenue	−2,175
increase in personal disposable income	+2,175
increase in consumers' expenditure at market prices	+1,977
increase in consumers' expenditure at factor cost	+1,621
initial increase in GDP	+989
multiplied increase in GDP	+1,315

The initial increase in GDP of £989m is simply the change in tax revenue multiplied by the marginal propensity to consume (b_3 in Table 1.7), along with the coefficients b_4 and b_5 which remove the indirect-tax and import contents of the increase in consumers' expenditure. The multiplied effect raises this by 1.33 to a figure which, with current-price GDP at an estimated £621bn (in 1992–3), is equivalent to a gain in total output of approximately 0.21%. This is the deviation in GDP from what it would have been in the absence of the tax reduction.

Changes in indirect taxation affect consumption by altering prices and the level of real personal disposable income. The effects of a change in VAT, for example, can be estimated approximately provided we know the effect on tax revenue. If taxes are reduced, the fall in revenue as a proportion of consumers' expenditure is equal to the proportionate change in prices. The latter leads to an increase in real personal disposable income, from which the effects on consumption and GDP may be estimated.[3] For a 1% fall in VAT, the Treasury estimates that revenue declines by £2,480 million.[4] Real personal disposable income will increase by this amount times the ratio of disposable income to consumption (i.e. the reciprocal of the APC). This leads to changes in consumption and GDP which can be found from coefficients already given for the multiplier:

---

[1]   See K.B.Church, P.R.Mitchell, D.S.Turner, K.F.Wallis and J.D.Whitley, 'Comparative Properties of Models of the UK Economy', *NIER*, August 1991.
[2]   Treasury, *Autumn Statement*, November 1991.
[3]   In terms of algebra we can denote the revenue change as ΔT, so that the change in consumer prices is $\Delta T/C$, where C is current consumption. The proportionate change in real disposable income, $\Delta Y/Y$, is equal to $-\Delta T/C$, and the absolute change, ΔY, is equal to $(-Y.\Delta T)/C$.
[4]   *Op. cit.*

	£m
change in tax revenue	– 2,480
increase in real personal disposable income	+ 2,755
increase in real consumers' expenditure at market prices	+ 2,505
increase in real consumers' expenditure at factor cost	+ 2,054
initial increase in GDP	+ 1,284
multiplied increase in GDP	+ 1,666

Here the effect of a 1% cut in VAT is equivalent to about 0.27% of GDP.

When discussing the effects of tax reduction it is important to remember that all changes in the budget balance have to be financed either by borrowing from the public or by increasing the money supply (or by some mixture of the two). These calculations must assume, therefore, that the money supply is increased in line with the demand for money, thus preventing an increase in rates of interest. If there is no monetary accommodation then fiscal expansion will lead to higher interest rates, and some expenditures – those sensitive to interest rates like investment and purchases of consumer durables – will be reduced (or 'crowded out').

The effects of *monetary policy* have in the past been the subject of a good deal of scepticism. On *a priori* grounds, however, it is difficult to see how higher interest rates can fail to have some effect on both investment demand and consumer durables, whilst higher mortgage rates involve a squeeze on consumer incomes that seems bound to reduce spending. The various econometric models give the effect of a 1% reduction in short-term rates of interest of between 0.19% of GDP (the Bank of England) to 0.41% (National Institute) in the first year of operation.[1]

3.7   Economic Forecasts

The analysis of movements in demand leads on naturally to the question of how GDP may be predicted over short periods of time. The first economic forecasts were developed by the Treasury in the late 1940s, and were used as an aid to demand management. Indications of their content were sometimes revealed in Budget speeches. They have been published since 1968, and, with the Industry Act of 1975, the Treasury has been obliged to publish them twice-yearly – in the Autumn Statement and the Financial Statement and Budget Report (FSBR). The published forecasts extend about 15 months ahead; that for March 1992, for example, goes forward to the first half of 1993.

The first problem encountered in constructing a forecast is that of establishing GDP estimates for the period extending from the last known figures to the month in which the forecast is assembled. A forecast made in February, for example, has to be made with the benefit of quarterly GDP figures which do not go beyond September of the previous year. A GDP estimate

---

[1] *NIER*, August 1991.

has to be assembled for the October–December quarter on the basis of monthly information which includes exports, imports, retail sales, industrial production and employment. Difficulties can arise because of the various gaps in coverage, and because different indicators sometimes tell conflicting stories, as, for example, when the employment and industrial production figures move in different directions.

Once the base period is established, the forecast proper (i.e. the part relating to the future) can be started. The methods by which this is done need not be described in detail. But for six months to a year ahead the task is made easier by the presence of a number of forward indicators which provide fairly direct information on the prospects for particular sectors of demand. The CBI, for example, conducts regular inquiries into whether its members intend to invest more or less in the next twelve months than in the previous period. The Department of Industry has its own inquiry, in which business is asked to estimate the percentage change in prospective investment. There are order series for engineering, machine tools and shipbuilding, which provide a forward view of production (for investment and export) in these industries. There are also figures for new orders received by contractors for private construction work, whilst in the field of housing investment figures are collected for orders received by contractors, for new houses started, and Building Society commitments and advances on new dwellings.[1] Government current expenditure and the government component of fixed investment can be predicted from information provided by government departments. Direct information, therefore, covers a fairly significant proportion of the autonomous element in total demand, and can be processed to provide forecasts for 6 to 12 months ahead. Some help towards the personal income and consumption forecasts is available from the record of recent wage settlements, whilst government forecasters will also have estimates of the pay and employment of public employees.

For longer-term forecasts, and for the more obviously endogenous components of GDP, the forecaster needs to have an integrated model, in which the relationships are either estimated econometrically or arrived at in some systematic way. The Treasury has a very large econometric model at its disposal, in which there are more than 1,000 equations. At the risk of simplification, this may be described as a highly complex and disaggregated multiplier model, with accelerator relationships for the main investment items, and with exports linked to world production and relative prices. The model includes links between wages, prices, and the exchange rate, and it also makes some use of interest rates as a determinant of investment. Imports are determined by GDP and competitive factors.[2]

The Treasury model is in a constant state of revision, if only because there are many different ways of formulating consumption and investment

---

[1] These figures are all published in *Economic Trends*.
[2] See T.Burns, 'The Interpretation and Use of Economic Predictions', *Proceedings of the Royal Society*, Series A, 407, 103–125 (1986).

functions, and it is never a simple matter to judge which of them is best. Thus, although the model is in constant use, it may be assumed that parts of it will be questioned by those responsible for getting the forecast right. The model, therefore, does not dictate the forecast to the exclusion of all argument and discussion, and there is plenty of room for judgement. There are often events which a model is unable to handle (strikes and fuel short-ages, for example) and which necessitate judgemental estimation of their effects upon economic activity.

The main upshot of the government forecasting work is a table in con-siderable detail of the course of GDP and its components, quarter by quarter, over a period of two to three years. The published version is less detailed and provides estimates by half-years.

The accuracy of the forecasts is a matter of some interest to policy-makers since they are still used to guide decisions on monetary policy, taxation and public expenditure.[1] Their accuracy is also an important test of the methods and hypotheses which lie behind them. Table 1.8 gives the main Treasury forecasts (published at budget time) for GDP, consumption and fixed in-vestment since 1979. The horizon chosen is the period from the second half of the previous year to the second half of the current year, this being the closest to a through-year change that can be derived from half-yearly figures. Thus for the March 1991 forecast, the period runs from the second half of 1990 to the second half of 1991.

As the table shows, the GDP forecasts have achieved an average level of accuracy of 1.3%, the largest error being 3.0% in 1979; they have also shown some tendency to underpredict. The consumption forecasts have been less accurate than those for GDP, and have shown a more pronounced tendency to underpredict, and the forecasts of fixed investment have, as might be expected, been the least accurate of the three.

The Treasury's forecasts are not as accurate as policy-makers would wish them to be. They contributed to the boom of 1986–8 by underpredicting the rise in GDP for three years in succession – thus encouraging tax cuts which might not have been made if they had been more accurate – and they failed to predict the downturn of 1991. The import and balance-of-payments forecasts were also misleading.

The more technical question, and one which is of particular interest to economists, is whether the forecasts have managed to improve on a state of ignorance. Here the best comparison is with a comparatively naive, or at least less informed forecaster, who for want of better knowledge, has to resort to predicting the average rate of change each year. The mean absolute errors from naive forecasts of this kind are shown in the bottom row of the table, and in all three cases they are, in fact, worse on average than those of the Treasury economists – by about one-third in the case of the GDP forecasts. Thus the conclusion is that the Treasury's forecasts, although

---

[1]   Burns, *op. cit.*, p. 117.

TABLE 1.8

Treasury Forecasts, 1979–92 (% changes to 2nd half-year from 2nd half of previous year)

	GDP			Consumption			Fixed Investment		
	Forecast	Actual	Error (F–A)	Forecast	Actual	Error (F–A)	Forecast	Actual	Error (F–A)
1979	-0.5	2.5	-3.0	1.2	3.0	-1.8	-0.5	6.1	-6.6
1980	-3.0	-3.8	0.8	1.0	0.1	0.9	-5.0	-9.3	4.3
1981	-0.2	0.8	-1.0	-0.8	0.5	-1.3	-1.0	-6.9	7.9
1982	1.5	1.4	0.1	0.7	2.1	-1.4	4.1	8.1	-4.0
1983	2.5	4.1	-1.6	2.0	4.3	-2.3	3.1	3.5	-0.4
1984	3.5	1.2	2.3	3.1	0.9	2.2	6.6	7.9	-1.3
1985	3.5	4.1	-0.6	3.4	4.5	-1.1	4.1	2.1	2.0
1986	3.3	4.2	-0.9	3.8	6.1	-2.3	5.7	6.3	-0.6
1987	2.8	4.9	-2.1	3.3	6.1	-2.8	4.7	12.6	-7.9
1988	2.3	3.6	-1.3	2.9	6.9	-4.0	5.7	10.0	-4.3
1989	2.0	1.7	0.3	2.2	2.5	-0.3	4.3	3.7	0.6
1990	0.6	-0.1	0.7	1.0	0.2	0.8	-3.2	-5.1	1.9
1991	-0.1	-1.9	1.8	-0.4	-1.6	1.2	-6.6	-8.3	1.7
1992	1.9			1.7			1.1		
Mean absolute error			1.3			1.7			3.3
Bias (mean algebraic error)			-0.4			-0.9			-1.7
Mean error from 'naive' forecasts			2.0			2.2			5.3

Sources: FSBRs, 1979 to 1992; ET(AS), 1991; ET, October 1991.

inaccurate and sometimes misleading, have nonetheless been better guides to the future than the guesses which might have been made without economic knowledge. Expertise has achieved something but there is much room for improvement.

4   INFLATION

4.1   Meaning and Measurement

Inflation may be defined as *any* increase in the general level of prices or, less widely, as any *sustained* increase.

In measuring the rate of inflation there is a choice of index numbers. The best index of the prices charged for all goods and services produced in the UK economy is the implied deflator for total final expenditure (TFE). This, like all implied indices, is not obtained directly from price data, but is the result of dividing the value of TFE by its amount at constant prices. If an index is required to measure the prices of goods purchased by UK residents, the best general measure is the implied deflator for total domestic expenditure, since this is the average of prices paid for consumption and investment goods, both privately and publicly purchased. Yet another implied index is the GDP deflator, or index of home costs, which is essentially an index of money incomes divided by real incomes, i.e. wages and profits per unit of output. This index leaves out import prices and indirect taxes, save in so far as they affect wages and profits.

If we are chiefly interested in the prices paid for consumer goods and services, we have a choice between the implied deflator for consumers' expenditure (the CPI) and the index of retail prices (RPI). The CPI is found by dividing the current value of consumers' expenditure by its volume as measured at constant prices.[1] By contrast, the index of retail prices (the cost-of-living index) is compiled directly from price data. It registers the prices of a collection of goods and services entering a typical shopping basket. Being a base-weighted index, it gradually becomes outdated in coverage. In periods of inflation, the composition of the index will tend to exaggerate inflation because consumers will switch their spending towards those goods which are rising least rapidly in price. The composition of the RPI is periodically revised for changes in the pattern of expenditure.

In the late 1980s the RPI became the subject of much criticism because of its inclusion of mortgage interest rates. Interest rates were being increased to counter inflation, and this had the paradoxical effect that policy against inflation raised inflation – at least to begin with. (The same thing could happen with a rise in indirect taxes.) For a while, official statements referred to an 'underlying inflation rate', which was the 12-monthly increase in the RPI with mortgage interest (which has a weight of 7.6%) omitted from the

[1]   The volume or constant-price estimates are derived from base-weighted quantity indices.

index. A more basic defect of the RPI is that mortgage payments are transfers between persons and not purchases of goods and services. When the mortgage rate is increased, income is simply transferred from borrowers to savers. Transfer payments do not figure in the various implicit deflators such as the CPI.

There is nothing new about inflation. The retail price index in 1990 was approximately 45 times its level at the beginning of the century. Prices fell in only 13 years – notably 1920–3 and 1925–33; and from 1933 to 1991 they rose every year. There was a fast inflation during and immediately after the First World War (13% per annum during 1914–20) – faster than in the Second World War when there were widespread price controls. The average rate of increase in prices was 3% per annum in the 1950s and 4% in the 1960s – despite the low level of unemployment. The lowest annual rise in prices recorded in this period was in 1959, when it was only 0.5%. It was not until the 1970s that inflation became really serious, with a record 24% increase in 1975 and an average rate for the decade of 13%.[1] The inflation rate was 18% in 1980, after which it fell to 3% in 1986, went up to 9% in 1990, and was falling again in 1991 and 1992.

4.2   The Inflationary Process

The primary generator of inflation in the UK is the domestic pressure of demand for labour and for goods, which tends to rise and fall with the trade cycle. To this must be added the outside influence of import prices, and the world price of oil. There have also been times when trade union pressure for higher wages seemed to be operating quite independently of demand pressures.

The main domestic element in the inflationary process is the degree of excess demand (i.e. demand less supply at going prices) in the various markets for goods and, particularly, for labour. Wages and prices in the individual markets may be expected to increase whenever demand runs ahead of supply. Their *rate of increase*, moreover, is related to the degree of excess demand in the market. In goods markets where there is excess supply there will be some tendency for prices to fall; and, in slack labour markets, wages may fall in real terms even though they are sticky in money terms. The balance of excess supply and demand in the labour market used to be measurable by either the rate of unemployment or by the vacancy percentage, but these two series have been moving away from each other for more than 20 years, and there is now some uncertainty about comparisons of the pressure of demand over long periods of time. (See section 4.3 below.)

The influence of import prices is important because imports of goods and services account for about 22% of TFE (Table 1.6). Some imports are in

---

[1]   This is the average of annual increases.

competition with home production, so that if their prices are raised home buyers may switch to domestic substitutes. But a large part of UK imports cannot be made at home at all. Certain foods, most raw materials and many semi-manufactures are in this category, and as demand for these goods is highly inelastic, increases in world prices for such commodities are followed by increases in the level of UK costs and prices. UK prices will rise if there is an increase in the world price of oil, which is the one major primary commodity it produces at home.

In the period since 1970 the main example of imported inflation was the fourfold rise in oil prices in 1973 and the increase in other import prices at the same time. UK import prices actually rose by a colossal 112% in the three years from 1972 to 1975, and were thus a major cause of the record inflation rate of 1975. There were also some large increases in import prices in 1976 and 1977 (see Table 1.9), but these were more directly due to a fall in the exchange rate, which was itself a consequence of the UK's high rate of inflation relative to the rest of the world.

Wage-pushfulness has to be kept in mind as a separate force because wages are widely fixed by a bargaining process, the outcome of which need not necessarily conform to market pressures of demand and supply. Alterations in union strength and solidarity, or in the readiness to strike for political reasons may act as an independent force (i.e. independent of market forces) in determining wage increases.

There was evidence of a wage-push inflation in the 1970s. In the 'pay explosion' of 1970 the rate of wage increase was substantially faster than could be explained on the basis of the traditional Phillips Curve; and it was also well above what was predictable from other models in which proper allowance was made for price changes.[1] The explosion may have been a reaction to the incomes policy of 1966–9, and to the belief that wage-earners were entitled to respectable pay rises after several years of regulation.

In the next few years there was further evidence of wage-push inflation in terms of a tendency for money wage rates to press ahead of prices. There was concerted opposition to the Conservative government's trade union legislation (the Industrial Relations Act of 1971) and to its incomes policy. Some very high wage demands were put in during this period – sometimes in flagrant breach of the government's wage guidelines.[2] Finally, the 'Winter of Discontent' of 1978–9 saw further outbreaks of union militancy and opposition to incomes policy. The very high figures for days lost in trade union disputes during these periods help to confirm a wage-push explanation for 1970, 1971–72 and 1979 (see Table 1.9). In the 1980s, however, this kind of wage inflation entirely disappeared – probably because of union legislation and the abandonment of incomes policy after 1979.

---

[1] M.J.Artis, 'Some Aspects of the Present Inflation', *NIER*, February 1971, reprinted in H.G.Johnson and A.R.Nobay (eds.), *The Current Inflation* (Macmillan, 1971).
[2] For an account of this period see M.J.Stewart, *Politics and Economic Policy in the UK since 1964* (Pergamon, 1978).

The pressure of domestic demand and changes in import prices can now be considered as the main exogenous forces in inflation. But the impulse effect of either will tend to be amplified by the interaction between wages and prices – the so-called wage-price spiral. As each wage rise leads to higher prices and so back to higher wages, the effects of an inflationary shock will tend to reverberate for several years after the event.

When the exchange rate is flexible, another interaction in the system is that running from domestic prices to the exchange rate and back to import prices. When UK inflation is faster than elsewhere, the exchange rate will decline, thus leading to higher sterling import prices. This leads on to higher industrial costs and to higher final prices, including higher export prices. Hence the exchange rate will fall again, and the process repeats itself. This process, however, only operates when the exchange rate is variable. It was at work in the late 1970s and 1980s, but has been neutralized by entry into the ERM.

The main forces in the inflationary process are illustrated in Figure 1.6. A possible omission is any direct influence of excess demand upon price increases, an effect for which there is some evidence in so far as profit margins vary with the cycle. Thus the profit margins of non-oil industrial and commercial companies fell by about four percentage points in the downturns of 1973–5 and 1978–81, and they rose in the ensuing recoveries.[1] But these are fairly small changes and the main influence of demand pressure still seems to work through the labour market.

Inflation is no different from the process of real output expansion in that it directly raises the transactions demand for money, and if this is not accommodated there will be a rise in interest rates. The assumption of most inflation models, therefore, must be that the money stock is flexible. Inflationary processes may be initiated in various ways, but they are usually supported by permissive increases in the stock of money. This does not rule out the monetary causation of inflation *per se* since additions to the quantity of money, for example, through open-market operations, can lead to increases in wages through the medium of a lowering of interest rates and an increase, therefore, in the pressure of demand for labour. Monetary inflation is not a special case of its own, but a variety of demand-pull inflation.

There are two other possible interactions between wages and prices, both of them operating through the effect of rising prices upon *expected future* prices. The first of these is the possibility that price expectations, rather than compensation for past price increases, is the operative factor in wage bargaining.[2] It has been suggested quite widely that the expectation of a price increase of, say, 10% in the next twelve months will induce trade unions and employers to settle for increases in nominal wages also of 10%.

---

[1] See the discussion in *NIER*, November 1982, pp. 21–2.
[2] E.S. Phelps, 'Phillips Curves, Expectations of Inflation and Optimal Unemployment Over Time', *EC*, N.S. 34, pp. 254–81 and M. Friedman, 'The Role of Monetary Policy', *AER*, Vol. 58(1), pp. 1–17.

This hypothesis assumes a degree of sophistication in the process of wage bargaining which is probably uncharacteristic of 'real-world' procedures. Wage claims are normally based on the *actual* rather than the *expected* rise in the cost of living; and it could be argued that the trade union representative who bases his case for a wage claim on anything as flimsy as a price forecast would not get very far. But the employers' side must not be neglected, and there may be something in the idea that the propensity to grant wage increases is influenced by their expectations of price increases on the part of their competitors.

There is also a possible link between price expectations and the level of demand. As consumers become aware that prices are going to rise, they may react by attempting to buy now rather than later (effectively switching out of money into goods). The consequence will be to raise the pressure of demand and thus add to the inflation rate. In general, this seems to be a

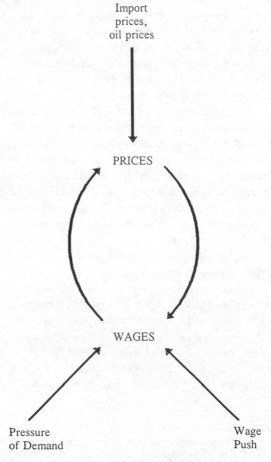

Figure 1.6   Inflationary Processes

characteristic of much faster inflations than those so far experienced in the UK.[1]

4.3   Excess Demand, Unemployment and Vacancies

The pressure of demand for labour is the principal domestic generator of inflation in the UK. For many years it was taken for granted that a reasonably reliable, but inverse, measure of demand pressure was provided by the unemployment percentage – which is an approximate measure of aggregate excess supply. Aggregate excess demand (which is the sum of excess demand in all those labour markets where demand exceeds supply) could be assumed to be related inversely to excess supply, and so to the unemployment percentage.

Excess demand, however, is much more germane to the determination of wage increases than excess supply. Excess supply (and unemployment) may cause wages to be downwards-sticky, but *increases* in wages (which is what we are interested in) are likely to occur in markets where there is positive excess demand. Their rate of increase, moreover, will be related to the degree of (positive) excess demand in those markets. It is excess demand which drives wages up, not excess supply which drives them down.

This means that the ideal statistic for monitoring wage inflation is the number of vacancies, not the number of unemployed. The actual vacancy figures, however, are incomplete – and certainly much less complete than those for unemployment. They are reported by employers only if it is worth their while to notify them. They may prefer to recruit through the local newspapers rather than through job centres. And an employer who has already notified the job centre of vacancies for a particular kind of worker will not need to register new vacancies because the original notice will suffice. Thus the vacancy statistics are an incomplete record of what ought to be measured. It is officially recognized that only about one-third of all new vacancies are notified to the Department of Employment.

The question is whether this matters. If the ratio of recorded to unrecorded vacancies remains a constant, then the figures will function as a reliable index of excess demand. And whilst there have been suggestions[2] that the recording ratio did, in fact, rise with the introduction of job centres, the Department of Employment, which is responsible for the figures, does not report that this is so.[3]

For many years the unemployment and vacancy statistics moved in close,

---

[1]   See, for example, A.J.Brown, *The Great Inflation* (London, 1955) and P.Cagan, 'The Monetary Dynamics of Hyperinflation' in M.Friedman (ed.), *Studies in the Quantity Theory of Money* (Chicago, 1956).
[2]   A.Budd, P.Levine and P.Smith, 'Unemployment, Vacancies and the Long-term Unemployed', *EJ*, December 1988.
[3]   'About one-third of all vacancies nationally are notified to job centres' (*EG*, March 1992, p. S42). 'Less than half of all vacancies are in fact notified' (Department of Employment, *British Labour Statistics, Historical Abstract 1886–1968*, 1971, p. 18).

consistent relationship to each other. The same unemployment percentage
was always observed against the same given vacancy rate, and changes in the
two percentages were the same in absolute magnitude. It was possible,
therefore, to regard either measure as an index of excess demand, whilst the
unemployment percentage also served as an indication of the degree of
personal and social distress caused by lack of work.

Since the late 1960s, however, there has been a gradual change in the
relationship of unemployment to vacancies. A given level of vacancies is
now associated with much higher unemployment than before. The extent of
the change can be seen from the following comparisons:

	Unfilled vacancies, UK		*Unemployment, UK*	
	(000s, percentages in brackets)			
Demand peaks:				
1965–6 (average)	262	(1.0)	346	(1.5)
1973–4 (average)	302	(1.2)	598	(2.1)
1979	241	(0.9)	1 296	(4.1)
1988	249	(0.9)	2 319	(8.4)
Demand troughs:				
1962–3 (average)	147	(0.6)	497	(2.2)
1971–2 (average)	139	(0.6)	794	(2.8)
1975–6 (average)	139	(0.5)	1 121	(3.7)
1982–4 (average)	134	(0.5)	3 060	(10.3)

The figures illustrate a continuing tendency for unemployment to increase
relative to a given vacancy percentage. Thus the unemployment rate associated with a vacancy rate of 0.6% increased from 2% in the early 1960s to
10% in the early 1980s – a rise of eight percentage points. In the peak year of
1988, there were 9 unemployed for each available vacancy, whereas in
1965–6, a period of similar demand pressure, the ratio was only 1 to 1.

The reasons behind this very large change in the numbers unemployed
(U) relative to vacancies (V) are not as fully understood as they ought to be.
But one suggestive indication of what has happened is available in the
responses to the questionnaire which the Confederation of British Industry
(CBI) sends to its members about the factors limiting output. In 1965–6 the
percentage of firms reporting that shortages of skilled labour were limiting
their output was 27% and in 1988 it was about the same at 22%. But the
difference was that in 1965–6 far more firms reported that their output was
limited by unskilled labour than in 1988: 15% in 1965–6 as against 4% in
1988. In the 1960s the unskilled labour figure averaged 8% of firms, whereas
in the period since 1974 the figure has only once been higher than 5%. The
inference is that the supply of unskilled labour does not pose problems even
at the peak of the cycle, whereas shortages of skilled labour have become
more serious.

This seems to suggest that the unemployed have become more mis-
matched to the available vacancies. What might have happened is that the
recessions of 1973–5 and 1979–82 led to substantial shake-outs of unskilled
and marginal labour, whilst the demand recoveries that followed were
concentrated on labour with specific skills. The unemployed were not

equipped to fill the vacancies. This problem could have been made worse by the exceptionally large flow in the 1980s of unskilled and unqualified entrants to the workforce. And the mismatch of skills would have been intensified by regional mismatch, and by the difficulties encountered in moving from low rent areas – mainly in the North – to areas such as the South-East where there were vacant jobs but a shortage of cheap, rented accommodation.

The mismatch explanation has been disputed, however, on the grounds that the mismatch of unemployed with vacancies, if measured proportionately across occupational groups and regions, has not greatly altered.[1] But if the *number* of unemployed is much larger, then the *magnitude* of the mismatch is more serious than before. It is also questionable whether measurements based on a small number of occupational groups and regions (the only available data) are sufficient to deal adequately with the question. On balance it seems likely that the demand for skilled workers has outgrown the supply; that the supply of unskilled workers has outgrown the demand, and that, within the skilled sector, there is some occupational and locational mismatch.

A related reason for the rise in unemployment relative to vacancies is that unemployment has become less involuntary. Whilst the unemployed start out by being involuntarily unemployed, they become less interested in the search for work as time goes on. Once they have been made redundant (through no fault of their own) their resolve to return to work is eroded by the experience of repeated applications and rejections in a situation where there are far more applicants than vacancies. Employers, moreover, normally prefer to take on those who have been in a job quite recently, with the result that the long-term unemployed become 'unemployable' in the sense that this is the way they are seen both by themselves and by employers. (This is sometimes called 'the discouraged worker effect' and the word to describe the whole phenomenon of unemployment going up but not coming down is 'hysteresis'.[2]) It is also the case that the sheer rise in the amount and generality of unemployment has had the effect of breaking down the old social stigma attached to being on the dole. There was also, in the late 1970s, some rise in the level of unemployment benefit relative to average earnings, and this tended to prolong the period of unemployment once a worker is made redundant.

There are also some purely statistical reasons for the change in the U–V ratio which relate to the way in which unemployment is officially measured. Between 1966 and 1981, the ratio of recorded to actual unemployment increased. Thus for male unemployment the ratio of the registered

---

[1] R.Layard, *How to Beat Unemployment* (Oxford University Press, 1986), pp. 55–8. But see also A.Wood, 'How much Unemployment is Structural?', *Oxford Bulletin of Economics and Statistics*, February 1988.
[2] The term 'hysteresis' refers to the process whereby a variable is determined by its past history and where there is no tendency for it to return to its former value.

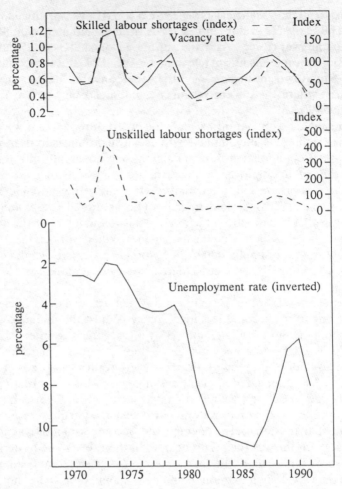

Figure 1.7   Indicators of the Degree of Labour Shortage: Vacancy Rate (%), Unemployment (%), CBI Reports of Skilled and Other Labour Shortages as Limiting Factors on Output
(*Sources: ETAS*, 1991; *EG*, March 1992; Confederation of British Industry)

unemployed to the numbers shown as unemployed in the population census increased from 56% in 1966 to 71% in 1971 and around 100% in 1981.[1] This effect, however, will have been counteracted after 1981 by the series of statistical revisions to the official unemployment figures. The main changes were the effect in 1981 of removing from the register people on special employment and training schemes, the change in 1982 from a registered to a

[1] For further discussion, see Budd *et al.* (*op. cit.*), *NIER*, November 1983, pp. 39–41; and A. Evans, 'Notes on the Changing Relationship between Registered Unemployment and Notified Vacancies: 1961–1966 and 1966–1971', *EC*, May 1977; S.J. Nickell, 'The Effect of Unemployment and Related Benefits on the Duration of Unemployment', *EJ*, March 1979; A.B. Atkinson and J.S. Flemming, 'Unemployment and Social Security and Incentives', *MBR*, 1978, and R. Layard and S. Nickell, 'The Causes of British Unemployment', *NIER*, February 1985.

claimant basis for the the figures, and the re-start interviews initiated in 1986. The Unemployment Unit has calculated the effects of these and other changes made since 1981 to have been about 900,000 by August 1988.[1]

It is not easy to make sense of what has happened. But the main statistical conclusion is that the unemployment rate can no longer be taken as a consistent indicator of excess demand in the labour market. If a single indicator has to be used to measure the pressure of demand for labour, there is much to be said for the vacancy figures. These, although incomplete, have remained in fairly close relationship with another indicator of labour shortage: the CBI's percentage for firms whose output is limited by shortage of skilled labour.

| | *Unfilled vacancies, UK* | *Per cent of firms limited by shortages of:* | |
		skilled labour	*other labour*
1965–6	1.0%	27%	15%
1973–4	1.2%	36%	17%
1979	0.9%	21%	5%
1988	0.9%	22%	4%

Sources: ET(AS), 1991; Confederation of British Industry.

Figure 1.7 gives a more complete picture of the various indicators of the pressure of demand for labour for the period.

4.4 Wage Increases and the Pressure of Demand

There is ample evidence that the pressure of demand for labour is a major determinant of the rate of inflation. Numerous studies in the 1950s and 1960s showed a strong negative relationship between the level of unemployment and the rate of change of money wage rates. One of the earliest studies of this kind, and certainly the most influential, was published in 1958 by Professor A. W. Phillips.[2] This examined unemployment rates and wage increases for nearly a century and, on the basis of data for 1861–1913, suggested that the rate of wage increase to be associated with different rates of unemployment was as follows:

Unemployment rate	1.0	2.0	3.0	4.0	5.0
% change in wage rates	8.7	2.8	1.2	0.5	0.3

The relationship became known as the *Phillips Curve*[3] and implied a

---

[1] *Unemployment Bulletin*, Autumn 1988. See also the discussion in Chapter 5 of this book.
[2] A.W.Phillips, 'The Relation between Unemployment and the Rate of Change of Money Wage Rates, 1861–1957', *Economica*, November 1958, although A.J.Brown, *op. cit.*, had illustrated the same relationship.
[3] The equation for the schedule was:

$$W' = -0.900 + 9.638U^{-1.394}$$

where W' is the percentage rate of wage change and U is the unemployment rate (Phillips, *op. cit.*).

downwards-sloping, non-linear, 'trade-off' between wage increases and the rate of unemployment.

One of the more remarkable features of the Phillips Curve, and one which distinguished it from many similar studies, was that it was able to predict increases in wages well outside the 1861–1913 period, the data for which were used to construct the relationship. Phillips was able to show in his article that there was an extremely close correspondence for 1948–57 between the wage changes implied by his relationship and those that actually took place.

The Phillips Curve continued to give accurate predictions of wage increases for a number of years after the study had been published. During the eight years from 1958 to 1965 there was not a single error in excess of 2.5% and the mean error (regardless of sign) was only 1.1%. The Curve also appeared to be unbiased, with the positive and negative errors tending to offset each other.[1] Forecasters today would be more than happy if their own equations behaved this well. It is fair to note, however, that these early successes occurred during a period when unemployment was very stable compared with the experience from which Phillips had started. In 1861–1913 unemployment rates ranged from 1 to 11%, whereas in 1948–66 they were between 1 and 2.3%. Thus it could be argued that postwar experience up to 1966 tested only a small part of the Phillips relation.

After the mid-1960s, the pure Phillips Curve became less reliable as a guide to the rate of wage inflation. It underpredicted by about 4.5% per annum in 1967–69, by 10–12% in 1970–3 and by more than 20% in 1974 and 1975. In the 1970s there was no recognizable relationship between statistics of the unemployment percentage and the rate of wage increase. There are, moreover, several quite satisfactory reasons for the breakdown of the Phillips relationship:

(i)   First, it is the upwards pressure of excess demand (as represented by vacancies) rather than the downwards pressure of excess supply (indicated by unemployment) which is the crucial determinant of wage inflation. In the 1950s, when unemployment and vacancies moved closely together, it did not matter greatly if unemployment was taken to represent (inversely) the degree of labour shortage. But as unemployment has drifted away from its relationship to vacancies, it has also lost its linkage with excess demand and the rate of wage increase.

(ii) A second major factor is the omission from the pure Phillips equation of the causal influence of price changes.[2] This would not

[1]   For a discussion of the predictive properties of various wage equations, see M.T.Sumner, 'The history and significance of the Phillips Curve', in D.Demery, D.W.Duck, M.T.Sumner and R.L.Thomas (eds.), *Macroeconomics* (Longman, 1984).
[2]   This omission would not have been denied by Phillips himself and was soon put right by R.G.Lipsey, 'The Relation between Unemployment and the Rate of Change of Money Wage Rates in the United Kingdom, 1862–1957: A Further Analysis', *Economica*, 1960.

have mattered so much in the 1950s and early 1960s when inflation was moderate. But the omission became serious with inflation at the rate experienced in the 1970s and early 1980s.

(iii) Thirdly, the Phillips relationship was partly obscured by a number of attempts, notably in the late 1960s, 1972–4 and 1975–8, to control wage increases by incomes policy.

(iv) A fourth factor is the influence of 'wage-pushfulness' by the trade unions, which, as we have discussed in section 4.2, appears to have been prevalent in the 1970s.

(v) Finally, there is the possibility that wage increases became more sensitive to price increases as a result of learning to live with inflation. As inflation became more rapid, a growing number of trade-union negotiators would have been led to insist on full compensation for price changes in wage negotiations, whilst others would have sought negotiations at more frequent intervals. There may have been some tendency to follow the 'expectations-augmented Phillips curve', with expected rather than actual price changes being taken as the basis for wage awards.

These factors – particularly (i) and (ii) – help to explain why the old wage-increase/unemployment relationship failed to hold after the mid-1960s. They lend support to the position that the principle behind the Phillips relationship – that the rate of wage change is geared to the excess demand for labour – can still be accepted. Indeed, there is ample evidence in the 1980s for such a principle in terms of the relationship between the rate of increase in earnings and the vacancy rate, once the influence of price increases is taken into account.

Earnings and the Vacancy Rate: Money earnings can be seen to forge ahead of prices more strongly when the vacancy rate is high – as in 1979 and 1988 – than in recessions such as 1980–2. The evidence is presented in Figure 1.8, where the changes in earnings are measured at the end of the year. They are the October–March averages compared with those of a year earlier, whereas the rise in retail prices is the calendar-year increase – an effective lag of six months.

The reason for the 6-month lag is the assumption that the earnings index is similar to an index of negotiated wage rates. As such, its level in one particular month will be an average of wage negotiations by different groups of workers over the previous twelve months. This means that one-twelfth of the index will have been negotiated 12 months ago, one-twelfth this month, and the 'average' group will have been negotiated six months before the date of the index. For a wage-rate index recorded at the end of December, therefore, the relevant price index is that for the calendar year. The lag means, for example, that the end-1992 rise in earnings is governed by the vacancy rate for calendar year 1992 and by the rise in retail prices for 1991–2.

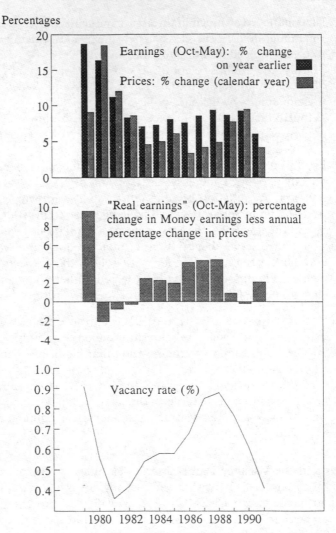

**Figure 1.8   Percentage Change in 'Real' and Money Earnings and the
Vacancy Rate, UK, 1979–91**
(*Sources: ET(AS)*, 1986, 1991; *ET*, March 1992)

(In Figure 1.8, the excess of the earnings change over the lagged price
change is referred to, unconventionally, as 'real' earnings, although it is, of
course, more usual to measure real earnings without the lag.)

It is possible to carry the analysis further by estimating the relationship of
the rate of change of earnings to the vacancy rate and the lagged rate of
inflation, using the standard method of least squares regression. In the
previous edition of this book a relationship was estimated for the period
1975–88, the main features of which were that the percentage change in
earnings, measured from October to March, was given as:

(i) about $7\frac{1}{2}$ times the vacancy rate for the calendar year
(ii) plus about $\frac{3}{4}$ times the annual percentage rise in the retail price index
(iii) minus a constant term of 0.74[1]

The relationship was estimated for the period from end-1974 to end-1988.

It is now possible to put this relationship to a proper test by asking how well it has managed to predict changes in earnings over the three years which have elapsed since the estimate was made. The actual and predicted changes in earnings, and the data for prices and vacancies are as follows:

	Vacancy rate (%)	Rate of price change (%)	Predicted change in earnings (%)	Actual change in earnings (%)	Error (%)
1989	0.78	7.8	10.9	8.7	2.2
1990	0.61	9.5	11.0	9.3	1.7
1991	0.43	5.9	6.9	7.5	− 0.6

The results appear to be fairly satisfactory, although a three-year test period is a bit short. They seem to corroborate both the general hypothesis that wage changes are determined by demand pressure and by prior price changes and the magnitudes of the coefficients. The 1989 error may be the kind of error which has to be expected from relationships of this kind, or it may be partly a consequence of the government's attempts to hold down wages in the public sector. Macroeconomic forecasting is not a precise science, and estimates of coefficients obtained by the method of least squares are not necessarily 'true' in the sense of being the *ceteris paribus* effects of one variable on another.

With three more years at our disposal it is possible to re-estimate the equation for the period 1980–90, a period which was wholly free from the effects of incomes policy. When this is done the new equation gives the change in earnings (E') for October–March over the same period a year earlier as:

(i) about 5 times the vacancy rate(V) for the calendar year
(ii) plus about $\frac{2}{3}$ times the annual percentage rise in the retail price index (P')
(iii) plus a constant term of 1.1

or more precisely the equation is:

$$E' = 1.09 + 5.16V + 0.65P' \qquad (1)$$

---

[1] The actual equation was

$$E' = 7.68V + 0.74P' - 3.00IP + 3.00CU - 0.74$$

where E' is the rise in earnings (%), V vacancies at job centres as a percentage of the workforce, P' the rise in retail prices (%), and IP and CU are dummy variables for 1974–7 and 1978–9 to allow for incomes policy and the catch-up after it.

This equation was estimated using data for 1980–90 so that its prediction for 1991 is a test of the equation with independent data. The equation predicts the October–March rise as 7.2%, and the actual rise was 7.5%.[1]

The equation is not so very different from the relationship in the last edition, but the slight change in the values of the coefficients should be taken as a warning that the apparent precision of the estimate is not to be taken as an indication of their reliability. The change in the value of the coefficient on the vacancy rate is quite small, bearing in mind that the vacancy rate is itself a very small figure.

Although the precise figures need not be taken too seriously, it is worth drawing attention to what they imply for wage inflation at different levels of demand pressure. During the period from 1979 to 1991 there was a major recession in 1979–81 with the vacancy rate falling to 0.36%, whilst at the cycle peaks in 1979 and 1988 vacancies were about 0.9% of the workforce. If it is assumed that prices are stable (so that the term P' is zero) then the implications for the rate of increase in earnings over the relevant range of vacancy rates are as follows:

vacancy rate (%)	0.3	0.5	0.7	0.9
increase in earnings (%)	1.6	2.6	3.6	4.6

If productivity is increasing at about 2% per annum, then wage costs per unit of output will be stable, according to this schedule, only if the vacancy rate is somewhere between 0.3 and 0.5%. This is not a welcome conclusion for policy – and it should, perhaps, be hoped that the relationship is wrong. But the schedule does, if anything, underestimate the implications, since it makes no allowance for the constant term.

Some consideration must also be given to the coefficient on prices. It is plausible to suppose that most groups of workers will try to obtain wage increases which are at least sufficient to compensate them for the rise in the cost of living – thus maintaining the real value of their earnings. This would mean, however, that the coefficient on price increases should be unity – rather than the value of 0.65 suggested by equation (1). It is possible, however, that the process of compensation is spread over more than one year, in which case the coefficient may be acceptable, although the equation will then be incomplete in that it allows for only one year's rise in prices.

The main general conclusion, however, is that there is reasonably strong evidence for the influence of the pressure of demand and the lagged inflation

---

[1]   The standard error of the residuals was 0.8% of earnings, r-squared 0.92, and the t-ratios on the two coefficients were respectively 2.9 and 9.2. The data were:

	1980	1981	1982	1983	1984	1985	1986	1987	1988	1989	1990
V	0.56	0.36	0.42	0.54	0.58	0.59	0.68	0.85	0.88	0.78	0.61
P'	17.9	12.0	8.6	5.0	4.6	6.1	3.4	4.2	4.9	7.8	9.5
E'	16.4	11.2	8.3	7.1	7.3	8.1	7.6	8.6	9.4	8.7	9.5
E' (estimated)	15.7	10.8	8.9	6.9	7.3	8.1	6.8	8.2	8.8	10.2	10.4
Residual	−0.7	−0.4	0.6	0.2	0.0	0.0	−0.8	−0.4	−0.6	1.5	0.9

rate on the rate of increase in money earnings. Relationships of this kind have been observed for many years, and our own relationship has stood up fairly well to the test of forecasts outside the estimation period.

4.5   Price Changes

A commonsense view of prices is that they are determined by a constant mark-up over variable costs, and this means that each change in costs would be followed, after a short time-lag, by a change in prices of the same percentage amount. Costs themselves divide into earnings (as an approximation to employment costs) and import prices, so that it must follow from what was said about earnings in the previous section that the rise in prices will be given by three variables: the pressure of demand for labour, the prior rate of inflation and the rate of rise of import prices.[1]

It should be possible to estimate the determinants of the change in prices either directly by the use of input–output tables, or indirectly by regression methods. The direct method suggests that, in the absence of any changes in indirect taxes, the percentage change in TFE prices should be given as:

(i)   0.66 times the percentage change in employment costs;
(ii)   plus 0.34 times the percentage change in import prices

since the coefficients 0.66 and 0.34 are the proportions in which employment costs and import prices are combined.[2]

The indirect method is to estimate the change in prices as a function of the change in import prices, along with the two determinants of the change in earnings: the lagged vacancy rate and the previous year's price increase. The result of doing so for the period from 1980 to 1990 is as follows:

$$P'_t = -3.91 + 8.00V + 0.62P' + 0.19Pm' \qquad (2)$$

where P'_t is the rate of change in retail prices for January–June over the same period a year earlier, V is last year's vacancy rate, P' last year's inflation rate, and Pm' is the October–March change in the unit value index of import prices.[3]

---

[1]   If $E'_t = aV_{t+1} + bP'_{t-1}$
and $P'_{t+\frac{1}{2}} = cE'_t + dPm'_{t+\frac{1}{2}}$
then $P'_{t+\frac{1}{2}} = c(V_{t-1} + bP'_{t-1}) + Pm'_{t+\frac{1}{2}}$
where a, b, c and d are coefficients; Pm' is the rate of increase (%) in import prices, and the subscripts relate to six-monthly time intervals.
[2]   *BB*, 1988, p. 29.
[3]   The standard error of the residuals was 1.1% of the price level, r-squared 0.87, and the t-ratios on the three coefficients were respectively 2.8, 3.0 and 2.8. The data were as given for the earnings equation together with:

	1980	1981	1982	1983	1984	1985	1986	1987	1988	1989	1990
Pm'(Oct–Mar)	5.2	12.8	7.9	7.6	12.7	−5.9	3.0	−2.2	2.1	10.1	−1.3
P' (Jan–June)	12.2	10.2	4.4	5.1	6.2	3.9	4.0	3.8	8.0	8.7	7.3
P' (estimated)	12.7	8.8	6.3	4.7	6.3	3.4	4.2	5.1	6.7	9.0	6.6
Residual	0.5	−1.4	1.9	−0.4	0.1	−0.5	0.2	1.3	−1.3	0.3	−0.7

This relationship makes no allowance for changes in indirect taxes or mortgage interest rates. But its coefficients appear to be fairly plausible. The constant term incorporates the average rise in productivity, whilst the coefficient on import prices is somewhat less than the input–output coefficient. The coefficient on the vacancy rate is larger than that given for the earnings equation, but this could reflect the direct effect of the pressure of demand on profit margins; that on lagged prices is about right, given the wage content of variable costs.

This relationship can also be used to answer the question of what inflation rate can be associated with the range of vacancy figures experienced in the 1980s. On the assumptions that import prices are unchanged and that there was no increase in the retail price index in the previous year, the inflation rates to be associated with the various vacancy percentages are as follows:

vacancy rate (%)	0.3	0.5	0.7	0.9
increase in RPI (%)	−1.5	0.1	1.7	3.8

These implications are consistent with those of the earnings relationship in the previous section. The *critical vacancy rate*, which could be expected to give price stability when there is no built-in inflation and import prices are stable, appears to be in the region of 0.5. Bearing in mind that this was about the rate experienced in 1982–84, the conclusion is again unwelcome. But the caveat must be made about undue precision. Much more work would be needed to be confident of this conclusion.

A further implication is that if the economy is run at a pressure of demand which is higher than the critical vacancy rate, then the rate of inflation will rise year by year as each wage increase feeds into prices and then back to wages. This is the so-called 'acceleration hypothesis' associated with theories of the expectations-augmented Phillips Curve. It applies in equal measure to the wage-price spiral. But the main conclusion to be drawn from this section is that the rate of inflation is intimately connected with the pressure of demand in the economy, and that this has to be quite low if prices are to be stable.

4.6   Note on Alternative Wage Relationships

The earnings hypothesis presented in 4.4 is based on the principle of demand pressure measured by the vacancy rate and augmented by the previous year's price change. The role of the price term may be seen as the attempt by workers to restore their real wages to the level of last year's wage settlement – which means that it is in some sense a 'real wage hypothesis'.

A number of economists have belittled the view that wage changes are related to the pressure of demand, and have sought to show that if such a relationship exists it is small and insignificant. The way to do this is to choose unemployment, which is a poor indicator of demand pressure, and well known to be lagged 6 months or a year behind, as the demand variable, and to relate it to wage changes quarter by quarter. By choosing the wrong variable and also the wrong time-lags it is not difficult to miss the key connection – rather like going to *Macbeth* and not finding Hamlet.

Some work on these lines has favoured the 'real wage hypothesis', a wage-push view in which the lagged level of the real wage is believed to have a negative effect on the rate of rise of money earnings, the other variables being the change in prices (a 'proxy' for price expectations), the change in unemployment and the lagged quarterly rise in earnings.[1]

The principal alternative hypothesis, however, is the expectations-augmented Phillips Curve, which has been popular since the work of Phelps.[2] But as we have pointed out earlier in this chapter, it is scarcely credible that price expectations, as distinct from actual price increases, can form the basis for a wage bargain. There is no direct evidence that unions or employers behave in this way. Only one or two of the econometric investigations of this hypothesis have used data on actual price expectations, and the vast majority have simply used the actual change in prices as a presumed proxy for price expectations. The claim that there is great support for the role of price expectations in wage inflation is based almost entirely on the renaming of prices as 'price expectations'. But as Abba Lerner once wrote, 'even if I call the tail of a sheep a leg that will not turn sheep into quintapeds'.[3]

The other problem with the expectations-augmented Phillips Curve is that it holds so tenaciously to the use of unemployment as the indicator of excess demand when it is well known that there has been an enormous shift in its relation to vacancies, and when, in our view at least, it is clearly labour shortages which drive wages up, not unemployment which holds them down. This is a principal reason why the best known estimate of the EAPC, and one which does use expectations data, has proved to be such a hopeless predictor.[4]

4.7   Inflation since 1970

Between the 1960s and 1980s the inflation rate was rising at given rates of unemployment because unemployment was moving gradually away from its old relationship to vacancies and the pressure of demand. The 1970s witnessed a number of major disturbances which accounted for the record inflation of the period, and there may also have been some strengthening of the wage-price spiral – as the result of an increased sensitivity of wages to prices. In the early 1970s, the main exogenous disturbances were the 'wage explosions' of 1970 and 1972, when wages rose much faster than could be

---

[1] M. Artis and M. Lewis, *Money in Britain* (Philip Allan, 1991).
[2] *op. cit.*
[3] A. P. Lerner, 'The Burden of Debt', *Review of Economics and Statistics*, vol. 43, 1961, pp. 139–41.
[4] M. T. Sumner, 'Wage Determination', in M. Parkin and M. T. Sumner (eds), *Inflation in the United Kingdom* (Manchester University Press and Toronto University Press, pp. 75–92), the predictive failings of which are pointed out in M. Artis and M. Lewis, *op. cit.*

TABLE 1.9

Inflation and Inflationary Pressures 1960–91

	(1) Change in retail prices (%)	(2) Change in average weekly earnings (%)	(3) Unemployment percentage	(4) Unfilled vacancies percentage	(5) Days lost in industrial disputes (m)	(6) Change in import prices (%)	(7) Change in exchange rate (%)	(8) Change in money stock (M4) (%)
1960–69 (av.)	4	6	1.9	0.8	4	2	−1	—
1970	6	12	2.6	0.7	11	4	−1	12
1971	9	11	2.6	0.5	14	5	0	17
1972	7	13	2.9	0.6	24	5	−4	24
1973	9	14	2.0	1.2	7	28	−9	22
1974	16	18	2.1	1.2	15	46	−3	11
1975	24	27	3.1	0.6	6	14	−8	10
1976	17	16	4.2	0.5	3	22	−14	11
1977	16	9	4.4	0.6	10	16	−5	15
1978	8	13	4.4	0.8	9	4	0	15
1979	13	15	4.1	0.9	29	7	7	14
1980	18	21	5.1	0.5	12	10	10	17
1981	12	13	8.1	0.3	4	8	−1	21
1982	9	9	9.6	0.4	5	8	−4	12
1983	5	8	10.5	0.5	4	9	−7	13
1984	5	6	10.7	0.6	27	9	−4	14
1985	6	9	10.9	0.6	6	5	−1	13
1986	3	8	11.1	0.7	2	−4	−9	16
1987	4	8	10.0	0.8	4	3	−2	16
1988	5	9	8.4	0.9	4	1	6	17
1989	8	9	6.3	0.8	4	7	−3	19
1990	9	10	5.8	0.8	2	4	−1	12
1991	6	8	8.1	0.4	1	0	0	6

Sources: *ET(AS)*, 1986, 1991; *ET*, *FS*, March 1992; *EG*, March 1992.

Notes: Col. (2) earnings in whole economy linked to earlier indices. Col. (3) UK unemployed as percentages of mid-year workforce. (N.B. There are discontinuities in the definition of unemployment after 1979.) Col. (6) unit value of merchandise imports on balance of payments basis. Col. (7) sterling exchange rate index. Col. (8) end-year, seasonally adjusted.

attributed to their normal relationship with prices or with the pressure of demand. The 1970 explosion may have been partly or wholly a 'catch-up' from incomes policy, whereas that of 1972 seems to be either inexplicable or attributable to direct union push associated with discontent over the Industrial Relations Act of 1971 and the policies of the Conservative government. The sharp rise in the numbers involved in industrial disputes bears witness to this explanation (Table 1.9).

Between 1972 and 1975, fresh factors took over. Undoubtedly, the most important was the colossal rise in oil and other import prices. The increase of 112% in import prices must, with imports comprising 22% of TFE, have added well over 20% to the level of retail prices. But the inflation was helped, rather than hindered, by Stage III of Mr Heath's incomes policy, where under the 'threshold agreements', wages were effectively linked one-to-one with prices. This was in 1974, and the linkage was continued during the first half of 1975. But, as the figures show, the inflation of 1973 and 1974 was greatly helped by an extremely high pressure of demand for labour, with vacancy rates higher for two years than they had ever been before. High rates of monetary expansion (or, more particularly, low real rates of interest) helped to raise the pressure of demand to unprecedented levels, but could hardly be regarded, as some commentators believed at the time, as the sole cause of the inflation.

After 1975 there was a sharp decline in the inflation rate for three years, and by 1978 the rate had fallen 16 points to 8%. This decline was partly attributable to the lower pressure of demand in 1976 and 1977, but the main factor responsible was the introduction in July 1975 of an incomes policy which won the consent of the trade union movement. Phase I of the policy set a limit of £6 a week on wage increases, whilst Phase II which began in July 1976 imposed a limit of 5%. Thus the rise in average earnings fell from 27% in 1975 to 9% in 1977.

The rise in the inflation rate between 1978 and 1980 can be traced to a number of influences, of which the first was the revival of demand pressure in 1978 and 1979. Oil prices rose sharply between 1978 and 1980, with the OPEC price more than doubling between these years. A more serious factor, however, was the withdrawal of union co-operation with incomes policy and the wage increases associated with the 1978–9 'winter of discontent'. But a further four percentage points were added to retail prices by the budget decision of June 1979 to raise VAT from 8 to 15%. Without this increase the task of reducing inflation in the next three years might well have proved easier.

During the 1980s the inflation rate subsided from that of the seventies, and in all other respects followed the principle that demand pressure (measured by the vacancy figures) was the principal determinant of wage changes, and through them of price changes. These have been explored in the previous two sections. Between 1980 and 1986 the inflation rate fell by 15 percentage points, although the decline would have been less without the VAT increase. World primary product prices were falling at this time (in terms of dollars), but UK import prices (in sterling) rose each year at a fairly steady 8–10% and were not, as some commentators have suggested, a cause of the lowered inflation rate. The cause of the reduced rate of inflation in this period, primarily internal, was the low pressure of demand and the low vacancy rate (see Figure 1.8). The figures for industrial disputes also show a marked reduction over this period.

After 1986, the rate of inflation was creeping up again, mainly as a consequence of the gradual rise in the pressure of demand for labour. Thus by the end of 1988, earnings were increasing at 9½% a year compared with 7½% two years earlier; profit margins were increasing too; and a sharp rise in mortgage interest rates was estimated to have added about 1½% to the index of retail prices. The recession that followed brought a sharp reduction in the pressure of demand – almost as sharp as in 1981 – with a consequent reduction in the growth of money earnings and retail prices. The rise in import prices was also abating during this period.

5   MACROECONOMIC POLICY

5.1   Demand Management

The traditional objectives of short-term macroeconomic policy were the maintenance of a high level of employment and a reasonably stable level of prices. This tradition, however, belongs to normative thought. It is open to any government to break with tradition if it chooses. Thus the period since the end of the Second World War can be divided into two, or perhaps three, sub-periods. In the first of these, the era of demand management, which lasted from 1944 to about 1974, governments of both the main political parties sought to achieve both high employment *and* price stability. In the third period, starting when Mrs Thatcher took office in 1979, and continuing until the present time, price stability has been the main macroeconomic objective, and the employment objective has taken a low priority except in so far as it coincided with the desire to cut taxes. Between these periods, from 1974 to 1979, the situation was, perhaps, more like the third than the first. The huge inflation of 1974 and 1975, and the balance-of-payments difficulties which followed, were major constraints on the Labour government's economic policy. Unemployment, which was high by the standards of earlier years, was allowed to rise, although not to the heights experienced in the 1980s and nineties.

During the demand-management era, governments developed a systematic approach to the problem of maintaining high employment, many features of which remain today. The objective was announced in the White Paper on *Employment Policy* (Cmd.6527) issued by the wartime coalition government. The White Paper stated that:

> The Government believe that, once the war has been won, we can make a fresh approach, with better chances of success than ever before, to the

task of maintaining a high and stable level of employment without sacrificing the essential liberties of a free society.

The White Paper recommended that there should be a permanent staff of statisticians and economists in the Civil Service with responsibility for interpreting economic trends and advising on policy. The execution of employment policy was to be examined annually by Parliament in the debate on the Budget. The White Paper foresaw that high levels of employment were likely to endanger price stability, and pointed out the need for 'moderation in wage matters by employers and employees' as the essential condition for the success of the policy.

For nearly thirty years the task of maintaining a high level of employment proved to be less difficult and less inflationary than had been feared. Employment levels were higher than the authors of the 1944 White Paper had hoped for, and inflation, at 3% per year in the 1950s and 4% in the 1960s, was moderate.

As was noted in section 2, however, the postwar economy passed through a series of fluctuations, minor until the 1970s, with the annual unemployment rate varying within a narrow range. Part of the reason for these fluctuations could be found in the different views taken by successive governments (or sometimes by the same governments at different times) as to the most desirable pressure of demand. The aim of high employment was always in some measure of conflict with the balance of payments and with price stability. Fiscal and monetary measures which affect employment were sometimes directed towards the required balance of payments, with the consequence that the employment objective sometimes took second place. This conflict was noticeable in two periods: from early 1956 to early 1959 when the Conservative government was aiming at a long-term balance-of-payments surplus (and when there was also concern about inflation), and the period immediately preceding and following the devaluation of sterling in November 1967.

An attempt to resolve the conflict between the employment objective and price stability was the occasional resort to incomes policy – in the sense of voluntary or compulsory guidelines for the rate of increase in wages and prices. But this was unpopular and seldom successful. The conflict remained unresolved, and together with the balance of payments, helps to explain why governments did not always aim to achieve the same level of employment. The targets for demand management tended to fluctuate according to circumstances and the priorities of the government of the day.

Once the government had decided on its preferred level of output and employment, the problem of how to attain it could be seen as a largely technical one – a matter of forecasting demand and output some period ahead, and then of adjusting the instruments of policy so as to bring the forecast level up (or down) to the target level.

Forecasts were necessary because of the time-lags and delays in the operation of policy instruments. The key statistics of the economy are all out of date by at least one month and, in some cases, much longer; civil servants may take time to advise the appropriate action; Parliament may take three months to enact it; and even after the policy is put into force, the full economic effects may not appear for some months afterwards. With reliable forecasts, the problem of delay between the need for intervention and its effects could be taken care of.

Thus the system adopted under demand management was for the Treasury to keep a constant watch on the main economic time-series and to make forecasts of GDP, employment, prices and the balance of payments for a period running 12–18 months ahead. The forecasting exercises took place three times a year, of which the most important were those preceding the public expenditure decision in the autumn and the main Budget in March or April. On receipt of the forecast, the Chancellor of the Exchequer was in a position to decide whether the situation foreseen was acceptable – in terms of employment, inflation and the balance of payments – or whether it needed adjustment. The adjustments might consist of changes in government expenditure or in tax rates, although in general the Treasury took the view that public expenditure was not a suitable instrument for fine-tuning because (i) its level was determined by quite separate political and social considerations which could not be subordinated to employment policy, and (ii) it was difficult to monitor the timing of government projects.[1] Thus the more usual instruments of demand management were changes in tax rates, particularly income tax and indirect taxes. For these, a 'ready reckoner' was drawn up to indicate the effects of given changes in tax rates on GDP and other key variables, such as unemployment, the balance of payments and prices. This followed the lines set out in the discussion of the multiplier above (sections 3.5 and 3.6). Thus, the Chancellor could decide by how much taxes should be raised or lowered in order to achieve what he saw as the most satisfactory level of demand. The system of demand management improved over the years as a result of developments in economic statistics – particularly the production of quarterly GDP account with seasonal adjustments – and some improvement in forecasting methods.

There were various shortcomings in the system, not all of them serious. They concerned the 'fine-tuning' of fiscal adjustments to forecasts which were not wholly accurate; the tendency for the balance of payments to deteriorate whenever the government attempted to stimulate demand; the use of fiscal instruments to win elections; and the claim (a disputed one) that policy was 'destabilizing' in the sense either that it made fluctuations worse than they would otherwise have been or that policy interventions sometimes or generally took the economy further from the government's short-term objective than it would have been if policy had been neutral. In retrospect, the most serious failing may have been that over the whole period governments attempted to run the economy at too high a pressure of demand, with

---

[1] J.C.R.Dow, *The Management of the British Economy, 1945–60* (Cambridge University Press, 1964), pp. 180–1.

the consequence that inflation, although quite moderate, became endemic and difficult to eliminate.[1]

The system of demand management can be used to influence either employment or inflation, and, although the name is consciously avoided today, there is no great difference between the current system of inflation control and the older approach to employment policy. The objectives and instruments have changed, but the system of forecasts and budget judgements related to them remains the same.

5.2 Debt and Deficits

Government action to expand the economy and to restore a tolerable level of employment leads inevitably, to a 'deterioration' in the budget balance, and in most circumstances to a budget deficit. The initial stimulus to demand, whether it is a tax cut or a rise in public spending, has this effect and, although the process of rising incomes tends to raise tax revenues, this will not be enough to offset the initial increase in the deficit.

A budget deficit, therefore, is the more or less certain consequence of any attempt to use fiscal measures to restore employment, and this raises two questions:

(i) The Technical Question: The first question is the technical issue of how the deficit is to be financed. Can it be done by printing money, or does the finance have to be raised by issuing interest-bearing bonds to the public? The answer, briefly, is that monetary finance can be used in the initial stages of the recovery, but when 'full employment' is reached the main source of finance has to be debt issue. This is because a perpetual growth of the stock of money when the demand for money is unchanging can only result in a progressive lowering of interest rates, and, therefore, in levels of demand which are higher than optimal – leading to more inflation than the government is able to accept. (It may help to simplify the problem by assuming that the optimal level of demand is one at which there is no inflation at all.)

If it is assumed that there is no recovery in private investment, then the deficit will not go away, and each year will have to be financed by the same annual addition to the stock of bonds. The National Debt, therefore, which is the cumulative sum of all bond issues, will rise indefinitely. So too will the ratio of debt to national income. This will also mean that the ratio of debt interest to personal income will rise indefinitely, a situation which is quite possible because the interest receipts are transfer payments. Recall that personal income consists of transfer payments as well as employment income and dividends, so that it is quite possible in principle for personal income (before tax) to be well in excess of GDP (see section 3.5).

---

[1]   For a further discussion and an account of the accuracy of forecasts over this period, see the 12th and earlier editions of this volume.

(ii) The Policy Question: The policy question is concerned with whether or not the budget deficit and the consequential rise in the National Debt can be accepted with equanimity.

Here the argument can become confused if the national debt is seen as being analogous to individual debt. If an individual gets into debt, he or she will know that the debt must be repaid, and that this will impose a burden in the form of more work or less consumption. The national debt, however, does not have to be repaid in the same way, and as a matter of history, has grown steadily larger for most of the period since its origin in 1694. The government is, of course, obliged to honour its promises to purchasers of bonds, and will do so by repaying them on maturity. But the government can, and usually does, borrow again, so that the debt in total is not repaid. The national debt is largely owed to ourselves, and does not impose a repayment burden in the same way as private debt.[1]

So does a rise in the national debt matter? The Keynesian answer is that the question must be judged, not by an appeal to doubtful notions of fiscal propriety, but by an appraisal of the consequences of the policy – all the consequences. This is one of the main postulates of Lerner's Theory of Functional Finance.[2] The crucial question is how to choose between two sets of circumstances: on the one hand, a situation in which there are deficits, a rising debt and, at the same time, 'full employment'; or the alternative situation of a balanced budget, an unchanging debt, but large-scale unemployment. (Choosing between these two situations may be called the Keynesian Problem of the national debt, and should be distinguished from the Classical Problem of the debt, which is the question of whether a government already at full employment is better off financing a rise in its expenditure by new taxes or by issuing bonds.)

One of the consequences of a rising national debt is that the interest payments on the debt must rise, and must, in fact, rise continuously. To pay for these it is necessary to raise taxes – also continuously. Higher taxes are needed not only to finance the secondary deficit created by the interest payments, but also to hold down personal incomes to the level deemed to be consistent with full employment and no inflation. There is, therefore, a redistribution of income from the taxpayers to the recipients of debt interest. This may raise some problems if the transfer is not consistent with the government's policy for the distribution of income. But for many, this is merely a 'nuisance' and not sufficiently serious to prefer unemployment to full employment. Underemployment implies a loss of real output, whereas

---

[1] This elementary proposition is not always understood or appreciated, and there is a flourishing school of macroeconomists – the 'new classical' school – which assumes that the national debt has to be repaid and that there is a limit to the debt–income ratio. For a helpfully sceptical account of this school see K.D.Hoover, *The New Classical Macroeconomics* (Blackwell, 1988).

[2] A.P.Lerner, 'Functional Finance and the Federal Debt', *Social Research*, February 1943; reprinted in M.G.Mueller, *Readings in Macroeconomics* (Holt, Rinehart and Winston, New York, 1966).

the debt interest problem is simply a transfer problem. It is not a burden in the sense of lowering national income.

This conclusion, however, is a normative one – acceptable to most Keynesians – but not compelling for all. Someone who attaches an extremely high priority to not redistributing income could take a different view – as could someone who holds the constitutional view that it is wrong to impose a tax burden on future generations when they are not represented at the time the decision is made – which is one of the positions taken by Professor Buchanan.[1] Our own (normative) view is that the 'burden' of the interest tax is not too serious, and that future generations can change taxes if they wish to. So we conclude that the problem of a rising national debt is not an obstacle to full-employment policy. There may be other obstacles, but debt problems are not serious enough to stand in the way of fiscal expansion to raise output and employment.

This conclusion does not lie easily with the new guidelines laid down by the Maastricht Treaty, under which public-sector deficits should not exceed 3% of GDP. This rule, if strictly applied, could become an impediment to full-employment policies, although at the time of writing a number of countries (including the UK, Belgium, Greece, Italy, Portugal and Spain) appear to be in violation of the guideline. But it remains to be seen whether the rule will be insisted on.

At the time of the 1992 Budget the Chancellor of the Exchequer published a forecast that the Public Sector Borrowing Requirement (PSBR) – which is the combined deficit of the central government, local authorities and public corporations – would be £28bn in 1992–3. At $4\frac{1}{2}\%$ of money GDP, this was not only at variance with the Maastricht guidelines but was widely condemned as 'irresponsible'. But the Chancellor's critics did not say how they, themselves, would have avoided the deficit – what taxes they would have raised or what expenditures they would have cut. The Chancellor was right to reply that a fiscal deficit was quite acceptable in a period of recession. He might also have said that to eliminate the deficit would have entailed making the recession larger than it was already. As Abba Lerner pointed out many years ago, fiscal actions must always be judged by their consequences.

5.3 Economic Policy and Inflation

Under flexible exchange rates, inflation does not itself reduce the average level of real income, although policies to counter it may have this consequence. Under fixed rates, however, a faster inflation in the UK than elsewhere will lead to lower output and employment in the export sector. The other main effect of inflation is that it brings about an arbitrary transfer of real income from some groups to others: from members of weak trade

---

[1] J.M.Buchanan, *The Public Principles of Public Debt* (Irwin, 1958). See also J.M.Buchanan, C.K.Rowley and D.Tollison (eds), *Deficits* (Blackwell, 1987).

unions to members of stronger unions, from the old to the able-bodied, and from those dependent upon non-indexed retirement incomes to those in work.[1]

Fast inflation produces sharp declines in real income between one annual wage settlement and the next, and this can cause unrest. It acts as a 'tax' on cash holdings, reducing their purchasing power; and if nominal interest rates are sticky, it reduces the real value of certain types of asset – thus leading to transfers of wealth between different groups of people. Finally, the prospect of inflation creates the fear that living standards will drop, and destroys confidence in the government's management of the economy.

In the period when inflation was merely creeping it may have been possible to regard it as a small price to pay for high employment. A gently rising trade-off between inflation and unemployment made the problem of political compromise minimal compared with the situation in the 1970s and after. The arrival of fast inflation transformed the policy problem. It meant that real incomes were rapidly eroded between wage settlements, and it transformed economic behaviour. Economic units learned how to live with inflation and sought to defend their real wages either by insisting on a full compensation for past increases in the cost of living or, perhaps, by bargaining on the basis of price forecasts. This meant that there were two main methods of bringing inflation under control. One was to deflate domestic demand to such a low level that its downwards effect was sufficient to offset any upwards effect coming from prior price increases. Given that prices were increasing at rates of 10 or 20%, this would have necessitated either intolerably high unemployment or an unbearably long period of correction. The other alternative was an incomes policy under which the rate of wage increase was subjected to statutory or firm quasi-statutory control.

A statutory incomes policy was tried by the Conservative government in 1972–4 after its attempt at a voluntary policy had failed. The new policy led to unrest, chiefly because one trade union, the National Union of Mineworkers, was prepared to 'go slow' and finally strike rather than accept its terms. It was this which led to the early election of 1974, and, it is argued, to the defeat of the Conservative Party.[2] Stage III of the policy provided for the effective indexation of wages to the cost of living. But this stage coincided with a major rise in import prices, and had the unfortunate consequence, therefore, of linking wages directly to the import price inflation.

The incoming Labour government continued the indexation provisions under the 'Social Contract' but little further was done to prevent inflation until July 1975, when a voluntary incomes policy was introduced in three stages, starting with a maximum increase of £6 per week. The rate of change of earnings fell from 27% in 1975 to 9% in 1977, and in prices from 24% in

---

[1]   For a further discussion of the effects of inflation, see W. Eltis, 'How Inflation Undermines Industrial Success', *National Westminster Bank Review*, February 1991, and J. Fender, *Inflation* (Harvester Wheatsheaf, 1990).
[2]   See M. J. Stewart, *Politics and Economic Policy in the UK since 1964, op. cit.*

1975 to 8% in 1978 (Table 1.9), and for the first time since the 1960s an incomes policy could be said to have made a significant impact upon the rate of wage inflation. It was estimated in the 12th edition of this book that the effect of the policy was to reduce wages below what they would otherwise have been by about 3% per annum for three years. But in the 'catch-up' that followed, the estimates suggest that these effects were partly eliminated.[1] Other work has suggested less effect, but whatever the numerical results of incomes policies, few governments would be prepared to accept a repetition of the spate of industrial disputes – a direct reaction to the policy – which occurred during the 'winter of discontent' of 1978–9.

5.4   Counter-Inflationary Policy Since 1979: The MTFS and After

The Conservative government which was returned in May 1979 was determined to reduce inflation without recourse to incomes policy. The government was also pledged to reduce income tax, and in the Budget of June 1979, the standard rate was lowered from 33 to 30p in the £. The revenue effects were counterbalanced by an increase in VAT from 8 to 15%, an act of policy which was itself inflationary – adding an estimated 4% to the RPI directly and still more via the wage-price spiral.

The chosen method for dealing with inflation was the imposition of monetary targets under the Medium Term Financial Strategy (or MTFS) introduced with the *Financial Statement and Budget Report* (FSBR) of March 1980. The strategy set target rates for the growth of the broad money stock (£M3) over a four-year period together with a planned reduction in the public sector borrowing requirement (PSBR), which is the combined deficit of the central government, local authorities and public corporations:

Financial Year	1980/81	1981/82	1982/83	1983/84
Target growth of £M3 (%)	7–11	6–10	5–9	4–8
Projected PSBR as % of GDP	3.75	3.0	2.25	1.5
Actuals: growth of £M3 (%)	19.4	12.8	11.2	9.4
PSBR as % of GDP	5.6	3.4	3.2	3.2

The ideas behind the MTFS reflected a variety of views and attitudes. One element was the crude 'monetarist' belief that inflation is caused by prior increases in the stock of money. On this assumption, a progressive reduction in the money stock was seen to be a necessary condition for a gradual fall in the inflation rate. But given that the budget deficit (and PSBR) were financed by a mix of money creation and debt issue, the fall in money creation would mean that new issues of debt would be increasing over time.

---

[1] S.G.B.Henry, 'Incomes Policy and Aggregate Pay', in J.L.Fallick and R.F.Elliott (eds.) *Incomes Policies, Inflation and Relative Pay* (Allen and Unwin, 1981); see also K.Mayhew, 'Traditional Incomes Policies', *Oxford Bulletin of Economics and Statistics*, February 1983. The effects of wage-reduction are, of course, multiplied via effects on prices and back, via the spiral, to wages.

The effect of this addition to the demand for loanable funds would be to raise interest rates and 'crowd out' private-sector investment – something the government did not wish to happen. Hence the solution chosen by the government was to enforce a decline in the PSBR itself, and projections to this effect were included in the FSBR.

A second idea behind the MTFS was the belief that expectations were of key significance in the inflationary process, and that these in turn were determined by the expected growth of the money stock. In some quarters, it was even believed that this would affect wage demands. Thus the 1980 FSBR stated that 'the speed with which inflation falls will depend crucially upon expectations both in the United Kingdom and overseas'. The MTFS also gained support from those who believed it would act as a discipline for budgetary policy, ensuring that the recession would not be countered and would thus, on Phillips Curve lines, bring down the rate of wage inflation by creating unemployment. Finally, it appealed to those who thought that public expenditure was too high.

In the first two years of the MTFS, the projected PSBR was treated as an inflexible target, and this meant that when unemployment rose by more than had been allowed for in the FSBR projection, the government felt impelled to look either for cuts in expenditure (which made the recession worse) or for increases in nationalized industry prices (which made inflation worse). In this latter sense the policy was counterproductive.

The MTFS failed to achieve its monetary targets, which were exceeded by 8% in 1980/81 and 3% in 1981/82, a result which put in question the Bank of England's ability to control the stock of money at all precisely. The renewal of the MTFS in 1981, when unemployment was well over two million and the policy was under attack from inside the government as well as outside, had the effect of making the recession worse than it need have been. This was at a time when the rise in the exchange rate (due mainly to North Sea oil and high interest rates) had severely damaged the export and manufacturing sectors. The combined effect was to induce a state of extreme slack in the labour market, such that wage increases abated, and the inflation rate, which had been 18% in 1980 (after the VAT increase) fell to 5% in 1983 and 3% in 1986 (Table 1.9). The MTFS could, perhaps, take credit for this achievement, but its success was due not so much to the monetary strategy as to the recession which it helped to bring about. There is no way of knowing whether it had significant effects through the medium of expectations.[1]

After 1983, the MTFS was retained in name but not in substance. The term figures annually in the *Financial Statement and Budget Report*, but its character changed. Increases in the money stock, which had been seen as precursors of the inflation rate, were now regarded as related to 'nominal

---

[1] For further discussion, see J.C.R.Dow and I.D.Saville, *A Critique of Monetary Policy* (Oxford, 1988), C.Allsopp, 'Monetary and Fiscal Policy in the 1980s', *OREP*, Spring 1985, and C.Allsopp, T.Jenkinson and D.Morris, 'The Assessment: Macroeconomic Policy in the 1980s', *OREP*, Autumn 1991.

income' (GDP in money terms). The crude monetarist belief that monetary growth precedes and causes inflation gave way to more technical considerations such as the proposition that – given the right definition of money – there is a stable demand for money or a stable velocity of circulation. The broad monetary aggregates, including £M3, were found to have unstable velocities of circulation, and in 1986 M0 replaced £M3 as the target variable on the grounds of its more stable velocity. But, in substance, M0 consisted solely of notes, coin and bankers' balances at the Bank of England. It does not include current-account deposits, and, at barely one-tenth the size of M3, it could hardly rank as an important monetary aggregate – even if it was thought to be controllable. It is difficult to believe that its 'targeting' was of any real significance. But the retention of something that could be called a monetary target helped to preserve the illusion that the MTFS was still in business. One-year targets for the growth of M0 were still being mentioned in the Medium Term Financial Strategies of 1991–2 and 1992–3.[1]

With the rise in inflation rates after 1986, ministerial discussion of inflation moved away from concern with monetary growth rates to the exchange rate, import prices, wage demands, and the pressure of demand in the economy – in short, all the factors which the Treasury used to believe in before the 'monetarist revolution' (and which were discussed in section 4 of this chapter). The reduction in inflation rates between 1990 and 1992 was achieved partly through an investment-led recession, which would probably have come anyway, and partly through the high level of interest rates which was needed to secure a capital inflow into the balance of payments. The higher interest rates helped to reduce investment further and caused some fall in consumer spending. The adoption of a fixed exchange rate regime was seen as providing a framework for more stable prices.

5.5   The Inflation–Unemployment Dilemma

The dependence of the rate of increase in wage rates (or earnings) upon the pressure of demand for labour has for many years been taken to signify an important and serious dilemma between the two main policy objectives. According to the original Phillips relationship, the *critical rate of unemployment* in the 1950s was about $2\frac{1}{4}\%$ of the labour force, this being the rate where the increase in wage rates, at 2% per annum, is exactly offset by the annual average rise in productivity – thus holding unit labour costs constant. The critical rate is analogous to the NAIRU (or non-'accelerating'-inflation rate of unemployment) encountered in the theory of the expectations-augmented Phillips Curve.

In section 4, where the vacancy rate was the preferred indicator of excess demand, the *critical vacancy rate* was put at somewhere between 0.3 and 0.5% of the workforce. These rates represent an extremely low pressure of demand, and when experienced in the 1981–4 period were associated with

---

[1]   *FSBRs*, March 1991, March 1992.

unemployment rates of about 10%. If these rates are correct estimates, and it was pointed out that they were by no means welcome, the implication is that to achieve price stability in the UK economy without further intervention it is necessary to have a permanent level of unemployment of something like 2½ million people – a shocking waste of people's energies and resources. And whilst it is possible for macroeconomic policy to reduce unemployment below this level, such reductions come at the cost of positive and increasing rates of inflation – as they did, for example, in the Lawson boom of 1987–9.

The dilemma of price stability *versus* employment is extremely hard to resolve. One approach is to use supply-side measures to reduce the mismatch of vacancies to unemployment – perhaps by measures which aim to train the unskilled unemployed in skills which employers need, at the same time ensuring that the school system produces properly qualified recruits to the labour force. Another is to adopt an incomes policy which effectively cuts real wages by preventing full compensation for price increases. The climate for conventional incomes policies such as those tried in the 1970s might be more favourable in the 1990s than it was then. And alternatives such as the National Economic Assessment in the Labour Party's 1992 manifesto, or the tax-based policy suggested by Professor Layard, could be considered.[1] The move towards wage bargaining at the plant rather than the national level may be of some small help. But without some new policies it is difficult to see how the problem of attaining price stability, or something close to it, without mass unemployment at the same time, is going to be solved.

5.6   The Balance-of-Payments Dilemma

Along with the problem of inflation there is a further dilemma with the balance of payments. The UK balance of payments on current account has been in deficit since 1987. The deficit reached 4% of money GDP in 1989 and, at £4.4bn in 1991, was not far off 1% of GDP even in a year of recession. Any recovery in the economy is likely to make the deficit worse, since imports always rise with GDP and generally must faster. This could lead to an enlargement of the current account deficit, and in the absence of policy measures, to a run on sterling and a threat to the exchange rate. In such circumstances the government can either accept that it should devalue, or adopt alternative measures.

Devaluation within the ERM, which is now advocated by a number of economists, would certainly give a stimulus to exports and employment and a short-term improvement in the external position.[2] But it carries with it the

---

[1] Layard, *op. cit.*
[2] See for example S. Wren-Lewis, *LBS Economic Outlook*, February 1992, the Cambridge Economic Policy Group, *Observer*, 19 April 1992, and J. Grieve Smith, *Guardian*, 28 April 1992.

danger of a progressive price increase which, in the longer term, would erode the whole of the competitive advantage gained from devaluation. This is because devaluation automatically raises the sterling price of imports, which adds immediately to the domestic price level. This, however, is only the beginning, since the effects of higher domestic prices will be passed on in wage bargains with the result that a second round of domestic price increases occurs – and via the wage-price spiral leads to a series of further increases.

To take a simple example, suppose that the £ is devalued by 10%. With imports at approximately 30% of total variable costs, the initial effect is to add 3% to the level of domestic prices. Wage rates will respond, however, with an increase also of 3%. And, since wage costs are weighted 70% in variable costs, the effect of this will be a second-round increase in domestic prices of 0.7 times 3%. Each price rise leads to a further increase which is 0.7 times the previous one, with the result that the series of period-to-period increases in domestic prices is as follows:

$$3(1 + 0.7^2 + 0.7^3 + 0.7^4 + \ldots + 0.7^n) \text{ per cent}$$

This (like the multiplier process) is a geometric progression tending to a limiting value, which in this case is:

$$\frac{1}{1 - 0.7} \text{ of } 3\% = 10\%$$

The effect, therefore, is an eventual rise in the prices of domestically produced goods, including exports, of 10%. The effect of the inflationary process is thus to raise the sterling price of exports by exactly the same percentage as their foreign price was initially reduced by the fall in the exchange rate, thus wiping out the whole of the competitive advantage gained by the devaluation.

The implication of this rather simplified example is that devaluation, if it is the chosen policy, has to be accompanied by ancillary measures which hold down real wages. This may be done either by an incomes policy which breaks into the wage-price spiral and prevents the wage reaction to the first price rise; or, by a supporting deflation of demand, which, besides reducing total output, will also tend to lower real wages by causing money wages to increase less rapidly than prices.

It is clear, therefore, that devaluation, although a possible solution, is not a simple one. Direct measures, such as import controls, are ruled out by international treaty obligations, as well as having unsatisfactory effects on economic welfare. The only other alternatives are a full fiscal deflation of demand or a regime of high interest rates. The first of these has the obvious consequences of depressed output and employment, which are exactly what devaluation tries to avoid. The second method – that of holding interest rates higher in London than in other financial centres – is the policy which was followed (both for domestic and balance-of-payments reasons) after 1988. It operates by attracting loan capital from abroad, thus balancing a current-account deficit with a capital-account surplus. This policy could be followed for a long period of time, but it has the undesirable effect of making fixed investment in the UK less profitable than elsewhere. This means that the stock of capital grows less rapidly than it otherwise would, and the long-term growth of the economy is correspondingly retarded. High interest rates, therefore, impose a resource burden on future generations, and by impairing the ability of UK industry to equip as fully with new technology as its competitors leads to a long-term, further deterioration in the balance of payments.

History shows that it is possible for countries to run current-account deficits for many years, but this is usually in circumstances where the real rate of return on direct investment is high and the country is a natural importer of capital – as, for example, was Canada in the early years of the twentieth century. But when the natural rate of return on physical investment is not so high, as in the case of the USA in the 1970s and the UK in the 1990s, the alternative is a high loan rate of interest. This will attract portfolio investment, but at the cost of retarding domestic capital formation and growth.[1]

6   ECONOMIC PROSPECTS AND POLICIES

During the six-year period from 1986 to 1992 the UK economy moved from a phase of rapid expansion into recession. The peak pressure of demand was reached in 1988; GDP growth fell in 1989 and 1990; and GDP fell in 1991. Unemployment, which declined from 3.1 million in 1986 to 1.6 million in 1990, was up to nearly 2.7 million in March 1992, although inflation, which

TABLE 1.10

Economic Trends and Prospects, 1986–93

	1986	1987	1988	1989	1990	1991	1992	1993 (forecasts)
GDP (% change)	3.6	4.5	4.2	2.2	0.8	−2.4	1.0[a]	3.0[a]
Consumption (% change)	6.2	5.2	7.4	3.5	1.0	−1.7	1.0[a]	3.0[a]
Imports (% change)	6.9	7.8	12.3	7.4	1.3	−2.9	4.1[a]	8.1[a]
Balance of payments on current account (£bn)	0.2	−4.2	−15.5	−20.4	−15.5	−4.5	−6.5	
Unemployment rate (%)	11.1	10.0	8.4	6.3	5.8	8.1	9.5[b]	11.2[b]
Vacancy rate (%)	0.68	0.85	0.88	0.77	0.61	0.43		
Inflation rate (RPI, %)	3.4	4.2	4.9	7.8	9.5	5.8	3.75[c]	3.25[c]
Earnings (Oct.–Feb. %)	7.6	8.6	9.4	8.7	9.5	6.9		

Notes: GDP, consumption and imports of goods and services – all by volume.
[a] Treasury forecasts, *FSBR* 1992–3, March 1992: 2nd half 1992, 1st half 1993.
[b] National Institute forecasts, *NIER* February 1992: calendar year.
[c] Treasury forecasts: 4th qtr 1992, 2nd qtr 1993.

---

[1]   See G. Davies 'The Capital Account and the Sustainability of the UK Trade Deficit', *OREP*, Autumn 1990.

had been 9.5% in 1990, was down to 4.0%. The balance of payments on current account, which might have been expected to be in surplus during a period of depressed output, was in deficit in 1991 – by £4.5bn or 0.8% of money GDP. (See Table 1.10 opposite for the principal figures.) Nominal interest rates had come down from the high levels of 1989, when bank base rates were 15%, but were still very high in early 1992. With base rate at 10% in May 1992 the real rate of interest was still over 7% for most borrowers.

The economic prospects reported by the Treasury in the FSBR of March 1992 were for a small rise in GDP in 1992, but some recovery in the pressure of demand in the first half of 1993, when GDP was predicted to be 3% higher than a year earlier. The balance-of-payments deficit was forecast at £6.5bn in 1992, although other forecasters were suggesting a higher figure: the National Institute's February forecast was for £8.3bn in 1992 and £9.5bn in 1993; and the Cambridge Economic Policy Group were suggesting £8.5bn and £10.0bn for 1992 and 1993.[1] Retail price inflation was put by the Treasury at 3.75% for the 4th quarter of 1992 and 3.25% for the 2nd quarter of 1993. Similar forecasts were being made by other institutions.

The objectives of macroeconomic policy were stated in the MTFS of 1992 as permanently low inflation and a move into the narrow band of the ERM with a parity of 2.95 Deutschmarks. At the same time it was being stated that a principal aim of policy was recovery from the recession. The Treasury's assumptions in the MTFS were for a slow, gradual recovery in output and, perhaps surprisingly, a simultaneous decline in the rate of inflation:

% increase on previous financial year	1991–2	1992–3	1993–4	1994–5	1995–6	1996–7
Real GDP	−2.0	2.0	3.25	3.75	3.50	3.25
GDP deflator	7.0	4.5	3.50	3.00	2.50	2.00

It is questionable whether these assumptions – published shortly before a General Election – were mutually consistent. The growth rate of potential output, which was estimated (in section 2) to have been about 2.2% per annum for 1978–89, was not likely to be appreciably higher in the 1990s. Thus the Treasury's assumption that GDP would grow at rates of 3.25 to 3.75% over 1992–7 implied a gradual tightening of the labour market, and this was likely to *raise* the inflation rate, not lower it, as the Treasury was assuming.

If the government had really wanted to reduce inflation further it would either have had to introduce an effective incomes policy – which it was not likely to do – or it might have allowed the economy to remain in recession until money earnings were rising less fast than prices. That is the unpleasant implication of sections 4 and 5 of this chapter. But to envisage a rise in GDP that was faster than potential combined with a *falling* rate of inflation, appeared to be wishful thinking.

---

[1] *NIER*, February 1992; *Observer*, 19 April 1992.

The Treasury's GDP assumptions would also have meant a fast growth of imports – faster than GDP – although exports, even with some recovery in the world economy, would be likely to grow less fast. The balance of payments, therefore, appeared in early 1992 to be more likely to deteriorate than to improve over the next few years, thus raising the question of what policy measures would have to be taken: devaluation, a return to higher interest rates, or demand deflation?

The tendency for the UK economy to inflation and balance-of-payments deficits – even at undesirably high levels of unemployment – was pointed out in sections 4 and 5 of this chapter. But in early 1992 there were no signs of a determined approach to these very difficult problems. The reader will be able to see for herself whether the 'stop' of 1991 will be followed by a 'go', with falling unemployment, and then another 'stop', as the inflation rate rises and the balance of payments becomes more critical.

REFERENCES AND FURTHER READING

C.J.Allsopp, 'Monetary and Fiscal Policies in the 1980s', *OREP*, Spring 1985.
C.Allsopp, T.Jenkinson and D.Morris, 'The Assessment: Macroeconomic Policy in the 1980s', *OREP*, Autumn 1991.
M.Artis and D.Cobham (eds), *Labour's Economic Policies 1974–1979* (Manchester University Press, 1991).
P.Browning, *The Treasury and Economic Policy 1964–1985* (Longman, 1986).
Central Statistical Office, *United Kingdom National Accounts* (1991 edition, HMSO). The CSO Blue Book.
Charter for Jobs, *We Can Cut Unemployment* (London, 1985).
G.Davies, 'The Capital Account and the Sustainability of the UK Trade Deficit', *OREP*, Autumn 1990.
J.C.R.Dow and I.D.Saville, *A Critique of Monetary Policy* (Oxford University Press, 1988).
W.Eltis, 'How Inflation undermines Industrial Success', *National Westminster Bank Review*, February 1991.
C.Feinstein and R.Matthews, 'The Growth of Output and Productivity in the UK: The 1980s as a phase of the post-war period', *NIER*, August 1990.
N.Gardner, *Decade of Discontent: the Changing British Economy since 1973* (Blackwell, 1987).
J.Grieve Smith, *Full Employment in the 1990s* (Institute of Public Policy Research, 1992).
Sir Bryan Hopkin, M.Miller and B.Reddaway, 'An Alternative Economic Stategy – a Message of Hope', *Cambridge Journal of Economics*, March 1982.
P.Jenkinson, 'The Assessment: Inflation Policy', *OREP*, Winter 1990.

R.Layard, *How to Beat Unemployment* (Oxford University Press, 1986).
R.C.O.Matthews, C.H.Feinstein and J.C.Odling-Smee, *British Economic Growth 1856–1973* (Stanford University Press, 1982).
National Institute Economic Review.
M.Stewart, *Politics and Economic Policy in the UK since 1964* (Pergamon, 1978).
Treasury, *Financial Statement and Budget Report 1992–93*.

2

Money and finance: public expenditure and taxation

Richard Harrington

1   INTRODUCTION

Chapter 1 considered the UK economy from the macroeconomic point of view. As well as examining the main categories of expenditure and considering some of the main macroeconomic problems, the chapter also dealt with government policies for managing aggregate demand. Such policies involve adjusting the levels of public expenditure and of taxation (budgetary policy), and varying the cost of funds in the financial markets, so as to increase or decrease amounts of money and credit available to the economy (monetary policy).

The policies are likely to have many repercussions on the economy over and above their effects on aggregate demand. Further, how well any particular policy works is likely to depend on the structure of the economy. That is to say, macroeconomic policy, like other policies, does not operate in a vacuum. In planning and in assessing policy, governments must take into account potential side-effects of policy actions; equally they have to consider the influence of changes in structures on the effectiveness of policy.

Consider first budgetary policy. The prime purpose of public expenditure is not as a means of regulating aggregate demand. We have public expenditure because we want the things it buys: hospitals and people to work in them, schools and school-teachers, fighter aeroplanes and pilots, etc. The many services provided collectively and paid for out of taxation are of importance in their own right. Demand management should, therefore, be conducted in ways which do not adversely affect the efficiency of publicly provided services. One way that budgetary policy can work adversely in this manner is when policies are changed too frequently. If, in attempts to adjust finely the level of demand in the economy, governments continually alter their expenditure plans, it becomes difficult for those responsible for providing public services to plan ahead and efficiency is likely to suffer.

So attempts to use public expenditure as a means of influencing aggregate demand are constrained by the need not to chop and change spending plans too frequently. For this reason, budgetary policy has tended to rely more on tax changes. But here also, policy is constrained by concerns other than demand management. Taxes have many side-effects. Changes in the taxation of company profits may affect the ability or willingness of firms to invest. High marginal rates of taxation on persons may diminish productive effort and increase the time and resources devoted to tax avoidance. And frequent changes of tax regime will be justly unpopular with companies trying to predict their cash flow and with the Inland Revenue, responsible for collecting direct taxes such as income tax and corporation tax.

The effectiveness of taxes can vary over time as economic circumstances change. An example is the stamp duty imposed on transactions in ordinary shares. For many years this tax produced modest sums of revenue and there was little scope for avoidance. But in recent years, there has been a rapid internationalization of finance, and many transactions in shares, including shares of large UK companies, can now be carried out equally well outside the United Kingdom as within it. There is increasing scope for the tax to be avoided by switching share-dealing abroad. To lessen the incentive for this, the Government reduced the tax from 2% to $\frac{1}{2}$% in two stages in 1984 and 1986.

Consider now monetary policy. The problems are the same in principle, but in practice they have become more acute. During the 1950s and 1960s the authorities could think in terms of a national financial system and could impose a variety of constraints on financial intermediaries in order to influence the availability and/or cost of finance. But the process of internationalization of finance has gone so far, that by the 1990s, it makes more sense to view the British financial system as part of a world financial system. And it is a world financial system in which much business is mobile and in which different centres such as London, New York, Tokyo, Zurich, are in competition with each other. The UK authorities, not unnaturally, wish to see London maintain its position as a key financial centre, with all the earnings and jobs that go with it, and so they have had to adjust policy accordingly. Constraints on financial institutions which reduce their ability to compete with foreign institutions, or which create incentives for business to be done abroad, have been dropped. The authorities have had to completely rethink their methods of implementing monetary policy.

Enough has been said to show that one cannot properly understand macroeconomic policy unless one understands the context and the institutional environment in which it takes place. This requires both an understanding of the working of the financial system and that important subset of it, the monetary system, and also an understanding of the size and composition of public expenditure and its financing. Of course, knowledge of private finance and of public finance is not only necessary in order to comprehend policy. Both are crucial for all aspects of economic life. It is the purpose of this chapter to explain first private finance, then public finance in the UK. We consider first the financial system and the many important changes that have occurred in recent years and then we turn our attention to the composition of government spending and the sources of government revenue.

2   THE FINANCIAL SYSTEM

2.1   Nature and Functions

A financial system is composed of institutions and markets which fulfil a variety of economic functions. Central to all is arranging or facilitating the lending of funds from one economic agent to another. Most other financial services are ancillary to, or derived from, this one. The lending of funds from one economic agent to another – from lender to borrower – can be accomplished in many different ways; but all can be classified into just two distinct approaches.

Firstly, the lender can lend direct to the borrower, albeit perhaps with the assistance of brokers who act in an agency capacity. This is what happens when a person subscribes to a new issue of government stock, deposits money with a local authority or buys a share in a public company. In each case, the person is lending direct to the borrower and is incurring all the risks that such lending involves. This may be called direct finance.

The second approach, which may be called indirect finance, involves a financial intermediary standing between borrower and lender. The lender lends his funds to the intermediary, e.g. a bank or a building society. The intermediary collects the funds from many lenders and decides to whom it will lend. Borrowers approach the intermediary and, if creditworthy, they receive loans. There is no direct contract between lender and borrower. Each deals with the intermediary, each has his contact with the intermediary; instead of one transaction, there are two.

This form of finance seems at first sight to be more roundabout, and to involve the use of more real resources of capital and labour than direct finance. But financial intermediaries are numerous and indirect finance more common than direct finance. What, then, are its advantages? They are many, and they derive from the ability of financial institutions to use their size and expertise to transform financial claims, so that they can offer savers a wider choice of assets than ultimate borrowers are able to do. At the same time, they can offer borrowers a more varied choice of credit terms than ultimate lenders are able to do. To fully appreciate this, consider the most important financial intermediary: the general-purpose bank.

Such a bank accepts deposits of all sizes and on a variety of terms. In the United Kingdom, the largest banks each have many millions of individual deposits, which in the aggregate sum to more than £50bn. They know that, every day, many depositors will withdraw money, but that many others will make new deposits. The law of averages, in normal circumstances, ensures that the total sum of money deposited does not vary greatly. In consequence, banks can allow depositors the freedom to withdraw funds at little or no notice, whilst at the same time making loans to borrowers which last for many years. The banks are said to engage in *maturity transformation*, that is, they borrow short and lend long. It is not only banks that do this. Building Societies lend money on mortgages for periods up to thirty years, whilst still allowing most depositors to withdraw funds on demand or at short notice.

Financial intermediaries not only transform maturities, they also transform risk. With direct finance, the ultimate lender bears the risk of default by the borrower, e.g. a person who buys a share in company X stands to lose money if company X goes into liquidation. The retail banks, who between them have millions of loans outstanding, also stand to lose when borrowers default. But because they are large institutions with trained staff able to judge to whom it is safe to lend and to whom it is not, they are usually able to keep loan losses to a small proportion of total sums advanced. And as past experience enables them to estimate the likely amount of bad debts, they can allow for this by adding a risk premium to the interest they charge borrowers. In this way banks, like other intermediaries, can bear risks and absorb losses, whilst depositors, in normal times, can know that their deposits are virtually riskless.[1]

Financial intermediaries provide other services. Retail banks not only offer deposits withdrawable on demand, they also provide facilities for deposits to be transferred from one account to another, and thereby provide a money-transfer system. Sight deposits in banks have become a superior form of money to notes and coin for most purposes, other than small day-to-day transactions. Life assurance companies, whose main business nowadays is accepting regular payments from lenders of funds, over a number of years, and then providing either a lump-sum payment or an annuity, combine this business with insurance against death. Thus, while the lender expects to receive a certain sum of money after, say, 20 years, he knows that should he die prematurely, the same or another guaranteed sum will be paid to his dependants.

So financial intermediaries perform many functions. And for this reason, many lenders and borrowers find it preferable to deal with intermediaries, rather than to deal direct with each other. This is especially true of small lenders and borrowers, for whom the time-and-trouble costs of direct dealing would normally outweigh any gain in terms of a more favourable interest rate. But there is still need for direct finance. Many wealthy persons are prepared to incur risk by lending direct to private enterprises in the hope of earning extra returns. If the enterprises fail, they lose money, but if the enterprises prosper, they receive increased returns in the form of both higher dividends and capital gains. Further, many persons, rich and poor alike, are happy to lend direct to the Government as here the risk of default is considered negligible. Those with large sums to lend can buy gilt-edged stock (marketable government bonds) but small savers can also lend direct to the Government by purchasing such assets as savings certificates and premium bonds.

---

[1] Which is not to say they are totally riskless or to say that banks never fail. We return to this issue in section 6 below.

During the last 20 years, the financial system, both in the United Kingdom and elsewhere, has been changing rapidly. Banks have introduced new financial instruments; they have developed new techniques of raising funds and making loans; new financial markets have been created. This process – known as financial innovation – has had a profound impact on the way in which financial services are provided, what costs are involved, and where financial services are provided. For this reason it is important to understand what is going on and why.

2.2   Internationalization

The world is shrinking rapidly. Advances in technology have made communications of all sorts easier and faster. People can travel rapidly by air between different parts of the globe and they can communicate easily and cheaply by telephone, telex and fax. Computer networks can be operated on a worldwide basis and information made instantly available to people in different countries. For many economic purposes, national frontiers are of less and less significance, and it is now possible for large firms to run their operations on a global basis. Of course, multinational firms are not new in themselves. But, in earlier times, such firms could not easily integrate their worldwide operations, as communications between head office and foreign subsidiaries were slow and costly. Subsidiaries tended to operate with a considerable degree of autonomy. Now, it is possible for head office to be in almost continuous contact with foreign subsidiaries and branches and to co-ordinate operations in one worldwide strategy.

These changes have been particularly evident in banking and in other areas of finance. Large banks have established networks of offices around the world. These offices can deal actively in the financial markets where they are situated and still report promptly to head office full details of all business done. In consequence, senior officials in head office can monitor closely the worldwide position of the bank in many different financial markets. And if they wish, they can undertake new business, designed to offset or to complement the activities of offices abroad, so as to keep the bank's global balance-sheet in line with what is desired.

At the same time, new international markets have grown in short-term financial assets, in bank loans and in securities. These markets are worldwide, although they tend to be dominated by a limited number of major financial centres. London, with over 500 banks, is the largest, but other centres are important as well; and since much business is potentially mobile, international financial centres are inevitably in competition with each other. International bank loans arranged in New York could be arranged in Paris or Amsterdam: international securities issued in London could be issued in Brussels or Zurich. Success in this competition depends upon things such as good telecommunications facilities, the availability of skilled labour, the tax regime, reserve requirements imposed on banks, the time zone in which a centre finds itself, and many others. This, in turn, means that governments and central banks, if they are concerned about the size of their financial industry (and most of them are) now have to consider carefully how policy actions may affect their national share of what has become an international business.

2.3   Technological Change

Developments in micro-electronic technology have been a crucial factor in the internationalization of banking, but they have also had other effects on banking, as well as on other areas of finance. This is of complex topic, about which books have been written, so what follows should only be seen as a brief summary.[1]

The initial uses of computers in financial institutions were in keeping records and in automating labour-intensive activities such as cheque clearing. As computers became more sophisticated and computing power cheaper, it became possible for records to be updated with increasing frequency and for information to be accessed more easily. This was of great importance: decisions in banking depend on information. Decisions about new business depend on what existing loans are outstanding, to which firms and industrial sectors, in which geographical areas, on the bank's position in short-term financial markets, and on many other aspects of the existing portfolio. Banks which have such information readily available are able to take quicker decisions than banks which do not. In modern banking, keeping track of one's position is not just for purposes of record, it is a key input into new business decisions.

Computers have also made it possible for financial institutions to cope with a much wider range of business. This is one reason for the fading of traditional demarcations between different types of financial institution. When calculations were done manually, it was cost-efficient to keep operations simple and this meant undertaking only a restricted range of business. But now that all sorts of complex calculations can be performed instantaneously, banks and other intermediaries can introduce a more varied range of assets and liabilities, they can deal easily in assets and liabilities denominated in many different currencies (including composite currencies such as the ECU) and they can more readily envisage competing for new types of business. And however complex the balance sheet, however variegated are assets and liabilities, if a bank has access to appropriate computer hardware and software, its managers can still keep track of credit exposures to firms and industries; of mismatches between the maturities of assets and liabilities; of risks due to financing fixed-interest loans on a basis of variable-rate deposits and so on.

---

[1]   An authoritative survey of developments in this area is provided by J.R.S. Revell, *Banking and Electronic Fund Transfers* (OECD, 1983).

New technology has changed dealing rooms out of all recognition. Dealers, whether in foreign exchange, in short-term financial assets or in securities, now use the latest micro-electronic equipment. They have access to screens on which any one of a number of pages of information on interest rates, exchange rates, etc., can be displayed at the touch of a button. Telephone contact with money brokers, with foreign-exchange brokers and with other leading banks is also instantaneous, and deals once struck can be automatically recorded in seconds. This considerable mechanization of dealing has both permitted and encouraged the surge in money-market activity that has occurred during the last two decades, both in London and elsewhere.

The foregoing can be described as back-office technology; it is not seen by most bank clients. But the use of new technology has spread to the front office, to the point of direct contact between banks and clients. The most obvious manifestation to date is the growth in usage of automatic teller machines (ATMs) which permit depositors to withdraw cash and carry out other simple transactions automatically and outside normal banking hours. At the end of 1990, there were over 12,000 ATMs in the UK and the number of cash withdrawals through ATMs is now of the order of 800 million a year.

For a time, the banks were experimenting with a system of electronic funds transfer at point of sale (EFT/POS) designed to replace many payments by cash or by cheque. It required retailers to have specially designed computer terminals and it required bank customers to have their own debit cards. If a card was inserted in a terminal and at the same time the card-holder registered his personal identification number, then payment for purchases would be made automatically by immediate debit to the buyer's account and credit to the retailer's account. But the system would have been expensive, and after much discussion and argument it was abandoned early in 1990 in favour of a less sophisticated but cheaper alternative. The banks have issued debit cards to their customers and these can be used instead of payment by cash or cheque but there is no immediate movement of funds. When a debit card is used, a voucher has to be completed and this has to be processed, with the result that the actual transfer of funds between accounts will take place some four days later.

Another way in which new technology directly affects relations between banks and their customers is through what is called 'office banking'. In essence, what this means is that corporate clients, provided they have adequate computing facilities, can communicate directly with their bank's computer to obtain details of their accounts or to initiate any of a number of transactions. The finance director can send instructions to the bank to make payments, to move money between accounts, to buy or sell foreign exchange or to buy any of a number of short-term financial assets, simply by tapping at a keyboard in his office. For important clients, banks guarantee fulfilment of the instructions within agreed limits. In some cases, involving large clients and large banks, such direct computer links can be international. ·

A number of banks and building societies are offering analogous facilities to personal clients under the name of home banking. This enables anyone with a home computer and a telephone to call up details of his account and to initiate a number of transactions.

3 BANKS, BUILDING SOCIETIES AND MONEY MARKETS

3.1 The Bank of England

The Bank of England was established as a joint-stock company by Act of Parliament in 1694. In return for a large loan to the then Government, it was granted important monopoly rights. Over the years, while still a privately owned institution, it came to exercise a number of important public functions, notably holding the nation's stock of gold and (later) foreign-currency reserves. The Bank (as it is known in financial circles) was nationalized in 1946 and made subject to the authority of the Treasury. It is now unambiguously an arm of government and its main purpose is to carry out a number of important public functions, although it continues to provide banking services for a number of private clients, comprised chiefly of banks, of members of its staff, and a small number of old-established clients who have had accounts with the Bank from the days when it was still a joint-stock company.

Of the many functions of the Bank of England, the following are the most important:

(a) banker to the Government;
(b) banker to the clearing banks;
(c) holder of the nation's stock of gold and foreign-exchange reserves;
(d) manager of the issue of notes and coins;
(e) implementation of government monetary policy;
(f) supervision of banks and of certain other financial institutions.

The Bank of England is banker to Her Majesty's Government; that is to say, it keeps all the main government accounts, receives tax revenues and makes payments in respect of government expenditures. The Bank also arranges borrowing for the Government through the issue of new gilt-edged stock. In most years since World War II, this has been necessary and the Bank of England has been regularly engaged in selling bonds on behalf of the Government. During the years 1988–90, the public-sector accounts were in surplus and, rather than selling new stock, the Bank used the surplus to buy back previously issued bonds. In 1991, the more usual pattern of a public-sector deficit reappeared and the Bank resumed net sales of government stock.

There is a large amount of outstanding government stock (currently over £130bn in total) and this is actively traded by investors and by gilt-edged market-makers. The Bank of England is in a position to exert an influence over this trading and can thereby have some impact upon market expectations of future interest rates. However, in recent years, the Bank has tended to sell or buy stock at rates in line with prevailing market interest rates and has chosen to exert its main influence on interest rates by means of operations in short-term bill markets.

The Bank of England is also banker to the clearing banks, i.e. those retail banks which operate the system through which cheques are cleared and monies transferred from one bank account to another. Although the gross sums transferred through clearing, each day, are large,[1] payments due from one bank to another are normally offset, to a great extent, by payments due in the reverse direction, and it is only necessary to settle a relatively small net balance. This is done, each working day, by transfers between bankers' accounts at the Bank of England.

The Bank of England holds, on behalf of the Government, the nation's stock of gold and foreign-exchange reserves and can use this stock to intervene on the foreign-exchange market. If it is policy to maintain the value of the pound against other currencies (as is now the case with the UK having joined the exchange-rate mechanism of the European monetary system), the Bank can intervene on the foreign-exchange market and buy sterling if it is weak or sell it if it is strong.

The Bank of England acts as note-issuing authority and (on behalf of the Government) manages the minting and issue of new coins. This is a large task: notes wear out, and old notes have to be continually withdrawn from circulation and new ones printed and distributed to the banks. Also, as the economy expands and as inflation erodes the value of money, there is a need for more notes and coins, so the Bank has to see that the supply is continually augmented. There are also seasonal fluctuations, with demands for extra notes and coin at Christmas and over bank-holiday weekends.

The Bank implements government monetary policy. In some accounts of monetary policy, there has been confusion about the division of responsibility between the Bank and the Treasury; but the position is, in principle, quite clear. It is the Government, acting through the Treasury, which is responsible for monetary policy, and it is the Chancellor of the Exchequer who has to defend government policy to Parliament. The Bank can give advice, and given its knowledge and experience of financial markets, its advice will often be influential, but ultimate responsibility lies with the Government.

Once the broad outlines of policy have been decided, it is the task of the Bank of England to implement policy. In order to do this, the Bank is allowed a considerable degree of autonomy. This is quite usual; central banks in other developed countries are also granted autonomy in day-to-day operations. The reason is readily apparent. Monetary policy is conducted largely through operations in financial markets where conditions change

---

[1] About 10 million cheques are cleared each day and in addition there are many credit items (e.g. direct debits) cleared and a small number of high-value items paid by electronic transfer without the use of a cheque. The total of all debit and credit items cleared amounts to approximately £100bn per working day.

from hour to hour, or even minute to minute. Thus, while the objectives of policy may be clear, the Bank must still use discretion over how best to pursue these objectives. For instance, if it is policy to support the international value of the pound, the Bank has to decide when, and by how much, to intervene on the foreign-exchange market. If there is heavy selling of sterling, the Bank may judge that immediate intervention would be futile. On the other hand, if there are signs that dealers are hesitating and are unsure of official intentions, even modest intervention by the Bank may be effective in halting a decline. Similarly, in dealing in the domestic markets in government bonds and in short-term bills, the Bank has to exercise discretion in the timing and in the amount which it buys or sells.

The supervision of the financial system has become of increasing importance. Many modern financial institutions are of such size that were they to fail there would be serious consequences for thousands, or even millions, of persons and firms, with obvious secondary effects on the economy as a whole. In Britain, the Bank of England is the supervisor of the banking system and the associated money markets. This aspect of its work is discussed in section 6 below.

3.2   The Retail Banks

Banking is a diverse business and there are a number of different types of bank. It is common to classify these into four main groups: retail banks, merchant banks, other British banks and foreign banks. And for many purposes, it is convenient to add, as a fifth group, the building societies, as much of their business is similar to that of banks. Figure 2.1 shows, for each of these groups, the amount of deposits outstanding in sterling and in foreign currencies.

The retail banks, as their name suggests, are banks which offer retail banking services to business and personal clients, both small and large, through a network of branches. Such services traditionally cover the taking of deposits at sight and at notice, the provision of chequebooks and the clearing of cheques, the making of loans, sale and purchase of foreign currency and travellers' cheques, dealing with international remittances, safe-deposit facilities, financial advice and maybe insurance broking. In recent years, banks have been actively seeking to increase business and other services have been introduced, notably automated teller machines, eurocheques (cheques which may be written in foreign currencies), long-term mortgage lending, and opportunities for mutual investment in securities through bank-managed unit trusts. The larger banks either own or have established links with security traders and also offer facilities for buying and selling securities.

Retail banking is nowadays contrasted with wholesale banking which involves dealing in large sums of money (typically one million pounds and over) in both sterling and foreign currencies. A large part of such business is

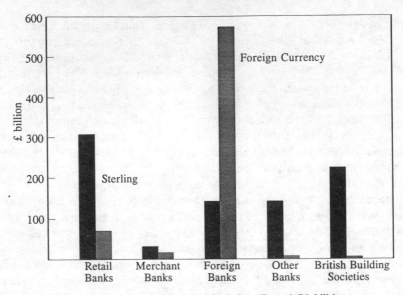

Figure 2.1   Banks and Building Societies – Deposit Liabilities
(*Sources: BEQB*, Nov. 1991; *FS*, April 1992). (*Note:* 'Deposit Liabilities' includes all liabilities other than items in suspense and transmission and capital. Compiled from figures for banks as at 30 September 1991 and for building societies as at 31 December 1991.)

undertaken in organized short-term financial markets in international centres such as London, New York, Tokyo and Paris. The distinction between retail and wholesale banking is conceptual rather than legal and most of the banks classified as retail banks are, in reality, mixed banks which undertake both types of banking. Other banks specialize largely or entirely in wholesale banking.

Published balance-sheets of the different groups of banks are drawn up in the same way, so it is only necessary to discuss these once. Accordingly, we shall discuss in detail the combined balance-sheet of the retail banks, and will then confine ourselves to noting the main differences when we look at other groups of banks.

The banks classified by the Bank of England as retail banks are (at 31 December 1991) as follows:

Abbey National plc
Abbey National Treasury Services plc
Allied Irish Banks, plc
Bank of England, Banking Department
Bank of Ireland
Bank of Scotland
Barclays Bank plc
Clydesdale Bank plc
Co-operative Bank plc
Coutts & Co.
Girobank plc
Lloyds Bank plc
Midland Bank plc
National Westminster Bank plc

Northern Bank Ltd
The Royal Bank of Scotland plc
TSB Bank plc
TSB Bank Northern Ireland plc
TSB Bank Scotland plc
Ulster Bank ltd
Yorkshire Bank plc

Of these banks, Barclays, Lloyds, Midland and National Westminster are the main retail banks of England and Wales; Bank of Scotland, Clydesdale Bank and Royal Bank of Scotland are the main retail banks in Scotland, although the last named also has a number of branches in England and Wales; and Allied Irish Banks, Bank of Ireland, Northern Bank and Ulster Bank are the main retail banks in both Northern Ireland and in the Republic of Ireland.

A subset of the retail banks, comprising the main English and Scottish banks, owns the Cheque and Credit Clearing Company which operates the daily clearing of cheques. Each bank presents for payment cheques that it has received from clients and receives for payment cheques drawn by its clients and paid into other banks. Banks may also present cheques for payment on behalf of other banks who do not participate directly in the clearing and for whom they act as agents. There is a separate electronic clearing system for direct debits, standing orders etc., where the participants include a slightly wider range of banks as well as three large building societies. A third clearing company deals with all high-value same-day clearings which include electronic credit transfers from across the country and high-value cheques (over £100,000) drawn on and paid into certain bank branches within the City of London. The participants here are again the main English and Scottish banks plus a few other banks actively involved in City of London money markets. Banks involved in the clearing of payments are known as clearing banks and settle debts between themselves by payments in or out of accounts at the Bank of England.

The combined balance-sheet of all the retail banks as at end September 1991 is given in Table 2.1. The table covers all business, including wholesale business, on the books of their UK offices.

Liabilities and assets are classified according to whether they are denominated in sterling or in foreign currencies. On the liabilities side of the balance-sheet, it will be noticed that most sterling deposits are from the UK private sector, although significant amounts are also received from other banks and from abroad. Most foreign-currency deposits come from abroad, although there are also important sums derived from other banks as well as from non-bank domestic residents. The items labelled 'CDs' refer to term deposits taken against the issue of a certificate. These certificates of deposits (CDs) are negotiable and hence allow lenders of money to make deposits for fixed periods of, say, three or six months, whilst having the option to sell the CD if they wish to get back their funds before the end of the period. Since CD prices fluctuate in value, an early sale may involve a capital gain or loss.

TABLE 2.1

Retail Banks: Balance Sheet, 30 September 1991 (£m)

Sterling Liabilities

Notes issued	1,584
Deposits: UK banks	25,799
UK public sector	4,326
UK private sector	228,568
overseas	24,305
CDs & other short-term paper	22,554

Foreign Currency Liabilities

Deposits: UK banks	8,027
other United Kingdom	11,068
overseas	42,400
CDs & other short-term paper	8,234
Items in suspense and transmission, capital and other funds (sterling and foreign currencies)	67,068
Total Liabilities	443,933

Sterling Assets

Notes and coins	2,947
Balances with Bank of England (including cash-ratio deposits)	1,100
Market loans: secured money with the discount market	6,979
other UK banks	30,660
UK bank CDs	8,966
UK local authorities	213
overseas	4,624
Bills: Treasury bills	4,040
eligible bank bills	9,913
other	186
Advances: UK public sector	505
UK private sector	241,862
overseas	4,583
Banking Department lending to central government (net)	1,282
Investments: UK government stocks	2,586
others	14,414

Other Currency Assets

Market loans and advances: UK banks	11,547
UK banks CDs	1,469
other UK	11,355
overseas	39,492
Bills	1,909
Investments	13,742
Miscellaneous (sterling and other currencies)	29,557
Total Assets	443,933
Acceptances outstanding	5,688
Eligible liabilities	254,945

Source: BEQB, November 1991.

The small item 'notes issued' refers to private banknotes issued by Scottish and Northern Ireland banks. These banks alone retain the historic right to issue their own notes, although apart from a small fiduciary issue, they have to be backed by holdings of Bank of England notes. The last item on the liabilities side covers items held in suspense for whatever reason (e.g. uncertainty as to who is the rightful owner of a deposit); items in transmission between accounts; and banks' long-term liabilities to shareholders and to bondholders.

Retail bank assets have become very diverse, as Table 2.1 shows. Of the sterling assets, firstly there are holdings of notes and coin (till money), together with balances at the Bank of England. The former are necessary for retail banks on account of their large volume of sight deposits, and the need to be able to convert these into currency, on demand. Other banks, whose main business is wholesale banking and who have few deposits subject to cheque, keep only negligible amounts of notes and coin in their tills. Balances with the Bank of England are composed of obligatory cash ratio deposits and also of those deposits that banks choose to keep with the Bank for their own convenience.

Sterling market loans are sums of money lent to one of several short-term money markets. Secured money with the discount market represents loans against the security of bills or bonds made to the eight discount houses. Loans to 'other UK banks' represent short-term interbank lending. The sterling interbank market is a very active over-the-telephone market in which banks borrow and lend large sums of money of £1m and above. It is used for many purposes. Banks temporarily short of funds can borrow; banks temporarily with excess funds can lend; those who wish to, can improve liquidity by, say, borrowing for two months and lending for two weeks; and those prepared to take risks, in the hope of earning extra profit, can anticipate future interest-rate movements by borrowing short and lending long (if rates are expected to fall) or by lending short and borrowing long (if rates are expected to rise).

Holdings of UK bank CDs represent another form of interbank lending: lending to other banks by purchasing their certificates of deposit. This has the same advantage to a bank as it does to non-bank purchasers of CDs; the loans are more liquid in that the CDs can always be sold prior to maturity. Loans to UK local authorities are short-term loans for periods ranging from a few days up to one year. Loans made to overseas residents include many loans to banks abroad.

Banks also make many loans by discounting bills. Bills are short-term IOUs which may be issued by the Government (Treasury bills), local authorities (local authority bills) or private companies (commercial bills). They are usually issued for three months and are sold to banks, discount houses or other purchasers, at a discount from their value on redemption. The discount is calculated so as to give the purchaser a rate of interest in line with current market rates for similar types of lending. For example, if a bank buys a 91-day commercial bill worth £1,000,000 at a 2% discount, it pays

£980,000. That is to say, it is lending, for 91 days, a sum of £980,000 in the expectation of earning interest of £20,000. It is easy to calculate that this represents a rate of interest of 2.04% over the 91 days, or 8.19% at an annual rate.

Bills are highly marketable, and a bank having made a loan in exchange for a bill is free to rediscount it (i.e. sell it) if it wishes to do so. The Bank of England uses the bill market as a means of influencing the liquidity of the banking system. When it wishes to take money out of the system (and hence raise interest rates), it sells bills. When it wishes to put money into the system (and hence lower interest rates), it buys bills. All Treasury bills are eligible for rediscount at the Bank of England, but only certain local authority bills are eligible and only those commercial bills which bear the acceptance of a bank which has fulfilled certain conditions laid down by the Bank of England are. Such commercial bills are described as eligible bank bills.

Advances represent the main form of sterling lending to non-bank customers. It will be seen that the greater part of such lending is to the UK private sector – persons and firms – with a relatively small amount being lent to customers abroad, and an even smaller amount being lent to the UK public sector. But this does not represent total bank lending to the public sector. We have already seen that banks lend to local authorities via money market loans and by discounting bills. And banks lend to central government in a number of ways, including discounting Treasury bills and buying government bonds.

For statistical purposes, the Banking Department of the Bank of England is included within the retail-banking sector. This may seem anomalous, but it will be recalled that the Bank of England as well as being banker to the Government and to the banks also has a number of private accounts. Lending by the Banking Department to central government is shown net, and can be either positive or negative, but in recent years it has usually been positive (i.e. net lending to the Government).

Sterling investments cover bank holdings of securities, chiefly British government bonds, but also a number of other securities, including sterling-denominated bonds issued by foreign borrowers.

Foreign-currency assets are dominated by interbank lending (within the UK) and by lending overseas, much of which is to banks abroad, but significant sums have also been used for lending to the UK private sector.

'Acceptances outstanding' and 'eligible liabilities' do not constitute additional actual liabilities. Acceptances relate to bank acceptances of commercial bills. A bank accepts a commercial bill when it puts its own name on the bill as a guarantee that, if the company due to redeem the bill should default, the bank itself will pay all monies due. For this service the bank is paid a fee. As it is only in the case of a prior default by another party that the bank becomes liable, acceptances outstanding represent contingent liabilities rather than actual liabilities.

Eligible liabilities are a subset of total liabilities and are defined, broadly speaking, so as to represent, for each bank, total sterling resources derived from deposits and available for lending to non-bank borrowers. More formally, eligible liabilities comprise the following:

(1)   all sterling deposits from non-bank sources with an original maturity of two years or less;
(2)   net sterling interbank borrowing;
(3)   sterling CDs issued less sterling CDs held;
(4)   any net deposit liabilities in sterling to overseas offices;
(5)   any net liability in currencies other than sterling
        less
(6)   60% of the net value of transit items.[1]

This magnitude is of importance, as it is the volume of its eligible liabilities that determines for each bank the amount of 'cash ratio deposits' that it must make with the Bank of England. Since August 1981, all banks with eligible liabilities in excess of £10m have been required to deposit a percentage of these eligible liabilities in a non-interest-bearing account with the Bank. Initially, this was set at 0.5%, but since January 1991, it has been 0.4%. Cash ratio deposits are not, at present, of significance for monetary policy, but are used as a means of providing resources and income to the Bank of England to enable it to carry out its functions.

3.3   Merchant Banks and Other British Banks

In Bank of England statistics, the domestically-owned banks which are not retail banks are divided into two groups: British merchant banks and other British banks. The former group is comprised of large and often old-established institutions that, as well as providing banking services for a limited range of companies and wealthy individuals, act as advisers on corporate finance; in particular they tend to be involved with mergers and acquisitions. It includes well-known names such as Rothschilds, Warburgs and Barings.

The banking business of the British merchant banks is composed largely of wholesale banking – dealing with large corporate clients and operating in the short-term money markets. Their retail business is small and only a minority of such banks have offices in mainland Britain outside London. An abridged balance-sheet for the British merchant banks is given in Table 2.2. It can be seen that approximately one-third of deposits are in currencies other than sterling. Nearly 20% of all deposits originate abroad and over 30% of all deposits are derived from the interbank markets. Correspondingly, on the assets side of the balance-sheet, much lending is through the various money markets. Large sums are lent on the domestic interbank

---

[1]   These components of eligible liabilities are described in detail in 'Reserve Ratios: Further Definitions', *BEQB*, December 1971.

TABLE 2.2

British Merchant Banks: Abridged Balance Sheet, 30 September 1991 (£m)

Sterling Liabilities	
Deposits: UK banks	10,063
other United Kingdom	16,327
overseas	2,064
CDs & other short-term paper	3,423
Foreign Currency Liabilities	
Deposits: UK banks	5,368
other United Kingdom	2,935
overseas	7,588
CDs & other short-term paper	669
Items in suspense and transmission, capital and	
other funds (sterling and other currencies)	8,546
Total Liabilities	56,983
Sterling Assets	
Notes, coins and balances with Bank of England	
(including cash-ratio deposits)	75
Market loans: UK banks and discount houses	9,658
UK bank CDs	4,442
UK local authorities	152
overseas	1,761
Bills	217
Advances: United Kingdom	15,204
overseas	1,634
Investments	3,827
Other Currency Assets	
Market loans and advances: UK banks (including CDs)	3,730
other United Kingdom	1,912
overseas	9,669
Bills and investments	1,915
Miscellaneous (sterling and other currencies)	2,787
Total Assets	56,983
Acceptances outstanding	3,789
Eligible liabilities	17,940

Source: BEQB, November 1991.

market and a large amount is lent abroad, much of it to banks abroad. Direct advances to non-bank customers represent a smaller proportion of total assets than in the case of the retail banks. Eligible liabilities are relatively low.

Merchant banks also undertake a number of other financial activities. They act as issuing houses; that is to say, they act for companies wishing to offer shares to the public and make all arrangements necessary including drawing up the prospectus, receiving applications for shares and making the initial allotment. They also act as fund managers and manage the investments of wealthy individuals, companies, pension funds, etc. Many run unit trusts, and a number are prominent as financial advisers, notably in the field of corporate mergers and takeovers.

The category of 'other British banks' comprises a large number of banks of varying origins. Some are specialized subsidiaries of other financial institutions, some have more the characteristics of a charitable trust but are obliged to register as banks in order to be able to accept deposits. But for many the main business is that of a finance house: raising money in the wholesale markets and lending to industry, for the purchase of capital equipment, and to persons, for the purchase of consumer durables. Many of these banks are relatively small.

An abridged balance-sheet of the other British banks is given in Table 2.3. It can be seen that the main business of these banks is in sterling and consists of taking deposits from other banks and from non-bank sources and making

TABLE 2.3

Other British Banks: Abridged Balance Sheet, 30 September 1991 (£m)

Sterling Liabilities	
Deposits: UK banks	16,152
other United Kingdom	15,307
overseas	5,312
CDs & other short-term paper	759
Foreign Currency Liabilities	
Deposits: UK banks	904
other United Kingdom	1,347
overseas	5,787
CDs & other short-term paper	266
Items in suspense and transmission, capital and	
other funds (sterling and other currencies)	10,612
Total Liabilities	56,035
Sterling Assets	
Notes, coins and balances with Bank of England	
(including cash-ratio deposits)	107
Market loans: UK banks and discount houses	10,822
UK bank CDs	602
UK local authorities	49
overseas	248
Bills	46
Advances: United Kingdom	31,686
overseas	234
Investments	1,700
Other Currency Assets	
Market loans and advances: UK banks (including CDs)	1,891
other United Kingdom	730
overseas	5,523
Bills and investments	940
Miscellaneous (sterling and other currencies)	1,459
Total Assets	56,035
Acceptances outstanding	150
Eligible liabilities	24,951

Source: BEQB, November 1991.

loans to UK residents, almost entirely private-sector residents. Eligible liabilities amount to nearly 45% of total liabilities.

3.4   Foreign Banks

On 31 December 1991 there were 343 different foreign banks operating in the UK, of which 38 were American and 32 were Japanese. Most had only the one office in or near the City of London. A small number of North American and Western European banks have had a London office since before World War II, in some cases since the nineteenth century, but for the most part these foreign banks are comparative newcomers. Most arrived during the 1960s and 1970s.

It was during these decades that a new international banking system was developing. This system, often referred to as the eurodollar market or, more accurately, the euro-currency markets, proved a magnet to banks world-wide. All large banks, as well as many medium-sized ones, sought to become involved. And while the euro-currency markets were truly international, with active dealing in many centres in Western Europe and elsewhere. London was, and still remains, the single most important centre. So it was to London that most foreign banks went, when they decided to compete for a share of the new international banking business, although, naturally, the larger banks also established offices in other important centres of the market as well.

The growth and functioning of the euro-currency markets are discussed below. For present purposes it is sufficient to note that virtually all of the foreign banks have as their main business wholesale banking in foreign currencies, and that much of this business is conducted with companies, persons and banks outside the UK. This is evident from inspection of the abridged balance-sheet for foreign banks in Table 2.4.

Table 2.4 shows all assets and liabilities on the books of UK offices of foreign-owned banks at 30 September 1991. It will be seen that total assets and liabilities are greater than total assets and liabilities held by all British-owned banks. The business of the foreign-owned banks is primarily in foreign currencies, and sterling deposits account for less than one-fifth of total deposits. Of the foreign-currency deposits, over 70% come from abroad (much of it from banks abroad) and approximately a further 11% is accounted for by borrowing in the London interbank market. On the assets side of the balance-sheet it will be seen that much lending is to foreign residents, of which a large proportion goes to banks abroad. There is also substantial domestic interbank lending.

Although sterling business of the foreign banks only represents a small proportion of total business, it is far from negligible. Eligible liabilities, which give a good indication of sterling business with the domestic sector after netting out interbank transactions, amounted to £102,163m, or 40% of the eligible liabilities of the UK retail banks. Having come to London

TABLE 2.4

Foreign Banks: Abridged Balance Sheet, 30 September 1991 (£m)

Sterling Liabilities	
Deposits: UK banks	32,922
other United Kingdom	41,426
overseas	44,127
CDs & other short-term paper	24,030
Foreign Currency Liabilities	
Deposits: UK banks	62,218
other United Kingdom	44,064
overseas	408,298
CDs & other short-term paper	58,758
Items in suspense and transmission, capital and	
other funds (sterling and other currencies)	20,892
Total Liabilities	736,736
Sterling Assets	
Notes, coins and balances with Bank of England	
(including cash-ratio deposits)	509
Market loans: UK banks and discount houses	30,368
UK bank CDs	6,582
UK local authorities	156
overseas	17,004
Bills	441
Advances: United Kingdom	80,457
overseas	8,944
Investments	7,625
Other Currency Assets	
Market loans and advances: UK banks (including CDs)	65,868
other United Kingdom	64,444
overseas	396,843
Bills and investments	45,073
Miscellaneous (sterling and other currencies)	12,424
Total Assets	736,736
Acceptances outstanding	14,657
Eligible liabilities	102,163

Source: BEQB, November 1991.

primarily to do international banking, many of the foreign banks have, nonetheless, been ready to compete for domestic business as well. In a small number of cases, foreign banks have opened offices in provincial centres, such as Birmingham or Manchester.

3.5 Building Societies

The building societies began as part of the self-help movement among skilled workers during the Industrial Revolution. Early societies pooled the savings of members to build houses for them. Often, lotteries were used to decide in what order members had access to the houses as they were finished. When all members were housed, the society was wound up. But, over time, the societies ceased to do their own building and evolved into purely financial institutions. They also largely ceased to be terminating societies and the word 'permanent' entered the name of many societies.

The building societies have grown rapidly in the period since World War II, playing the dominant role in the finance of the growth of owner-occupancy. Their traditional business is simple to describe. They are mutual societies which collect money from many millions of savers in the form of shares and deposits. The word 'share' is a misnomer and shareholders do not participate in profits. The difference between shares and deposits is that shareholders are members of the society and are entitled to vote at annual general meetings. They receive a slightly higher rate of interest but rank below depositors, as creditors, in the event of a dissolution of the society. But since the risks of investing with building societies are low, most investors opt for the higher interest offered by shares and the amount of money held as deposits has dwindled.

The societies devote nearly 80% of their funds to making loans on the security of first mortgages on residential property. The remaining 20% finances modest amounts of other lending to clients but is used mainly as a reserve of liquidity and is invested chiefly in money market assets such as term deposits with banks and CDs.

But whilst the traditional business of collecting savings and providing mortgages to owner-occupiers remains central to their activities, the building societies, like other parts of the financial system, are going through a period of change. The Building Societies Act of 1986 and subsequent Orders in Council have considerably widened the powers of the societies. On the liabilities side of their account, they now offer a wide range of 'shares' at differing rates of interest and they have also to moved into money transmission, with many societies offering accounts subject to cash withdrawals by cheque and through automatic teller machines. The building societies have also become large borrowers in the wholesale money markets, borrowing from banks and selling CDs and short-term and medium-term bonds. On the assets side, the societies are now permitted to lend limited amounts of money on second mortgages and also to provide unsecured personal loans up to a maximum of £10,000.

The building societies have also been empowered to undertake a range of other financial services including estate agency, insurance broking, fund management, and financial advice: societies may, if they wish, take an equity stake in both life and general insurance companies and in stockbrokers.

These new functions represent a considerable extension of building society activities and are another example of the de-specialization that is taking place in finance and of the growth of conglomerates providing a wide range of financial services. Many observers see these changes as the thin end of the wedge and predict that many of the building societies will in time evolve into all-purpose banks. Significantly, the 1986 Act permits building societies to shed their mutual status and to convert to a limited company, whereon they may seek authorization as banks. One large society, the Abbey National, has exercised this option and now has banking status.

With the possible conversion of other large societies into banks and the continuing trend to merger among smaller societies, it is likely that the number of independent societies will continue to fall. In 1960, there were over 700 societies, by 1985 the number had fallen below 170 and it has fallen since then to close to 120.

Although the building societies are still distinguished from other financial intermediaries by their concentration on housing finance, the developments of recent years have brought them much closer to the retail banks. They offer easier withdrawal of funds than hitherto, they have begun to diversify lending and they are active participants in the wholesale money markets. From the other side, the banks now offer mortgage finance. The liabilities of both types of institution are now included in the official definitions of narrow and broad money supply.

Table 2.5 shows the assets and liabilities of building societies at end-December 1991.

TABLE 2.5
Building Societies: Balance Sheet, 31 December 1991 (£m)

Liabilities	
Retail shares and deposits	178,934
Wholesale deposits and commercial paper	19,881
CDs	8,868
Bonds	14,112
Other liabilites and reserves	25,403
Assets	
Sterling bank deposits, including CDs	27,889
Other liquid assets	10,945
First mortgages on owner-occupied property	193,639
Other lending	10,657
Other commercial assets	4,068
Total assets = total liabilities	247,198

Source: BEQB, February 1992.

3.6   Measures of Money

Given the number of different banks in the UK and the variety of types of deposit and other liabilities, there can be no unambiguous definition of what constitutes money. Indeed, the notion of *the* money supply is almost as much an abstraction as the economist's concept of *the* rate of interest. All one can do is to aggregate different sets of assets and derive different measures of money. And this is what is now done in all developed economies, with central banks publishing data for a number of definitions of money. The Bank of England used to publish information on a variety of definitions, spanning the range from M0 (the narrowest) through to M5 (the broadest) and with, in addition, subdivisions in some cases. But recently there has been a rationalization and the Bank now publishes regular information on three series only: a monetary base (M0), retail money (M2) and a broad monetary aggregate (M4).

The narrowest definition, **M0**, covers notes and coin in circulation plus banks' operational balances at the Bank of England. Operational balances exclude required cash-ratio deposits that banks have to maintain. This is not really a measure of money in the conventional sense, more a measure of the potential cash reserves available to support further bank expansion of credit. But, nowadays, there is no attempt to control bank deposits by limiting the availability of cash reserves, so M0 is a somewhat artificial construct. However, it tends to be dominated by the component notes and coin, and holdings of these tend to move in line with spending, with the result that M0 is a good coincident indicator of aggregate expenditure in the economy. Since the 1984 Budget, the Government has set annual targets for the growth of M0.

M2 seeks to be a measure of the money holdings of private-sector residents apart from large wholesale or money-market deposits. It comprises the resident private sector's holdings of notes and coins and sterling retail deposits with banks and building societies. Retail deposits are defined as the sum of:

(a)   all non-interest-bearing deposits;
(b)   chequable sight or time deposits, i.e. deposits subject to cheque or to withdrawal on demand in any form;
(c)   other deposits of less than £100,000 (excluding certificates of deposit) withdrawable within one month without significant penalty.

To avoid double counting, all deposits of banks and building societies themselves are excluded. **M4**, which seeks to be an inclusive measure of money, comprises the holdings of private-sector residents of notes and coin and of all sterling deposits (including certificates of deposit) at banks and building societies, again excluding deposits in the names of banks and building societies themselves.

It has to be stressed that there is no one 'correct' definition of money. Nor, in a time of financial innovation, is there one definition of money which gives clear and consistent predictions of changes in the price level in accordance with the quantity theory of money. Financial innovation means that the relative advantages and attractions of financial assets will be changing and as a result public holdings of these assets will be likely to change independently of changes in the price level or in real income. There need be no close association in the short run between changes in money holdings (on any definition) and changes in output and/or prices. Those who believe that monetary influences are nonetheless an important influence on aggregate demand (and ultimately on output and/or prices) have to monitor a range of monetary indicators. As noted above, M0 is widely seen as a useful co-incident indicator of aggregate demand, although it is necessary to make allowance for a secular rise in its velocity of circulation, i.e. the ratio to M0

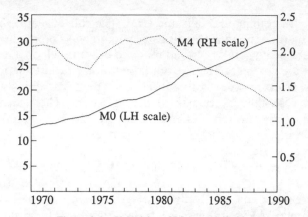

Figure 2.2   Velocities of Money 1969–90
(*Sources: NIE* (The Blue Book), 1991; *ET (AS)*, 1992). (*Note:* Velocity is measured by annual gross domestic product (average estimates) divided by the mid-year values of the monetary series (seasonally adjusted).)

of national income (GDP) has been declining for many years. With M4 it is the reverse; after fluctuating considerably in the 1970s, M4 has exhibited a trend decline in velocity of circulation since 1980, i.e. the ratio to M4 of national income has been rising. The velocity of circulation of M2 has also been declining, albeit more slowly than in the case of M4.[1]

Figure 2.2 shows the changes in velocity for both M0 and M4 for the years 1969–90.

3.7   The Sterling Money Market (Discount Market)

The sterling money market or discount market involves a number of discount houses, other traders in bills, a large number of banks and the Bank of England. The market plays a central role within the monetary system. Discount houses borrow money, mainly from banks but also from other sources, and invest in short-term financial assets, notably bills and certificates of deposit. The funds they borrow are almost wholly short term, either overnight or at call (i.e. can be recalled without notice) and are secured against the financial assets they hold. Thus, the discount houses provide the banks with a convenient form of liquidity which can be added to, or subtracted from, on a day-to-day basis. Banks finding themselves with temporarily surplus funds can add to their deposits with the discount market; banks with a shortage of funds can call back monies already lent to the market. Deposits with discount houses earn a competitive rate of interest and, as they are fully secured, any risk is slight.

The discount market's role in providing liquidity does not end here, for the discount houses also act as market-makers in Treasury bills, local

---

[1] For a discussion of trends in velocity, see Bank of England: 'The Determination of the Monetary Aggregates', *BEQB*, August 1990.

authority bills, commercial bills and CDs. The role of market-maker is an important one. For financial assets to be negotiable (i.e. readily tradeable), there have to be dealers who stand ready to buy and sell on a regular basis. Assets that are not negotiable are not liquid; and efficient financial markets need liquid assets in order that market participants can quickly respond to changes in cash flow by buying or selling assets. The discount houses' willingness to buy and sell bills and CDs ensures their negotiability and so makes them that much more useful as liquid assets, both for banks and for other market participants.

It is not only banks who benefit from an active market in bills; the Bank of England uses the bill market for purposes of monetary policy, to put money into, or take money out of, the banking system. The operations of the Bank can be summarized as follows. Each day, there are large flows of funds between the commercial banks and the Bank of England. Since the Bank acts as banker to the Government, all payments to the Government involve money flowing from the commercial banks to the Bank. Similarly, all payments by the Government involve money flowing from the Bank to the commercial banks. And the Bank of England will also be making and receiving other payments as well, e.g. on account of foreign-exchange transactions, or due to payments by banking clients of the Bank other than the Government. These movements of money both ways will only exactly cancel out by accident; usually there will be a net balance either way. This will mean that the banking system will normally find itself with either a surplus or shortage of cash. Whichever is the position, it will quickly be communicated to the discount market, as banks either offer new deposits or call for the repayment of existing ones. When the market is in surplus, the Bank of England will sell bills in order to absorb the surplus. When the market is short of funds, the Bank will announce its willingness to buy eligible bills, but will leave the discount houses individually to decide at what price to offer these. If the Bank is happy with the level of short-term interest rates implied by the offers from the discount houses, it will then buy the bills, thereby relieving the shortage of cash. On the other hand, if the Bank is not happy with the interest rates implied by the offers of any discount houses, it can reject those offers. The discount houses will then have to seek a 'lender-of-last-resort' loan from the Bank and will pay a penal rate for it.

In this way, the Bank of England uses the bill market and the discount houses to smooth out shortages or surpluses of cash in the banking system. Its tactics are designed to avoid always imposing a pattern of interest rates on the market, whilst still leaving itself free to influence such rates when it deems this desirable.[1]

---

[1] This description of Bank of England operations in the money market is, necessarily, a brief one. For a detailed account, the reader should refer to 'The Role of the Bank of England in the Money Market', *BEQB*, March 1982, and to 'Bank of England Operations in the Sterling Money Market', Annex 3, 'Bank of England Dealings in the Sterling Money Market: Operational Arrangements', *BEQB*, August 1988.

Although the Bank of England may, at times, make loans direct to certain financial institutions, e.g. dealers in government securities, it is traditionally through the discount market that the Bank deals with the banking system. And whilst, on occasions, the Bank will deal direct with one or more clearing banks, it is still the case that only the discount houses are formally entitled to request loans from the Bank of England as lender of last resort.

3.8   Other Domestic Short-Term Money Markets

The sterling money market is the traditional money market in London. For a long time it was the only significant short-term financial market in Britain but, since the mid-1960s, a number of new and more important markets have been created where short-term financial assets are actively traded. This is an important development and one that has occurred in virtually all advanced economies. In this section, we look briefly at the importance of the new domestic markets in short-term financial assets; in the next section we consider the corresponding short-term international markets.

This distinction, while useful for purposes of exposition, is becoming somewhat artificial. Among developed nations, most financial markets are increasingly international. However, as the greater part of all sterling business is still transacted in London, we may refer to short-term markets in sterling as domestic markets. But it should be borne in mind that just as there is considerable borrowing and lending of foreign currencies in London, if for whatever reason British banks were to become inefficient, much sterling business could easily migrate to Brussels, Paris or other centres.

In London, the main markets for short-term funds are the interbank market, the market in large time deposits from non-bank sources and the market in certificates of deposit. All of these include deals in sterling (and also dollars and a number of other currencies). There are also markets for deposits with local authorities and with finance houses (in sterling) and, since the mid-1980s, markets have also existed for short-term deposits denominated in composite currency units (such as the ECU) and Special Drawing Rights (SDRs). Transactions in these markets are in large round sums (£1m and upwards) and are agreed over the telephone, often through specialist money brokers but also, on occasion, direct between the contracting parties.

The growth of short-term money markets where rates of interest are determined by supply and demand for funds is something new. Traditionally, most banks in the UK had their interest rates tied to the Bank of England's discount rate (Bank rate), which meant that rates were administered rather than being competitively determined. It also meant there was little scope for price competition between banks and, apart from some elements of non-price competition, most banks were in the position of just accepting passively such deposits as were offered. Lending was restricted in accordance with funds available as well as by frequent official credit-control measures. Credit rationing was an entrenched feature of the UK financial system.

All this started to change when banks began to compete with each other on price and to bid for new deposits. It started with the growth, in the 1960s, of the market in dollar deposits. The market was international and not subject to the many traditional restraints on domestic sterling business. It was a new development and there was no established customer loyalty among depositors. It involved sufficient numbers of banks from many different countries that agreements on rates of interest were unlikely. The market began as a highly competitive market and has remained so.

The growth of an international market in dollar deposits, centred in London, precipitated an influx of foreign banks, which banks, being newcomers to the United Kingdom, were outside all traditional agreements on interest rates. In addition, they had no existing stock of sterling deposits. If they were to do any business in sterling they would have to compete for deposits by offering a competitive rate of interest. And since they were already competing actively for dollar deposits, this was not a difficult step to take. The process snowballed as domestic banks sought, where possible, to match the rates being offered elsewhere. In 1971, the Bank of England introduced new monetary measures, known as Competition and Credit Control, which abolished all the old controls and agreements on rates of interest. Thenceforth, all banks were free to set their own rates of interest and to compete for funds.

For many banks, it soon became the case that virtually all deposits were taken at market-determined or market-influenced rates of interest. And even for the large retail banks, who for many years had had large volumes of modestly remunerated deposits, the position was changing as competition spread downwards with better terms being offered, even on comparatively small deposits. In 1989, these banks, in the face of competition from smaller banks and some building societies, began to offer interest-bearing chequing accounts. This trend, inevitably, meant a higher average cost of funds and, in turn, greater pressure on banks to maximize the return on assets. Non-obligatory reserve assets and especially unproductive cash holdings were cut to a minimum. This could be done without increasing the risk of illiquidity, as banks were able to use the new markets, and especially the interbank market, as a means of lending funds short term. In this way, they could maintain liquidity at little sacrifice of interest.

So, the short-term financial markets served the dual function of providing funds for those banks that needed them and providing remunerative short-term assets for banks with surplus funds. Both functions were a source of liquidity. Banks can regard their short-term assets as being a source of liquidity, in the traditional manner, but they can also, quite legitimately, regard their ability to borrow new funds at short notice as an additional source of liquidity.

As markets grew, both in number and in depth, so banks became more confident of being able to borrow and lend as they wished. 'Liability management' – the continual adjusting of short-term liabilities – became accepted as a part of modern banking and as a necessary complement to the more traditional asset management. Non-bank borrowers and lenders also adjusted their behaviour. Cash management became the order of the day with finance departments of large companies devoting considerable resources to monitoring market trends and ensuring that their own borrowing and lending were on the best terms.

This process of marketization of banking now appears irreversible. The short-term markets have become an integral part of the financial system, and much business is premised on their continued existence. And for many banks, their standing in the short-term markets and their ability to deal quickly and in large amounts is an important weapon in the competitive struggle for business. We saw above that many banks, as part of their office-banking packages, were ready to guarantee, within limits, the fulfilment of clients' orders for foreign exchange or for the purchase or sale of short-term assets. Such guarantees can only be given by banks confident of their own ability to deal instantly in the relevant financial markets.

The existence of active markets in a number of different currencies means that banks and other dealers will frequently wish to buy or sell particular currencies, so a foreign-exchange market is a necessary complement to these short-term markets. In fact, such is the importance of London as a financial centre, that its foreign-exchange market is, in terms of turnover, the largest in the world. A survey conducted by the Bank of England in April 1989[1] produced estimates of turnover of $187bn per day; of which 27% was accounted for by trading between sterling and the US dollar and a further 22% by trading between the Deutschmark and the US dollar. Most trading is between banks and about half of it is conducted through the intermediation of specialist foreign-exchange brokers. Parallel surveys conducted in a number of other centres showed New York to be the second largest market in foreign exchange ($129bn per day) and Tokyo to be the third ($115bn per day).

There are also a growing number of markets in financial futures and in traded options. A financial future is a financial asset, e.g. a three-month bank deposit or a long-term government bond, which is traded today for delivery in the future. A traded option contract is a saleable right to buy or sell a standard quantity of a given financial asset at a fixed price within a given period of time. Both futures and options markets include contracts to buy or sell currencies, as well as contracts to buy or sell a number of financial assets denominated in sterling or in dollars. It may seem surprising that

---

[1] The results of the survey are given in 'The Market in Foreign Exchange in London', *BEQB*, November 1989.

people should wish to deal, now, in contracts that only come into force (or may be exercised) in the future. But such contracts can be used to manage risk. For instance, a bank makes a six-month, fixed-interest loan on the basis of a three-month deposit. It runs the risk that in three months time, when it replaces the maturing deposit, rates of interest will have risen and it will lose money on the deal. It can hedge the risk by negotiating, now, a three-month deposit, at an agreed rate of interest, for delivery three months hence.

3.9   International Money Markets

Of the short-term markets, the largest are the so-called eurocurrency markets. In broad terms, these markets can be defined as international markets for short-term time deposits and for bank loans (not necessarily short-term) in currencies other than that of the country where the trans-action takes place. That is to say, the eurodollar market is a market in dollar deposits and loans outside of the United States of America; the euro-Deutschmark market is a market in Deutschmark deposits and loans outside of Germany, etc. And for completeness, it should be added that, in addition to loans and deposits, the markets now trades certificates of deposit and other short-term financial instruments.

This raises the obvious question: what is so important about location? Why is a dollar deposit in a bank in London different from a dollar deposit in a bank in Chicago? After all, apart from location, there is no difference in the actual dollars themselves; the holder of either deposit could use them to acquire goods and services in America in the normal way. The answer, essentially, is that dollar deposits held in the USA are subject to all the rules and regulations of the Federal Reserve Board and other American regu-latory agencies; dollar deposits held outside the USA are not. It is a question of jurisdiction. The position of other monies is analogous, but to explain this point more fully we shall remain with the US dollar.

Dollar deposits held outside the USA are not normally subject to reserve requirements. This is so with dollar deposits in most European countries, including the UK. Since reserve requirements in the USA, as in most countries, earn no interest, they are a significant cost to banks. In their absence, banks can operate on narrower margins and hence can offer better terms to both lenders and borrowers of money. Other costs are lower too. The eurodollar market is a wholesale market dealing in sums equal to or in excess of $1m. Deposits and loans are for a fixed term and there are virtually no retail deposits. So the first advantage of the non-resident dollar market is low costs which enable banks to offer more favourable rates of interest.

A second advantage is freedom from exchange controls. This was illustrated in the 1960s when the American authorities introduced a range of measures designed to curb the high level of capital exports from the USA. These included restraints on resident US banks lending dollars abroad. But the demand for dollars in the rest of the world remained high and this demand was channelled into the eurodollar market, where rates of interest rose above the level of rates in the USA. This led non-American residents, not subject to US regulations, to switch dollars from American to European banks, including European branches of American-owned banks. Also, those who received dollars in the normal way of business (e.g. exporters to the USA) and wished to hold them, rather than sell them for another money, naturally chose to keep them in Europe rather than in America. Even central banks switched some of their dollar holdings to commercial banks in Europe. In general, the American measures were a failure and were abolished in January 1974, but not before most of the internationally mobile dollar funds had shifted to Europe.

The eurodollar market is not subject to national restrictions on interest rates. This was also an important influence on developments in the 1960s. Twice during that decade, the US authorities put an effective ceiling on the interest rates that resident American banks could pay on time deposits. The ceiling did not apply outside the USA, so again there was scope and reason for higher rates of interest to be paid on dollar deposits in Europe. Analogous situations have occurred with other monies. On occasions, the German authorities, in attempts to curb speculative buying of Deutschmarks, have ordered domestic banks to pay zero or low rates of interest on new mark deposits by non-residents. The chief result was not to discourage non-residents from holding mark deposits, but to ensure that they held them with banks in Luxembourg or Zurich not subject to the German controls.

During the 1960s and 1970s, the eurodollar market and the parallel markets in other currencies grew rapidly. During much of the 1980s, due, *inter alia*, to the international debt problem, growth was more subdued. But the markets remain large, unfettered, competitive markets for both time deposits and for term loans. Their very size is an attraction in itself, as loans can be arranged for larger amounts than would be possible in most domestic markets. Large loans are usually syndicated, i.e. shared by a group of banks.

A key element in eurocurrency trading is the active interbank market. This market fulfils the functions described in section 3.7 above, and in the process, effectively knits together the many hundreds of different and disparate banks into one coherent market. General shortages or surpluses of funds are quickly reflected in demands for borrowing or in offers of funds in the interbank market and have prompt effects on interest rates there.

Such rates are a barometer of market conditions and are widely used as a basis for determining rates on loans to non-bank customers. The most important rate is the London interbank offered rate for dollar deposits, or LIBOR. It is the rate at which larger banks are prepared to lend dollars. The key rate is for three-month loans although there are also LIBORs for six-month dollar loans, for one-month loans, etc. There are also LIBORs for a number of other currencies traded in London. But since the dollar remains the dominant currency in international banking, it is the LIBOR for dollar deposits which is of most significance.

Most eurocurrency deposits are short term, but lending to non-bank borrowers is often for a period of years. In order to make such medium-term (1–5 years) and long-term (over 5 years) loans, banks have to regularly replace or renegotiate maturing short-term deposits. But they cannot know in advance what interest rates they will have to pay in the future. It follows that it would be risky to offer loans stretching over a number of years at fixed rates of interest. The solution adopted has been to make loans on a variable-rate basis, where the interest rate is expressed as LIBOR plus a percentage and is recalculated every three or six months. The percentage depends on the borrowers' credit standing. In this way, banks avoid a direct interest-rate risk, although they only do so by passing the risk to the borrower, which is not always a satisfactory solution.

3.10   The Determination of Short-Term Interest Rates

It was pointed out in the section on the sterling money market, that the Bank of England exercises a key role in that market which enables it to influence short-term rates of interest. With many payments made each day between the Government and the private sector, it will frequently be the case that there will be a net balance in favour of the Government. This will mean a net loss of funds to the banking system which will be translated quickly into a shortage of money deposited with the discount houses. Only the Bank of England is in a position to relieve this shortage and it is able to decide the price it will charge for so doing and thereby influence short-term rates of interest in the market.

In the discussion of other short-term domestic markets, it was pointed out that these were competitive markets where interest rates were set in accordance with supply of and demand for funds. It was partly due to the growing importance of these markets that official controls over many rates of interest paid and charged by retail banks were abolished. Since 1971, all banks in Britain have been free to set their own rates and nowadays most rates, even in retail banking, follow the trend of rates in the wholesale markets.

This sometimes gives rise to confusion: is it the case that the authorities set the rates, or is it the case that rates are determined by supply and demand? The position, in reality, is quite clear. The authorities no longer impose specific rates of interest on particular financial institutions. Nor, at present, do they seek to control long-term rates of interest. Therefore, they do not directly control the pattern or structure of *relative interest rates*. Supply of and demand for funds is free to exert its influence, and those intermediaries or groups of intermediaries which are more efficient are free to quote better rates than their rivals.

But the Bank of England, through its own market operations, can alter the supply of funds and hence can push the *general level of interest rates* up or down as it sees fit. And whilst the Bank normally only operates in the one market, arbitrage ensures that changes in short-term rates there will promptly be mirrored elsewhere. In fact, the Bank's powers are so well understood that it only needs a sign that the Bank is ready to see rates move one way or another for the banks to move their rates into line.

So the position is that it is the authorities, operating through the Bank of England, who effectively determine the general level of short-term sterling rates of interest. It is then up to market forces to determine the pattern of different relative rates of interest.

In fact, once short-term money market rates change significantly, the banks will also promptly adjust their base rate, i.e. the rate which determines the cost of bank loans for persons and for companies. Building societies also tend to adjust mortgage rates as well as rates paid to savers after changes in money-market rates.

The position is similar in most other developed countries. Thus in the USA, the Federal Reserve Board has the power to determine the level of short-term interest rates. Given this level, it is up to other market participants to decide how to react: what rates they are prepared to pay; what rates they can afford to charge.

None of this says that the authorities, in the UK or in other countries, will exercise their power over short-term rates of interest regardless of the consequences. For instance, low short-term sterling rates of interest would be expected to cause an outflow of funds and a possible fall in the value of the pound. If the British authorities do not want the pound to depreciate, then they cannot, at the same time, operate so as to bring about low short-term rates of interest.

The exchange rate is, at present, the main constraint on the authorities' choice as to levels of rates of interest. By joining the exchange rate mechanism (ERM) of the European Monetary System in October 1990, the British government committed itself to maintaining the value of sterling within a narrow band (a maximum deviation of 6%) against all other ERM currencies. In practice, the Deutschmark plays a dominant role in the ERM and if the UK interest rates were to fall much below German interest rates, it is likely that there would be an outflow of money from Britain putting downward pressure on sterling. So short-term rates in Britain have to be maintained at or slightly above German rates. And since Germany itself is now struggling with the difficult problems consequent upon re-unification and has a higher rate of inflation than is normal, the German central bank – the Deutsche Bundesbank – is keeping short-term rates of interest at relatively high levels. So British rates of interest in 1991 and early 1992 have also remained high, despite the continuing recession.

4   THE CAPITAL MARKET

4.1   Securities, New Issues and Secondary Trading

The capital market is a general term which covers the markets in which securities – equity shares, preference shares and bonds – are bought and sold. Essentially, there are two related markets: the new issue market, where new securities are offered by borrowers wishing to raise new funds; and the secondary market, where existing securities are bought and sold.

In principle, the capital market is an example of what we earlier termed direct finance: lenders of funds lending direct to the ultimate borrower, without the intervention of a financial intermediary. In some cases this is so, as for instance when many individuals subscribed to the sale of shares in British Telecom. But, it is by no means always the case. The majority of the securities listed on the British Stock Exchange are now held by institutional investors such as insurance companies, superannuation funds, unit trusts and investment trusts. Over the years, many personal holders of securities have chosen to sell out and to entrust their financial wealth to intermediaries; so indirect finance has increased. This has been encouraged by a tax system which has favoured saving via superannuation funds and (until 1984) life assurance. Conservative governments in the 1980s tried to reverse the trend and to encourage more personal share-owning. They met with some initial success, but it is too early to say how durable this will be.

Although their detailed terms and conditions can vary widely, most securities fall into three main categories. Firstly, there is the equity share[1] which represents a share in the ownership of a company; the equity shareholders jointly own the company and each has the right to vote at general meetings. If a company makes a profit, that profit belongs to the shareholders and some or all of it may be distributed to them in the form of dividends. But if a company makes a loss, then not only may shareholders receive no dividend, they may also see the market value of their shares fall. Equity shares are risky assets because they represent a claim on a residual; the shareholders own what is left after all other creditors have been paid, and if the company cannot pay all its creditors – it becomes insolvent – then the equity shareholders get nothing.

Secondly, there is a somewhat less risky security – the preference share. Preference shareholders are entitled to dividends paid out of profits but only up to a fixed maximum; but, on the other hand, the claims of preference shareholders take precedence over those of equity shareholders. There is less scope for capital gain and less likelihood of loss. Preference shares do not normally confer voting rights.

Thirdly, there are bonds which, for the most part, are fixed-interest securities. Bondholders lend a sum of money for a stated period of time and in exchange they are entitled to regular payments of interest and the

---

[1]   Equity shares are also known as equities, ordinary shares and (in America) common stocks.

eventual repayment of the principal sum lent. Beyond this, they have no share in profits but their claims normally have precedence over those of both equity shareholders and preference shareholders.

Both types of share are only issued by commercial undertakings where there is an expectation of profit. Bonds are issued by commercial undertakings and also by governments, by provincial and local authorities and by other public bodies including international organizations.

Not all securities are offered for sale to the public in general or to large institutional investors. Most small companies and a number of not-so-small ones remain as private companies where their shares are held by a limited number of owners and there is no formal means of trading them.

The new issue market is concerned with securities that are to be offered to investors more widely. There are two main ways in which this may be done ; securities may be offered for subscription by the general public or they may be placed with (i.e. sold to) a limited number of large investors such as insurance companies and pension funds. Of the two, the public offer for subscription is the more expensive and nowadays tends to be used only by companies going public – i.e. hitherto private companies which wish to raise fresh funds and need to sell new shares – and by the Government for sales of bonds.

A public offering of equity shares will normally be managed by one of the larger security dealers. Much legal and administrative work has to be done and a detailed prospectus prepared giving information on the owners and managers of the firm, on its history, its past and present trading performance and also giving audited profit figures for a number of years. This prospectus will be distributed to other security dealers, banks, investment managers and financial advisers in the United Kingdom and (for larger issues) abroad as well. It must also be advertised in a number of national newspapers. The issue will probably be underwritten, that is to say, a number of institutional investors will, for a fee, agree to take up any shares which remain unsold. The managers of the issue have to arrange for applications for shares to be received and checked and shares allocated among would-be purchasers.

In the case of an issue of UK government bonds,[1] the procedure is somewhat simpler. The issue is managed by the Bank of England. A prospectus is issued and published but it is shorter than a company prospectus because (a) the Government is a regular borrower and (b) the affairs of the Government are already public knowledge in a way that those of a company are not. But it may be noted that, if a foreign government wishes to raise money in Britain, it does have to produce a lengthy prospectus including information on the recent political and economic history of its country. For UK government bonds, issues are usually made in large amounts – £1,000m or more – and applications are invited at or above a specified minimum price (in the case of an issue by tender) or without any minimum price (in the case

---

[1] Government bonds are also known as government stock, gilt-edged securities or just gilts.

of an auction). If there is unsold stock, this will be taken on to the books of the Bank of England as a 'tap stock' and sold on tap to the market as demand materializes. The Bank usually expects to have at least one such stock available so that it can always make sales whenever there is a demand.

A placing of securities direct with institutional investors is a cheaper method of issue than an offer for sale to the public at large. There is no requirement to publicize a lengthy prospectus and the issuers have far fewer purchasers and potential purchasers to deal with. Most bond issues, apart from issues by the Government, are now issued in the form of a placing and a number of companies have also issued limited additional amounts of equity shares in this way.

There is no legal requirement on issuers of new securities to seek a listing on the Stock Exchange, but most do and those that do not make other arrangements to ensure the securities are easily negotiable. People are more likely to buy securities if they know they can sell them again. Neither persons nor corporate bodies can reliably predict their financial circumstances far into the future and know what needs for money may arise. They will not wish to be locked into investments for many years; so assets that can easily be resold will be more attractive than those which cannot. This is the importance of secondary financial markets.

Complying with the requirements for a full listing on the Stock Exchange is expensive and a trading record of a minium of three years is required. But, so as not to discourage smaller companies from making a public offering of shares, the Exchange permits trading in what are called unlisted securities, i.e. securities not admitted to the official list. The conditions to be fulfilled before a company can have its shares traded on the unlisted securities market (USM) are not negligible, but they are less onerous and less costly than for a full listing and the minimum trading record is only two years. A number of companies have gone public through this route. In January 1987, a Third Market was started aimed at even smaller companies but this failed to attract interest and was closed in 1990.

The London Stock Exchange was traditionally the dominant secondary market where securities issued in the United Kingdom were traded. Prior to 1973, there were a number of small exchanges operating in provincial cities but in that year they, along with exchanges in Cork and Dublin, joined with London to form a single Stock Exchange for the entire British Isles. Subsequently, whilst many brokers continued to operate from provincial offices in Britain and Ireland, the trading of securities soon became confined to London (for UK securities) and Dublin (for Irish securities).

Trading on the Stock Exchange (as the combined exchange was called) followed the pattern of the former London Stock Exchange and involved a sharp distinction between the roles of stockbroker and stockjobber. The broker was the person in contact with the public and all persons and firms wishing to buy or sell securities had first to approach a stockbroker. The broker acted as agent for his client and for this he charged a commission.

In order to execute his client's instructions, the broker had to deal with a stockjobber (market maker) on the floor of the Exchange who had portfolios of securities and who stood ready to buy and sell for his own account. There were a number of competitive jobbers, each specializing in a range of securities and brokers were free to shop around and do business with whoever quoted the most favourable price. Stockjobbers were restricted to dealing only with stockbrokers and did not deal direct with the public. All trading was conducted on the floors of the Exchange, apart from some after-hours business conducted over the telephone.

This system imposed what was called 'single capacity', i.e. a firm that was a member of the Stock Exchange either dealt as agent for non-members or it traded for its own account, in which case it did not deal directly with non-members. The system had a number of advantages, notably in avoiding conflicts of interest and it had long been defended by many member firms of the Exchange. But whether it was a good system or not, it was not the way the rest of the world operated. In national markets abroad and in international security dealing, there was dual capacity: large firms combined the roles of broker and jobber and held portfolios of securities in their own name, while still dealing direct with investors. And trading in securities, like other financial activity, was becoming increasingly international. During the 1960s and 1970s, a large new international market in bonds – the eurobond market – had grown up with many of its leading traders based in London. It clearly represented a threat to the traditional British way of dealing in securities.

4.2   The International Eurobond Market

The eurobond market is an international capital market in which securities – predominantly fixed-interest securities but also including some variable or floating rate notes (FRNs) – are issued and sold worldwide. The market is dominated by a number of international security houses and international banks which act both as issuing houses and as market makers. The main borrowers of funds are international organizations, public corporations and large well-known companies. Securities are issued in a range of currencies, but the US dollar is the dominant one. There is no physical market place and the market functions as a worldwide over-the-telephone market. London is the single most important centre.

The issue of new securities involves a lead manager or managers and a syndicate of subscribing banks and security houses. The lead managers arrange the details of the issue: size, currency, duration, interest terms, etc. and then assemble the syndicate of subscribers. Members of the syndicate will intend to place the securities with clients and will subscribe for that amount of securities they feel they can re-sell. The syndicate will normally be international, and in this way, the securities will end up spread among a wide range of investors in a number of countries. Secondary trading is facilitated by one or more security houses, normally including the original lead manager(s), making a market in the securities, i.e. standing ready to quote prices at which they will buy or sell.

Several features of the market are noteworthy. Firstly, it is a market which is subject to minimal official regulation; for while dealers are subject to laws against fraud and malpractice in the countries where they operate, they are not subject to long lists of rules such as those which apply to issues of new securities to be listed on the London or New York Stock Exchanges. No lengthy prospectus is prepared for a new issue and there is no requirement to advertise a proposed new issue in national newspapers. This is justified on the grounds that eurobonds are not offered for sale to the general public; they are 'placed' with professional dealers and only sold to a relatively narrow range of professional investors. This argument seems to have been accepted by the UK authorities when framing the 1986 Financial Services Act. The result is that issue costs are low and considerably less than for a public offering of securities. But, at the same time, the scope for worldwide distribution of eurobonds means that large sums of money – often well in excess of $100m – can be raised.

The market represents an internationalization of security dealing in the same way that the eurocurrency markets represent an internationalization of banking. It also represents a diversification of business for a number of banks who through this market have become actively involved in the issuing and trading of securities. In many cases, banks are doing business in the international capital market that they would not be allowed to do in their own domestic market. In Japan and the USA, national laws still impose a separation of banking and security trading.

In the eurobond market, there has never been a separation of stock-brokers and stockjobbers as was the case on the UK Stock Exchange. The dealers are the security houses and the banks who buy and sell shares on their own behalf and who combine the functions of jobber and broker. For this reason, British stockbrokers and stockjobbers had been unable to participate in what was a fast-growing market; the jobbers because the regulations of the Stock Exchange prevented them from dealing direct with clients; the brokers because the regulations prevented them from dealing as principals. And the newer markets were taking away business from the Stock Exchange: a number of large UK companies chose to issue international bonds rather than raise funds on the domestic market.

4.3   The London Market: The 1986 Reforms and After

By the early 1980s it had become apparent to the more far-sighted that the Stock Exchange in Britain would have to change. In effect, member firms, jobbers and brokers, faced a stark choice: they could continue their traditional ways of doing business and lose the chance of becoming involved in the growing international security market, or they could change their practices to bring them more into line with those elsewhere. But it so happened that, at the time, the Stock Exchange authorities were preoccupied with preparing a defence of their rule book prior to a hearing before the Restrictive Practices Court. The rules of the Exchange had been referred by the Office of Fair Trading (OFT) to the Court under the previous Labour government and, given the complexities of the Exchange rule-book, it was taking time for both the OFT and the Stock Exchange to prepare their respective arguments. But with a growing awareness that this hearing was proving a distraction from the real issues and that other reforms were urgent, the Department of Trade and Industry reached an agreement with the Stock Exchange authorities in July 1983 to drop the case before the Restrictive Practices Court on condition that the Exchange abandon the fixing of commissions for buying and selling securities. Competitively negotiated commission rates were expected to be lower than the hitherto fixed rates, and it was soon accepted that they would not be adequate to support the expensive system of dual capacity. So it was decided that, along with the move to negotiated commissions, the Exchange would permit dual capacity: the combining within one firm of the roles of market maker and broker.[1]

By now, it was a question of the total reform of the Stock Exchange: and one thing led to another. The new market makers would need sufficient capital resources, for market makers necessarily hold blocks of securities so as to be able to sell as well as buy on demand; and whilst they hoped to make profits over the long run, no market maker can always avoid short-term capital losses when security prices are falling. To be able to absorb such short-term losses, it is necessary to have adequate capital reserves. This was the experience of the large American and Japanese security houses, but previously the London stockjobbers had had only modest capital resources and the brokers, whose function had only been that of agent, had had virtually none. So it was necessary for the would-be market makers to acquire new capital – and fast – and this meant outside shareholders. The only likely candidates with sufficient funds to spare were banks, both British and foreign, and certain foreign security dealers.

And there was the question of new technology. Security prices could be displayed on screens, deals could be agreed over the telephone; this is how the eurobond market worked already; so was a trading floor necessary any longer? It was decided to create the infrastructure for a computerized trading system but to leave firms the choice of whether to deal over-the-telephone or to deal between representatives on the floor of the Exchange.

---

[1] The details of the negotiations between the Stock Exchange and the Department of Trade and Industry and their political background are admirably described in Chapter 2 of Margaret Reid, *All Change in the City* (Macmillan, 1988).

After discussion of whether the reforms should be introduced piecemeal or altogether, it was decided to go for the latter option with most of the changes occurring in one 'big bang' on Monday, 27 October 1986.

Big Bang, as it became known, saw the greatest reform of security trading in Britain this century. Large new market makers were created, usually by mergers of broking firms and/or jobbing firms and bank interests. Many were owned by banks or overseas security houses who saw this as a unique opportunity to become established in the London security markets and who were prepared to pay considerable sums of money for the privilege. It was soon found to be more convenient to deal over the telephone, and face-to-face trading on the floor of the London Exchange ceased. Following agreements between the governing body of the Exchange and a similar body representing Eurobond dealers, the Exchange was reconstituted as the International Stock Exchange of the United Kingdom and the Republic of Ireland, although, for brevity, the shorter name 'The Stock Exchange' is still widely used. The new Exchange is a Recognised Investment Exchange (RIE) within the terms of the Financial Services Act of 1986.

Under the new system, firms which opt to be market makers in specified securities agree to display their prices by means of the Stock Exchange Automated Quotations system (SEAQ) and this makes them accessible on screens to other traders. For widely-traded securities, market makers are committed to dealing, up to published maximum amounts, at the prices displayed; for securities that are less widely traded, the prices displayed are indicative rather than guaranteed. As one would expect, the selling price is slightly above the buying price and market makers earn income from this difference. They are also free to charge commission on all transactions, but for most large transactions competition has resulted in commission levels of zero or close to zero. Many brokers, notably the smaller firms of brokers and the provincial brokers, did not become market makers, and have continued to act in an agency capacity, buying and selling securities in transactions with market makers on behalf of clients. But, in contrast to what went on before, clients, at least the larger ones, are free to deal direct with market makers: they are not obliged to use the services of a broker.

The new system did attract new capital into the market and it resulted in a more competitive system with more firms of market makers competing for business in all the regularly traded securities. Commission rates have fallen for large transactions and there has been a tendency for the 'market touch', the gap between best buying and best selling price, to narrow as well. Also, London has significantly increased its business in foreign securities. This said, however, it must be noted that the initial success of Big Bang owed much to the fact that, at the time, share prices were rising strongly. It is always easier for dealers to make money in a rising market. But in October 1987, share prices fell dramatically and subsequently turnover fell. A number of security firms made losses and some withdrew from market making.

By the early 1990s, things had improved and more firms were trading profitably although it remains likely that there will be more market makers who will have to exit the industry. It was inevitable that such major changes should produce a period of uncertainty and continuing adjustment but, on balance, the reform appears to have been a notable success. Security trading in London is more competitive, as is shown by the growth in dealing in foreign securities and by the many reforms that have been introduced in other European securities markets in order to stay competitive with London.

An indication of the importance of the capital market can be gained by looking at the sums of money raised on the new issue market, and by looking at turnover on the secondary market. During the three years 1989–91, new issues of all listed securities, excluding UK government bonds, averaged £9,355m a year. Of this total, just over 60% was accounted for by rights issues, i.e. issues of additional shares by existing public companies and offered, in priority, to existing shareholders. A certain amount of out-standing fixed-interest stock was redeemed each year, both by public companies and by local authorities, so the net amount of new money raised was less than the gross figure given above. For public companies and all overseas borrowers, total net new money raised, in 1989–91, averaged £7,047m a year. In addition, net issues on the USM raised an average of £455m a year over the same period.

Although these are large amounts, they are not large relative to net lending by banks or by building societies. But it must be borne in mind that equity capital is a strategic form of fund raising in that it is risk-bearing. All firms require risk-bearing capital in order that small or temporary losses can be sustained without the existence of the firm being called into question. This is as true of banks as it is of industrial and commercial companies, and many banks have figured among the companies raising new capital in recent years. The capital market is not the largest source of funds to domestic enterprises, but it remains a crucial one.

Throughout the 1970s and early 1980s, new funds raised for the Govern-ment by sales of bonds were usually large and often exceeded the amounts raised for the private sector by sales of all securities. In the late 1980s, the public sector moved into financial surplus and the Government began to repay debt. During the three years 1988–90, there was a net redemption of over £30bn of government stock. But in 1991, the public sector again became a net borrower and in the first three quarters of that year nearly £7bn net of government stock was sold. All projections – official and unofficial – are that the public sector will remain in substantial deficit for the foreseeable future.

Turnover on the Stock Exchange during the years 1989–90 averaged slightly over £1,640bn a year, or over £6,500m per working day. Of the annual average, over £960bn was accounted for by transactions in UK government stock and nearly £600bn was accounted for by transactions in equity shares, of which a growing proportion was in foreign shares. By 1990, the volume of trading in foreign equity shares was almost as large as that of trading in domestic (British and Irish) shares.

5   OTHER FINANCIAL INTERMEDIARIES

5.1   Life Assurance Companies and Pension Funds

Both life assurance companies and pension funds must be classed as financial intermediaries in terms of the description given of financial intermediaries in section 2.1 above. Both take funds from savers and lend to borrowers. The difference between them and most of the institutions previously considered is that they do not provide liquid financial assets. Both offer savers long-term investment possibilities.

The most popular form of life assurance contract nowadays is the endowment policy, although this can come in a number of forms including policies linked to investment in unit trusts. The essential feature of an endowment policy is that the assured pays either a single premium or makes regular payments over a number of years and at the end of this time, the insurance company guarantees to pay a lump sum. If the policy is without profits, this will be a known amount (the sum assured) agreed at the outset; if the policy is with profits, it will be a basic sum assured plus bonuses; if the policy is directly linked to investments in a unit trust, it will depend upon the returns to the investments.

Should the policyholder die before expiry of the policy, his dependants will receive the sum assured and extra profits (if any). Thus, an endowment policy is a mixed financial instrument. It is largely a straightforward long-term financial contract, in which what is returned reflects what has been paid, an element of accrued interest and, maybe, returns on investments, but it also includes insurance cover against death within the currency of the policy.

There are a number of other forms of life assurance contract, but almost all involve either a single large payment or regular payments by the assured over a number of years in exchange for a guarantee of an eventual lump sum payment to the assured, or to his dependants.

Life assurance has been a popular form of saving in the United Kingdom and was, until the 1984 Budget, encouraged by tax relief on premiums paid. The life assurance companies comprise a number of specialist life companies as well as the large general insurance companies who also offer marine, fire and accident insurance. The latter categories of insurance do not represent financial contracts, as we are here using the term, as there is no lending or borrowing involved. The person who insures his house or his car buys a service (indemnity in the event of loss) for which he pays a price. His payment represents consumption expenditure, not saving.

Total accumulated funds held by all life assurers (specialist and general insurance companies) amounted, at end-1989, to £247,827m. Nearly half of this sum was invested in equity shares, domestic and foreign, while large amounts were also invested in property and in British government securities.

Pension funds are set up to provide pensions for members of a particular occupational group, or for employees of a particular firm or public-sector body. The principle is simple: those covered by the fund make regular contributions over a number of years and, upon retirement, are entitled to a regular pension until death. This pension may be of a fixed amount or it may allow for adjustments to compensate for inflation.

The number and size of pension funds have grown during recent decades as more and more firms have set up funds to cover their employees. In some cases of large firms or public corporations, the pension funds now administer considerable sums of money and are numbered among the largest discretionary managers of funds in the country. At end-1989, total net assets of pension funds amounted to £339,675m.

About two-thirds of total assets are invested in equity shares, domestic and foreign, and most of the rest is spread over investments in British government securities, in property, and in short-term assets.

Life assurance companies also provide pensions both for individuals (notably the self-employed) and for groups. For many small firms, it is easier to make pension provision for staff through a life assurance company, than to set up one's own fund. All pension funds, whether administered by independent pension funds or by life assurance companies, have a favourable tax status and do not pay tax on interest and dividends received on their investments.

5.2   Other Institutions

Unit Trusts and Investment Trusts: There are two forms of mutual investment common in the United Kingdom: unit trusts and investment trusts. The intention of mutual investment is to enable small investors to pool resources in order to gain the benefits of diversification which would not be available to each one individually. There are high fixed costs of dealing in negotiable securities and a small investor with, say, £5,000 to invest would not be able to spread this over a number of different companies. He would, more likely, have to put all his eggs in one basket and invest all the money in one company. That would be a risky strategy. But if 1,000 investors, each with £5,000 to invest, were to come together and put their money in a common pool, they would have £5m to invest. This could be diversified over many companies, so reducing the risk. This is the principle of mutual investment.

Unit trusts are legally constituted as trusts with a trust deed and a trustee. The trustee, usually a bank or an insurance company, holds the assets of the unit trust on behalf of the beneficial owners – the unitholders. The trust is managed by a professional manager who is responsible for decisions about investment policy, subject to the provisions of the trust deed. Units can be sold at any time and the sums raised added to the pool of investible resources. Similarly, units can be sold back to the manager, who is then obliged to sell some investments to repay the unitholder. Unitholders are each entitled to a *pro-rata* share of the value of the invested funds of the trust and the Department of Trade and Industry lays down rules for calculating the value of individual units.

Investment trusts are not, in fact, trusts in the legal sense. They are limited companies which issue their own shares and which use the proceeds to invest in other companies. Thus, anyone who buys shares in an investment trust automatically buys a diversified investment. Investment trusts have their shares listed on the Stock Exchange and they are bought and sold like other equity shares.

At end-1990, funds managed by unit trusts amounted to nearly £42bn of which the greater part was invested in equity shares, both in the United Kingdom and abroad. The total assets of investment trusts are somewhat smaller and, at end 1989, amounted to something over £19bn and again most was invested in ordinary shares.

Finance Houses: There are a number of finance houses and consumer credit companies active in the UK. They tend to be small as most of the larger institutions have now taken the status of bank and are included within the category 'other British banks', discussed above. Many are specialized institutions set up to finance the products of particular manufacturers or retailers. Funds are raised largely by issuing bills and by borrowing from banks. At end 1990, such companies had assets outstanding of £9,832m, of which over £7bn was accounted for by loans to persons and to industrial and commercial companies.

6   REGULATING THE FINANCIAL SYSTEM

Financial activity is a large and important part of the modern economy. In Britain, in 1990, financial services accounted for approximately 18% of gross national product. And finance is not a separate activity from others: all firms and all individuals depend on the efficiency and the probity of financial institutions. There is, therefore, a clear public interest in both the competence and the integrity of financial practitioners and this has resulted in increased official regulation of the financial system.

Traditionally, financial institutions were governed by a number of different Acts of Parliament, each relating to different aspects of their business but, more recently, Parliament has sought to provide comprehensive regulation within the framework of a limited number of Acts covering specific financial institutions. The 1979 and 1987 Banking Acts cover the activities of all banks; the 1986 Building Societies Act regulates the building societies and the 1986 Financial Services Act seeks to regulate all trading of securities, of life assurance and of a wide range of ancillary activity.

The 1979 and 1987 Banking Acts require that all firms undertaking banking business be authorized by the Bank of England and lay down detailed conditions for authorization. These include requirements to supply the

Bank regularly with statistical information, to open one's books for inspection upon request from the Bank and to respond to any directives given by the Bank. It is apparent that the Acts give considerable power to the Bank of England, although there is provision for any bank refused authorization to appeal to the Treasury. The regulations cover all engaged in banking within the United Kingdom, both British-owned and foreign-owned banks.

The main public efforts of the Bank, to date, have been in the areas of capital adequacy and of liquidity. It has laid down, for all banks, minimum requirements of capital (i.e. equity capital, reserves and other irredeemable or long-term funds) dependent on both the volume and composition of bank assets. These requirements follow the proposals put forward in 1988 by the Committee on Banking Regulations and Supervisory Practices which is composed of representatives of central banks and supervisory authorities of twelve developed countries[1] and which meets regularly in Basel, Switzerland. These proposals were accepted by the competent authorities in the twelve countries and have since been adopted in whole or in part by many other countries worldwide. The Basel committee worked in close consultation with the European Commission with the result that the 1989 EEC directive on the capital resources of credit institutions closely resembled its own proposals.

The internationally agreed capital standard is a minimum requirement and the Bank of England reserves the right to treat each bank individually and to impose stricter standards where it feels these to be appropriate. The Bank also imposes requirements on each bank as to its liquidity, meaning both its short-term borrowing operations and its holdings of liquid assets.

The provisions of the Building Societies Act of 1986 have already been touched on in section 3.5 above. As well as laying down detailed rules about what activities building societies could and could not engage in, the Act also created a Building Societies Commission with powers over the societies analogous to those of the Bank of England over the banks.

The Financial Services Act of 1986 was a wide-ranging measure designed to regulate the activities of security traders, brokers, agents and advisers. For all of these it is now necessary to be authorized in order to carry on business and authorization requires compliance with a set of rules of conduct.

The Act established a Securities & Investment Board (SIB) with powers of supervision over all firms engaged in financial investment but with power to delegate this supervision to approved regulatory organizations. It was intended that such organizations should be set up for different sections of the industry and that they would include representatives of the firms being regulated, i.e. there would be an element of self-regulation. This was seen as

[1] The twelve countries are Belgium, Canada, France, Germany, Italy, Japan, Luxembourg, Netherlands, Sweden, Switzerland, United Kingdom, United States.

desirable as much of modern financial activity is complex and the only people with a detailed understanding of it are those who are actually engaged in the business.

Four self-regulatory organizations (SROs), have been set up. They are:

(1)   the Securities and Futures Authority (SFA), covering all traders and brokers in securities and in futures and options;

(2)   the Life Assurance & Unit Trust Regulatory Organization (LAUTRO), covering all life assurance companies and unit trusts;

(3)   the Investment Managers Regulatory Organisation (IMRO), covering all fund managers; and

(4)   the Financial Intermediaries, Managers & Brokers Regulatory Association (FIMBRA), covering all agents, brokers and other intermediaries not already covered by one of the other SROs.

Each of these self-regulatory organizations establishes and publishes its own rules of conduct but these rules have to be approved by the Securities & Investment Board. Thus it is incorrect to say that the system is wholly one of self-regulation: it is a mixed system in which self-regulation is permitted but subject to the ultimate authority of a statutory body. It was the Government's hope that this would produce an effective system of regulation but without the bureaucracy and the legalistic approach believed to be inherent in the American model with a single powerful statutory body; the Securities & Exchange Commission.

The Financial Services Act also established the idea of recognized investment exchanges (RIEs). SIB will recognize an exchange where it is satisfied that it provides an efficient and well-run market with adequate financial resources to safeguard investors. Where firms transact business on an RIE, the requirements on them are less onerous than where transactions are carried out on unrecognized exchanges.

The Act also provides for certain professional bodies (e.g. solicitors, accountants) to be recognized by SIB so as to enable their members to continue with traditional financial activities without having to join one of the SROs. But recognition does require the professional bodies to have adequate rules to ensure investor protection.

Following the coming into force of the Act, there were widespread complaints about the length and detail of rule books with accusations of regulatory overkill and concern about the cost of compliance. SIB responded by simplifying its rule book (which serves as a model for the rule books of the SROs) and establishing a set of principles of good conduct as a substitute for many specific rules.

Over the years, the involvement of the EC in financial regulation has grown. The objective of the European Commission is to achieve a single European financial market with financial institutions and their clients able to do business anywhere in the Community unhindered by artificial obstacles and constraints. The Commission has pursued this objective with a three-pronged approach. Firstly, there should be a minimum necessary harmonization of rules and regulations so as to bring about fair competition and to ensure adequate consumer protection. Secondly, institutions should not require authorization to do business in each country; once duly authorized by the competent authorities in one member country, they should be free to operate throughout the Community. Thirdly, all activities of each institution within the Community should be supervised by the authorities in the country in which its chief office is situated (the principle of home country control).

To date, the Commission has largely achieved its ends as far as banking is concerned. A number of directives have been proposed, discussed and finally accepted by the Council of Ministers and have become part of EC law. Banks now have considerable freedom to operate throughout the EC. But the position is very different as far as security dealing is concerned. Although certain measures regarding company prospectuses, financial reporting by listed companies and the marketing of mutual funds have been agreed, what was to have been the main directive on investment services covering security trading, investment advice, portfolio management and dealing in derivative contracts such as futures and options remains the subject of disagreement in the Council of Ministers. A directive was adopted by the Commission in December 1988 and it has been much discussed since, but without agreement. National systems of security trading are more varied than was the case with banking; moving to a common European approach will require more in the way of concessions and compromises. But beyond issues of principle there are also important questions of national self-interest; it appears that many countries fear that, in an open market, London will quickly become the dominant market for European equities, as it is already for international bonds.

But if securing agreement on financial regulation is one problem, enforcing it is another, as a number of recent financial scandals has shown. These have provided several well-publicized instances of individuals or institutions deliberately breaking the law and, as a result, causing large losses to depositors and/or other creditors. This is not the place for a blow-by-blow account of particular scandals but two are worthy of comment: the enforced closure of the Bank of Credit and Commerce International (BCCI) and the collapse of the business empire of the late Mr Robert Maxwell. Both occurred in 1991.

BCCI was a bank originally established by Pakistani interests but which had since passed into the majority ownership of the Sheikh of Abu Dhabi; it was registered in Luxembourg, had interests in many countries but the bulk of its business was in Britain. In the summer of 1991, the Bank of England, working in collaboration with banking supervisors in other countries, withdrew authorization from the bank and brought about its immediate closure. All depositors, large and small, lost access to their money and found themselves in the position of creditors of an insolvent company. Following its closure, it became apparent that BCCI had been engaged in fraud on a large scale which had been disguised by systematic false accounting. There were also allegations of other serious misdemeanours, such as money laundering for terrorist organizations, about which the full truth has yet to be revealed.

No system of regulation – of finance or of other human activities – can ever guarantee that no wrongdoing will ever take place. But the controversy surrounding the closure of BCCI has been about whether the Bank of England acted promptly enough once it had evidence of wrongdoing. This issue was much discussed by the Treasury and Civil Service Committee of the House of Commons which conducted hearings before issuing a report in March 1992.[1] The Bank had evidence which would have justified closing BCCI over a year before it did so, but had chosen not to do so in the hope that a change of management and an injection of fresh funds from the principal shareholder would enable BCCI to operate correctly and would avoid losses to depositors. The Bank's concern for depositors was legitimate but others have suggested that the Bank may also have been influenced by worries about the reputation of London and about the risk of a diplomatic upset to relations between the UK and Abu Dhabi. Be that as it may, the Committee took the view that probity should be paramount and that, once there was evidence of serious wrongdoing, the Bank of England should have acted immediately without waiting to see whether new management could be drafted in and past losses made good.

What became known as the Maxwell affair was a very different matter and did not concern banking supervision directly. The late Robert Maxwell ran a group of companies, including one national daily newspaper, and was a well-known public figure. After his death by drowning in November 1991, it rapidly became apparent that large parts of his business empire were insolvent and that many creditors, including a number of British and foreign banks, stood to lose large sums of money. Up to this point, it is the story of a corporate failure, albeit a large one, and does not have any special implications for financial supervision. But as more was learned about the affairs of the Maxwell companies, it became evident that Robert Maxwell had taken some £400m from the pension funds of companies under his control. This was money which had been invested, on behalf of present and prospective pensioners, by two fund management companies duly authorized by the Investment Managers Regulatory Organization (IMRO).

Quite clearly, the owner of a group of companies should not be able to raid pension funds in this way. Another parliamentary select committee, this time the Social Services Committee, looked at the question and concluded that changes in the law were necessary. At present, pension schemes are governed by the law of trusts and there are areas where the precise ownership of the funds held in trust is unclear. But the Committee also had some harsh things to say about many of the advisers and regulators involved with the Maxwell pension funds. It found that they had taken a blinkered view of

---

[1]   Treasury and Civil Service Committee, Fourth Report: *Banking Supervision and BCCI: International and National Regulation* (HMSO, 1992).

their responsibilities and that regulation of the two fund managers by IMRO had proved no obstacle to the wrongdoing of the late Robert Maxwell.

Given the importance of pension funds to so many people, it may be expected that, sooner or later, the Government will take steps to clarify the legal position on the ownership of the funds where this is in doubt and to ensure that trustees are able to safeguard the monies in trust against attempts by owners or managers of companies to use these for their own ends.

No system of financial supervision can prevent all improper or criminal behaviour. Cases where this does occur should be studied to see if they could have been prevented and if any loopholes in the letter or the practice of regulation could be blocked so as to prevent similar behaviour in future. But ultimately, financial supervision, like all policing, involves striking a balance between inadequate regulation which fails to stop unlawful activities and excessive regulation which hampers lawful activities.

7   GOVERNMENT EXPENDITURE

7.1   Volume and Composition

Government expenditure accounts for a large part of national income. In the financial year to end-March 1991, total expenditure of general government (i.e. central and local government combined) amounted to £221bn, or 40% of gross domestic product. But not all of this represented purchases of goods and services by the public sector; nearly one-half was accounted for by transfer payments such as pensions, unemployment benefits and sickness payments. For many purposes, it is important to distinguish these two categories of expenditure. General government expenditure on goods and services represents a claim on the resources of the country: government hires the services of schoolteachers, policemen, etc., it purchases warships from shipbuilders, ambulances from car manufacturers, etc. Transfer payments, on the other hand, involve no direct claim on resources. Government collects the money in the form of taxes and national insurance contributions and promptly redistributes it as cash payments to pensioners, social-security claimants and others. Transfer payments represent a redistribution of income and it is only when the recipients of the pensions, benefits, etc., spend the money that there is an actual claim on resources.

Government expenditure has grown over time. This is true of expenditure on goods and services and of total expenditure inclusive of transfer payments, both of which have risen in absolute amount and both of which, for many years, were rising as a share of national income. These trends, which are of long standing and date back to the nineteenth century, continued for much of the period since World War II. This is illustrated in appendix Table A-5 on page 371, which shows general government current expenditure in absolute amounts over the years 1980–90 and in Table 2.6, which shows general government expenditure on goods and services and total

TABLE 2.6

General Government Expenditure as a Percentage of GDP, 1946–90

	Expenditure on goods and services	All expenditure including transfer payments
1946	23.9	45.6
1950	19.8	34.6
1955	20.3	33.4
1960	19.7	34.7
1965	20.9	37.1
1970	22.3	40.5
1975	26.4	48.5
1980	23.6	45.1
1985	22.9	45.9
1986	22.9	42.8
1987	21.9	40.2
1988	20.9	38.1
1989	21.2	38.5
1990	22.2	38.9

Note: All expenditure includes net lending by government less any privatization receipts. GDP is GDP at market prices.
Source: Economic Trends, annual supplements, 1986, 1989, 1992.

government expenditure, both expressed as percentages of GDP, for selected years during the period 1946–90.

It can be seen that both series, after dropping back from high wartime levels, showed a tendency to rise subsequently. By the mid-1970s, both expenditure on goods and services and total expenditure accounted for higher shares of national income than they had done in the immediate post-war year of 1946. But, during the 1970s, the size of public expenditure and the level of taxation became major political issues. Firstly, the Labour government, with Dennis Healey as Chancellor of the Exchequer, made efforts to curb the growth of government expenditure and then, in 1979, a Conservative government was elected on a programme which gave priority to controlling public expenditure and reducing the 'burden of taxation'. Attempts to implement this programme had mixed results: for some years, total government expenditure continued to absorb an increasing share of GDP, but by the mid-1980s, a definite downward trend was established. By the financial year 1988–9, total government expenditure was below 40% of GDP for the first time in over 20 years. It remained below 40% for a further two years but in financial year 1991–2 it was back to a preliminary estimate of around 42%.[1]

British experience with public expenditure is not out of line with what has happened abroad. This is evident from Table 2.7 which shows, for seven industrial countries, the average share of total government expenditure in GDP, in four different time periods between the years 1960 and 1989. The figures have been standardized, as far as possible, to make them

---

[1] See the *Financial Statement & Budget Report*, various years (H.M. Treasury).

TABLE 2.7

Total Government Expenditure: Seven Industrial Countries (% of GDP, average figures)

	1960–7	*1968–73*	*1974–9*	*1980–9*
United States	28.3	31.0	32.6	36.0
Japan	19.1	20.2	28.4	33.2[a]
West Germany	35.7	39.8	47.5	47.6
France	37.4	39.0	43.7	50.3
United Kingdom	34.7	39.9	44.4	44.9
Italy	31.9	36.0	42.9	48.7
Canada	29.4	34.7	39.2	45.0

Source: OECD, *Historical Statistics 1960–1989*, Table 6.5.
[a] Average for years 1980–8.

comparable. It will be seen that the trend increase in the share of government expenditure was common to all seven nations. The share of government expenditure in the UK over the entire period has been broadly similar to the shares in France, West Germany and Italy. The relative size of the public sector is larger in these European countries than in the USA and Japan.

The composition of government spending in Britain during 1990 is shown in Figure 2.3. It is also shown in more detail in Table 2.8, which gives figures for 14 separate categories of expenditure for the years 1979, 1985, 1989 and 1990. In addition to the two latest years for which data were available, 1979 and 1985 have been included to show trends in public expenditure since the election of the Conservative government under Mrs Thatcher. In view of the considerable public discussion about cuts in government expenditure, it is of interest to know what actually happened to spending in all the different spheres of government activity over the period 1979–90. The percentage change in nominal spending over 11 years is shown, for each category, in the last column of the table. During this period, prices rose by an estimated 120.2%; therefore, increases greater than this can be seen as a rise in real expenditure, increases of less than this can be seen as a decline in real expenditure.

But comparisons of this sort involve a number of difficulties, so it is important to be clear what is involved. The stated increase in prices of 120.2% is an approximation, but it is the best indicator available of the movement of all prices within the economy. It is derived from the so-called GDP deflator, which in turn is derived from a comparison of index numbers of nominal output and real output across the whole economy. As such, it is an attempt to capture the change in all prices, including those of exports, capital goods and publicly provided services, not just those of consumer goods. It shows that expenditure on a representative basket of goods and services produced in the UK would have had to rise by 120.2% over the years in question in order to purchase the same volume of output. In this sense we can talk about a constant level of real expenditure.

But not all expenditure is on a representative basket of goods and services. Some prices rose more than average, some less. Constant real

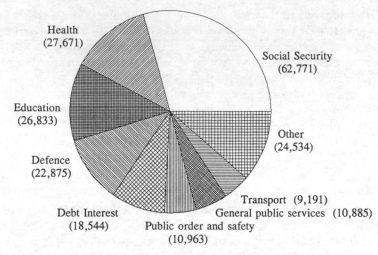

Figure 2.3   Government Expenditure 1990 – Main Categories
Source: NIE (The Blue Book), 1991). (*Note:* Includes expenditure by both central
and local government. Figures in parentheses are millions of pounds.)

expenditure on goods whose prices were in the former category would be
insufficient to maintain a constant volume of output; constant real expenditure on goods whose prices were in the latter category would be more than
sufficient to do so. The cost of providing government services is normally
estimated to rise faster than prices generally, although there are severe
problems in making any estimate at all due to the near-impossibility of
deriving measures of real output for much of government activity. For

TABLE 2.8   General Government Expenditure by Category (£m)

	1979	1985	1989	1990	% change 1979–90
General public services	3,706	6,013	9,469	10,885	193.7
Defence	8,969	18,213	20,961	22,875	155.0
Public order and safety	2,893	6,225	9,433	10,963	278.9
Education	10,310	17,283	24,837	26,833	160.3
Health	9,082	17,889	25,102	27,671	204.7
Social security	20,998	46,246	57,341	62,771	198.9
Housing & Community Amenities	7,250	7,008	7,995	7,923	9.3
Recreational & Cultural Affairs	1,138	2,241	3,185	3,570	213.7
Fuel & Energy	1,218	1,079	−1,880	−3,780	−
Agriculture, Forestry & Fishing	1,163	2,622	1,972	2,618	125.1
Mining & Mineral Resources, Manufacturing & Construction	2,463	2,375	1,572	1,274	−48.3
Transport & Communication	3,216	4,094	7,129	9,191	185.8
Other Economic Affairs & Services	1,876	4,348	4,946	6,413	241.8
Other expenditure	11,414	22,025	24,774	25,060	119.6
Total	85,696	157,661	196,839	214,267	150.0

Source: BB, 1988, 1991.
Memorandum Item: Increase in prices (GDP deflator) 1979–90 = 120.2%.

instance, due to technological development, the cost of military equipment tends to rise faster than the average level of prices: as new equipment is purchased, should we view this as an increase in the efficiency of the military services and, therefore, an increase in output of defence provision, or should we view it as an increase in the cost of providing the same level of output? There is no space to discuss this issue here, but the point to bear in mind is that constant real expenditure does not mean a constant volume of any particular type of output. This is as true at the national level as it is at the personal level. In what follows, we are concerned with expenditure.

It is clear from Table 2.8 that the largest categories of spending are social security, health, education, defence and the final 'other expenditure' category. Social security expenditure, which in the two years 1989 and 1990 accounted for nearly 30% of all government expenditure, is largely composed of transfer payments: grants and allowances paid direct to beneficiaries. Expenditure has been increasing for many years. The largest single item is the retirement pension and as the number of pensioners has risen steadily, so, inevitably, has the cost of pensions. This cost, at £22bn in 1990, was nearly double the real cost of pensions twenty years earlier. Other large items of expenditure in 1990 were income support (supplementary benefits) which amounted to nearly £9bn, family benefits which were over £5bn and invalidity benefit which had risen to over £4bn. Payments of unemployment benefit amounted to less than £1bn.

Expenditure on health, most of which is accounted for by the cost of the National Health Service, has been rising rapidly since 1950 and has accounted for a steadily increasing share of public expenditure. It is reasonable to expect this trend to continue whichever political party is in government.

Real expenditure on education (which includes expenditure on the research councils) has grown only slowly since the early 1970s; but this is unsurprising when it is recalled that the number of children of school age has declined for much of this period. Expenditure on primary and secondary schools accounts for some 60% of this item.

Defence expenditure has also risen in real terms but, in most periods since 1950, its growth has been slow and, until 1979, it represented a declining share of total public expenditure. During the early 1980s, there was a temporary reversal of this trend and defence spending rose sharply but it has subsequently fallen back with real expenditure again rising only moderately.

The category 'other expenditure' is dominated by interest payments on the national debt. Growth, in recent years, has been largely due to the high levels of interest rates.

The category 'housing and community amenities' includes, as well as housing, water, sanitation, street lighting and other community services. Expenditure on housing, which usually accounts for over one-half of the total, is a mixture of capital expenditure, subsidies and grants. This category has been cut heavily since 1979. The figures shown are for expenditure net of receipts from sales of council houses. If we count such receipts as income, and not as negative expenditure, then the reduction in expenditure is somewhat less, but it is still substantial.

Public order and safety covers expenditure on police and fire services, law courts and prisons. Here, real expenditure has increased by 72%, since 1979, and this increase has been spread over all four sub-categories.

General public services include the costs of running the apparatus of government, i.e. expenditure on the home and foreign civil service, local government administration, Parliament and tax collection, as well as the UK contribution to the EC and foreign aid. In real terms, expenditure under this heading has risen, since 1979, by about 33%.

Expenditure on transport and communication covers government expenditure on road, rail, air and water transport, pipelines and communications. In real terms, expenditure has risen by about 30% since 1979. All of this has occurred in the last three years and is due to a growth in capital expenditure on transport infrastructure.

There is a problem in interpreting the statistics for the category 'fuel and energy' which covers government expenditure on coal mining, petroleum and natural gas, nuclear fuel and electricity. The figures shown are net of receipts from sales of assets (privatization receipts) and from repayments of debt to the Government by public corporations. Without these two items, total expenditure in 1989 and 1990 would have been positive and there would have been no clear trend over the 1980s.

The heading 'mining and mineral resources, manufacturing and construction' is self-explanatory, except to add that it excludes expenditure on fuel resources, dealt with elsewhere, and that it includes expenditure on consumer protection. The bulk of expenditure is accounted for by transfer payments, notably capital grants to the private sector and the provision of capital for public corporations. There has been a reduction in expenditure on the latter of these items since 1979 and this more than accounts for the substantial fall in total spending.

The remaining two specific categories of expenditure – 'agriculture, forestry and fishing' and 'recreational and cultural affairs' – are largely self-explanatory. Real expenditure under the former heading rose sharply between 1979 and 1985 but has fallen back since. Expenditure under the latter heading has tended to grow steadily year by year. The final category – 'other economic affairs and services' – covers government expenditure on the distributive trades, hotels and restaurants, tourism, multipurpose development projects, other economic and commercial affairs and general labour services. Total expenditure, in real terms, increased considerably in the years to 1985 but has fallen back subsequently.

This discussion of public spending has been in terms of aggregate expenditure by general government, i.e. central and local government combined. The share of local government is slightly less than 30%. In 1990, total expenditure by all local authorities amounted to almost £66bn, of which education alone accounted for over £21bn. Other large claims on local authority resources are public order and safety, social security, housing, and interest on debt.

7.2   The Budget

The Budget is presented annually by the Chancellor of the Exchequer to the House of Commons. It is the most public of the several occasions on which the Government sets before Parliament its economic forecasts and its policy proposals. The Budget serves several purposes. Firstly, it is the normal occasion for the Government to propose changes in taxation. These changes may include the introduction of new taxes or the abolition of existing taxes, they may include changes in tax rates, and they almost certainly will include changes in the law concerning what persons or what activities are liable to tax. Proposed changes in the law include both substantive changes, i.e. where the Government is introducing a new policy, and changes designed to block loopholes in existing laws that are being exploited to avoid paying tax. The Government's proposals become effective either on Budget Day itself, or on an announced date thereafter; but they still require the subsequent approval of the House of Commons. After debate and possible modification, the Budget proposals are presented to the House of Commons in the form of a Finance Bill. When passed by the House, this becomes the Finance Act and is the definitive legal statement of the changes in taxation.

A summary statement of the proposed tax changes and of their effect on Exchequer revenues is given in the *Financial Statement and Budget Report* (*FSBR*), published immediately after the Chancellor's statement to the House of Commons. This document also gives details of estimated tax receipts for the past financial year and forecasts of tax receipts for the forthcoming one. Table 2.9 reproduces the figures given in the *FSBR*, 1992–3. Appendix Table A-5 shows government receipts over the period of 1980–90.

It can be seen that the greater part of tax receipts is accounted for by the collections of the Inland Revenue (broadly speaking, direct taxes) and the Customs & Excise (broadly speaking, indirect taxes). In addition, there are a number of other receipts of which the most important is provided by local authority rates and the community charge. Social security receipts are not officially classed as taxation although, from the point of view of those who pay them, they are virtually indistinguishable from other taxes. But, however they are classified, it can be seen that they produce substantial amounts of revenue.

Traditionally the Budget was the occasion for announcing some changes in government expenditures. It was also the time when the Supply Estimates, i.e. the estimates for the coming year of tax-financed public expenditure, were presented to the House of Commons. But the expenditure changes announced in the Budget were usually small in size and the Estimates only repeated what had already been made public. The main

TABLE 2.9   Receipts of General Government (£bn)

	1991–2 Latest Estimate	1992–93 Forecast
Inland Revenue		
Income tax	58.0	59.6
Corporation tax	18.4	16.8
Petroleum revenue tax	−0.2	0.1
Capital gains tax	1.2	1.1
Inheritance tax	1.3	1.3
Stamp duties	1.7	1.5
Total Inland Revenue	80.4	80.4
Customs & Excise		
Value Added Tax	35.5	40.0
Petrol, derv duties, etc.	10.9	11.8
Tobacco duties	6.1	6.6
Alcohol duties	5.0	5.3
Betting and gaming duties	1.1	1.1
Car tax	1.2	0.7
(EEC own resources)		
customs duties	1.8	1.9
agricultural levies	0.2	0.0
Total Customs & Excise	61.8	67.4
Vehicle excise duties	3.0	3.2
Local authority rates and community charge	21.5	22.1
Other taxes and royalties	4.4	4.6
Total taxes and royalties	171.1	177.8
Social security receipts	36.3	38.7
Interest and dividends	6.1	5.5
Gross trading surpluses and rent	3.8	3.7
Other receipts	4.8	4.0
General government receipts	222.1	229.8

Source: Financial Statement and Budget Report, 1992–93.

discussion of public expenditure was when the Government produced its annual Public Expenditure White Paper, usually well before the Budget, either in late Autumn or early in the New Year. This White Paper gave firm projections of government expenditure for the financial year ahead and more tentative projections for the two following years. The figures were broken down into the main categories of expenditure and within each category there was a further breakdown, giving a detailed picture, item-by-item, of public expenditure.

Until recently, it was a frequent criticism of the annual Budget procedures that tax changes were presented separately from public expenditure changes. In addition, there was the problem that the Budget only concentrates on the tax revenue of central government and does not consider local authority revenues. Similarly, the annual Supply Estimates presented with the Budget proposals covered only expenditures financed by these tax revenues. For many years, there was no attempt to give an overall picture of total public spending and total public receipts.

But this is changing. In 1980, the Government introduced, as part of its economic policy, a medium-term financial strategy (MTFS) in which total public expenditure and total public revenue were central elements. This strategy proved to be highly flexible in practice and the intermediate targets of policy were frequently changed,[1] but it remained the case that much attention was devoted to the total spending and total receipts of general government, both in the Budget speech and in the FSBR. The Government's need to borrow or ability to repay debt continues to be seen as an important policy variable. It was therefore a logical step, long overdue, when in his 1992 Budget speech, the Chancellor announced that, starting in 1993, the Budget would be presented in December and would include detailed government proposals on both revenue and expenditure.

7.3   The PSBR and the PSDR

In most years since the end of World War II, general government revenues from taxation, national insurance, royalties, etc., as well as from sales of publicly owned assets, have been insufficient to finance total expenditure. In consequence, government has had to borrow. Central government has financed most or all of the borrowing needs of local government and it has also loaned funds to public corporations. In this way the bulk of the borrowing of the public sector has been centralized and managed by the central government. The total need to borrow each year – the public-sector borrowing requirement or PSBR – was given a prominent role under the Government's Medium Term Financial Strategy.

The importance of the PSBR, it was argued, had to do with how it was financed. The authorities had a basic choice: they could borrow from the banking system (including, for this purpose, the Bank of England), in which case the money supply would rise; or they could borrow from the non-bank private sector, in which case there would be no effect on the money supply. As it was a central objective of the MTFS to limit the growth of the money supply, there was a clear preference for the latter. But, other things being equal, the more the authorities borrow from the non-bank private sector, the more they will bid up rates of interest. And high rates of interest were seen as undesirable in that, other things being equal, they would be expected to act as a disincentive to capital investment. So we had the situation that the Government wished to control the money supply, and wished to do this without pushing up rates of interest any more than necessary. The implication was that the Government should limit its own borrowing; hence the importance of controlling the PSBR.

---

[1] A detailed account of the changes in the MTFS is given in M.J.Artis and M.K.Lewis, *Money in Britain* (Philip Allan, 1991).

In its immediate objective, the Government was, for a time, remarkably successful. The PSBR which, during the years 1979–84, had averaged over £10bn per annum, was greatly reduced in 1985 and 1986 and became a surplus in 1987. In 1988, the surplus was of the order of £14bn or 3% of GDP and there were further, if smaller, surpluses in 1989 and 1990. These surpluses were used to repay outstanding government debt, hence the term public-sector debt repayment or PSDR.

But public expenditure grew rapidly in 1991 and was forecast to continue to do so in 1992. This, plus a lower growth in tax revenues due to the recession, brought about a return to substantial public-sector borrowing. In the FSBR accompanying the 1992 Budget, the PSBR for the financial year to end March 1992 was estimated at just less than £14bn and the PSBR for the following financial year was predicted to be double that amount. The Chancellor of the Exchequer claimed that such a large borrowing requirement was essentially due to cyclical factors, i.e. the recession, and was compatible with a balanced budget over the entire economic cycle. This claim should be taken with a pinch of salt: it seems improbable that during the boom phase of the cycle the Government will wish to run a surplus or PSDR of £28bn. It would appear that only part of the deterioration in government finances is due to the recession; the rest is due to a more rapid growth in government expenditure without any attempt to raise more tax revenue.

The relationship between government borrowing and the growth of the money supply has, in fact, been very weak. Notwithstanding the switch from public-sector deficit to surplus in the late 1980s, all the main measures of money showed rapid growth (see appendix Table A-6) and at the same time output grew rapidly, the balance of payments deteriorated and inflation again became a serious problem. The result was that in 1988 interest rates had to be raised to high levels (short-term rates over 15%) in order both to curb bank lending and to encourage an inflow of foreign capital to finance the deficit on the current account of the balance of payments. The high rates of interest had the intended effect; economic activity weakened and money supply growth slackened (this was most notable in the case of M4), this notwithstanding the fact that public-sector finances were now moving from surplus to deficit.

8   Taxation

8.1   Income Tax

Income tax is the single most important tax in terms of revenue produced. It can be seen from Table 2.9 that, in financial year 1991–2, it yielded an estimated £58bn, or just over one quarter of total government receipts. Income tax is also one of the oldest taxes, having been first introduced by William Pitt in 1799. It is straightforward in principle, but complex in practice. All personal incomes are assessable to tax, but each taxpayer is allowed to earn up to a certain amount before starting to pay tax. This amount is known as the personal allowance. There are a number of other possible allowances. For instance, expenses necessarily incurred in earning income are not taxable and constitute an additional tax allowance. The sum of all allowances is deducted from total income and what is left is taxable income. It is this that is subject to tax.

There are different personal allowances for the single and for the married. The single person's allowance in financial year 1992–3 is £3,445, which means that a single man or woman, without other allowances, can earn £287 a month or over £66 a week before starting to pay tax. For married couples, one spouse can claim an additional allowance, which in 1992–3 amounts to £1,720. Therefore, a married man, claiming the higher allowance, but with no other allowances, can earn just over £430 a month or almost £100 a week before starting to pay tax.

Income tax in Britain, as in most other countries, is a progressive tax, that is to say, the share of income that is taken in tax rises as income rises. Those with higher taxable incomes pay a larger proportion of their income in tax. This is justifiable on the principle of ability to pay: those with higher taxable incomes are presumed to be able to afford to contribute a larger proportion of their income in tax. It is also justifiable if one accepts that the taxation system should serve as a means of income redistribution. Progressivity is achieved by having different tax rates apply to different levels of taxable income. For many years, there were as many as six different tax rates, each applicable to different levels of income. But, in 1988, most of these were abolished and the system was reduced to one of just two rates: a basic rate and a higher rate. For 1992–3 a new lower rate was introduced and the rates for that year are as follows:

Tax rate (%)	Taxable income (£s)
20	2,000
25	2,001–23,700
40	over 23,700

Personal allowances, rates of tax and the tax bands to which they apply are announced each year in the Budget speech. The Chancellor is free to vary these, although he is now under a requirement to state what upward variation would be required to compensate for inflation. This means that proposed tax changes can be promptly judged by their real not just their monetary effects. Clearly, if annual inflation were 10% and personal allowances were only raised by 5%, then people would start to pay tax at lower levels of real income than before. Similarly, if the higher rate threshold was raised by less than 10%, people would find themselves moving into the higher tax band at lower levels of real income than before. If such changes are deliberately sought, the Chancellor can alter allowances and thresholds accordingly, but he now has to do so openly and compare the changes he is making with neutral (i.e. inflation-adjusted) changes.

There are a number of problems with the present system of income tax. It must be accepted that some problems are inevitable, and one should not look for perfection in a system which involves several hundred tax offices assessing the incomes of over 20 million people, all of whom have their own unique circumstances. However, it is desirable to improve equity and efficiency as far as is possible. One source of general dissatisfaction for many years was the taxation of husbands and wives. Traditionally their incomes were aggregated and treated as one, with the result that a married couple where both were earning would move more quickly into higher tax brackets than would two unmarried people living together in the same house. There was a potential tax penalty on marriage.

This particular anomaly was ended by the reform of personal taxation which took effect in April 1990. Husbands and wives are now taxed separately both for income tax and for capital gains tax, and so do not start to pay higher rates of taxation any earlier than unmarried people. But the reform has not achieved neutrality: a married couple where both are earning now pay less tax than they would do if they were not married. This is because both can claim the full personal allowance and in addition there is the married couple's allowance.

This extra allowance (currently worth almost one half of the personal allowance – see above) was originally introduced as the married man's allowance at a time when fewer married women took paid employment. It was reasoned that the married man's income was supporting two people (at least) and therefore, on the principle of ability to pay, he should be required to pay less tax than a single person on the same level of income. This seems reasonable, but the extra allowance (now claimable by either spouse) is still given when both parties to the marriage are working and both are claiming individual personal allowances. This means that the amount of income a married couple can earn before paying tax (in 1992–3) is $2\frac{1}{2}$ times that of a single person. It also means that a married couple where only one spouse earns will pay more tax than would a married couple where both earn, even if the total income of the two households is the same.

There is no obvious equity in this. It seems anomalous, in an age of separate taxation, that a married couple can, in effect, claim $2\frac{1}{2}$ personal allowances.

People who earn income are also liable to pay national insurance contributions. These payments, which are made by the employed, by employers and the self-employed, are used to finance the social security funds which in turn provide state pensions, sickness and disablement benefits, unemployment benefit and a range of other allowances and grants. But despite the name, national insurance is not insurance in the sense that it is based on actuarial principles; contributions are standardized and are not related in any close way to expected claims on the social security funds. This is true at the level of the individual contributor and also at the level of the funds themselves; no attempt is made to see that total payments in equal total payments out. Each year, the Treasury makes a payment from general taxation revenues as a grant towards the cost of social security, while confusingly the social security funds also make a contribution towards the cost of the National Health Service. In reality, national insurance payments

TABLE 2.10

Marginal Rates of Deduction from Income: Tax and National Insurance (NI) Combined

Annual Income	Tax	NI	Tax + NI
0–2,807	0	0	0
2,808–3,445	0	9	9
3,446–5,445	20	9	29
5,446–21,060	25	9	34
21,060–27,145	25	0	25
Over 27,145	40	0	40

Notes: The table shows the position as it applies in financial year 1992–3 to an employed single person aged under 65. No allowance has been made for entitlement to tax relief other than the personal allowance. The person is assumed not to be contracted out of the state earnings-related pension scheme.

National Insurance is, in practice, assessed on weekly income but has here been shown in relation to annual income so as to make it comparable with income tax.

Given that once income exceeds £2,808 per annum one must pay, in addition to 9% marginal rate of national insurance, a 2% rate on the first £2,808 of income, it is clear that anyone crossing the threshold would have a sudden very high rate of marginal deduction, e.g. if income rose from the weekly equivalent of just below £2,808 per annum to £2,908 per annum, annual national insurance payments would rise by £65.16.

are more akin to taxation than to insurance and for many purposes it makes sense to consider the two together.

By looking at both tax and national insurance, we can see the full position regarding deductions from income made by government and can get a more accurate picture of effective marginal rates of 'tax'. In financial year 1992–3, no national insurance would be paid if earnings were less than £2,808 per annum (£54 per week).[1] For incomes above this sum, and for persons not contracted out of the state earnings-related pension, national insurance is payable at the rate of 9% of income up to an upper level of income.[2] But, in addition, persons earning £2,808 per annum are also required to pay a contribution of 2% on this first £2,808 of income. If income does not reach this level, nothing is payable; once income does reach this level, 2% on the whole amount is payable. Both lower and upper levels of income for payment of national insurance are normally adjusted each year in line with inflation.

The rate of 9% is payable on incomes between £2,808 per annum and £21,060 per annum; after that no further payments are due. This is a concession to the notion of insurance – at the higher levels of income, people are judged to be paying an adequate level of premium. But any such argument is undermined by the fact that the employer's national insurance contribution continues to be paid without there being any upper limit on incomes.

---

[1] National insurance is assessed on a weekly basis. It is presented here on an annual basis so as to be comparable with income tax.

[2] Those who are contracted out of the state earnings-related pension scheme pay at a rate of 7%.

Table 2.10 shows marginal rates of deductions from income for both tax and national insurance calculated on the basis of rates and tax bands applying for financial year to end March 1993.

8.2   Corporation Tax and Oil Taxation

Corporation tax is levied on company profits. As with persons, companies can take advantage of a number of allowances against earnings, and it is the total of profits less allowances which is subject to tax. For many years, the rate of tax was relatively high at 52% but, at the same time, there were generous provisions whereby much capital expenditure constituted an allowance against income and served to reduce taxable profits. The result was that the yield from corporation tax was low: many companies, in spite of earning substantial profits, paid little tax.[1] In 1984, the Government initiated a reform of the tax which involved the progressive reduction of the rate of tax to 35% and the simultaneous phasing out of some of the more generous tax allowances. In March 1991, the standard rate of corporation tax was further reduced to 33%. For companies with profits below £250,000 a reduced rate of 25% applies. For companies with profits between £250,000 and £1,250,000 there is partial relief from the full rate of 33%.

The tax payable by a company depends directly on the size of taxable profits and is unaffected by whether profits are distributed to shareholders or are retained in the business. But the tax is paid in two parts: advanced corporation tax (ACT) and mainstream corporation tax, and the division between these two parts does depend on how much is paid to shareholders in the form of dividends. For when dividends are paid, these are treated as net-of-tax payments and the company has to pay tax on behalf of the shareholders at the basic rate of income tax. It is these payments which constitute ACT. The system is best explained by an example.

Assume a company with taxable profits of £100m. Its total liability for corporation tax is £33m. That is fixed. Now, suppose the company pays to shareholders, dividends of £20m. Since these payments are regarded as being net-of-tax, they have to be grossed-up in order to determine the shareholders' gross income and the company's liability to ACT. The principle of grossing-up is straightforward. If a taxpayer with a marginal tax rate of 50% receives a net-of-tax payment of £500, it can easily be seen that the gross payment must have been £1,000: the taxpayer needed to earn £1,000 in order to be left with a net £500 after tax. If the marginal rate of tax had been 25% (the basic rate in 1992–93), a net-of-tax payment of £500 would have corresponded to a gross payment of $100/75 \times £500 = £666.7$. On the same basis, shareholders who have received £20m net of tax are deemed to have received a gross income of $100/75 \times £20m = £26.7m$, of which £6.7m is tax

[1]   See J. A. Kay and M. A. King, *The British Tax System*, fifth edition (Oxford University Press, 1990).

due. And this is the amount that the company has to pay in ACT. Subsequently, it will pay mainstream corporation tax of £33m less the £6.7m already paid.

For shareholders liable to tax at the basic rate of income tax, there is no further tax liability. They are deemed to have received a gross income equal to 100/75 of dividends received and to have had tax paid on their behalf by the company. For shareholders whose marginal tax rate exceeds 25%, additional tax is due on the deemed gross payment. Conversely, shareholders such as pension funds, who do not pay tax, can claim a refund of the tax paid on their behalf.

Of the allowances which companies can set against income, the most important are in respect of depreciation. In order to produce, and to generate, profits, all companies require some capital. But capital depreciates in value due to use and due to age. If a company is to remain in business, it has to set aside sufficient funds to be able to replace worn-out plant and machinery. So not all corporate earnings can be viewed as profit, in the sense that they could be distributed and spent by shareholders: some earnings have to be set aside in order to maintain intact the capital stock. This is recognized by the tax authorities and corporation tax is levied on profits after provision for depreciation. To avoid the trouble and expense of trying to assess physical depreciation for each company separately, general rules are laid down. Physical depreciation is translated into accounting depreciation and standard percentage allowances are granted in respect of plant and equipment and in respect of industrial holdings.

There are two common methods that accountants use to calculate depreciation. These can be explained by the following example. Assume a depreciation allowance of 20% a year applied to a machine costing £1,000. We could assume that, each year, the machine loses 20% of its existing value. So, in year 1, it loses £200 in value and is then worth £800. In year 2, it loses 20% of £800, i.e. £160 and is then worth £640. In year 3, it loses 20% of £640, i.e. £128 and so on. This is the declining balance method and it results in depreciation allowances being greater in the early period of life of capital equipment. Alternatively, we could assume that, each year, the machine loses 20% of its initial value. This would mean that depreciation was a constant £200 a year, and that the machine was fully depreciated after five years. This is the straight line method. Both methods are used at times by the Inland Revenue.

Depreciation allowances have been widely used in the years since World War II as a means to try to stimulate investment. Governments have increased the permitted rate of depreciation so that firms installing new equipment could get the tax relief earlier, and they have also granted initial allowances or first-year allowances whereby a large part of the new investment became tax deductible in the year in which it was installed, regardless of any actual physical depreciation. This was carried to its logical conclusion in 1972, when all capital expenditure on plant and machinery, excluding passenger cars, was made subject to a first-year allowance of 100%. This meant that a company purchasing a machine worth £10,000 could immediately reduce taxable income by this amount and, at the then rate of corporation tax, save £5,200 in tax. Subsequently the initial allowance in respect of industrial buildings was raised to 75%.

These first-year and initial allowances were phased out between 1984 and 1986. After 1 April 1986, allowances are limited to 25% (on a reducing balance basis) in respect of plant and machinery and to 4% (on a straight line basis) in respect of industrial buildings, agricultural buildings and hotels.[1] These are the standard allowances, but additional allowances, as part of regional policy, are given on certain categories of expenditure in development areas, special development areas and in Northern Ireland. (There is a discussion of regional policy in Chapter 5 below.)

Oil Taxation: Oil taxation involves three separate elements: royalties, petroleum revenue tax (PRT), and corporation tax. Royalties, which are now charged only on certain oil and gas fields, are a direct levy on the value of all production. PRT is a tax levied on the receipts from the sales of oil and gas – above an exempt initial amount – less operating costs and royalties. Both royalties and PRT are imposed on oil and gas fields individually. Corporation tax is applied normally to the profits of oil and gas producers, but after deduction of royalties and PRT.

This range of taxes, which, at first sight, appears unduly complicated, was designed to ensure a high yield to the Exchequer from the profitable large fields whilst, at the same time, not overtaxing smaller or more costly fields. To further ensure that taxation should not deter the extraction of oil and gas from marginal fields, the Secretary of State for Energy is given the power to refund royalties and to cancel PRT in cases where the profitability of a field is low.

In the early 1980s, there was concern that the most promising geological areas had already been exploited and that companies were increasingly unwilling to look for oil in other offshore areas, many of which were in less congenial situations and involved drilling at great depths below sea level. To provide additional incentive, the Government announced, in the 1982 Budget, the abolition of royalties on newly-developed oil and gas fields, apart from onshore fields and those in the relatively shallow waters of the Southern Basin of the North Sea (between 52°N and 55°N). It was officially estimated that this change and the subsequent changes in corporation tax and in investment allowances would have the result of reducing the marginal rate of taxation of new offshore oil fields, outside the Southern Basin, from 88% to 83.75%.

Total revenues from all royalties and taxes on oil and gas production depend closely on the sterling price of oil and gas. These depend on changes

---

[1] For a discussion of investment allowances in general and of the specific changes introduced in the 1984 Budget, see J.R.Sargent and M.F.G.Scott, 'Investment and the Tax System in the UK', *MBR*, Spring 1986.

in world prices expressed in dollars, and on the pound–dollar exchange rate. Receipts were at a peak during financial years 1984–5 and 1985–6 when they averaged some £12bn per annum but due, *inter alia*, to a decrease in world oil prices, they have fallen back considerably since then. In financial year 1991–2, receipts from all royalties and taxes were officially estimated at the time of the March 1992 Budget to be no more than £1bn. Total North Sea revenues now represent around ½% of total tax revenue as compared with over 9% when they were at their peak in the mid-1980s.

8.3   Capital Gains Tax

Tax is levied on capital gains: for persons it is levied at a rate equal to that which would apply if the gain were treated as additional income; for companies it is levied at the corporation-tax rate. The case for such a tax is partly one of equity: why should a person who receives £1,000, in the form of a capital gain, pay no tax, when a person who receives the same sum, in the form of income, has to pay tax? But there is also a case for such a tax on the grounds of efficiency: without it, much energy will be spent on seeking ways to convert income into capital gains, in order to avoid tax. The case for capital gains tax (CGT) is strong.

But there are inherent difficulties in implementing fairly such a tax and, in consequence, the present tax represents something of a compromise between what is desirable in theory, and what is convenient in practice. Many assets are exempt entirely from the tax. These include a person's principal private residence, agricultural property, motorcars, most life assurance policies, assets donated to charities, winnings from gambling, National Savings instruments and government stock and most corporate fixed-interest securities. There are provisions for allowing losses on assets subject to CGT to be offset against gains; and to avoid the high cost of collecting many small amounts of tax, there is an annual personal allowance, whereby gains below a certain amount are exempt from taxation. For fiscal year 1992–3, this allowance has been set at £5,800 for individuals and £2,900 for most trusts.

A complication of capital gains tax is that gains usually accrue over time and hence it is desirable to distinguish between real and monetary gains. A person who bought a share in company X in 1979 for £1,000 and sold it in 1989 for £2,000 made a gain on paper; but since the general level of prices approximately doubled over the same period, there was no real gain. Since March 1982, CGT has been on an indexed basis and only real gains have been subject to tax.

8.4   Inheritance Tax

There is a good case on grounds of equity for a tax on wealth. If two people earn the same income, but one also owns a large personal fortune whereas the other has no capital, it would normally be presumed that the former had a greater ability to pay than the latter. But there are a number of severe practical problems that arise in attempts to tax wealth directly. While income usually accrues in the form of money, which means there is no special problem in making a money payment of taxes, much wealth is in illiquid form and may be indivisible. Thus, a person who owns a stately home, but who has little other wealth, may find himself unable to pay even a modest rate of wealth tax, without selling the home. Similarly many farmers and many small businessmen (who often have more debt than liquid assets) would find themselves unable to pay a wealth tax without selling part of the farm or the business. But governments usually wish to encourage both an efficient agriculture and a productive small business sector, and this is one main reason why they have shied away from direct wealth taxes which would make difficult the accumulation and productive use of wealth.

A common fall-back position has been to tax wealth when it changes hands at death. This was the approach in Britain between 1894 and 1974. But in practice estate duty, as it was known, yielded only modest amounts of revenue. There were a number of exemptions from, and reductions in, duty in respect of certain assets (e.g. agricultural land) and, in any case, those with large estates could transfer them to their heirs during their lifetime. Provisions were introduced to levy estate duty on property disposed of within a specified period prior to death, and this period was progressively extended to seven years. But, in spite of this, it was still commonly alleged that estate duty was an avoidable tax.

In 1974, the new Labour government replaced estate duty by a capital transfer tax (CTT), under which disposals of property were made subject to tax, whether made during life or at death. Tax was levied, at a progressive rate, on the cumulative value of all gifts over a period of ten years. That is to say, in calculating tax due, gifts in any one year were aggregated with the cumulative total of gifts in the preceding nine years. It was the total of all gifts over the ten-year period which determined which rate of tax should apply.

There were a number of exemptions. Transfers of property between husbands and wives, in life and at death, were free of all tax, as were outright gifts and bequests to charities. Gifts, during any one year, to one individual, up to the value of £250 were exempt from duty, and so also were total gifts, during any one year, up to the value of £3,000. After allowing for exemptions, all transfers of property were cumulated. Of the cumulative total, an initial amount (£67,000 in 1985–6) was free of duty and then tax rates increased as total transfers increased. In financial year 1985–6, the maximum rate was 30% for lifetime gifts and 60% for bequests, and was reached when cumulative transfers of property reached £300,000.

In 1986, the Government abolished the tax on lifetime gifts between persons. Gifts into, or out of, trusts and gifts involving companies remain subject to tax. Gifts, at death, are taxed as before and provisions to tax gifts made within seven years of death have been reintroduced. The reason given for the change was that CTT deterred lifetime giving, had the effect of freezing the ownership of assets, especially the ownership of family businesses and that this was often detrimental to such businesses. The tax now applies mainly to transfers of property at death and has been renamed the inheritance tax. Since 1988, a flat rate of 40% has been levied on all taxable transfers in excess of an initial exempt amount. This amount, in recent years, has been raised annually in line (at least) with the increase in retail prices. For the financial year 1992–3, it stands at £150,000.

8.5   Value Added Tax

Value added tax (VAT) is, after income tax and social security receipts, the largest producer of revenue to the Government. It is intended as a broadly based expenditure tax and was introduced, in 1973, following the accession of the United Kingdom to the EEC. VAT had, by then, become part of the process of fiscal harmonization within the Community, although, since for many years there was no attempt to harmonize *rates* of tax, it remained, at best, only a partial harmonization. The tax is intended to be non-discriminatory and is levied on producers of intermediate goods as well as on producers of final goods. This raises considerably the costs of collection which fall both on the revenue authorities – the Customs & Excise – and on the taxpayers themselves. But since complete non-discrimination would have undesirable redistributive effects, there are different rates of VAT, so the objective is not achieved in practice.

The tax is levied at all stages of production and is imposed on the value added by each producer. How it works in practice can be illustrated by the following simple example. We assume a VAT of 15% which was the standard rate in force in the United Kingdom between 1979 and 1991. A manufacturer purchases raw materials at a price of £115 inclusive of VAT, i.e. the cost of the raw materials is £100 and tax is £15. This latter is known as the input tax. The manufacturer then uses capital and labour to produce a finished article which he sells to a retailer for £230 including VAT. £30 is the output tax, and the manufacturer has to pay to the Customs & Excise the difference between output and input taxes, namely £15. So the cost of the product, net of tax, is £200 and tax, at the rate of 15%, has been paid. The initial suppliers of raw materials added value of £100 and so paid £15 in tax; the manufacturer also added value of £100 and so paid the same amount in tax. If, now, we assume that the retailer will earn £20 net on each product he sells, then this sum is the value added at the retail stage, and tax is due thereon. The retailer will sell the product at a price of £253; his output tax will be £33, his input tax was £30, so he is liable to pay VAT of £3. The total amount of tax paid (£33) is equal to 15% of the total net-of-tax sale value of the product. It has been collected, at each stage of the production process, by taxing each producer according to his value added.

VAT is costly to collect for the authorities and complex, and therefore

costly, for many of those who pay it. Large firms with sophisticated accounting systems cope without difficulty but, for many small businesses, the costs
of calculating VAT are high.

The standard rate of VAT was raised from 15% to 17.5% in April 1991. If
this rate were levied on all items, it would bear heavily on the poor: unlike
income tax, where no tax is payable on low incomes, the full tax would be
levied all expenditures. To prevent this and to introduce some progressivity into the tax, certain items, which form a large proportion of the
expenditure of those on low incomes, are zero-rated. Not only is no VAT
levied on the production and sale of these commodities, but producers can
also reclaim VAT paid by suppliers of intermediate goods. Such items
include food, fuel and power, transport and children's clothing. There is a
third category of goods, those that are exempt from VAT. Exemption is not
the same as zero rating: producers of exempt goods pay no VAT themselves, but cannot reclaim what has already been paid on inputs supplied to
them. Exempt goods and services include health care, education, insurance
and financial services, postal services and land. Very small firms with turnover less than a prescribed amount are also exempt from VAT. In financial
year 1992–3, the amount is £36,000 per annum.

VAT is rebated on exports but is charged on imports. This means all goods
sold in the United Kingdom are taxed at the appropriate British rate regardless of their origin; all goods sold in France are taxed at the appropriate
French rate, etc. This arrangement has enabled the EC to function with
widely different VAT rates in the different member states although it has
relied on border checks and complicated customs formalities. But the 'single
European market' is due to come into force from the beginning of 1993 and
this is likely to involve a reduction in border controls and maybe, in some
cases, their disappearance altogether.[1] With this in mind, the European
Commission proposed in 1987 the harmonization of VAT rates throughout
the Community. Specifically, it proposed that there should be just two rates
for all member countries: a standard rate fixed between 14 and 20% and a
reduced rate between 4 and 9% for items judged to be basic personal
necessities. This proposal met with opposition from a number of countries,
including Britain, where the Government wishes to maintain its zero
rate.

In the light of this opposition and in recognition of the fact that any
harmonization of VAT rates prior to January 1993 was improbable, the
Commission put forward revised proposals in 1989. These proposals showed
more flexibility; they did not exclude the maintenance of a zero rate of VAT

---

[1] Article 8A of the Single European Act defines the internal market as an area without
internal frontiers. The European Commission interprets this to mean all internal border
controls should go. Some member countries, including the UK, are resisting this and claiming
the right to maintain certain controls.

for certain categories of consumer goods and they envisaged a transitional VAT regime for a number of years after January 1993. This will enable the EC to continue to live with the existing wide difference in VAT rates. Tax will continue to be rebated on exports and charged on imports, but it is planned that an EC-wide computer system linking national tax authorities will co-ordinate this instead of the existing customs formalities.

The European Commission has also sought to narrow the range of items subject to existing lower rates of tax and has taken a number of cases to the European Court of Justice. As a consequence, the UK government had to levy the standard rate of VAT on items previously zero-rated, such as non-residential construction (subject to VAT from April 1989) and fuel and power supplied to business and water and sewerage services supplied to industry (all subject to VAT from April 1990).

8.6 Excise Duties and Customs Duties

Excise duties are duties levied on goods, whether produced domestically or imported, and have as their prime objective the raising of revenue. Customs duties are duties levied specifically on imported goods and where the objective may be to protect domestic producers, to raise revenue, or both. Following the entry of the United Kingdom into the EC, and after an initial transitional phase, customs duties have no longer been levied on imports from other member states of the EC; and those that are levied on imports from non-member countries are now determined jointly for all EC members in order to maintain a common external tariff. Receipts of customs duties are regarded as part of the 'own resources' of the Community and remitted to Brussels.

The most significant excise duties, in terms of revenue raised, are clearly those on oil, tobacco and alcohol. As can be seen from Table 2.9 these three duties raised, in financial year 1991–2, an estimated £22bn. It could be asked why one should single out for tax, in what is a highly discriminatory way, these three commodities? The first answer is that all three have inelastic demands, i.e. increases in price have only a small effect on demand, so they are eminently suitable as a means of raising revenue. This, and the fact that the duties are all of long standing and have become accepted (albeit grudgingly), are probably sufficient reasons for most Chancellors of the Exchequer. But other good economic reasons can be advanced. The consumption of tobacco, as a widely accepted cause of cancer, has a very high human cost in terms of suffering and premature death. Alcohol abuse, which is widespread, has both a high human cost and a high social cost. Motoring has high social costs in terms of congestion, pollution and the expense of policing, while the large numbers of accidents to which it gives rise have both high human and social costs.

The duties on oil, tobacco and alcohol are all stated as fixed monetary amounts. So, unlike VAT – defined as a percentage rate – they are not automatically indexed for inflation. Increases in the duties are regularly made at the time of the Budget, but for many years during the 1960s and 1970s there was a tendency for increases to fall short of the rate of inflation, with the result that the real value of the duties fell. Increases in excise taxes inevitably raise prices, and so themselves contribute to measured inflation, and this appeared, on occasions, to have dissuaded Chancellors from making sizeable increases. During the 1980s, duties were raised more systematically and tended to maintain or even to increase their real value with the tax on cigarettes rising considerably and the tax on leaded petrol also rising in real terms.

The question of harmonizing excise taxes throughout the EC, which had previously been discussed in a somewhat leisurely manner, has acquired greater importance with the approach of 1993 and the 'single European market'. If, as is foreseen, customs checks at borders are fewer or are abolished altogether, then one may expect goods subject to excise taxes to be purchased where rates are low and imported into those countries where rates are high; something which already happens but which at present is limited by border controls. But if this means there is a strong case for reducing the disparities in excise duties within the EC, the practical problems remain formidable. Existing levels of duty vary widely and in those countries where rates are high (Denmark, Ireland, the United Kingdom) there would be difficulties in making significant reductions both on grounds of loss of revenue and from concerns about matters such as health and the environment; in those countries where rates are low (Greece, Spain) there would be political difficulties about making large increases.

The European Commission has made proposals that excise duties on tobacco, mineral oils and alcoholic drinks be harmonized, with all countries moving towards the present average rates of duty in the twelve countries. To date, there has been little support for this and the proposal has made no progress.

8.7   Local Taxation

Local taxation has long been a controversial and somewhat unsatisfactory area of British public finance. Until recently, the only significant tax raised by local authorities was the annual levy (rates) on immovable property which had been in existence for centuries. This tax, which was levied on housing as well as industrial and commercial property, was much disliked by householders and, in order to keep down the charges made upon them, successive governments increased the grants to local authorities made out of central government revenues. The result was that a rising proportion of local government expenditure was financed not from local rates but from national taxation. In the mid-1950s, some 45% of local authority current expenditure was so financed; twenty years later the proportion was around 60%. And since much of what was collected in rates was derived from industrial and commercial companies, it meant that local residents, those who voted in local elections, were paying directly only a low and diminishing proportion of the cost of expenditures made in their name. By the mid-1970s, less than 20% of all current expenditure of local authorities was financed directly by those who voted for the councils which decided the expenditure.[1]

This raised the obvious problem of local accountability; local electors have every incentive to vote for more services if they know they will only pay a small part of the cost of providing them. Such a situation can be avoided if central government grants are for a known amount, fixed in advance; then local ratepayers will know that marginal additions to expenditure will have a significant impact on their own rate bills. But prior to the mid-1970s, there were frequent changes in central government support for local authorities and this tended to respond to the size of local government expenditure and to political pressure and lobbying on behalf of ratepayers. The result was that local government expenditure continued to rise rapidly. Between 1958 and 1976, the current expenditure (i.e. excluding investment) of all local authorities tripled; total rates paid doubled while central government grants more than quadrupled (all in real terms, after taking account of inflation).

After 1976, central government support was less readily forthcoming and did not increase in real terms. For a time, local authorities reduced their expenditure but with the election of a Conservative government in 1979, the scene was set for a period of confrontation. The Conservative government was committed to trying to curb public expenditure with a view to reducing the tax on personal and corporate incomes and sought to reduce government grants to local authorities. But many of the larger local authorities (those in the metropolitan counties and in Greater London) were run by Labour councillors and chose not to cut expenditure but instead to increase sharply local rates which, of course, conflicted with the central government's objective of reducing taxation.

There was a period of years in which the Conservative government in Westminster sought to gain greater control over local authority spending while many of the authorities themselves responded with a variety of measures designed to circumvent government controls. In a small number of well-publicized cases, councils set out openly to defy the Government. The latter responded by abolishing certain councils (the Greater London Council and the equivalent authorities in the metropolitan counties), by taking powers to impose legal ceilings on the rate demands of those authorities whose expenditure was deemed excessive, and then by deciding to abolish rates altogether as far as households were concerned and to bring under central government control the rates levied on industrial and commercial companies.

---

[1] See N. Hepworth, *The Reform of Local Government Finance*, Transactions of the Manchester Statistical Society, 1985–86.

The Government seems to have been motivated by concerns about the question of accountability, believing that local electors were voting for what it saw as high-spending councils because a large proportion of the electorate paid very little by way of rates towards local expenditure. Since rates were a property tax, households comprised of several persons paid no more than households comprised of one person; those on social security were entitled to rate rebates and others, such as students, were not liable to pay any rates at all. Accordingly, it decided to switch from a tax on property to a tax on persons, a tax which would require some payment by every adult citizen with very few exceptions.

The new tax – the community charge or, as it soon became known, the poll tax – was introduced in Scotland in April 1989 and in England and Wales in April 1990. It was a tax levied on persons unrelated to property and, above a certain minimum level, unrelated to income. Its supporters claimed that since it would widen the number of people who paid directly for local government, it would give more people an incentive to scrutinize the behaviour of their local authority and to demand value for money. Opponents stressed the flat-rate nature of the tax and its not being related to ability to pay, a criticism which was only partially met by exempting certain categories of persons from all payments and by reducing the liability of others. Those exempt included children under 18 and all persons still at school, and severely mentally handicapped, long-term hospital patients and those living in nursing homes or hostels and certain members of religious communities. Those benefiting from a reduced liability included full-time students (who paid only 20%) and those on low incomes who could claim a rebate up to 80% of the tax depending upon their economic circumstances.

Business rates were retained but removed from the control of local authorities. Instead of each authority setting its own rate, the Government would set a uniform rate which would apply to all business premises across the country.

Few taxes are popular, but the community charge proved to be exceptionally unpopular and provoked street demonstrations and a campaign of non-payment resulting in many summonses being issued and a small number of people actually being sent to prison. The tax was widely seen as unfair even by many of those who duly paid it, and it soon became apparent that the cost of collection would be high. It rapidly came to appear as a political liability to the Conservative government that had introduced it, and after the change of leadership in November 1991, the Government announced that the community charge would go. There was a period of hasty deliberation and in early 1992 Parliament enacted legislation to abolish the community charge and to introduce another new tax – council tax – to come into force throughout Great Britain in April 1993. This is primarily a tax on property rather than on persons.

The council tax is similar to the old rating system, but there are differences. Each local authority will levy a charge on all residences in its area and the amount payable will depend upon the value of the residence. But whereas, with rates, value was a notional rental value (assessed by valuation officers), under the new tax, value is capital or sale value. This is an improvement, as the old notional values were largely subjective, often out of date and widely seen as arbitrary. Capital values can be fixed more closely to the objective values arising from the regular buying and selling of private houses.

Further to simplify matters, each residence will cease to have its own individual valuation but will instead be classed as belonging to one of eight valuation bands. The lowest rate of council tax will be paid by households living in residences of value of £40,000 or below; the next lowest rate will be paid by households living in residences of value in excess of £40,000 but below £52,000 and so on up to the highest rate payable by those occupying properties worth in excess of £320,000. (The figures quoted apply to England; the valuation bands in Scotland and Wales have been set at lower levels.)

There is one charge per property and it applies regardless of whether the property is in owner-occupation, is privately let or is let by a local authority or housing association. One departure from the principle of a property tax is that where a property is occupied by only one eligible taxpayer, there is a reduction of 25% on the amount otherwise due; where a property is unoccupied, there is a reduction of 50%.

In order to lower the amounts due in the final years of the community charge and to try to ensure that the new tax did not involve large increases in tax liability for large numbers of people, the Government introduced a further shift in local authority finance from local taxation to central taxation. Local authorities were compelled to reduce their community charge (and will have their council tax demands tightly controlled) while direct grants from central government were increased, being paid for out of a rise in VAT from 15% to $17\frac{1}{2}$%. Announcing this measure in his 1991 Budget, the Chancellor of the Exchequer stated that the net yield from local taxation would fall to £7bn. When this is set against local authority expenditures (in 1991) of around £66bn, it can be seen just how great has been the shift from locally-controlled to centrally-controlled finance in recent years.

The community charge was introduced with the claim that it would make local government more accountable to local electors. The end result of this ill-considered measure has been precisely the reverse.

Before leaving this vexed question, it is worth pointing out that, notwithstanding the political controversies of recent years, there remains a strong economic case for a tax on immovable property. The case is that the incidence of such a tax will fall largely on economic rent and will not, in the long run, affect the cost of the property. For the purchase price of private houses, just like that of office blocks, does not usually depend wholly, or even mainly, on cost of production but on scarcity and location. If people pay £500,000 for a luxury house in exclusive parts of Berkshire, this is not because such houses cost that amount to build – many were built years ago at a fraction of this sum – but because wealthy people wish to live there and because suitable properties are scarce. Similarly, office blocks in the City of London can be worth over a hundred million pounds, not because they cost such sums to produce but because, for many businesses, a City address is valuable and the number of good addresses is limited. In both cases, high demand and an inelastic supply combine to raise firstly property prices and ultimately the price of the scarce factor, i.e. land.

It is well known and explained in most economic textbooks[1] that high demand for land will raise its value and will, in the process, create Ricardian rent. The returns accruing to landowners are rent precisely because they are not a cost of production but are a return to scarcity. And rising rents do not increase the supply of land because the supply to the economy as a whole is fixed. So why not levy a tax on economic rent, which is what a property tax is?

Other things being equal, the value of land will increase as output and wealth in the economy expand. Greater competition for the fixed supply of land will raise its price and hence the returns to landowners. But this return does not, for the most part, stem from any effort on the part of landowners but rather from the efforts of all who contribute to greater economic prosperity. It seems desirable, therefore, that some of the returns to land should accrue to society in general in the form of taxation.

But if there is a good economic case for some form of property tax, this is nevertheless a tax on wealth and has the practical disadvantages associated with such taxes that were mentioned earlier in the discussion of CTT. Many people, especially the elderly, live in houses which reflect past rather than present income. They resented paying high rate demands but equally, and not unnaturally, did not wish to sell a home they had spent many years saving to buy.

There are obviously conflicting interests and a compromise is desirable. The new council tax, which is a property tax but which includes a reduction for one person living alone, is an attempt at a compromise of a rough and ready sort.

8.8   Taxation and the EC

Membership of the European Community has already produced a number of changes in taxation in the UK and is likely to produce further changes in the future. The UK has to pay some tax revenue to the EC while the structure and rates of certain taxes are influenced by, or are likely to become influenced by, Community requirements. Further, the European Commission has recently proposed a new Community tax on non-renewable sources of energy as part of its programme for the environment.

The tax paid to the EC is comprised of (a) all customs duties arising from

---

[1]   See, for instance, R. G. Lipsey, *An Introduction to Positive Economics* (7th edition, Weidenfeld & Nicolson, 1989).

the common external tariff; (b) the levies applied to imports of agricultural products from outside the Community; and (c) the proceeds of a percentage rate of VAT levied on a specified collection of goods and services up to an agreed maximum rate, currently 1.4%. There is also provision for additional payments related to national GNP if total EC receipts from these three sources of funds are insufficient to finance the Community budget. The amount actually paid in any one year will depend upon the size of the Community budget and this, in turn, depends upon negotiations every five years between the European Commission and the governments of the member states. In the case of the UK, the amount actually paid will also depend on a special rebate to which it is currently entitled and which is effected by an abatement of its VAT payments.

This special rebate was granted to the UK in 1984 after a series of acrimonious discussions within the European Council and elsewhere. The British government argued that the rules determining contributions to the EC budget and the pattern of EC spending resulted in Britain making a net contribution to the EC which was excessive given that real incomes in Britain were somewhat less than the Community average. This argument was reluctantly accepted by Britain's EC partners and a compromise was agreed whereby a rebate would be paid annually to the UK amounting to 66% of the difference in the previous year between its contributions to the Community's VAT receipts and its share in expenditures from the 'allocated' Community budget. The allocated budget accounts for over 90% of Community expenditure and covers all main categories of expenditure apart from foreign aid.

The EC budget continues to be a source of controversy. The European Commission is usually keen to extend its activities and accordingly is usually looking to increase its resources, while those countries which expect to have to pay the most, notably Germany and the UK, are usually concerned to limit the Commission's spending. Prior to 1988, an upper limit on this spending was set by putting a maximum percentage on the VAT payments that the EC could claim. For the five-year budget period 1988–92, this was changed with the limit on the size of the EC budget being expressed as a percentage of Community GNP. Annual expenditure by the EC was subject to a maximum equivalent to 1.15% of Community GNP in 1988 rising to 1.20% of Community GNP in 1992.

A new five-year budget has to be agreed for the period 1993–7 and the European Commission published proposals early in 1992 which make a claim for a large increase in its resources. The Commission would like the revenue ceiling to rise to 1.35% of Community GNP by 1997, permitting the Community budget to rise to ECU 87.5bn (£58.5bn) in that year compared to planned expenditure of ECU 66.6bn in 1992. The reaction of the British government and a number of others to this proposal has been hostile. Germany, coping with the high costs of reunification, is reluctant to increase payments to Brussels and has suggested that the British rebate should be re-negotiated. It is likely that the EC budget and its financing will remain a vexed issue.

The EC is concerned to harmonize certain taxes levied by member states. This has been touched on already in the section on value added tax, where Commission proposals for maximum and minimum rates of VAT were discussed, and in the section on excise taxes, where the pressure for a degree of harmonization was briefly considered. Other areas where there has been talk of the need for minimum common standards are the taxation of interest and dividends and the taxation of company profits. The traditional exchange controls which restricted international capital movements have been abolished in most EC member states and are due to be phased out in the remaining countries within the next few years. A number of governments fear that the ability of persons to invest abroad freely will lead to an increase in tax avoidance and favour the imposition of a Community-wide withholding tax, i.e. a tax at source on all payments of interest and dividends. This view has found some support in the European Commission in Brussels but it is opposed by Luxembourg and the UK, both of whom are concerned at the potential effects of a withholding tax on their international financial business.

More recently, the European Commission has proposed an EC-wide tax on fossil fuels and other non-renewable forms of energy at a rate equivalent to $3 per barrel of crude oil in 1993, rising to $10 per barrel by the year 2000. (7.35 barrels = 1 metric ton.) The intention is that the tax receipts would be retained by national governments who would make offsetting reductions in other taxes so that the burden of taxation would not rise. The proposed tax is an environmental measure designed to raise the price of fossil fuels to the consumer, cut down demand and thereby assist EC countries to control levels of carbon dioxide emissions. But at the time of writing (early May 1992) there has been no agreement in the Council of Ministers for this tax to be introduced.

Taxation is one of those areas of EC activity where new measures still require the unanimous support of all member countries. This goes some way towards explaining why so few of the Commission's proposals have been adopted.

Apart from concerns to harmonize tax rates or to promote common taxation arrangements, the EC authorities are concerned to see that member countries should not use excise duties so as to discriminate in favour of domestic produce and against the produce of other member states. In 1983, the European Court of Justice decided that British excise duties on alcoholic beverages were discriminatory in that beer, largely home produced, was less heavily taxed than wine, most of which was imported from other EC countries. As a result, in the 1984 UK Budget, tax on beer was raised more than was necessary to keep pace with inflation, while tax on wine was reduced.

More recently, the European Court has ruled that the reduced rate bands of VAT (zero in the case of Ireland and the UK) should only apply to items which can be seen as necessary personal consumption and not to items which are bought for commercial use. As a result of a judgement on 21 June 1988, the UK had to impose VAT on non-residential construction and property development, and on fuel, power, water and sewerage services supplied to business.

SUGGESTIONS FOR FURTHER READING

M.J.Artis and M.K.Lewis, *Money in Britain* (Philip Allan, 1991).

A.D.Bain, *The Economics of the Financial System* (2nd edition, Blackwell, 1992).

Bank of England Quarterly Bulletin.

M.Hall, *The City Revolution: Causes and Consequences* (Macmillan, 1987).

J.A.Kay and M.A.King, *The British Tax System* (5th edition, Oxford University Press, 1990).

B.Kettell, *Monetary Economics* (Graham & Trotman, 1985).

A.R.Prest and N.A.Barr, *Public Finance in Theory and Practice* (7th edition, Weidenfeld & Nicolson, 1985).

M.Reid, *All Change in the City: The Revolution in Britain's Financial Sector* (Macmillan, 1988).

3

The balance of payments

C.J.Green[1]

1   THE OVERALL BALANCE OF PAYMENTS

1.1   Introduction

The importance to the UK of the balance of payments, foreign trade and foreign investment is probably too obvious to require emphasis. The growth of the UK economy, the level of employment, and the standard of living have been, and will continue to be, greatly influenced by external economic events. The purpose of this chapter is to outline the main features of the external relationships of the UK and to discuss economic policies adopted to influence these external relationships, with the primary focus of attention being on the years 1979–91.[2]

Major events since the publication of the previous edition of this volume are the UK's entry into the exchange rate mechanism of the European Monetary System (EMS) in 1990 and significant revisions to the treaty arrangements underlying the EC, agreed at Maastricht in 1991. Previous editions of this volume contained a separate section on the European Community (EC). The integration of the UK into the EC is now such that this treatment no longer seems appropriate, and discussion of EC topics appears throughout the chapter. For comparison with previous editions, coverage of general UK–EC relations is now contained in section 1.6; the EMS is discussed in section 2; and trade-related issues (including the Common Agricultural Policy (CAP), the Community budget, and the Single European Market (SEM)) are covered in section 3.

It is often said that the UK is a highly 'open' economy and an indication of the meaning of this is given by the fact that, in 1990, exports of goods and services were 24.2% of GNP (at market prices) and imports of goods and services were 26.6% of GNP. These percentages are substantially larger than the comparable figures for the mid-1960s, with the most rapid increase coming immediately following the UK's entry into the EC in 1973.[3] A high

---

[1]   I am very grateful to Robin Bladen-Hovell for assistance in preparing the manuscript for this chapter.
[2]   1979 coincides with the coming to power of the first Thatcher administration as well as the coming on stream of major North Sea oil wells. Earlier editions of this volume contain a discussion of external developments between 1945 and 1979. See, in particular, the 5th edition (1974), and the 12th edition (1989).
[3]   In 1965, the export-GNP ratio was 18.2% and the import-GNP ratio was 19.2%.

degree of openness implies that the structure of production and employment is greatly influenced by international specialization. For the UK it also means that over 30% of the foodstuffs consumed and the bulk of raw materials necessary to maintain inputs for industry have to be imported. In the sense defined, the UK is a more open economy than many industrial nations e.g. Germany and France, but less open than some others such as Belgium.

1.2 Basic Concepts

The Balance-of-Payments Accounts: The concept of the balance of payments is central to a study of the external economic relationships of a country but, as with any unifying concept, it is not free from ambiguities. Such ambiguities stem from at least two sources, viz. the different uses to which the concept may be put and the different ways in which we may approach the concept – either as a system of accounts or as a measure of transactions in the foreign-exchange market.

From an accounting viewpoint, we may define the balance of payments as a systematic record, over a given period of time, of all transactions between domestic residents and residents of foreign nations. In this context, residents are defined as those individuals living in the UK, and UK government agencies and military forces located abroad. Ideally, the transactions involved should be recorded at the time of the change of ownership of commodities and assets, or at the time specific services are performed. In practice, trade flows are recorded on a shipment basis, at the time when the export documents are lodged with the Customs and Excise, and at the time when imports are cleared through Customs. As the time of shipment need bear no close or stable relationship to the time of payment for the goods concerned, this method gives rise to errors in the recording of the accounts. All transactions are recorded as sterling money flows, and when transactions are invoiced in foreign currencies, their values are converted into sterling at the appropriate exchange rate. Because sterling is a 'key' or 'vehicle' currency, and is used as an international medium of exchange, it transpires that around 76% of UK exports and 38% of UK imports are invoiced directly in sterling.[1]

Like all systems of income and expenditure accounts, the balance-of-payments accounts are an *ex post* record, constructed on the principle of double-entry bookkeeping. Each external transaction is in principle entered twice, once to indicate the original transaction and again to indicate the manner in which the transaction was financed. The convention is that credit items, which give rise to a flow of funds into the UK (e.g. exports of goods

---

[1]   S. A. Page, 'The Choice of Invoicing Currency in Merchandise Trade', *NIER*, No. 98, 1981.

and services and foreign investment in the UK), are entered with a positive sign, and that debit items, which give rise to a flow of funds out of the UK (e.g. imports of goods and services and investments by UK residents overseas) are entered with a negative sign. It follows that, by definition, the balance-of-payments accounts always balance – the total of credit items must equal the total of debit items. Thus, the interpretation of the accounts depends on dividing them up in particular ways. As there are many ways of dividing up the accounts, they cannot be used to present one unambiguous picture of a country's external economic relationships.

The Structure of the Balance of Payments: In common with most other countries, the UK balance-of-payments accounts are itemized in a manner which generally follows the recommendations laid down by international agreement through the offices of the International Monetary Fund (IMF). However, the grouping and aggregation of individual items in official UK balance-of-payments statistics have changed over the years. Such changes have not always enhanced the analytical value of the statistics, whereas the IMF has recommended a useful standard presentation which has not changed markedly over many years. For these reasons, the summary statement of the UK's balance of payments for 1987–91, contained in Table 3.1, follows with one exception the IMF's presentation rather than that in official UK sources.[1]

The first major feature of the IMF presentation is the distinction between current and capital accounts and, for many purposes, this is the most convenient summary division of the accounts. The current account records all trade in goods and services, including current transfers (Table 3.1: lines A1–A5); whereas the capital account records all transactions in assets and liabilities, including capital transfers (Table 3.1: lines A6–A13).

First in the current account are the so-called 'visible' trade items consisting of the exports (A1) and imports (A2) of commodities. These are shown separately in Table 3.1, whereas all subsequent items are shown on a net basis, i.e. receipts less payments. Full details of separate debit and credit items are given in the official sources. Exports are recorded 'free on board' (f.o.b.), that is at their value at the port of exit excluding the cost of international shipping and insurance. Import statistics are more usually collected c.i.f. (cost, insurance, freight), that is at their value inclusive of international shipping and insurance. As shipping and insurance are not part of the producer cost of a product, it has become conventional to adjust import data to their f.o.b. basis for reporting in the balance of payments.

The remaining items in the current account are the so-called 'invisibles'.

---

[1]   It should be emphasized that the individual items in the accounts emanate directly from UK official statistics; it is their aggregation and grouping in Table 3.1 which follow the IMF presentation. For a readable summary of the IMF presentation see 'Guide to Analytical Presentation of the Balance of Payments', *IMF Survey*, 6 February, 1978. UK balance-of-payments statistics are published annually in the CSO, *United Kingdom Balance of Payments*, HMSO; also known by its cover as 'The Pink Book'.

TABLE 3.1

UK Summary Balance of Payments 1987–91 (£m: credits + / debits −)

	1987	1988	1989	1990	1991
Current Account					
A1. Exports (fob)	79 153	80 346	92 389	102 038	103 704
A2. Imports (fob)	−90 735	−101 970	−116 987	−120 713	−113 823
B1. Balance of Visible Trade					
A1 + A2	−11 582	−21 624	−24 598	−18 675	−10 119
A3. Services	6 745	4 574	4 685	5 201	5 471
A4. Interest, Profits & Dividends	4 078	5 047	4 088	4 029	1 580
A5. Transfers	−3 400	−3 518	−4 578	−4 935	−1 332
B2. Balance of Invisible Trade					
A3 + A4 + A5	7 423	6 103	4 195	4 295	5 719
B3. Balance on Current Account					
B1 + B2	−4 159	−15 521	−20 403	−14 380	−4 399
Capital Account					
A6. Capital Transfers	−	−	−	−	−
A7. Direct Investment	−10 737	−10 644	−4 376	7 295	2 163
A8. Portfolio Investment	24 913	5 282	−17 359	−7 213	−9 582
A9. Other Capital nie					
A9.1 + A9.2 + A9.3	−849	15 354	28 306	10 607	18 821
A9.1 Government	−282	163	−71	−548	−3 011
A9.2 UK Banks	492	12 571	16 581	7 179	8 909
A9.3 Other	−1 059	2 620	11 796	3 976	12 923
A10. Foreign Authorities'					
Sterling Reserves	4 494	2 413	904	1 465	na[1]
B4. Balance on Capital Flows					
A6 + A7 + A8 + A9 + A10	17 822	12 407	7 475	12 158	11 402
A11. Balancing Item	−1 651	5 875	7 488	2 299	−4 421
B5. Balance for Official Financing					
B3 + B4 + A11	12 012	2 761	−5 440	77	2 582
A12. Allocation of SDRs and IMF					
Reserve Tranche Position	−	−	−	−	−
A13. Official Financing					
A13.1 + A13.2 = (B5 + A12)	−12 012	−2 761	5 440	−77	−2 582
A13.1 Official Reserves					
(Increase −)	−12 012	−2 761	5 440	−77	−2 582
A13.2 Change in Net IMF Position	−	−	−	−	−

Source: Pink Book and *ET.*
[1] Not available separately, included in A9.1 and A9.2.

Services (A3) include receipts and payments arising from charges for the insurance and shipping services associated with the international exchange of goods. When imports are adjusted from a c.i.f. to an f.o.b. basis, much of the adjustment is imputed back into the accounts as part of the debit items in respect of services purchased. Other services arise independently of the exchange of goods, notably the expenditures of tourists when abroad, and the burgeoning activity of consultancy services. Remittances on account of interest, profits and dividends (IPD) (A4) arise when, for example, British firms pay dividends to foreign shareholders (a debit) or vice-versa (a credit). Shareholders and holders of other assets perform a service in lending capital funds to firms and governments; the dividend or interest payments are their rewards for performing this service. Note therefore that, whereas interest and dividend income from assets appear in the current account, revenues from the purchase or sale of an asset appear in the capital account. Current transfers (A5) are so-called 'unrequited' in nature, as they do not directly arise from the sale of goods and services or of assets. Remittances home by immigrant workers, payments to and from the EC, and foreign aid payments or receipts are the main examples.

Turning to the capital account, capital transfers (A6) are difficult in practice to distinguish from current transfers and, apart from certain exceptional governmental transfers of assets, identifiable transfers are all typically recorded in the current account. Direct investment (A7) consists of transactions undertaken to acquire or extend control over a foreign enterprise; portfolio investment (A8) consists of transactions aimed at securing investment income or capital gains. The distinction between these two classes is clearer in practice than it might appear. In general, direct investment abroad by the UK involves the construction and equipping of factories abroad or the acquisition or sale of foreign subsidiaries by British firms. Thus, direct investment, whether by UK firms abroad, or by foreign firms in the UK, is carried out mainly for the purpose of undertaking production of goods or services in a foreign country. In contrast, agents undertaking portfolio investment act 'at arms length' and have no direct managerial interest in the activity in which the investment is made. Portfolio investment involves the purchase or sale of securities of overseas companies or governments. Such securities are typically held by financial institutions, such as pension funds, as part of their overall investment operations.

Other capital not included elsewhere (n.i.e.) is, as its name implies, relatively heterogeneous. Government transactions recorded in this section (A9.1) include various long-term intergovernmental transactions: for example, subscriptions to international bodies such as the World Bank; and all short-term borrowing apart from two items recorded specifically else-where. The latter consist of the borrowing which is counted by overseas monetary authorities as part of their reserves (A10) and loans from the IMF which, along with government liquid asset transactions, are shown in official financing (A13). Transactions by UK banks (A9.2) consist of the vast majority of their sterling and foreign-currency transactions with overseas residents, including all their loans and deposits but excluding their trans-actions in long-term bonds which are recorded under A8. Finally in this group, 'Other' (A9.3) consists of the identifiable transactions of other sectors. Items of note here include overseas borrowing by Public Corpor-ations, and transactions in respect of trade credit. The immediate counter-part of a high proportion of export and import payments is the trade credit, usually of between one and six months, granted by the supplier to the purchaser. The amount of such credit outstanding at any one time is very large, although it has a rapid turnover. However, the balance-of-payments accounts record only the net changes in trade credit outstanding during the year, and these amounts are usually relatively small.

We will defer consideration of line A10 until later and come next to the balancing item (A11) which is the residual in the accounts, and which is required to compensate for the total of measurement errors and omissions. These can arise from a variety of sources. In general, the two sides of any given transaction cannot be recorded simultaneously. For example, the value of commodity exports is recorded mainly by the Customs and Excise Department but the proceeds from these exports are recorded only indirectly using statistics provided by banks and other financial institutions. Although, in principle, the accounts should balance, in practice numerous discrepancies in recording procedures generally give rise to a positive or negative balancing item. A positive balancing item reflects unrecorded receipts, and a negative balancing item reflects unrecorded payments. The major source of errors and discrepancies in the accounts arises when data are collected mainly by sample surveys, especially if respondents have an incentive to under- or over-report. These circumstances occur particularly in the recording of trade in services and in capital-account items other than those reported by government or financial institutions. Particular problem areas include revenues and expenditures associated with tourism, and trade credit flows. As discussed in section 1.4, the large size of the balancing item has been a source of concern in the UK's accounts for some years.

Line A12 relates to the UK's membership of the IMF. Allocations of Special Drawing Rights (SDRs) to the UK are treated as a credit item, even though they do not correspond to any actual transactions, because an allocation effectively increases the UK's reserves (A13). Likewise, when the UK's quota in the IMF is increased, the UK is required to subscribe 25% of the increase to the IMF (the so-called 'reserve tranche') in the form of SDRs or other 'convertible' foreign currencies,[1] and the official reserves fall by the corresponding amount.

The remaining lines of the balance of payments constitute official financing. The sum of lines A13.1 and A13.2 gives the amount by which the country's foreign-exchange reserves increased($-$) or decreased over the year. Foreign-exchange reserves consist of the immediately liquid foreign-currency assets of the central bank, together with its automatic drawing rights at the IMF. These play a specific role in balance-of-payments and exchange-rate policy. The transactions which make up the balance of payments involve a myriad of individual decisions to make transactions with other countries, many of which involve a purchase or sale of foreign currency. There is no guarantee that, in aggregate, demands by domestic residents to purchase foreign currency in exchange for pounds will exactly match sales of foreign currency for pounds. Given the price of foreign

---

[1] A currency is said to be 'convertible' if it can be freely exchanged into other currencies by domestic and foreign residents. Many countries impose tight restrictions on the convertibility of their currency.

currency, an excess demand or supply of foreign currency has to be met from some source. It is the central bank in a country (in the UK the Bank of England) which acts as the last line of defence in supplying foreign currency if there is an excess demand for it, or in acquiring it if there is excess supply. Of course, excess demand or supply could lead to a change in price – of the foreign-exchange rate – but this is a large subject in its own right and is deferred to section 2. In reckoning a country's official foreign-exchange reserves, only assets are included as these are immediately available. In a crisis, central banks can find it difficult to borrow without the attachment of conditions. Indeed, the inclusion of a country's automatic drawing rights in the IMF in this reckoning acknowledges that the only guaranteed source of foreign-currency borrowing for a central bank resides in these rights. An amount equal to 25% of a country's quota (the reserve tranche position) may be used automatically. Along with other IMF member countries, the UK has further access to four credit tranches, each of which corresponds to 25% of quota, but access is dependent on the country concerned adopting economic policies which meet with the approval of the IMF, this being particularly so for drawings beyond the first credit tranche. Borrowing in the credit tranches is recorded separately under official financing in line A13.2. The main point of IMF borrowing is that it is the only form of unsecured foreign assistance for a central bank which is always certainly available, subject to the conditionality required by the IMF.

We return finally to line A10, which consists of movements of funds arising from transactions made by overseas monetary authorities (mainly central banks) who hold sterling assets as part of their own official reserves. These assets include ordinary deposits with UK banks and with the Bank of England, as well as holdings of government bonds and Treasury Bills. The IMF recommends the recording of this item as part of official financing on grounds of symmetry so as to ensure that the sum of all countries' official financing surpluses worldwide is, in principle, equal to the sum of official financing deficits. This procedure has never been followed precisely by the UK and a number of other countries because movements in these funds are largely outside the control of the domestic monetary authority and they can therefore equally well be seen as generating a requirement for official financing as much as they can be seen as contributing to that financing.[1] With currency exchange rates floating, central banks around the world have found it prudent to hold relatively diversified portfolios of major currencies in their official reserves, and this includes sterling, holdings of which for official reserves purposes amounted to £18.8bn at end-1990, up from £14.6bn at end-1980. In this chapter, we take the view that movements in these funds are best thought of as generating a requirement for official financing and we therefore depart from the IMF presentation and show them separately as

---

[1]   These funds correspond to what were formerly called 'the sterling balances', movements in which did cause reserve management problems for the UK authorities during the sixties. For a full account of the sterling balances see the 11th edition of this book.

contributing to the balance on capital flows. It should be emphasized, however, that this is just one of many occasions when the appropriate classification is a matter of judgement and no one view can be regarded as unambiguously 'right' or 'wrong'.

Main Balances in the Balance of Payments: As we have seen, in an accounting sense it can be said that the balance of payments always balances. The interpretation of the accounts therefore depends on their being divided up in particular ways. It is customary to select a number of main 'balances' in the accounts which give a summary picture of different aspects of a country's overall balance of payments (Table 3.1, lines B1–B5). Two major balances are those on current account (B3) and on the capital account excluding the balancing item and official financing (B4). These two balances give, respectively, the net receipts or payments on account of all identified transactions in goods, services and transfers (the current account), and in assets and liabilities other than official financing (the balance on capital flows). The balance for official financing (B5) is also regarded as important for the reasons given above – it shows the amount of 'last resort' activity undertaken by the central bank in buying or selling foreign-currency reserves. The balance for official financing is often called the 'overall balance'. Within the current account itself, a distinction is made between the balance of visible trade (B1) and the invisible balance (B2). To some extent, this is because statistics on the visible trade balance become available more rapidly than other items in the accounts apart from official financing, and therefore provide a leading indicator of possible trends in the accounts.

Finally, reference may be made to the 'basic balance' which may be found in older treatments of the balance of payments, and which is defined as the sum of the current account and the net flow of long-term capital. The argument for including these items together is that they were thought to be largely 'autonomous' in nature, whereas the remaining short-term capital flows, including official financing, were thought to be more 'accommodating', being carried out mainly in order to finance trade and long-term capital flows. The basic balance is currently not widely used because it is extremely difficult in practice to distinguish 'long-term' and 'short-term' capital flows and to determine, other than arbitrarily, which are autonomous and which accommodating.

The Balance of International Indebtedness: The balance of international indebtedness is a reckoning of the net external assets and liabilities of a country. It therefore gives the value of all assets held abroad and borrowing from abroad by UK residents, as well as all assets held in the UK and borrowing from the UK by overseas residents. Whereas the balance of payments gives a record of transactions and therefore of flows of funds during some particular time-period, the balance of international

TABLE 3.2

UK: Net External Assets and Liabilities *1986–90 (£bn, End of Period)

	1986	1987	1988	1989	1990
1. Direct Investment	33.1	25.4	32.7	36.2	20.3
2. Portfolio Investment	96.6	54.8	78.2	116.8	88.4
3. Other Capital nie	−34.0	−26.4	−42.5	−79.2	−83.1
3.1 Government nie	(5.9)	(5.5)	(5.1)	(3.7)	(4.7)
3.2 UK Banks	(−45.9)	(−38.3)	(−51.1)	(−76.2)	(−76.9)
3.3 Other	(6.0)	(6.4)	(3.5)	(−6.7)	(−10.9)
4. Foreign Authorities' Sterling Reserves	−9.6	−13.8	−16.1	−16.2	−18.8
5. Reserves	17.4	27.0	28.7	26.3	22.7
5.1 Official Reserves	(17.4)	(27.0)	(28.7)	(26.3)	(22.7)
5.2 Net IMF Position	(−)	(−)	(−)	(−)	(−)
6. Net UK Assets	103.6	67.0	81.0	83.9	29.5
7. Change from Previous Year	23.3	−36.6	14.0	2.9	−54.4
8. Current Account Balance (Calendar Year)	0.2	−4.2	−15.5	−20.4	−14.4
9. GNP at Market Prices (Calendar Year)	388.0	425.3	472.9	515.5	554.6
10. Net UK Assets in per cent of GNP (%)	26.7	15.8	17.1	16.3	5.3

Source: Pink Book.
* Net Liabilities are shown with a negative sign.

indebtedness gives the stocks of assets and liabilities outstanding at a particular point in time. Thus the total balance of international indebtedness on any given date is equivalent to the UK's total net overseas assets. As far as possible, the stocks of assets and liabilities in this balance are valued at current market prices.

Table 3.2 gives the balance of international indebtedness for the UK over the 1986–90 period. It can be seen that the classification of this account is similar to that of the capital account of the balance of payments. Indeed this should not cause surprise, as the capital account shows transactions in the same assets and liabilities whose outstanding stocks are given in the balance of international indebtedness. However, it is important to appreciate that the capital account over any particular year is not simply equal to the change in the corresponding items in the balance of international indebtedness over that year. The differences are due in part to errors and omissions in the different procedures for estimating the stocks of assets and liabilities and for recording the net transactions which make up the balance-of-payments account. However, the differences also arise more particularly because the value of a nation's assets and liabilities can change for two reasons: first, new net lending or borrowing may take place: this is recorded in the capital account. Second, the price of an asset or liability may change and this is not recorded in the capital account because it does not correspond to any transaction but to a valuation change.

A major cause of changes in international asset values is exchange-rate movements. Thus, when the price of sterling in terms of foreign currencies falls, the pound is said to depreciate.[1] Each unit of foreign currency will exchange for more pounds than before. Hence UK residents holding assets overseas whose values are denominated in foreign currencies will experience an increase in the sterling value of their assets – they will make capital gains. UK residents who have loans denominated in foreign currencies will experience an increase in the sterling value of their liabilities – they will make capital losses, as increased sterling amounts will be required to repay the loan. The reverse is true when the pound appreciates. However, it should be emphasized that not all overseas assets and liabilities are denominated in foreign currencies; many are denominated in sterling, as for example when the British Government sells sterling gilt-edged securities (bonds) to overseas residents. The sterling values of such assets and liabilities are not directly affected by movements in the exchange rate.

In general, therefore, the relation between the capital account of the balance of payments and the balance of international indebtedness is not a simple one. Moreover, when the exchange rate of sterling changes, overseas residents who hold sterling-denominated assets or liabilities will make capital gains or losses in terms of their own currencies. Clearly, exchange-rate movements have complex effects on international assets and liability holdings and thus on individual decisions to adjust these holdings. These effects are considered in more detail in section 2.

1.3   Equilibrium and Disequilibrium in the Balance of Payments

It is obviously important, both for purposes of economic policy and historical analysis, to have clear notions of balance-of-payments equilibrium and disequilibrium. It would simplify matters if we could calculate easily the 'deficit' (or 'surplus') in the balance of payments, and thus refer to the balance of payments as being 'out of equilibrium' or 'in equilibrium' if the deficit (or surplus) were thought to be sufficiently large or small in magnitude respectively.

However, the formulation of such concepts is not easy and depends on the purpose for which they are to be used. The time-span over which equilibrium is defined is obviously important. A daily or even monthly time-span would be of little value and it is generally accepted that a sufficient span of years should be allowed so that the effects of cyclical fluctuations in income will have no appreciable net impact on external transactions. The exchange-rate regime in force and the degree of intervention by the authorities are also important. If the authorities are intervening in the external accounts in a variety of ways, it becomes necessary to consider which interventions are intended either to restore or perturb an equilibrium and which are carried

---

[1]   The terminology should be kept clear. When the price of sterling in terms of foreign currency falls, the pound is said to *depreciate*; when the price of sterling rises, the pound *appreciates*. Thus a move from £1 = US$1.70 to £1 = US$1.60 represents a depreciation of the pound *vis-à-vis* the dollar, and a move in the other direction represents an appreciation.

out for other purposes largely incidental to the balance of payments. Thus, sales of foreign-currency bonds to augment the official reserves on the one hand, and the granting of foreign aid on the other, both have an impact on the external accounts but decisions about the latter would not normally be thought of primarily as constituting 'balance-of-payments policy'. In practice, equilibrium in the balance of payments is usually defined with reference to one of the various balances introduced in section 1.2. Which of the balances is utilized depends on the purpose at hand.

Balance for Official Financing (Overall Balance): This is the most commonly used concept of equilibrium, and the Balance for Official Financing is often simply referred to as 'the balance of payments surplus' (or deficit). Its rationale arises from the role of the central bank in the foreign-exchange market. If the exchange rate is allowed to float freely to equate the supply and demand for foreign exchange, including central government foreign transactions incidental to balance-of-payments policy, then equilibrium in the market is always attained automatically and this coincides with the fact that the BOF will, under these circumstances, always be identically zero.

Since 1972, successive UK governments have allowed sterling to float but this float, like that of other currencies, has never been completely free. The authorities have intervened in the foreign-exchange market in a variety of ways and, as shown in Table 3.1, the BOF has never been identically zero but has often been quite large in magnitude. When the exchange rate is managed by the authorities to any degree, a key role is assigned to the central bank as the last-resort provider of foreign currency, although this is by no means the only instrument which can be used to influence the exchange rate. Thus the BOF is an appropriate indicator of the balance of pressures on the exchange rate. If the BOF is positive (in surplus), the Bank of England has been able to increase its reserves at the prevailing sterling exchange rate, suggesting an excess supply of foreign currencies at this rate and consequent upward pressure on the exchange rate; whereas the existence of a deficit on the BOF suggests an excess demand for foreign currencies and consequent downward pressure on the exchange rate.[1]

A further advantage of the BOF is that it shows the potential increase (decrease) in the UK money supply as a result of a surplus (deficit) in the balance of payments and hence gives an estimate of at least the general direction of expansionary (contractionary) forces in the economy emanating from the external accounts. The link between the BOF and the supply of money arises through the central-bank balance sheet. As a matter of necessity, an increase (decrease) in central-bank foreign assets must be exactly balanced by an increase (decrease) in its liabilities. In general, the counterpart of a purchase (sale) of foreign exchange by the central bank is an

---

[1]   This and succeeding arguments must all be subject to the caveat noted earlier that there is not necessarily universal agreement about the appropriate definition of the BOF.

increase (decrease) in its sterling deposit liabilities to the commercial bank from which it purchased the currency. Such deposits are included in a commercial bank's 'operational deposits', and an increase (decrease) in these deposits therefore allows an expansion (contraction) in the commercial bank's loans and hence in its deposit liabilities, thus leading to an increase (decrease) in the money supply. The central bank can offset this effect by carrying out what is commonly called 'sterilization'. A sale (purchase) of Treasury bills or bonds to the commercial bank in question will sterilize the monetary implications of the surplus on the BOF by drawing down (increasing) the commercial bank's operational deposits to their original level. Thus, while the link between the BOF and the potential change in the money supply is a direct one, the link between the BOF and the actual change in the money supply is a good deal more tenuous, depending as it does on the sterilization policy of the authorities and the exact responses of commercial banks to changes in the levels of their operational deposits.[1]

A final argument for focusing on the BOF is that most other definitions of surplus or deficit involve some element of arbitrariness in classifying the accounts. In particular, all other definitions fail to take into account the balancing item which, by its very nature, cannot be allocated among the identified items in the accounts. Such definitions are therefore inherently subject to some degree of mismeasurement and hence misinterpretation.

There are, however, arguments for not focusing exclusively on the BOF, the main one having to do with the role of the authorities. Acquisition or use of reserves is not the only nor even the most common method for the authorities to influence the balance of payments and the exchange rate. The level of interest rates in the economy has a direct influence on the exchange rate, as discussed in section 2. More generally, the level of income is a powerful determinant of many of the transactions which make up the balance of payments, and few policy measures exist which do not have at least some effect on the level of income in the economy. Thus, the authorities may pursue policies which produce equilibrium in the BOF but which result in unacceptable levels of interest rates, unemployment, or inflation in the economy. This implies that the authorities have to keep in mind other policy objectives as well as equilibrium in the BOF and, in designing policies, must recognize the interactions between the balance of payments and the rest of the economy.

The Current Account Balance: This is of interest because it marks the division between trade in goods and services and transactions in assets. Examination of the current account balance also brings out the relationship between the balance of payments and the national income and expenditure accounts. In discussing this relationship it is helpful to use some notation.

---

[1]   For useful accounts of the links between external transactions and the domestic money supply, see 'External Flows and Broad Money', *BEQB*, December 1983; and 'Measures of Broad Money', *BEQB*, May 1987.

Let: Y = GDP at Market Prices; C = Consumers' Expenditure; G = Government Expenditure; I = Private Investment; X = Export of Goods and Services; Z = Imports of Goods and Services; S = Private Savings; T = Tax Revenue; and F = Net Transfers Abroad. Using this notation, GDP calculated from the expenditure side can be written as:

$$Y = C + I + G + X - Z \qquad (1)$$

In this identity, we see that the balance on goods and services ($X - Z$: equal to the current account balance exclusive of transfers) is arithmetically identical to the excess of domestic income (Y) over domestic expenditure ($C+I+G$). This fact often leads to a statement that a deficit in the goods and services balance is *caused* by an excess of domestic expenditure over domestic income. Since one is simply identical to the other, attribution of causation is incorrect; it is necessary to look more deeply for the causes of the excess of domestic expenditure over income. However, it is true that, if it were thought desirable to reduce a deficit on goods and services, this would of necessity involve a cut in domestic expenditures *relative* to domestic incomes. More generally, any policy which influences the balance between domestic incomes and expenditures (and few policies will not do this in some measure) will also necessarily affect the current account.

It is also illuminating to write the disposition of the GDP by income recipients as:

$$Y = C + S + T + F \qquad (2)$$

Deducting (2) from (1) and rearranging the resultant identity gives the following:

$$(X - Z - F) = (T - G) + (S - I) \qquad (3)$$

Current Account = Government Budget + Private Sector
Surplus/Deficit   Surplus/Deficit   Surplus/Deficit

In other words, the current account surplus (deficit) is arithmetically identical to the sum of the government budget surplus (deficit) and the private sector's surplus (deficit) of savings over investment. Since (3) is an identity, we still cannot describe either side of the identity as causing the other, but we can again state that policies which influence saving and investment and the government budget balance will, unless they are exactly offsetting, of necessity affect the current account balance.

The current account balance is also related in an important way to the balance of international indebtedness. The private sector surplus (deficit) is equivalent to its net acquisition of financial assets (liabilities); likewise the government budget surplus (deficit) is equivalent to net government lending (borrowing). By analogy, the current account surplus (deficit), which is identical to the capital account deficit (surplus), is equivalent to the net acquisition (sales) of overseas assets by UK residents. As we have seen, the value of the UK's net external assets may change either because of net new lending or borrowing, or because of changes in the price of existing holdings of assets and liabilities. Net new lending or borrowing in total is equivalent to the current account surplus or deficit. Hence, the UK can only acquire net new overseas assets (liabilities) to the extent that it runs a current account surplus (deficit). In Table 3.2, the current account balance is shown together with the change in UK net overseas assets, the difference between the two being attributable to valuation effects and net errors and omissions.

The Concepts of Equilibrium Compared: It should be clear that whereas the BOF focuses on the role of the authorities, the current account position draws attention to the interaction between the balance of payments and the economy as a whole. A reasonable summary of their relative uses would emphasize that the BOF is a relatively short-run equilibrium concept while the current account balance is of more interest in the longer run. Thus a substantial deficit on the BOF generally requires some immediate action on the part of the authorities. Indeed, in the era of relatively fixed exchange rates between 1945 and 1972, the IMF defined a 'fundamental disequilibrium' in the balance of payments as a deficit on the BOF which could not be financed or rectified by the authorities without a change in the exchange rate. On the other hand, a deficit on the current account can be financed for relatively long periods by capital inflows, but at a cost of steadily increasing international indebtedness, which ultimately must be repaid.

Finally, it should be emphasized that no single concept can be universally applicable. Different items in the balance of payments are interlinked. One obvious linkage is that while an outflow of capital may produce a once-for-all deficit on the capital account, the return flows of IPD in later periods will lead to a smaller but continuing inflow which improves the current account. Other less obvious linkages are too numerous to mention. Thus, the most firm guidance available is that whatever concept of equilibrium is used, it should be justified as being appropriate for the purpose to which it is applied.

1.4   Trends in the Balance of Payments and External Assets

The Historic Position: We turn now to consider more specifically the balance-of-payments performance of the United Kingdom. For this purpose we examine first Table 3.3, which contains average annual figures for the main items in the balance of payments covering selected periods since 1952, together with movements in the GNP and outstanding net external assets over the same periods. The first sub-period covers the 1950s, a time which in retrospect appears relatively tranquil. The second sub-period leads up to the devaluation of the pound in 1967. The end of the third sub-period is marked by the floating of sterling in June 1972. The end of the next sub-period coincides with the beginning of the major boost to export revenues from North Sea oil in 1979. The end of the next sub-period is marked by a sharp

TABLE 3.3

Trends in the UK Balance of Payments, Annual Averages for Selected Periods (£m)

	1952–62	1963–7	1968–72	1973–9	1980–5	1986–90
1. Balance on Visible Trade	−158	−326	−303	−3,182	−617	−17,208
2. Balance on Invisibles[1]	269	249	762	2,360	4,399	6,353
Government	(−277)	(−589)	(−733)	(−1,676)	(−3,489)	(−6,216)
Private	(546)	(838)	(1,495)	(4,036)	(7,888)	(12,568)
3. Current Account Balance	111	−77	459	−822	3,782	−10,855
4. Portfolio and Direct Investment	−145	−136	−99	−154	−8,726	−7,297
5. Capital Account nie	na[2]	171	10	765	3,181	16,400
6. Balancing Item	58	15	−65	1,039	1,212	4,212
7. Balance for Official Financing	24	−27	305	828	−551	2,460
8. Official Reserves and Net IMF (− increase)	−24	27	−305	−828	551	−2,460
GNP at Market Prices (£bn)	22.3	36.1	53.4	129.8	290.8	471.3
Net External Assets (£bn; end of period)[3]	1.5	2.3	6.4	12.1	73.8	29.6

Source: Pink Book and ET.
[1] The Government/Private split for 1952–62 is partly estimated.
[2] Not separately available.
[3] Amount outstanding at end -1962, end -1967 (etc).

fall in world oil prices, which subsequently stabilized at appreciably lower
levels than in 1980–5. The final sub-period brings the data essentially up to
date for comparison with Table 3.1. The averaging process hides substantial
variations in the accounts from year to year but it also helps uncover any
longer-term trends in the accounts.

A useful starting point is with the characterization of the UK balance of
payments given by Cooper in 1968.[1] This runs in terms of four main propositions: (1) the UK normally has a deficit on visible trade which is more
than offset by a surplus on invisibles. (2) This implies a surplus on current
account. In addition the UK is normally a net exporter (i.e., experiences net
outflows) of long-term capital. (3) The role of the UK as an international
banking centre, with the focus particularly on London, tends to produce
volatile short-term capital flows which have an important influence on the
overall balance of payments. (4) These activities are all carried out with a
very inadequate underpinning of official exchange reserves.

By and large, this was the picture throughout the 1950s and 1960s.
Through 1962, the UK generally experienced a modest current account
surplus and was able to add to its reserves at an average rate of £24m per
year. In 1963–7, the visible trade balance worsened sufficiently to produce a
deficit on current account. This precipitated a devaluation of the pound in
1967, followed by an improvement in the current account. Table 3.3 also
confirms the picture of the UK as a net exporter of long-term capital
(portfolio) and direct investment.

As far as reserves and short-term capital are concerned, Cooper's summary is again broadly accurate for the 1950s and 1960s. A convenient
reckoning of the strength of a country's official international reserve position is in terms of the number of months' imports which outstanding
reserves could be used to finance. The UK's official reserves were broadly
stable at about 3 months' imports over the period 1952–62, decreasing to 2.3
months' average over 1963–72. In comparison, industrial Europe as a whole
(excluding the UK) maintained reserve levels averaging about 6 months'
imports throughout the fifties and sixties.

The UK's reserve position might have been more tenable were it not for
the large swings in short-term capital to which Cooper refers. When the UK
balance of payments deteriorated, short-term capital flowed out of London
as its holders feared a possible devaluation of the currency. However, this
very outflow often turned a barely manageable position into a crisis and such
crises were a recurrent problem in the fifties and sixties. That these crises
were, to some extent, 'unnecessary' can be brought out by noting that the
magnitude of both the current balance and the BOF during the fifties and
sixties tended to decline in relation to GNP and also in relation to the UK's
overall net overseas asset position. It was shortage of international liquidity
in relation to short-term capital flows which was a major cause of the
periodic crises.

---

[1]   R. E. Caves (ed.), *Britain's Economic Prospects* (Allen and Unwin, 1968), Chapter 3.

After 1972, the UK balance-of-payments position underwent important changes, most of which can be traced back to three major factors. First, the floating of sterling in 1972 presaged a more general international move towards floating exchange rates by the major industrial countries. This, in turn, changed considerably the rules and constraints associated with balance-of-payments management. The second major factor was the UK's accession to the EC in January 1973 which, it is estimated, resulted in the UK running a larger balance-of-payments deficit or smaller surplus than would otherwise have been the case.[1] Third, and probably of most immediate importance for the UK, was the discovery and subsequent exploitation of North Sea oil. Accompanying these developments were dramatic changes in the world price of oil: sharp increases in 1973 and 1979, followed by a precipitate slump in 1985–6. The period immediately following the floating of sterling (1973–9) saw a sustained worsening of the visible trade balance and a succession of current account deficits. The deficit on long-term capital also persisted over this period, despite a substantial inflow of private capital in connection with North Sea oil exploitation.

Successive governments chose to accommodate the current account deficit to some extent by a substantial programme of official short- and long-term borrowing, with repayments effectively guaranteed by a portion of future North Sea oil revenues. Thus the UK was able to absorb a sequence of large current account deficits without having to undertake such a major adjustment programme as would otherwise have been required in the absence of North Sea oil.

Developments Since 1979:   The early eighties (1980–5) saw a dramatic turnaround in the balance-of-payments position. The oil price rise of 1979 coincided with the coming on stream of major North Sea oil-fields. Oil exports doubled between 1979 and 1981, even as the non-oil visible balance deteriorated further. The net result was a shrinking of the overall deficit on visible trade which, together with the continued strengthening of the invisibles balance, combined to produce a sequence of record current account surpluses. On the capital account, the abolition of exchange controls in 1979 accentuated the traditional pattern, and record outflows of long-term capital were experienced.

The net result of these developments was a massive increase in the net external assets of the UK from £12.1bn at end-1979 to £73.8bn at end-1985. However, the existence of a deficit on average in the BOF during this period illustrates the hazards of placing too much emphasis on one particular measure of the balance-of-payments deficit or surplus. Despite the underlying strength of the balance of payments, official reserves fell, as the UK continued its programme of repayments of official foreign debt.

The most recent period has been marked by a further dramatic shift in the

---

[1]   See M.H.Miller, 'Estimates of the Static Balance of Payments and Welfare Costs Compared', Chapter 6 in J.Pinder (ed.), *The Economics of Europe* (Charles Knight, 1971).

accounts. The fall in the price of oil in 1985–6 coincided with a levelling-off of output from the North Sea and resulted in a fall in the net oil contribution to the visible balance. This was felt most severely in 1986. In 1987 the net oil contribution remained at about the same level, but it fell further before stabilizing after 1988. Although non-oil exports increased, the visible trade deficit reached record proportions, averaging 3.6% of GNP during 1986–90 compared to 2.4% during 1973–9.

Thus, despite a continuing increase in the surplus on invisibles, and while still having substantial reserves of North Sea oil, the UK has returned to the pre-oil position of experiencing significant current account deficits. On the capital account, the five-year average data mask substantial year-to-year swings in individual items. However, the overall position remained one of substantial net outflows of long-term capital, more than offset by short-term capital inflows. In this period, despite the weakness of the current account, the authorities generally accumulated reserves particularly in 1987 when sterling was sold as part of an active policy of exchange-rate management aimed at preventing an excessive appreciation of the currency. Movements in the net external asset position reflected, at least qualitatively, the fluctuations in the current account with a sharp increase in 1980–5 being followed by an almost equally sharp fall in 1986–90.

Appraisal: The main concern about recent balance-of-payments performance has been the slide into massive current account deficit even while North Sea oil production is high and even while the economy is in recession. The figures for net external assets suggest that about two-thirds of the build-up in assets over 1980–5 were already run down by the end of 1990. These net asset data are subject to a wide margin of error, particularly the most recent figures. Nevertheless, the overall trend is relatively clear and disturbing. Moreover, despite the increase in official reserves, reserve levels were still under two and half months' imports at the end of 1990, about the same as in the mid-seventies. To some extent, as we discuss in section 2, the relatively poor performance of the non-oil trade account in recent years is simply the obverse of the high level of oil exports, and it is to be expected that the non-oil visible balance should worsen along with the expansion of oil activities. Moreover, the deterioration in the visible balance has been overlaid by continued strength in the invisibles account. It is sometimes remarked that, as a trading nation, the UK cannot survive solely by producing services, and as a literal statement this is true. However, the gloomy emphasis in such statements does overlook the UK's historic position as a major net exporter of services many of which are essential to the flow of trade.

One difficulty in interpreting recent balance-of-payments performance stems from the quality of the data, reflected in the large and mostly positive balancing item (Table 3.1). In general the balancing item is thought to relate to unrecorded capital flows, especially trade credit, and the increase in its size is attributed particularly to the abolition of exchange controls in 1979. The control procedure provided a relatively accurate source of capital account data. These are now gathered through a variety of survey sources, some of which are voluntary and inevitably less reliable than before. However, the sheer size, sign, and persistence of the balancing item must invoke caution in attributing it to any one source. If it did reflect entirely unrecorded capital inflows, then we would expect to see some impact on the invisibles account in the return outflows of IPD, and there is no discernible impact of this kind in any of the detailed items which make up this account. It is possible therefore that the balancing item may include unrecorded current account items, particularly services. Moreover, the recording of all balance-of-payments items is likely to prove increasingly difficult with the creation of a single market within the EC. (See section 3 for more details.)

In summary, the main feature of the UK's balance of payments in the early 1990s is that North Sea oil discoveries, despite their scale (see section 1.5), have provided only very temporary relief from the UK's historic balance-of-payments problems. Cooper's characterization of the UK continues to be strikingly accurate in broad outline. However, the particularly worrying feature in recent years has been the sheer size and apparent durability of the visible trade deficit, which is far too large to be covered by any foreseeable improvement in the invisibles account. While there have been signs of an improvement in the visible trade balance in 1990–1, it is unlikely that this improvement will be sustained as economic recovery gathers momentum. It remains to be seen whether the undoubted changes in the structure of the UK economy in the 1980s have made such an imbalance easier or harder to manage.

1.5   North Sea Oil and Gas

Apart from membership of the EC, the North Sea oil and gas discoveries constitute the single most important set of influences on the UK economy since World War II. Exploration began in 1960; the first gas production came on stream in 1964 and the first oil in 1975. However, most of the early production went to domestic consumption, effectively replacing imports, and net oil exports only began in 1980 when the UK became fully self-sufficient in energy.[1] The impact of the North Sea on the economy has been lopsided. Oil and gas production and processing contributed some 14.2% of the output of UK production industries, but only 5.3% of total GDP, in 1980. These percentages rose to peaks of 20.9% and 7.2% respectively in 1984, since when they have levelled off and begun to decline. However, the major effects of the North Sea fell disproportionately on the balance of payments and the government budget. These latter effects are discussed in

---

[1]   Throughout the period the UK has been both an exporter and an importer of crude oil. Refineries are built to utilize a particular balance of crude oil and UK refineries require a mix of domestic and foreign crude. Clearly it is the net balance of these transactions which is relevant for balance-of-payments purposes, and the term 'energy self-sufficiency' implies that the economy can sustain net exports of energy production.

section 2. Here, we look in more detail at the impact of North Sea oil and gas on the balance of payments as a whole and at some of the difficulties involved in forecasting its impact in the future.

When calculating the overall direct impact of North Sea oil and gas on the UK balance of payments, account has to be taken of several factors. First, is the net effect on the balance of trade in oil and gas, as home output is exported or substituted for imports. Second, is the net trade in equipment and technical services to discover and extract oil and gas. This is a particularly slippery concept, in that one could argue that, as UK-based oil equipment industries developed and began exporting their output, these exports could be regarded as contributing to North Sea oil-related revenues. In practice, such exports are rather indirectly related to North Sea oil and most calculations of balance-of-payments effects only cover imports of equipment which can be easily identified for North Sea exploration and extraction purposes. The third main item consists of the inflows of foreign capital required to help finance the extraction and development of oil; and fourth are the net IPD outflows remitted overseas by foreign firms operating in the North Sea, and reflecting the earnings on their invested capital.

The effects of North Sea oil were first felt well before the UK became a net exporter of crude oil. Prior to 1976 the net effects were relatively small as direct investment in the North Sea was, to a large extent, offset by imports of equipment and services. After 1976, the build-up in production generated substantial net benefits. These have arisen both in the form of direct exports and more particularly in import substitution: domestic production has replaced energy sources which would otherwise have to be imported. Through 1985, the cumulative balance-of-payments saving totalled approximately £115bn, more than one-third of the GDP in that year.[1] It should be emphasized that these calculations only estimate the proximate effects of the North Sea; they are not an estimate of the overall effects, nor indeed can they be used to predict what would have happened in the absence of North Sea oil. Developments in the North Sea also influenced the exchange rate and many other variables in the economy, which in turn affected production and consumption in all sectors. Thus far, all we can say is that the North Sea provided an unexpected windfall which substantially increased the wealth of the United Kingdom. A deeper analysis is required to ascertain more fully the ramifications which this increased wealth has implied for the economy and this is deferred to section 2.

Forecasts of the future development of the North Sea are also subject to considerable uncertainty. The two major elements in the calculations concern the size of recoverable reserves and the sterling price of crude oil. Recoverable reserves depend on the size of existing oil and gas reserves as well as on new discoveries and the state of technology. As technology

---

[1] For further details, see 'North Sea Oil and Gas: Costs and Benefits', *BEQB*, March 1982; and 'North Sea Oil and Gas', *BEQB*, December 1986.

evolves over time, it typically makes possible the recovery of an increasing proportion of the reserves which are known to exist, as well as making exploration possible in increasingly inhospitable sectors. Above all, however, the size of recoverable reserves depends on the price of oil, as this determines which segments can be profitably recovered and which not. As oil reserves constitute an asset, in long-run equilibrium they should earn the same rate of return (suitably adjusted for differences in risk) as other assets. Since oil reserves do not pay interest, the return from a fixed quantity of oil reserves which are held in the ground is simply the capital gain on such holdings, i.e. the proportionate change in the price of oil. In the long run, therefore, the real price of oil (its price relative to the general price level) should increase at a rate equal to the market rate of interest.[1] In the short run, this relationship is extremely tenuous as it is affected by the immediate balance of world supply and demand and by the structure of the world oil market. Fluctuations in income over the business cycle, the prices of substitutes for oil, and energy conservation measures are major influences on demand. Supply is affected by the continued advances in technology, which invariably increases recoverable reserves, as well as by events such as the Gulf War which may lead to temporary cuts or spurts in world output.

As far as market structure is concerned, OPEC was able to act as a cartel and enforce output restrictions and a substantial rise in oil prices in 1973 and 1979–80. However, the balance of world supply and demand moved to such an extent that in 1985–6 there was a collapse in the world oil price from which it scarcely recovered until the run-up to the Gulf War in late 1990. In the post-Gulf War period, prices have moved in a range around $20 per barrel.[2] In comparison, average North Sea oil production costs in 1985 were estimated to be about $10 per barrel and these will rise over time as more marginal fields are brought into operation. There seems little likelihood that OPEC will re-emerge as a major price-setting force in the world oil market in the immediate future. OPEC oil is a much smaller share of world energy than in the seventies and many OPEC economies face major costs in the wake of the Gulf War which will impel them to increase rather than restrict output.

The sterling price of oil is also influenced by the sterling exchange rate, particularly against the dollar, which is the currency in which world oil prices are currently set. The more sterling is appreciated against the dollar, the smaller will be net oil export revenues and the government's tax

[1]   One of the seminal papers which considers the issues involved in oil pricing is W. D. Nordhaus, 'The Allocation of Energy Resources', *Brookings Papers on Economic Activity*, 1973:3, pp. 529–70.
[2]   Prices quoted are spot market prices of Brent crude, the main price for North Sea oil. For details on world oil demand and supply prospects, see P. R. Odell, 'The Prospects for Oil Prices and the Energy Market', *LBR*, No. 165, July 1987.

revenues from the North Sea. Other aspects of government policy will also be important – in particular, the production and depletion policy adopted, and the levels of royalty and petroleum revenue tax charged, which will determine the proportion of profits left to oil producing firms.

Bearing in mind these uncertainties, it is nevertheless interesting to cite one set of calculations of future North Sea oil and gas benefits.[1] Adopting the assumption of a constant average price in real terms of US$20 per barrel, it transpires that oil production would peak in the mid-1990s and gradually decline to zero around the year 2025. Using the same assumption, the present value of the economic rents to be earned from North Sea production beginning in 1986, amounts to about twice the rents actually earned through end-1985. In short, nearly two-thirds of the total benefits of North Sea oil production have still to materialize, and should do so during the course of the next 35 years. It seems fair to assume, therefore, that the North Sea will continue to play an important role in the UK economy for some time to come.

1.6   The UK and the European Community (EC)

The UK became a full member of the EC along with Denmark and Ireland in January 1973. The Labour government of 1974 declared its intention to renegotiate the original terms of entry,[2] completed the renegotiations in March 1975[3] and then settled the question in favour of membership with a referendum in July 1975. Since then, the EC has been enlarged to twelve countries with the entry of Greece (in January 1981) and Portugal and Spain (in January 1986). EC membership has had increasingly profound implications for economic and social policies in the UK. In this chapter we concentrate chiefly on balance-of-payments and exchange-rate issues; other issues are treated in Chapters 2 and 4 of this volume.

Calculation of the economic costs and benefits to the UK of EC membership can be made under two headings. First are the 'static' gains and losses, which themselves arise from two sources: the formation of a customs union between the UK and other EC members with a common external tariff; and the inter-country transfers which result from aspects of the CAP and the Community budget. The second heading includes 'dynamic' gains and losses which may result from selling in a larger market: allowing, for example, the exploitation of economies of scale in production and consequent improvement in competitiveness. If the combined static and dynamic effects led to a

---

[1] For further details of these calculations see 'North Sea Oil and Gas', *BEQB*, December 1986.
[2] *Renegotiation of the Terms of Entry into the European Economic Community*, Cmnd. 5593 (April 1974).
[3] *Membership of The European Community: Report on Renegotiations*, Cmnd. 6003 (March 1975).

deterioration in the balance of payments, the UK would have to restore external balance, typically by a combination of a depreciation in the exchange rate and cuts in public spending or tax increases. These policies would impose a measurable real resource cost on the UK. The reverse would be true if entry were to produce an improvement in the balance of payments.

Calculations made at the time of pre-entry negotiations were virtually unanimous in finding that entry would impose a static balance-of-payments cost, probably of around one per cent of GDP in the long run.[1] Acceptable estimates of dynamic gains or losses have not so far been made. In fact, the UK's relative economic position in the EC has not changed markedly since entry. Since 1972, per capita GDP in the UK has fluctuated between about 93% and 104% of the EC average. This does not, however, answer the question: Would this performance have been better or worse if the UK had not been an EC member? In practice, of course, the benefits of UK membership of the EC are also concerned with the political gains to the UK of being a member of a larger grouping of nations which gives individual countries a greater say in world affairs through EC membership than they would have individually. However, such political gains have also proved elusive until recently as the EC was mired for almost a decade in a series of internal debates which centred, not surprisingly, on issues concerning income redistribution between member countries.

More recently, there have been many signs that the EC has found new life. Some progress has been on the thorny agricultural and budgetary disputes; the EMS has proved more durable and, arguably, more effective than its critics had thought possible; and planning for the SEM in 1992 has provided fresh impetus to Community efforts to reduce barriers to the free movement of goods, services and factors of production within the EC. These topics are discussed in detail in sections 2 and 3. More importantly perhaps, the EC has assumed a greater importance on a wider political stage. The spectacular collapse of the communist regimes in Eastern Europe culminating in the dissolution of the Soviet Union in December 1991 has focused attention on the EC. The former East Germany became a *de facto* member of the Community when Germany was reunified in October 1990, and several non-EC countries from both the European Free Trade Area (EFTA) and the former eastern bloc have already applied or have announced their intention to apply for EC membership. The new impetus in the EC is reflected in the December 1991 Treaty of Maastricht which sets out concrete steps and a conditional timetable for achieving economic, monetary, and ultimately political union. The Treaty contains clauses giving 'opt-out' rights to individual countries (in practice, the UK) and relating in particular to monetary union and social policy. However, the Treaty is broadly viewed as an important step on the road to European unification.

---

[1]   The 1970 White Paper, *Britain and the European Communities: An Economic Assessment*, Cmnd. 4289 (February 1970) suggested a balance of payments cost ranging between £100m and £1.1bn per annum.

2   ECONOMIC POLICY, THE EXCHANGE RATE, AND THE BALANCE OF PAYMENTS

2.1   Introduction

The coverage of this section is limited to a discussion of government policies where the prime concern is to influence the balance of payments and the exchange rate. In principle, *all* economic policy affects the balance of payments, since any non-trivial intervention in the economy is likely to produce at least minor alterations in the balance of forces affecting trade and payments flows and the exchange rate. Thus, policies to control inflation or to stimulate growth are likely to have substantial impacts on trade and capital flows, but these problems are discussed elsewhere in this book and are of interest for reasons other than those concerned with the balance of payments. For present purposes, such policies are not regarded as balance-of-payments policies. On the other hand, policies which are directed explicitly at trade and capital flows may have effects on other sectors of the economy. However, in this section we will concentrate primarily on the exchange and payments implications of such policies.

2.2   The Exchange Market Framework

Modern industrial economies have evolved by means of a progressive specialization of labour and capital, and one important pre-condition for this is the adoption of a single internal currency, to act as an intermediary in all economic transactions. At the international level, specialization has so far proceeded without this advantage. Since nations maintain separate currencies for internal use, it follows that, in general, international transactions must proceed with the simultaneous exchange of national currencies. This exchange of currencies takes place in the foreign-exchange market and it is there that the relative prices of different national currencies – exchange rates – are established. At the outset, therefore, an important policy issue which faces the government of any country is that of the degree of restraint which it wishes to place on the exchange of its own currency with the currencies of other nations. Not only may the chosen restraints limit the type and geographical direction of transactions which domestic residents may make with foreigners, but they will also have an important bearing upon the conduct of policy to achieve internal objectives such as full employment and price stability.

   Until 1979, successive UK governments had exercised their options in two ways: by placing direct controls on the currencies against which sterling may be exchanged for the purpose of specified transactions (exchange controls), and by adopting particular exchange-rate regimes within which to conduct economic policy. However, exchange controls were abolished in October

1979, and there seems little prospect that such controls will be reintroduced in the UK, except possibly within some EC context.[1]

Exchange-Rate Regimes: The period since 1945 can be divided into three phases in which the UK operated economic policy within successive and distinct exchange-rate regimes. In the first phase, between 1945 and June 1972, policy was operated in accordance with the rules of the par-value system.[2] This required the adoption of a fixed spot-market exchange rate for sterling ('the par-value')[3] which was maintained by the authorities buying or selling sterling whenever the exchange rate threatened to move outside a permitted band of fluctuation of 1% either side the par-value. A country with a 'fundamental disequilibrium' in its balance of payments, and after consultation with the IMF, was expected to change its par-value, as did the UK government in 1949 and 1967. In the market for forward exchange, the par-value system imposed no formal restrictions. There are, in fact, good reasons to believe that spot and forward exchange rates will necessarily be fairly closely related. The *Covered* Interest Parity Theorem states that, provided arbitrage funds are in perfectly elastic supply, the percentage difference between the spot and a forward exchange rate in any pair of currencies will equal the interest differential on assets of the corresponding maturity denominated in those currencies.[4] With arbitrage funds not in infinitely elastic supply, the forward rate will deviate from its covered interest parity value. Evidence for the period since 1960 is consistent with the view that forward exchange rates up to three months have mostly approximated their interest parity values quite closely.[5] The implication of covered interest parity is that, if spot exchange rates are fixed, similar restrictions on forward exchange rates will either be unnecessary or, in circumstances in which different countries' interest rates diverge very sharply, will probably be unenforceable.

The second phase in exchange-rate policy began in June 1972 when the UK abandoned its commitment to maintain a fixed (though adjustable) exchange rate, and instead allowed sterling to take whatever values the balance of demand and supply for foreign exchange might dictate. By the middle of 1973, sterling had been joined in floating by all other major

---

[1]   An account of UK exchange control regulations can be found in the 10th and earlier editions of this volume. See also the IMF *Annual Reports on Exchange Restrictions*.

[2]   A full discussion of the rules of the par-value system may be found in the 10th and earlier editions of this volume.

[3]   A distinction must be made between the spot-market and the forward-market exchange rates for a currency. The *spot exchange rate* is the price of foreign currency for immediate delivery, that is, at the time the rate for the transaction is agreed (or, strictly, within two working days). A *forward exchange rate* is the price for foreign currency for delivery at a specified date in the future. The most widely traded forward contract in practice is that for delivery in three months.

[4]   For a more detailed discussion see, for example, R. MacDonald, *Floating Exchange Rates: Theories and Evidence* (Unwin Hyman, 1988).

[5]   See the survey in D. L. Thornton, 'Tests of Covered Interest Rate Parity', *FRBSLR*, Vol. 71, No. 4, July/August 1989, pp. 55–67.

currencies. For the advanced industrial nations as a whole, the par-value system was effectively abandoned. A policy of allowing sterling to float does not mean that the exchange market ceases to be an object of concern. The government still has to decide to what extent sterling will float freely without official intervention in the exchange market by the authorities' buying or selling foreign currency. Moreover, even in the absence of official intervention, the authorities have considerable scope for influencing the exchange rate by less direct means, particularly involving capital flows. The main determinants of capital flows are the relative rates of return on domestic and foreign assets, allowing for the effects of risk and taxation. These rates of return are affected by variations in domestic and foreign interest rates, and also by anticipated exchange-rate changes which would result in capital gains or losses for holders of foreign currency assets. If a sterling depreciation is anticipated, for example, this will provide an incentive for wealth-holders to switch any sterling-denominated assets they hold into foreign-currency-denominated assets in order to avoid the expected capital loss on holdings of sterling assets. As it is relatively difficult to obtain forward cover for periods of much over 6 months, judgements about the expected future course of the exchange rate are a key ingredient in most foreign investment decisions.[1] Variations in the relative rates of return on domestic and foreign currency assets will affect capital flows and hence the demand and supply of sterling and, therefore, under a floating rate regime, will affect the spot exchange rate of sterling. It follows that any policy measure which affects domestic interest rates or the market's expectations of the future spot exchange rate will, given foreign interest rates, influence the current spot exchange rate and the forward rate.

Thus, the whole range of monetary policy actions which affect interest rates will also, to some extent, influence the exchange rate, and can be used explicitly for this purpose. It should, however, be emphasized that the effects of monetary policy on the exchange rate depend, *inter alia*, on the interest elasticity of arbitrage and speculative funds and on the elasticity of expectations of the future exchange rate with respect to movements in current interest rates and exchange rates. Thus, while the qualitative effect of monetary policy on the exchange rate may be relatively straightforward to work out, its exact quantitative effect is, in general, subject to a very high degree of uncertainty.

The third phase in exchange-rate policy began in October 1990 when sterling joined the Exchange Rate Mechanism (ERM) of the EMS. The ERM is the central feature of the EMS which came into existence in March 1979. The ERM is essentially a zone of stable but not fixed exchange rates

---

[1] Reference may be made here to *uncovered* interest parity, which is said to hold if the interest differential on assets of a given maturity denominated in different currencies is equal to the *expected* percentage change in the spot exchange rate between now and the maturity date of the asset. Uncovered interest parity holds when speculative funds are in infinitely elastic supply, but available evidence suggests that, in general, this is not the case.

within the EC, underpinned by a complex set of mechanisms intended to support and reinforce exchange-rate stability. While entry into the ERM does not necessarily mark a return to a fixed exchange rate for the UK, it does considerably reduce the scope for exchange-rate flexibility. In a floating-rate system, even though the exchange rate may be managed, the authorities always have the discretion to cease intervention and let the exchange rate adjust passively to other policy changes. The ERM resembles the par-value system in that the authorities are obliged to intervene to prevent sterling moving outside a permitted band of fluctuation about a central rate. However, ERM arrangements are intended to spread the burden of adjustment more widely than did the par-value system under which, in practice, the burden invariably fell on the countries with the weaker currencies. In addition, a central goal of the ERM is to promote policy 'convergence' within the EC, leading ultimately to monetary integration involving the replacement of national currencies in the EC by a single European currency. Insofar as policy convergence is achieved, it will automatically reduce at least some of the burden of adjustment for all countries.

At the present time, however, UK domestic financial policy is inevitably subject to the constraints imposed by the ERM and by sterling's central rate within the system. Thus, although sterling is still floating against other currencies (including those in the ERM), in its policy implications the current phase more nearly resembles a fixed-exchange-rate regime than a floating rate regime. The detailed arrangements of the ERM are complex and are discussed next. The general background to the ERM and its wider policy implications are discussed later in this section.[1]

The Exchange Rate Mechanism of the European Monetary System: The ERM consists of an exchange-rate structure and an intervention mechanism based on the European Currency Unit (ECU). The EMS also includes a system of credits for financing payments' imbalances between members called the European Monetary Cooperation Fund (EMCF). At the inception of the EMS, the UK along with other EC countries agreed to contribute to the ECU credit arrangements, but unlike the other countries, it declined to join the ERM, although special transitional arrangements were agreed for the Italian lira. The Spanish peseta joined the ERM in June 1989, the pound sterling in October 1990 and the Portuguese escudo in April 1991, then leaving the Greek drachma as the only EC currency outside the ERM.

The exchange-rate structure of the ERM consists of a 'currency grid'

---

[1]   Full details of the EMS mechanism are given in Commission of the European Communities, *European Economy*, July, 1979. A useful exposition is given in: 'The Exchange Rate Mechanism of the European Monetary System', *BEQB*, November 1990. The arguments for monetary integration are set out by the then President of the European Commission, R.Jenkins, in 'European Monetary Union', *LBR*, No. 127, January 1978.

TABLE 3.4

EMS Exchange Rates

	ECU central rates	Composition of the ECU	
	units of national current per ECU (effective 8 October 1990)	currency amounts (effective September 1989)	% currency weights (based on 12 October 1990 exchange rates)
Belgian/Luxembourg franc	42.4032	3.431	8.1
Danish krone	7.84195	0.1976	2.5
Deutschmark	2.05586	0.6242	30.2
French franc	6.89509	1.332	19.3
Irish punt	0.767417	0.008552	1.1
Italian lira	1538.24	151.8	9.8
Netherlands guilder	2.31643	0.2198	9.4
Spanish peseta	133.631	6.885	5.3
UK pound	0.696904	0.08784	12.8
Greek drachma	205.311	1.44	0.7
Portuguese escudo	178.735	1.04741	0.8

Source: BEQB.

within which each member's currency is assigned a central rate against other EC currencies, together with a permitted band of fluctuation of 2.25% either side of this central rate. The peseta, escudo and sterling each have a transitional arrangement allowing them a permitted band of 6% either side of their central rate. The central rates are not irrevocably fixed, but may be adjusted, or 'realigned' after consultation among EMS members, although one of the aims of the EMS is to prevent major exchange-rate adjustments which may turn out to have been 'unnecessary'.

To this end, central banks are obliged to keep their currencies within the margins of fluctuation but, in practice, this can create an asymmetric burden of obligation. The weak-currency country loses reserves and is always under pressure to adjust its internal policies to a greater extent than is the strong-currency country. To try and eliminate this asymmetry, the ERM includes an ingenious intervention mechanism an important part of which is the ECU, a basket of EC currencies which acts as numeraire for the ERM. The ECU is a composite currency containing specific amounts of the currencies of all member states (including those which are not members of the ERM) which to begin with were reviewed every five years. The composition of the ECU immediately following the last review in September 1989 is given in Table 3.4, together with the ECU central rates on 8 October 1990 when sterling joined the ERM. For a given currency composition, actual currency weights within the ECU will still change because of exchange-rate movements, particularly after realignments within the EMS, and Table 3.4 also gives the percentage currency weights immediately after the entry of sterling into the ERM.

The intervention mechanism is based on the currency grid of bilateral exchange rates among ERM currencies. The bilateral rates are those implied by the central rates of the currencies against the ECU. When a currency reaches 2.25% above or below any one of its bilateral central rates (6% for the peseta, escudo and sterling), the central banks of the strongest and the weakest currencies are obliged to intervene and can call on financing from the EMCF for this purpose. However, since any of the bilateral exchange rates can trigger an intervention, the degree of depreciation of a currency is limited to 2.25% against the *strongest* currency in the ERM, and the degree of appreciation is limited to 2.25% against the weakest currency. Thus, the effective range of fluctuation for any individual currency is less than the 2.25% bands would suggest, and will change continuously as the positions of individual currencies in the band change.

A further means of identifying currencies whose exchange rates are diverging from the others utilizes the 'Maximum Divergence Spread' (MDS), which measures the maximum percentage by which a currency's market rate against the ECU can change from its ECU central rate before that currency reaches its bilateral limit against any other ERM currency. The MDS is given by $+/- 2.25 (1 - w_i)\%$, where w_i is the weight of the currency in the value of the ECU basket. The divergence indicator is provided by the 'divergence threshold' whereby a currency may not deviate from its central ECU rate by more than three-quarters of its MDS.[1] The point of this arrangement is that, in general, a currency should reach its divergence threshold before it reaches any of the bilateral intervention limits defined by the currency grid, and, once this occurs, there is a presumption that consultation will be initiated with *all* Community members to decide upon intervention policy, possible changes in central rates *and* any necessary internal policy measures. These procedures were strengthened in September 1987 when it was agreed that non-mandatory intervention within the 2.25% limits could also be financed by drawings on the EMCF subject to the quota restrictions on individual countries' drawings from the fund. Although the onus is on the country whose currency is divergent to alter its policies, the divergent currency could be either appreciating or depreciating. Thus it was hoped that the burden of adjustment would be more equally shared within the Community, avoiding continued pressure exclusively on a weak-currency country.

An additional function of the ECU, besides acting as numeraire in the EMS, is as an instrument of settlement between EC central banks and

---

[1] When a currency diverges from its central rate it also pulls the values of the ECU with it to some extent. The adjustment $(1 - w_i)$ in the calculation of the MDS reflects this fact and ensures that the divergence range reflects deviations of a currency from other individual currencies in the ECU basket. An adjustment is also made for the wider margins applicable to Portugal, Spain and the UK and for the fact that the drachma, while a component of the ECU, is not a participant in the ERM. Any divergence of these currencies in excess of 2.25% is excluded when the value of the ECU is calculated for the purposes of the divergence indicator. The notional weight of sterling in the ECU at 12 October 1990 was 12.8%, giving a divergence range of $+/- 5.23\%$ for sterling against the ECU. The divergence threshold for sterling at that time would be 75% of this, or $=/- 3.92\%$.

ultimately, perhaps, as a single European currency. EC members currently deposit 20% of their gold and gross dollar reserves with the EMCF on a three-month renegotiable basis, and in return have access to a variety of credit facilities to finance payments imbalances within the Community and to support the currency grid.[1]

The Evolution of the Exchange Rate 1979–91: With sterling only one of many currencies engaged in a simultaneous float, there is no simple index of movements in the international value of sterling. Sterling may appreciate in terms of some currencies while, at the same time, it depreciates in terms of others. Current practice is to rely upon the 'effective exchange rate' index, which is a weighted average of the bilateral exchange rates between sterling and 16 other currencies, the weights being given by the relative importance of the countries concerned in the UK's trade in manufactured goods.[2] The evolution of the effective exchange rate (EER) since 1979 is shown in Figure 3.1.

The broad trends in the movement of the EER since 1979 can be divided conveniently into three phases. The first, to January 1981, was one of fairly rapid appreciation from a value of 103.9 in January 1979 (with 1985 = 100) to 133.4 in January 1981. From this time on, the EER moved into a second phase in which it was broadly depreciating, reaching a low of 86.4 in November 1986. In the final phase, from December 1986 to December 1991, the EER has moved in a fairly narrow band between 86.9 and 99.4. Taking the average of these two values as a central reference rate, we find that the EER has fluctuated within a range of about 6.7% either side of this central reference rate. It is evident from Figure 3.1 that this represents greater stability for the EER in comparison with the period 1979–86 (and indeed in comparison with the pre-1979 period).

It should be emphasized that sterling's entry into the ERM does not guarantee stability of the EER. First, as we have seen, sterling can fluctuate within limits against other ERM currencies. Second, the ERM currencies may themselves fluctuate against non-ERM currencies, notably the dollar and the Japanese Yen. Over the period 1981–5 (prior to sterling's entry into the ERM), the evolution in the EER was the product of divergent movements in sterling *vis-à-vis* the US dollar on the one hand, and the Japanese and European currencies on the other. The predominant feature of international currency markets over that period was the 64% appreciation of the US dollar between January 1981 and March 1985, followed by a yet more precipitate (72%) depreciation by end-December 1987. The fall and

---

[1] The gold contribution is valued at the average London fixing price during the six months prior to valuation, and the dollar portion is valued at the market rate of the two working days prior to valuation.
[2] For details of the current method of calculating the effective exchange rate, see 'Revisions to the Calculation of Effective Exchange Rates', *BEBQ*, November 1988, pp. 528–9. Reference to earlier methods of calculating the effective rate may also be found in this article.

subsequent partial recovery in the pound over the same period mirrored the movement in the dollar; sterling's movement against other European currencies and the Yen was much less marked and, until 1987, was generally one of steady depreciation. Since 1987 the EER has been more stable, as we have noted, and this stability has continued since sterling's entry into the ERM.

2.3   Economic Policy and the Exchange Rate

The Exchange Rate and the Adjustment Process: Before we consider the likely causes and implications of these movements in sterling, it will prove useful to outline some of the main economic aspects of floating exchange rates. The exchange rate plays an important role in the balance-of-payments adjustment process and an exchange-rate depreciation (appreciation) is generally thought to be a necessary component of any policy measures taken to eliminate a balance-of-payments deficit (surplus). However, the exact mechanisms by which an exchange-rate change influences the balance of payments are by no means universally agreed.

The 'elasticities approach' lays emphasis on the effect of an exchange-rate change in altering the relative prices of domestic and foreign goods and services, and thus altering the demands and supplies of these goods and services, thereby changing the current account balance. Thus, a depreciation raises the domestic price of imported goods, depressing the

Figure 3.1   Sterling's Effective Exchange Rate, 1979–91

demand for imports, and lowers the foreign price or increases the domestic profitability of export goods, thus tending to stimulate the export effort, and by these means improving the current account.[1]

The 'absorption approach' also focuses on the current account but lays stress on the fact, noted in section 1.3, that a current account deficit (surplus) is associated with an excess (deficiency) of domestic expenditure in relation to income. On this view, a depreciation improves the current account by stimulating incomes through the expansion in exports. Expenditures will typically rise by less than incomes as a part of the increase is saved, and so the current account improves. A depreciation may also depress expenditures by increasing domestic prices which may reduce demand directly, as well as indirectly through a rise in the rate of interest, if the quantity of money is being tightly controlled.

In the 'dependent economy' (or 'Australian') model, emphasis is placed on the role of traded and non-traded goods. The former are freely traded on world markets at competitive prices. The latter never enter international trade, either because, as for certain services, they are location-specific, or because international transport costs are such that the good can never be competitive in international markets. The prices of the non-traded goods are determined in each country by its own domestic supply and demand. Over time, goods and services may switch from being traded to non-traded or vice-versa, depending on the evolution of international transport costs. In this approach, a current account deficit (surplus) is associated with domestic excess demand (supply) for traded goods, given the relative prices of traded and non-traded goods and the level of overall domestic monetary demand in the economy. A devaluation (revaluation) increases (reduces) the domestic currency price of traded goods, and hence also increases (reduces) the price of traded goods relative to non-traded goods. This stimulates (depresses) production of traded goods for export and switches demand from traded goods previously imported into non-traded goods (or vice-versa in the event of a revaluation). This produces an improvement (deterioration) in the current account. However, to the extent that demand for non-traded goods has increased and supply fallen, in order to prevent a rise in prices of non-traded goods, typically some deflation of domestic monetary demand is required to sustain the current account improvement. To this extent, the dependent economy model synthesizes the elasticity and absorption approaches by providing a role both for changes in relative prices and for changes in domestic monetary demand.

Finally, the 'monetary approach' concentrates on the BOF, noting that a deficit implies that there is a net outflow of reserves and can thus be

---

[1] In the special case in which trade is initially balanced and supply elasticities of traded goods are infinite, then a depreciation improves the trade balance provided that the sum of foreign and domestic elasticities of demand for imported goods exceeds unity. For a discussion of the evidence on import and export elasticities, see J. Williamson, 'Is There an External Constraint?', *NIER*, August 1984, pp. 73–7.

interpreted as corresponding to an excess supply of money in the domestic economy relative to demand, with the excess being 'worked-off' through the balance-of-payments deficit. In this approach, a depreciation works primarily through the money market by increasing the price level and thus reducing the real supply of money in the economy, with the central bank being required to maintain tight control over the nominal money supply. A reduction in the supply of money in its turn has a familiar deflationary impact on the economy as a whole.

It should be evident that these different approaches are interlinked.[1] Different aspects of the adjustment process are important at different times but, in practice, exchange-rate changes work, at least to some extent, through all the channels listed above. However, different circumstances are likely to call for different sets of supporting policies to accompany an exchange-rate change. For example, at full employment, a depreciation will only increase domestic money incomes rather than real incomes, and emphasis has to be placed on deflating the economy while also switching domestic expenditures away from import goods.

Arguments for Floating Exchange Rates: In its simplest form, the case for floating exchange rates rests upon the efficiency and automatic nature of the free-market mechanism in reallocating resources in response to changing circumstances. In a dynamic world in which comparative advantages change over time and national inflation rates differ, changes in exchange rates are necessary if widespread misallocation of productive resources is to be avoided. The advantage of floating rates, it is argued, is that the amount and timing of the necessary changes can occur progressively at a pace dictated by the costs and profitability of resource allocation, and not, as in a fixed rate system, by periodic discrete jumps, often dictated by speculative pressures and political expediency.

Floating exchange rates also have important implications for macroeconomic policy. Under a floating-rate regime, the government is under less pressure to decide precisely what constitutes an equilibrium exchange rate, as this will be decided automatically within the foreign-exchange market. This does not, however, imply that the conduct of domestic economic policy, particularly demand management, can proceed independently of developments in the foreign-exchange market. Balance-of-payments problems do not disappear with the adoption of a floating exchange rate; they simply appear in different forms. Developments that would lead to a loss of reserves with a fixed exchange rate, lead to a depreciation in the foreign-exchange value of the currency if the exchange rate is allowed to

---

[1] For an entertaining account of these different approaches and their deficiencies, see A.P.Thirlwall, 'What is Wrong with Balance of Payments Adjustment Theory?', *RBSR*, March 1988, No. 157. For an empirical study of the adjustment process in the UK, see D.A. Currie and S. Hall, 'The Exchange Rate and the Balance of Payments', *NIER*, February 1986, pp. 74–82.

float. In the first case, a continuing loss of reserves will result in a policy-induced contraction in domestic income; while with a floating rate, the loss in real domestic purchasing powers occurs as the prices of tradeable goods rise and the real value of the money stock declines with the currency depreciation.

The main advantage of a floating exchange rate was traditionally thought to be that it allowed greater independence in domestic macroeconomic policy-making. As there is some value of the exchange rate which will give exactly a zero BOF at any level of employment, the objective of full employment may be more consistently pursued. Likewise, a floating rate tends to isolate the level of demand for domestic goods from changes in foreign incomes and preferences. An increase in foreign demand which, under a fixed rate, would generate a multiple expansion in UK output and employment, now generates an appreciation of the sterling exchange rate until the final increase in the value of UK exports is exactly matched by an appreciation-induced increase in the value of UK imports. The total demand for UK goods, and therefore UK output, will remain unchanged.

However, these arguments overlook the fact that, in a relatively free international capital market, the exchange rate affects not just the prices of internationally traded products but also the prices of internationally traded assets. The exchange rate which is determined in a free market depends on the demand and supply of foreign currency emanating from both trade in products and in assets. There is no reason to expect any immediate relationship between day-to-day transactions in foreign currency generated by product markets and those generated by asset markets, and the equilibrium exchange rate implied by product market considerations may be very different from that implied by asset market considerations.

It is now generally recognized that, in the short run, the exchange rate of a currency which is freely floating is determined mainly by asset market considerations, particularly by relative international interest rates and expectations of future economic trends. Product market factors may reassert themselves in the longer term, but it is unclear just what 'longer term' means in calendar time. For example, the four-year appreciation of the US dollar to March 1985 must have been caused to a large extent by a worldwide portfolio shift in favour of US dollars. The current account of the US balance of payments worsened continuously from a surplus of $6.9bn in 1981 to a deficit of $107.1bn in 1984 but this appeared to have little effect in checking the simultaneous rise of the dollar.

Floating Exchange Rates, Asset Markets and 'Overshooting': It was recognized for many years that floating rates might be volatile because of speculation in financial markets. If the markets for foreign exchange are to be cleared continuously without the intervention of the monetary authorities and without undue fluctuations in the exchange rate, it is essential that speculators take over the role of the authorities and operate in a stabilizing manner, selling sterling when the rate is temporarily 'too high' and buying sterling when the rate is temporarily 'too low'. Proponents of floating rates argued that speculative activity will be stabilizing because destabilizing speculation (buying when the rate is 'high' and selling when it is 'low') is unprofitable.[1] However, this presumes that speculators can predict the 'true' equilibrium value of the exchange rate. Opponents fear that the exchange market will be dominated by too much uncertainty for speculators to recognize the equilibrium rate. Waves of optimism and pessimism will follow the frequent revision of expectations and will generate substantial movements in exchange rates, which are unrelated to 'fundamental' economic considerations. The difficulty with the above arguments is that we have little factual evidence to decide either way. Certainly the post-1972 period with floating rates has witnessed some sudden, sharp movements in exchange rates. There is evidence, too, that exchange rates respond to the publication of new economic statistics, no matter how provisional the data. However, it is unclear whether movements of this kind can be regarded as excessive.

It must not be overlooked that destabilizing speculation can disrupt any exchange-rate framework and clearly did so with the par-value system. One of the major drawbacks of the par-value system was that it gave a one-way option to currency speculators. A currency under pressure would be pushed to one edge of the permitted band of fluctuation. This immediately signalled the possibility of a change in par-value, which could be in one direction only. This encouraged a large and cumulative movement of funds across the exchanges, which tended to precipitate the very par-value adjustment which speculators had predicted. An important advantage of floating exchange rates is that the problem of recurrent one-way speculative options at the expense of the authorities is eliminated.

It has also been argued that floating rates increase the uncertainty faced by international traders and investors to the detriment of the international division of labour. It is the volatility of exchange rates which may deter trade, and volatility will not be a serious problem insofar as speculation is able to stabilize floating exchange rates.[2] Moreover, many exchange risks involving trade in goods and services can be covered with simultaneous deals in spot and forward markets. For sterling transactions involving the major currencies, the forward exchange market currently provides active dealings for contracts up to one year in duration. Longer-term trade contracts and international investment projects will face problems, but it is unlikely that the exchange risks are more severe than the other risks which such projects routinely incur. Moreover, the markets in futures, options and other

---

[1]   See M. Friedman, 'The Case for Flexible Exchange Rates', in *Essays in Positive Economics* (University of Chicago Press, 1953).
[2]   For a review of the impact of exchange-rate volatility on international trade, see 'The Variability of Exchange Rates: Measurement and Effects', *BEQB*, September 1984, pp. 346–9. The managers of industrial firms frequently cite exchange-rate volatility as a deterrent to trade. See House of Lords, *Report from the Select Committee on Overseas Trade* (HMSO, 30 July 1985).

'derivative' instruments considerably widen the range of possibilities for traders to hedge their exchange risks.[1]

A more subtle argument which has gained credibility in the light of experience is that exchange rates 'overshoot': if a disturbance requires an appreciation of the pound, it will tend to over-appreciate in the short run and subsequently depreciate to its equilibrium value. This is explained by the flexibility of the exchange rate relative to other prices in the economy, particularly money wage rates. If a general adjustment in wages and prices is required, this will take time; in the meanwhile, asset prices, particularly the exchange rate, must 'over-adjust' to compensate for the sluggishness of wages and product prices.

In this connection, it is important to distinguish between the concept of *volatility* and that of *misalignment*. The exchange rate may be highly volatile on a day-to-day basis but nevertheless stay relatively close to its equilibrium value. However, when the exchange rate overshoots its equilibrium value for long periods, it can be said to be misaligned, and such misalignment may cause a systematic misallocation of resources in the economy. In this situation, a freely floating exchange rate may be detrimental rather than advantageous. As before, evidence is hard to find because of the difficulty of identifying the equilibrium exchange rate. However, as described below in section 2.4, the appreciation of sterling in 1979–81 appeared in part to correspond to an overshooting of the exchange rate.

Overall, the balance of argument and evidence is that some flexibility in exchange rates is desirable as a means of promoting efficient resource allocation and reducing the vulnerability of the economy to external disturbances. However, there is still considerable room for debate about the optimum balance between flexibility and management by the authorities. Thus, if undue volatility and overshooting of the exchange rate prove serious, the authorities can engage in 'official' speculation or exchange-market intervention. This implies that, even with a floating exchange rate, the authorities must maintain a stock of exchange reserves. Widespread adoption of exchange-management practices also requires the institution of international co-ordination and surveillance of exchange-rate practices, and these are precisely the functions of the IMF under its revised Articles (see section 5 below).

2.4   The Exchange Rate and the Balance of Payments 1979–91

In section 1.4 we outlined the changes in the UK's external position over the period since 1979, showing that the current account moved into substantial surplus between 1980 and 1985, followed by a very sharp swing back into deficit from 1986 onwards. The purpose of this section is to outline some of

[1]   G.T.Gemmill, 'Financial Futures in London: Rational Market or New Casino?', *NWBQR*, February 1981.

the major factors leading to the changes in the current account and the exchange rate during the period, and their relation to domestic and international events. To conduct the analysis it is helpful to distinguish between those factors which are related to changes in national price levels, and those which are related to the forces of production, consumer preferences, productivity and thrift. It is to the former that we turn first. In interpreting the events of the period, it must also be emphasized that the exchange rate for sterling was not allowed to float freely, but was managed quite actively, and this policy produced effects which were a mixture of those occurring under the extremes of fixed and freely floating rates.

The Real Exchange Rate: A convenient place to begin is the theory which relates the values taken by a currency's exchange rate to its purchasing power parity (PPP). Broadly speaking, this suggests that the equilibrium exchange rate between the currencies of two countries is proportional to the ratio of the price levels in the respective countries. Providing this factor of proportionality remains constant, the proportionate rate of change of the exchange rate will be approximately equal to the difference between the inflation rates in the two countries.[1] With the exchange rate in equilibrium, the current account would be in balance. To study movements in the exchange rate relative to its purchasing power value, it is helpful to calculate an index of the real exchange rate (REX).

Figure 3.2 shows the monthly movements from 1979 to 1991 in the sterling REX, measured as the ratio of the effective exchange rate (EER) of sterling (in the computation of which the OECD countries have a weight of 100%), to the consumer price index (CPI) in the combined OECD countries relative to that in the UK. In symbols:

$$REX = \frac{EER}{OECD\ CPI/UK\ CPI}$$

The larger the value of this index, the more appreciated is the sterling exchange rate relative to its PPP value. Thus, movements in REX correspond to deviations from PPP. However, it should be emphasized that the index only measures *relative* movements. It is normalized to 1985 = 100 for convenience, but we cannot infer that sterling was at its equilibrium purchasing power value in that year.

The main feature of the broad movements in REX since 1979 was its sharp appreciation in 1979–80, followed by an almost equally rapid depreciation. Between January 1979 and January 1981 REX rose by 37.9%, implying an equal loss in the relative price competitiveness of UK goods in international markets over the period. Over the succeeding two years REX declined by

---

[1] Probably the clearest statement of the purchasing power parity theory is still contained in J.M.Keynes, *A Tract on Monetary Reform* (Macmillan, 1923), pp. 70–93. A textbook treatment of exchange-rate theories can be found in R.MacDonald, *op. cit.*

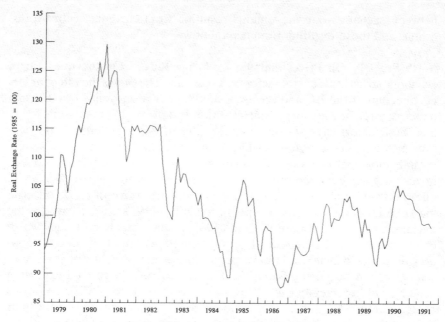

Figure 3.2   Sterling's Real Exchange Rate, 1979–91

28.2% but it was not until January 1985 that the REX had fallen back to its January 1979 level. These movements largely reflected the movements in the EER. UK prices rose relative to foreign prices throughout the period but, as we saw in section 2.2, the EER first appreciated sharply and then depreciated during 1979–86. Since 1986 the EER has been more stable. However, UK prices have continued to rise faster than the OECD average, increasing by 35.6% between November 1986 and October 1991, compared to the OECD average of 28.0% over the same period. As sterling EER did not display any discernible trend over this period, there was a modest appreciation in the REX. In 1991 the REX averaged about the same rate as it did in 1985, implying that sterling's relative purchasing power value was unchanged between the two years.

These calculations indicate that, even though PPP may capture the longer-term trend in the EER, in the short term there have been substantial deviations from PPP.[1] The proximate sources of these deviations can be found by considering three main factors: capital movements, structural factors such as North Sea oil, and monetary policy. As far as capital movements are concerned, a full analysis is contained in section 4; for the present the reader is reminded of the earlier discussion of the possible discrepancies

---

[1] There is fairly considerable evidence that the major currencies (including sterling) have deviated substantially from PPP. Cf. G. Hacche and J. Townsend, 'A Broad Look at Exchange Rate Movements for Eight Currencies, 1972–80', *BEQB*, December 1981.

between exchange-rate movements resulting from current account transactions and those resulting from capital flows.

North Sea Oil, Oil Prices and the Exchange Rate: On the question of
economic structure, several factors are relevant. The first is the effect of UK
membership of the EC and the associated longer-term trends in UK trade
patterns, discussed in more detail in section 3. *A priori*, it is impossible to say
how these factors have affected the PPP value of sterling. Certainly they are
slow-moving, persistent forces which would be unlikely to explain relatively
volatile movement in the exchange rate around PPP. Of much greater
importance has been the progression of the UK towards self-sufficiency in
oil production and the sharp changes in the world price of crude oil. The
market price of oil rose from $14 per barrel in June 1979 to $36 a barrel at the
beginning of 1981. Between 1982 and 1985, the combination of slack world
energy demand and increased oil output created persistent downward pressures on prices which would have been more acute were it not for a substantial cut in output by Saudi Arabia, the world's largest oil-exporting
country and key member of OPEC. In December 1985, OPEC countries
agreed to take steps, including an increase in production, to restore their
share of the world oil market. Spot market prices responded with a precipitate fall from $29 a barrel in early December 1985 to just $10 a barrel early in
April 1986. Oil prices recovered slowly in the late eighties, reaching $20 per
barrel in 1989–90, and rising abruptly to $30 per barrel in the run-up to the
Gulf War in late 1990. In the post-Gulf War period, prices have moved in a
range around $20 per barrel.

The oil price increase of 1979–80 coincided with the coming on stream of
major UK oil fields and the country's move into oil self-sufficiency. These
factors alone must have played a major role in the sharp appreciation of
sterling in 1979–80. The direct oil effect on the current account balance
was reinforced by indirect effects on confidence and capital flows. From
1979 there was, in effect, a favourable reassessment of the long-term prospects for sterling and the associated exchange risks of holding sterling-
denominated assets. A further structural influence on the exchange rate was
the depth of the UK recession. Between 1978 and 1981, UK industrial
output fell by 6.8% and unemployment rose sharply. The depth of the
recession was associated with a decline in domestic demand and therefore an
improvement in the current account. This in turn would have contributed to
the buoyancy of sterling. A final factor was the rise in UK nominal interest
rates, particularly short-term interest rates, relative to those in other OECD
countries. Throughout 1979 and much of 1980, UK short-term rates were
between 2% and 4% higher than comparable rates in the United States. This
would tend to induce a capital inflow into the UK and hence raise the value
of sterling. However, the 1979 abolition of exchange controls should, by
facilitating a capital outflow, have moderated the rise in sterling to some
extent. Overall, there remains some disagreement both about the relative
contribution of each factor to the appreciation of sterling and about

whether, when put together, they provide a complete explanation of this appreciation.[1] It seems certain that increased confidence in sterling as a petro-currency must have contributed to some part of the appreciation, but this is to assert little more than that we cannot fully explain why the pound rose so strongly in 1979–80.

Between 1981 and 1982 the pound depreciated again almost as sharply as it had risen. A part of this depreciation simply reflected the movement of the US dollar referred to in section 2.2, but the fact that the 1979–80 appreciation was so largely and rapidly reversed lends some support to the argument that sterling's overall movements in the 1979–82 period were consistent with the overshooting hypothesis. Sterling once more fell in 1985–6 as the world oil price tumbled but the depreciation was less marked than the movements at the beginning of the decade. After 1986, the authorities made more active efforts to manage the exchange rate than was the case in the early part of the decade. We turn to exchange-rate management below, but first we attempt an overall appraisal of the relationship between North Sea oil and the exchange rate.

These relationships have been hotly debated.[2] The benefit of oil resources can be spread across the whole community only if the oil is sold on the market and the government follows 'appropriate' monetary and fiscal policies to assure distribution of the benefits. Since all UK oil production represents an equivalent gross gain to the balance of visible trade, an increase in production will improve the current account and put upward pressure on the exchange rate. This depresses the production of non-oil tradeables in the UK and, since these are labour-intensive relative to oil, it has the effect of reducing the aggregate demand for labour at current levels of real wages. The non-oil tradeable sector consists largely of manufacturing industry and the adverse effects on manufacturing of a high exchange rate consequent on a resource discovery are known collectively as the 'Dutch disease', following the evolution of the Dutch economy after the discovery of natural gas in the sixties. The question is how far a sustained real appreciation of the currency, with its Dutch disease implications, is a necessary consequence of a resource discovery.

Forsyth and Kay argued that a high real exchange rate is the principal mechanism by which the benefits of North Sea oil can be realized. Since oil has to be traded for consumer goods, the terms-of-trade improvement allows UK consumers to purchase foreign manufactured goods more cheaply than would otherwise be the case. On this view, the real

---

[1]   For an appraisal of the causes of the rise in sterling, see W.H.Buiter and M.H.Miller, 'Changing the Rules: Economic Consequences of the Thatcher Regime', *Brookings Papers*, 1983:2, pp. 305–65.

[2]   The path-breaking contribution was P.J.Forsyth and J.A.Kay, 'The Economic Implications of North Sea Oil Revenues', *Fiscal Studies*, 1980, pp. 1–28. For a rebuttal, see T.Barker, *Energy, Industrialization and Economic Policy* (Academic Press, London, 1981). An official viewpoint is given in 'North Sea Oil and Gas: A Challenge for the Future', *BEQB*, Vol. 22, 1982.

appreciation did not imply a general deterioration in UK competitiveness but rather reflected a change in the UK's comparative international advantage: from a manufacturing exporter to a resource exporter. It does not follow that the authorities should have allowed an unchecked appreciation of sterling. It does, however, follow that the correct way to limit the appreciation was for the UK government to invest the oil proceeds largely overseas, or to encourage the private sector to perform this task by, for example, abolishing exchange controls as occurred in 1979. In effect, this policy implies the replacement (in part) of one national asset (oil) by others, such as overseas portfolio and direct investment assets.

The contrary argument is that the decline in UK manufacturing industry was caused by the real appreciation of sterling, was largely unnecessary and might be difficult to reverse as it is more costly to open new factories than it is to close old ones. On this view, North Sea oil revenues should have been invested by the UK government in a programme of industrial regeneration. In addition, the authorities should have expanded demand in 1979–80 in a deliberate effort to depress sterling and reduce the unemployment rate.

In assessing these views it is difficult to resist the conclusion that some real appreciation must follow from North Sea oil. A demand-led expansion of the economy was constrained by the need of the UK to run balance-of-payments surpluses in the 1980s to generate overseas assets, in part so that future generations can benefit from the oil wealth, but also to repay foreign (especially official) debt incurred in the seventies. Indeed sterling's appreciation did not prevent such surpluses from appearing, which would suggest that the currency was not overvalued in this period.

Turning now to the utilization of oil resources, it is clear that investing in sectors rendered unprofitable by the terms-of-trade shift would not of itself make those sectors more profitable. More plausible is the argument that there should be investment in non-traded goods industries whose profitability would increase as a result of the sterling appreciation. In the public sector this would include investment in roads and in health, education, and training. Through such investments, the North Sea oil benefit could be translated into physical and human capital assets, with positive effects on UK industrial competitiveness in the medium and long term when North Sea production declines.[1]

It seems clear therefore that North Sea oil development must produce a higher sterling exchange rate than would otherwise prevail, followed by a gradual depreciation as oil is depleted. Some structural change is certain to follow from this, with adverse consequences for employment in the production of traded goods. The pattern of comparative advantage has changed in a way which allows a higher average level of UK income than would otherwise prevail. The proper response is to devise policies aimed at accommodating North Sea oil resources with a minimum of transitional cost and maximum of

---

[1] Cf. *The Challenge of North Sea Oil* Cmnd. 7143 (HMSO, 1978).

longer-term benefit. The balance-of-payments experience of the late eighties suggests that such policies are still needed. The main impact of the 1985–6 fall in oil prices in combination with other forces was to produce a severe deterioration in the current account which has so far taken five years to reverse.

In summary, the UK has remained exceedingly vulnerable over the last decade to sharp and lasting movements in world oil prices. First an increase then later a decrease in prices has each been a major cause of structural changes to which the UK economy has adapted only slowly and apparently at some cost.

Monetary Policy and the Exchange Rate: So far we have looked at deviations from PPP in terms of shifts in various real factors impinging upon the exchange rate. Equal weight must also be given to monetary policy including government intervention in the foreign-exchange market. The next section deals with the theoretical issues involved in the use of monetary policy to manage the exchange rate, so here we simply record that the float of sterling has been managed in differing degrees since 1979. The management of sterling has been carried out in three main ways: by the use of reserves (intervention), by variations in interest rates, and more indirectly by the general stance of monetary policy.

From 1979 the authorities were committed to a regime of annual targets for the growth rate of the money supply. This was formulated in the MTFS, which is discussed in detail in Chapter 1. In a small open economy, strict adherence to monetary targets implies a loss of control over the exchange rate, and the official policy for much of the eighties was to rely on market forces to determine the exchange rate, given the monetary targets in place. In practice the MTFS targets were frequently overshot, and the authorities adopted various policies intended to have a more direct impact on the exchange rate.

In 1979–80, the authorities sold sterling and accumulated reserves amounting to $9bn in intervention aimed at stemming the sharp appreciation of the exchange rate. A similar episode occurred in 1987 when $21.5bn of reserves were accumulated in an effort to curtail the appreciation of sterling against the Deutschmark. Interest-rate policy was also used in a more discretionary way as the decade wore on; in October 1985, the authorities announced that policy would include adjustments to short-term interest rates required to help maintain the external value of the pound within a desired range. By the time that sterling joined the EMS in October 1990, the authorities had already been committed for some time to an active policy of exchange-rate management.[1]

---

[1] See, for example, the Chancellor of the Exchequer's 1985 Mansion House speech, reported in *The Financial Times*, 18 October 1985; and his speech to the House of Commons on 30 November 1988 when he stated, *inter alia*, that 'The Government's anchor against inflation is its determination not to allow a devaluation of the pound.'

2.5   Sterling and the EMS

The origins of the EMS can be traced to the 1970 Werner Report, which proposed the achievement of full monetary union within the EC by 1980. This timetable was abandoned almost immediately and it was not until 1979 that the EMS was established. Renewed impetus for monetary union was given first by the April 1989 report of the Delors Committee, and then by the December 1991 Maastricht agreement among EC heads of state, which laid down criteria and a timetable for the establishment of a common European currency.

The EMS, as presently constituted, amounts to a zone within which each industrial country pursues a mutually consistent exchange-rate target. However, the EMS is also seen as an important step on the road to European monetary integration, leading eventually to the establishment of a common currency. We look first at the theoretical arguments for and against targeting the exchange rate.

Exchange-Rate Target Zones: There are powerful constraints on the ability of any individual country to manage its own exchange rate, particularly if the proposed policy calls for a systematic appreciation or depreciation of the currency away from a level which would be set by the private market. First, in a world where all the major currencies are floating, governments may follow mutually inconsistent exchange-rate targets and find themselves in a situation of competitive exchange-rate management in which one country's policies are nullified by the actions of others. Second, when national authorities attempt to set an exchange rate which is very different from that which would be set by the private market, the resulting flows of speculative short-term capital tend to force a change in policy. Third, any disequilibrium exchange rate will, in general, be associated with a non-zero BOF and thus with changes in the stock of foreign-exchange reserves and the domestic money supply. Changes in the domestic money supply will change domestic prices until the exchange rate returns to equilibrium. This must be so since, as long as the exchange rate is out of equilibrium, the money supply and therefore domestic prices will be changing; when the exchange rate is in equilibrium there are no forces impelling any further price or exchange rate changes. It must be stressed that this is true only in the long run and that the links between reserve changes and the domestic money supply can, to some extent, be offset by sterilization. Moreover, the concept of an 'equilibrium exchange rate' is itself fraught with ambiguity. While PPP may provide a useful guide to long-run movements in the exchange rate, in the short run the equilibrium exchange rate depends *inter alia* on the tightness or ease of domestic monetary policy. Nevertheless, it can be concluded that the scope for exchange-rate management in the longer run is extremely limited.

In the short run, though, there are several arguments to suggest that some degree of exchange-rate management might be desirable. First, the authorities may view changes in the demand and supply of foreign exchange as temporary and so act as a speculator to prevent such changes influencing the exchange rate and causing costly changes in trade flows. The difficulty with this argument is that it presumes that the authorities are substantially better informed than private investors as to what constitute 'permanent' and 'transitory' changes. On some occasions this presumption may be correct but it is certainly not true *in general*.[1]

Exchange-rate management may also be viewed as an alternative to monetary targeting, according to which the authorities pursue a target value or, more likely, a restricted 'zone' of values within which the exchange rate is allowed to fluctuate. This can be achieved by varying domestic interest rates to influence the flow of international capital. If the authorities were to attach overriding importance to the achievement of an exchange-rate target, they could not in general simultaneously expect to attain a target for the quantity of money, for it is by varying the quantity of money that the authorities can influence interest rates in such a way that they do not unduly affect the value of the exchange rate.

The relative merits of monetary and exchange-rate targets are too complex to be debated in full here.[2] The choice of one or other should be determined by its ability to 'insulate' the economy from unwanted exogenous disturbances. Roughly, exchange-rate targets are likely to be preferable if the main disturbances to the economy originate in financial markets. An exchange-rate target helps prevent such disturbances from being transmitted to domestic production and prices.

A further argument for exchange-rate targeting relates to the credibility issue. Policy targets of any kind gain their effectiveness in part because they are taken seriously by agents in the private sector when they formulate their economic plans. If the government and private sector set mutually consistent goals and achieve these goals, the performance of the economy will typically be better in terms of higher output and lower inflation than would otherwise be the case. This is because when a plan is not achieved by one sector of the economy it imposes an unanticipated and invariably costly shock on other sectors. Such shocks may then be translated into increases in prices or unemployment.[3] In this calculus the activities of the government are obviously particularly important. If the government attains a reputation for achieving its targets, the private sector will generally plan on that assumption and such a government is said to have 'credibility' or 'a

---

[1] The assessment of the effectiveness of official stabilization operations is fraught with difficulty. See 'Intervention, Stabilization and Profits', *BEQB*, September 1983, pp. 384–91.
[2] For a clear exposition of the issues involved, see M.J.Artis, 'From Monetary to Exchange Rate Targets', *Banca Nazionale del Lavoro Quarterly Review*, September 1981, pp. 339–58.
[3] The need to distinguish carefully between anticipated and unanticipated shocks in studying the impact of economic policy was argued in a seminal (and difficult) article by R.E.Lucas, 'Expectations and the Neutrality of Money', *JET*, Vol. 4, No. 2, pp. 103–124. For a textbook treatment see C.L.F.Attfield, D.Demery and N. Duck, *Rational Expectations in Macroeconomics* (Basil Blackwell, 1985), especially Chapters 1–5.

reputation'. If, however, the government frequently misses its targets, it is not credible and this renders private sector planning more difficult, as well as imposing frequent costly shocks on the economy as outcomes differ from announced targets.

In this framework, policy targets should be achievable but should also carry some meaning.[1] The arguments for exchange-rate targeting in this context are twofold. First, the target is set in terms of a 'strong' currency with a low inflation experience, thus effectively ruling out the possibility that the home currency will depreciate. This provides a 'nominal anchor' against internally generated inflation. Second, the linkages between interest rates, capital flows and exchange rates appear to be strong and immediate if not necessarily very stable. This implies that the exchange-rate target can be met by varying domestic interest rates – raising them when the exchange rate tends to depreciate too far and vice-versa.

The problem with this strategy is that the interest-rate changes needed to achieve the exchange-rate target may conflict with other domestic policy goals. Thus, if the target value of the exchange rate is chosen wrongly or too inflexibly, then maintaining the target will have adverse effects on either output or inflation which may persist for some time. This suggests the need for making the targets *conditional* on other aspects of the economic situation, including domestic monetary conditions and the level of demand. However, when there is a potential conflict between the domestic and the external situation, it is far from clear which should be given priority.

In summary, exchange-rate management is fraught with problems, although it seems clear that some degree of management is desirable. It is not easy to judge the 'right' level of an exchange-rate target, or the priority which should be accorded that target. In 1973, the UK authorities set out their broad objectives of exchange-rate policy as being '... not to oppose any well-defined trend but merely to smooth excessive fluctuations'.[2] Sterling's entry into the ERM, implying as it does a relatively tight band of fluctuation for the currency, renders this judgement nugatory, and we turn next to the operation of the ERM.

The ERM in Practice: At the time of the establishment of the EMS, academic and government opinion in the UK was generally hostile to the idea of UK entry into the ERM.[3] Drawing on the apparent lessons from the

---

[1] Thus a government facing an ongoing inflation rate and money growth of 20% which sets a target for the following year of 20% for the growth in money may achieve its target, but it is unlikely to gain credibility, as the target effectively underwrites existing money growth and inflation rates, and does not convey any intent to reduce these rates.
[2] Bank of England, *Annual Report and Accounts*, 1973, p. 21.
[3] For an early evaluation of the EMS, see 'The European Monetary System', *NIER*, February 1979, pp. 5–12. Official viewpoints are contained in HC (1978–79) 60: *First Report of the Expenditure Committee*, 1978–79, para. 15; and in *The European Monetary System*, Cmnd. 7405, November 1978.

collapse of the par-value system, it was widely agreed that the substantial disparities of economic performance within the EC made it unwise to fix exchange parities within the limits set by the ERM. Other factors which appeared to weigh specifically against UK membership included the possibility that oil-price changes would pose unacceptable strains on the ERM because of the divergence of interest between the UK as an oil exporter and other countries as oil importers. In addition, there was a potential conflict between the MTFS, which emphasized the money supply as an intermediate target, and the EMS, which emphasizes the exchange rate.

During the eighties the actual experience of the EMS forced a reappraisal of the economics of the system, and progress towards European integration in the latter part of the decade impelled a reconsideration of the political economy of UK participation in the ERM. It is now widely agreed that, following a turbulent period immediately after the inception of the system, ERM countries have, since about 1983, been converging on lower and more stable inflation rates than existed before 1979, and this has been achieved with more stable interest rates and exchange rates than before. However, the extent to which the ERM has contributed to these outcomes and the magnitude of their costs and benefits are still matters of debate.[1]

The ERM has not worked exactly as originally intended, particularly in its allocation of the burden of adjustment. Given the exchange-rate structure, deficit countries are inevitably under more pressure than surplus countries. From the start, Germany has had low inflation, a strong balance of payments and a strong currency and, in practice, other countries in the system have had to adjust towards the German inflation rate. This is the 'German leadership' hypothesis and it is underscored by the fact that there has been little use of the divergence indicator as ERM members have typically reached their bilateral limits (usually against a strong Deutschmark) before reaching the divergence threshold. However, it also seems clear that the ERM has worked in this way partly because of the wishes of the (non-German) members, who have placed a high priority on reducing inflation in the eighties. The Deutschmark has therefore acted as the nominal anchor in the system, with the Bundesbank pursuing an anti-inflation policy and other ERM members tied to the value of the Mark.[2]

The evidence on exchange-rate stability under the ERM is also ambiguous. The system appears to have helped stabilize the rates of ERM members *vis-à-vis* one another but not necessarily *vis-à-vis* other currencies. Moreover, although there has been considerable dissatisfaction in the UK at the volatility of the sterling exchange rate, it is far from clear that volatility *per se*

---

[1] For a clear summary of the issues, see A.G.Haldane, 'The Exchange Rate Mechanism of the European Monetary System: A Review of the Literature', *BEQB*, February 1991, pp. 73–82.
[2] There is some debate about the German leadership hypothesis but it appears valid, at least in a weak form. See, for example, M.J.Artis and D.Nachane, 'Wages and Prices in Europe: A Test of the German Leadership Hypothesis', *Weltwirtschaftliches Archiv*, Vol. 126, March 1990.

is particularly harmful to the economy.[1] Misalignment of the exchange rate clearly is damaging, as discussed in section 2.3, but there is little evidence either way on the propensity of the ERM either to prevent or provoke misalignment in exchange rates.

Certainly the exchange-rate adjustment process has mostly been smoother within the ERM than under the par-value system. More recent exchange-rate adjustments have occurred within existing bands, thus ruling out a discrete jump in the market exchange rate which, under the par-value system, offered a one-way option to speculators. Moreover, there has been no general realignment since 1987. Some commentators have argued that these adjustments without excessive speculative pressures have been made possible by the existence of direct controls on international capital movements in most ERM countries.[2] However, capital controls have been increasingly relaxed and, for all the major countries, now abolished as a result of the 1988 Capital Liberalization Directive with, as yet, little adverse impact on the ERM.

Considerable attention has been devoted to the role of the ERM in enhancing the credibility of the (anti-inflation) policy stances of (non-German) ERM members. A central aspect of the credibility hypothesis is that ERM members should resist realignments since these involve the devaluation of some currencies, producing an upward impetus to inflation and destroying credibility. In practice, exchange-rate adjustments in each ERM realignment have typically been less than required to restore PPP relative to the previous realignment, and in this way have sought to mitigate the credibility problem associated with realignments. Credibility is difficult to measure and although there are many theories placing considerable emphasis on the importance of credibility, there is little concrete evidence on its importance in practice.

A more recent paradox in the ERM has been the relative strength of the high-inflation currencies. As capital controls were reduced and realignments became less frequent, European capital was increasingly attracted to countries with buoyant demand, higher inflation and therefore higher nominal interest rates.[3] This poses a dilemma for high-inflation countries, which was

[1] On all these issues, see HC (1984–85), 57–IV, *Thirteenth Report from the Treasury and Civil Service Committee*, 1984–85. For an overall evaluation, see M.J. Artis, 'The European Monetary System: An Evaluation', *Journal of Policy Modeling*, 1986.
[2] For an evaluation of this argument, see F. Giavazzi and A. Giovannini, *Limiting Exchange Rate Flexibility* (MIT Press, Cambridge, 1990).
[3] A distinction must be made between the nominal interest rate observed in the market and the real interest rate. The real interest rate gives the rate of return in constant purchasing power terms, i.e. adjusted for changes over time in the value of money. To a close approximation the (*ex ante*) real rate is equal to the difference between the nominal rate and expected inflation. The Fisher hypothesis predicts that increased inflation and inflation expectations will generate a rise in nominal interest rates with relatively little effect on real rates. Thus, in general, high-inflation countries will have higher nominal interest rates than low-inflation countries, and this appears to be broadly true. For a textbook discussion of the Fisher hypothesis, see M.J. Artis, *Macroeconomics* (Oxford University Press, Oxford, 1984).

highlighted by the then UK Prime Minister's personal adviser, Professor Alan Walters, in a book arguing *inter alia* against UK entry into the ERM.[1] In these circumstances, domestic considerations call for high interest rates, but the ERM exerts downward pressure on domestic interest rates to keep the home currency within the intervention limits. Lower interest rates fuel aggregate demand and exacerbate the inflation problem. This has been dubbed the 'excess credibility' problem but so far it has only affected the Italian lira in 1989 and, more stubbornly, the Spanish peseta for much of 1990–1.

Most commentators would agree that the ERM has been fairly successful in improving the control of member countries over nominal magnitudes such as inflation. However, there is less agreement on the costs of this success. Virtually all models of inflation that command serious support suggest that it is exceedingly difficult to reduce inflation without some, possibly temporary, cost in terms of higher unemployment. Moreover, the slope of the trade-off between unemployment and inflation is generally reckoned to differ among countries. (Chapter 1 contains a discussion of the UK case.) The striking feature of the eighties is that (non-German) ERM members have experienced persistently high unemployment rates along with gradually falling inflation rates. In most cases, unemployment rose sharply in the early eighties as the impact of deflationary policies was first felt. However, as inflation has fallen, unemployment has remained high in most ERM countries. The Netherlands has had a relatively good experience in this regard. Its inflation reached a peak of 7.1% in 1980; fell to zero in 1987 and rose back to 2.5% in 1990–1. Dutch unemployment rose from 4.1% in 1980 to a peak of 11.2% in 1983–4, falling back to 6.5% in 1990–1. Making the conservative assumption that the natural rate of unemployment in the Netherlands was 5.5% in this period, the figures show that cutting inflation by about 4.5% has so far cost the Netherlands a loss of output totalling approximately 32% of one year's GDP: on the face of it, an extremely high cost. The unemployment experience of other ERM members has been worse still.

The appropriate mix of inflation and unemployment in a country is largely a political choice for its citizens. Thus we cannot say if ERM members were mistaken in placing priority on reducing inflation in the eighties. However, the inflation–unemployment choice should be informed by a knowledge of the slope of the inflation–unemployment trade-off. On this count, (non-German) ERM members faced exceedingly severe trade-offs of this nature in the eighties. The costs of inflation are poorly understood and have proven hard to pin down, whereas the costs of unemployment (in terms of lost output) are clear to see, and it is difficult to believe that the gains from reduced inflation have outweighed the costs of high unemployment in any of

---

[1] See A.A. Walters, *Britain's Economic Renaissance* (Oxford University Press, Oxford, 1986).

the (non-German) ERM countries in this period. Of course, the inflation–unemployment trade-off does not depend exclusively or even mainly on the ERM, but on the economic and social institutions in each country. Where the ERM can be indicted, however, is in imparting a strong deflationary bias to a group of countries for which the costs of deflation appear clear and large, and for whom the benefits appear intangible and at best small. Overall, the ERM appears so far to have been a zone of low inflation and high unemployment. It remains to be seen how far this era will prove to have been a transitional one.

Did Sterling Join at the Right Rate?:   Notwithstanding these considerations, sterling joined the ERM on the 'wide' band basis on 8 October 1990 at a central rate of £0.0696904 per ECU and a bilateral central rate against the Mark of £1 = DM2.95. The main permissive factors in the UK's decision to enter were the lower world oil price, which had ceased to place upward pressure on sterling since the early eighties, and the growing disillusionment with monetary targeting, both in its difficulty of implementation and in its uncertain effectiveness in reducing inflation. Key positive factors in the entry decision were the anti-inflation characteristics of the ERM discussed above and which it was hoped would be effective in the UK, and the developing political momentum towards economic and monetary integration in the EC as a whole.

Nevertheless it is still useful to ask if the exchange rate chosen for sterling's ERM entry was 'the right rate'. As we have seen, determining the right exchange rate in general is exceedingly difficult. PPP provides only a very imperfect guide and, indeed, most calculations suggest that, according to PPP, sterling was somewhat *undervalued* when it joined the ERM. An alternative concept which has been widely used to calculate sterling's position in the ERM is that of the 'Fundamental Equilibrium Exchange Rate' (FEER). This is defined as the real exchange rate consistent with both internal and external balance in the long run. 'Internal balance' is defined as the natural (or non-accelerating inflationary) rate of unemployment. 'External balance' is defined as the sustainable current account surplus or deficit. Typically the FEER is calculated for a country by simulating an econometric model in which the authorities set fiscal policy to maximize a social welfare function subject to the government budget constraint and private sector behaviour. The exchange-rate trajectory in such a simulation gives the path of the FEER over time.

Calculations of this kind invariably suggest that sterling's central rate *vis-à-vis* the ECU on entry into the ERM was overvalued in comparison with its FEER by at least 10%.[1] Over time it can be expected that sterling's FEER will depreciate to some extent as North Sea oil is depleted and also because the UK appears to have a rather high income elasticity of demand

[1]   For an analysis of sterling's ERM entry exchange rate, see J. Williamson, 'FEERs and the ERM', *NIER*, August 1991, pp. 45–50.

for imports in comparison with its main trading partners both inside and outside the EC. A further factor in these calculations is the impact of German reunification which, it is anticipated, will tend to moderate the upward drift in the Deutschmark. However, the capital cost of reunification will also lead to higher German interest rates and, *ceteris paribus*, this will tend to raise interest rates across the EC.

These considerations suggest that sterling can only be maintained in the ERM in the long run either by devaluation as part of a general realignment, or by the UK maintaining a systematically lower inflation rate than that of Germany to offset the overvaluation and subsequent appreciation of the sterling exchange rate *vis-à-vis* its FEER value. An early devaluation of the pound would most likely cause the UK to lose its ERM policy credibility. However, the alternative is also likely to be costly in terms of the unemployment it may entail.

Immediately after entry, sterling moved to near the top of its intervention band but this configuration was soon reversed, and sterling was typically one of the weakest ERM currencies throughout 1991. However, this outcome was accompanied by a significant easing of monetary policy with base rate falling from 15% in September 1990, immediately prior to entry, to 10% in December 1991. As yet, therefore, it is too early to say just how severe will be the constraints that ERM membership will undoubtedly impose on domestic UK economic policy.

Monetary Union in the EC: The EMS is currently a zone of stable exchange rates, but it is increasingly viewed as a transitional phase in the move towards monetary union in the EC involving the establishment of a single European currency. The case for monetary union in the EC is often presented as analogous to the case for having a common market in commodities. Creation of a single currency reduces transactions costs and promotes exchange and the division of labour which, it could be argued, is necessary if the benefits of the EC are to be fully realized by member countries. Furthermore, it can be argued that as EC members develop intensive trade and investment links with one another, then adoption of a single currency is the only foreign-exchange-market policy consistent with price stability.

However, the costs of complete monetary unification may also be considerable. With a single currency throughout the EC, each country becomes a region within the larger currency area. A country in balance-of-payments deficit with the rest of the EC would have to adjust in much the same way as a region of the UK in deficit with the rest of the UK currently has to adjust. Since an exchange-rate change is ruled out, adjustment must be by a combination of domestic deflation and changes in regional taxes and subsidies. Within the EC, of course, the latter are largely ruled out for balance-of-payments purposes by the CET. In practice, the process of adjustment by a region within a single currency area depends to a large extent on the monetary effects of a balance-of-payments imbalance. A deficit, for example, will generate flows of money out of the region, depressing demand

and, ultimately, prices and wages within the region. The effectiveness of this process in restoring regional balance-of-payments equilibrium without sustained regional recession depends on the flexibility of wages and prices, and on the mobility of labour and capital between occupations and regions in response to changed profit opportunities.

There is no general agreement as to what constitutes the optimal area for a single currency. A high degree of wage and price flexibility and of labour and capital mobility within the currency area are likely to be important, but may be neither necessary nor sufficient conditions for optimality. An alternative criterion for optimality relates to the degree of openness of an economy. In a highly open economy with a very small non-traded goods sector, an exchange-rate change has its main impact on the price level, with relatively little impact on relative prices. In this setting the exchange rate is not effective as an instrument of balance-of-payments adjustment. Thus the optimal currency area consists of regions which are highly open *vis-à-vis* each other but relatively closed *vis-à-vis* the rest of the world.[1]

There is no reason why the optimal area for separate currencies should coincide with the jurisdiction of existing nation states and it would be wishful thinking to assume that the entire EC has ever constituted an optimal currency area. It seems unlikely that the EC will satisfy the wage flexibility or factor mobility criterion for optimality for many years to come. However, the process of trade integration is such that much of the Community may satisfy the openness criterion a good deal sooner.

The Convergence Problem: Currency unification is not just a special case of fixed exchange rates. Under fixed exchange rates, there always exists a risk that an exchange-rate change will in fact occur and this risk is related to the monetary and fiscal policies pursued by national currency authorities. In particular, there is no immediate constraint on the rate at which fiscal deficits can be monetized, since excessive simply leads eventually to a depreciation of the currency. With a unified currency, however, exchange-rate changes are impossible and this imposes new policy constraints. If EC countries were to adopt a single currency (say the ECU) with a single issuing authority (a European central bank), national governments could only monetize their deficits within the constraints of European central bank policy. However, the alternative policy of national governments issuing ECU-based debt may not be as tightly constrained in practice, with the result that high-deficit countries may impose sizeable externalities on other EMU member states.

Clearly this poses a range of immediate problems for currency unification. A measure of agreement on at least some of these problems in the EC was

---

[1] An old but still valuable survey of the theory of optimal currency areas is contained in Y. Ishiyama, 'The Theory of Optimum Currency Areas: A Survey', *IMFSP*, July 1975, pp. 344–83. A recent survey of the role and effectiveness of the exchange rate in correcting balance-of-payments imbalances is: P.R. Krugman, 'Has the Adjustment Process Worked?', *Institute for International Economics*, October 1991.

reached and codified in the December 1991 Treaty of Maastricht. The move to a single currency is scheduled to begin in 1996, when EC finance ministers will decide which countries meet certain 'convergence criteria'. If, at this stage, fewer than seven countries satisfy the criteria, there will be a further meeting before July 1998 which will decide which countries are ready for currency unification, and in this decision, the convergence criteria can be set aside. Those countries qualifying at this stage will automatically adopt the ECU as their single currency in January 1999.

The key to these developments is the set of convergence criteria which, in each country, call for the following:

(a) Price inflation to be no more than 1.5% above the average of the three EC countries with the lowest inflation.
(b) Long-term interest rates to be no more than 2% (200 basis points) above the average of the three EC countries with the lowest rates of interest.
(c) National budget deficits to be less than 3% of GDP.
(d) Outstanding public debt to be no more than 60% of GDP.
(e) The national currency should not have been devalued in the previous two years and must have remained within the 2.25% intervention bands of the ERM.

As of late 1991 only France and Luxembourg satisfied all these criteria, and seven out of the EC 12 failed to satisfy the public debt criterion, which is arguably the most difficult one to adjust towards rapidly and the one which is central to the achievement of most of the other criteria.[1]

The central feature of the convergence criteria is that they focus exclusively on nominal magnitudes. As we have seen, there has been considerable progress towards nominal convergence among ERM countries but at a cost of high and largely non-convergent unemployment rates. Convergence on real magnitudes such as unemployment would require the EC to move much closer to other optimal currency area criteria such as regional wage and price flexibility and factor mobility. If, as is likely, this does not occur, then the EC would need to offset regional payments imbalances by a much greater rate of fiscal transfers to deficit regions than heretofore. The Spanish government has dubbed this the policy of 'cohesion', but there is little immediate prospect that this will prove adequate until the Community budget is reformed as we discuss in section 3 below.

If adequate measures are not taken to ensure real convergence then the ERM and the putative European currency area promise to continue to be a zone of low inflation and high and divergent unemployment. This would not be a regime which would have commanded the respect of the founders of the

---

[1] For a discussion of convergence criteria, see 'Convergence in The European Community', *BEQB*, August 1991, pp. 328–31. For an appraisal of the progress of ERM members thus far towards convergence, see R.Anderton, R.Barrell, J.W. in't Veld, 'Macroeconomic Convergence in Europe', *NIER*, November 1991, pp. 51–62.

par-value system which, whatever its defects, gave as much emphasis to employment and growth as to stable prices.

3   THE CURRENT ACCOUNT

3.1   Long-Term Trends

The Structure of Trade: In this section we shall examine the major structural developments in the current account of the UK since 1950, concentrating in particular on the performance of merchandise trade, services and transfers, the latter in connection with the UK's membership of the EC. IPD are considered with the capital account in section 4.

Radical changes in the pattern of UK overseas trade have occurred in the last forty years. Table 3.5 shows the major changes in the geographical composition of trade. Several general trends are immediately apparent. Compared to the 1950s, the following years show a decreased dependence on trade with developing countries, a trend which has been primarily at the expense of trade with the less developed members of the OSA, and the four major Commonwealth nations, Canada, Australia, New Zealand and South Africa. The decline in importance of the oil-exporting countries as a source of UK imports since 1980 is the direct result of the exploitation of the UK's North Sea oil resources. As far as trade with the developed nations is concerned, the most striking trend is the increasing importance of trade with the EC. In 1972, the year prior to entry, the current twelve EC members accounted for approximately 30% of UK exports and imports; but by 1990, the export share had risen to 53.19% and the import share to 52.3%. In the light of the popular conception of Japanese strengths, it is interesting to note that Japan still only supplies 5.4% of UK imports, although the importance of Japan as a UK export market is smaller still.

The switch towards a greater trade dependence on the industrialized, high per capita income countries of Western Europe, Japan and North America has been matched by significant changes in the commodity structure of UK trade, particularly in respect of imports. The changing structure of UK import trade is shown in Table 3.6. Most important here is the increase in the proportion of imports of manufactures and the decline in the proportion accounted for by foodstuffs, beverages and tobacco. Imports of manufactures (SITC Codes 5–8) now account for over 75% of total UK imports. This same trend has also been experienced by other EC countries, although it remains the case that the UK has a higher proportion of imports of non-manufactures than does, for example, France or Germany.

On the export side, Table 3.6 shows that changes in structure have been less marked. It is clear that North Sea oil has had an important influence on trade structure. This can be seen in the significant decline in the import share of fuels and lubricants, and a corresponding rise in the export share of

TABLE 3.5
Area Composition of UK Merchandise Trade[1] 1955–90

	1955	1970	1980	1985	1989	1990
	EXPORTS					
	(fob: in per cent of total)					
Western Europe	28.9	46.2	57.6	58.3	59.2	61.8
EC[3]	(15.0)	(29.4)	(43.4)	(46.3)	(50.7)	(53.1)
North America	12.0	15.2	11.2	17.0	15.4	14.4
USA	(7.1)	(11.6)	(9.6)	(14.7)	(13.0)	(12.5)
Other Developed[2]	21.1	11.8	5.6	4.8	5.8	5.6
Japan	(0.6)	(1.8)	(1.3)	(1.3)	(2.5)	(2.5)
Total Developed Countries	62.0	73.2	74.5	80.0	80.4	81.8
Centrally planned economies[3]	1.7	3.8	2.8	2.0	2.0	1.4
Oil exporting countries	5.1	5.8	10.1	7.6	6.2	5.4
Other developing countries	31.2	17.2	12.4	10.1	10.4	10.5
Total	100.0	100.0	100.0	100.0	100.0	100.0
	IMPORTS					
	(cif: in per cent of total)					
Western Europe	25.7	41.5	55.9	63.1	64.9	64.8
EC[3]	(12.6)	(27.1)	(41.3)	(46.0)	(52.4)	(52.3)
North America	19.5	20.5	15.0	13.8	13.1	13.2
USA	(10.9)	(12.9)	(12.1)	(11.7)	(11.1)	(11.4)
Other Developed[2]	14.2	9.4	6.8	7.5	7.6	7.4
Japan	(0.6)	(1.5)	(3.4)	(4.9)	(5.8)	(5.4)
Total developed countries	59.4	71.4	77.7	84.3	85.6	85.4
Centrally planned economies[3]	2.7	4.2	2.1	2.2	1.9	1.4
Oil exporting countries	9.2	9.1	8.6	3.3	1.9	2.4
Other developing countries	28.7	15.3	11.3	10.0	10.0	10.1
Total	100.0	100.0	100.0	100.0	100.0	100.0

Sources: *AAS*, 1963, 1976, 1989; *MDS*, October 1991.
[1] There are minor changes over time of some of the classifications. The components do not sum exactly to 100% as items valued at less than £50 (1955, 1970); £200 (1980, 1985); £600 (1989, 1990) are not classified by area.
[2] Australia, Japan, New Zealand, South Africa.
[3] The former German Democratic Republic is included under Centrally Planned Economies through 1989 and under EC thereafter.

these products, reflecting, respectively, the import-substitution and export-generating aspects of North Sea oil that we discussed in section 1.

For services, both debits and credits in proportion to total merchandise imports have shown a tendency to decline since 1970, after rising somewhat in the years following 1955.[1] The positive balance on services in more recent years can be attributed largely to a rapid expansion in receipts from financial services (other than IPD) as receipts from travel and transport have increased more slowly.

---

[1] Some degree of stability in service credits and debits is to be expected because of the method of estimating certain invisibles, such as shipping and insurance, as a fixed percentage of the value of merchandise trade.

It will be apparent from this that UK trade is increasingly dominated by an exchange of manufactured goods and services for other manufactured goods and services with the advanced industrialized nations. These structural changes imply that British industry has experienced and will continue to experience greater foreign competition in home and export markets.

Competitive Performance: The trend towards increased non-oil visible trade deficits has often been interpreted as evidence of a general lack of competitive edge in British industry relative to foreign industry. Related evidence is provided by the progressive decline of the UK's share of the total exports of manufactured goods of the major industrial countries,[1] and by the increased import penetration of the UK market by foreign products. These trends have prompted fears of the 'de-industrialization' of the UK, with the manufacturing base so eroded by foreign competitors, that full employment and balance-of-payments equilibrium cannot, in the long run, be achieved simultaneously.[2] As discussed above, these fears have been heightened rather than quelled by the development of North Sea oil and its implications for the adjustment of the economy. At the very least, the UK may face a severe balance-of-payments constraint as North Sea oil is gradually depleted.[3]

The statistics of the decline in the UK share of world exports of manufactures are dramatic and indicate that the share fell steadily from 20.4% in 1954 to a low of 8.8% in 1974. Since 1974, however, the UK's share of world trade in manufactures appears to have stabilized at around 9.0%. Of itself, the decline in export share need not give rise to concern, since it may simply reflect a decline in the UK share of world manufacturing production, the natural result of her early industrial start. (In 1899, the UK accounted for 32.5% of world exports of manufactures and 20% of world manufacturing production.) However, the decline in the UK's share in world manufacturing production may itself reflect the same factors which hinder UK trade performance.

On the import side, there is also some evidence of a loss of competitive edge. Even though all the major industrialized nations, with the exception of Japan, have experienced a rising import share since 1955, the UK seems to be relatively more import-prone than her competitors and to have a relatively high income elasticity of demand for imports. A customary measure of import penetration is the ratio of imports to domestic consumption. For manufactured goods this ratio increased from 17% in 1968 to 26% in 1978 and again to 37% in 1989. This trend appears widespread across manufacturing industry and is not confined to any one sub-sector. However, some care is required in interpreting these figures since, in part, they reflect the

---

[1]   These consist of Germany, France, Italy, Netherlands, Belgium, Luxembourg, Canada, Japan, Sweden, Switzerland, USA and UK.
[2]   See the various contributions to F. Blackaby (ed.), *Deindustrialization* (Heinemann 1979).
[3]   See J. Williamson, 'Is There an External Constraint?' *NIER*, August, 1984, pp. 73–7.

TABLE 3.6

Commodity Composition of UK Merchandise Trade and Services, 1955–90

SITC Code	Description	1955	1970	1980	1985	1989	1990
		EXPORTS					
	Merchandise	(fob: in per cent of total merchandise exports)					
0,1	Food, Beverages, Tobacco	5.8	6.4	6.9	6.3	7.0	6.8
3	Fuel and Lubricants	4.8	2.6	13.6	21.4	6.6	7.5
2,4	Basic Materials	3.9	3.4	3.1	2.7	2.5	2.2
5,6	Semi-manufactures	38.9	34.3	29.6	25.3	28.6	28.0
7,8	Manufactures	43.5	49.9	43.9	41.7	52.8	53.2
9	Unclassified	3.0	3.4	3.0	2.5	2.5	2.2
	Total Merchandise	100.0	100.0	100.0	100.0	100.0	100.0
	Private Services						
	Transport and Travel	22.4	25.8	19.0	15.0	15.5	15.4
	Financial & Related Services	11.6	15.0	13.7	16.0	16.4	15.1
		IMPORTS					
	Merchandise	(cif: in per cent of total merchandise imports)					
0,1	Food, Beverages, Tobacco	36.2	22.6	12.4	10.9	9.4	9.8
3	Fuel and Lubricants	10.4	10.4	13.8	12.4	5.3	6.2
2,4	Basic Materials	28.7	15.1	8.1	6.3	5.3	4.8
5,6	Semi-manufactures	19.2	27.7	27.1	25.0	26.4	26.0
7,8	Manufactures	5.2	22.9	35.6	43.7	52.3	51.9
9	Unclassified	0.3	1.3	3.0	1.6	1.2	1.3
	Total Merchandise	100.0	100.0	100.0	100.0	100.0	100.0
	Private Services						
	Transport and Travel	19.0	23.1	16.6	14.4	14.3	14.4
	Financial & Related Services	4.8	5.7	4.8	5.5	4.6	4.7

Sources: AAS, 1963, 1976, 1989; *MDS*, October 1991; *Pink Book*.

increasing division of labour in the international economy which has occurred since 1958. Thus, similar calculations on the export side show a corresponding, albeit less marked, trend increase in the proportion of UK output which is exported, with the average ratio of UK manufacturing exports to manufacturing production rising from 18% in 1968 to 26% in 1978 and 30% in 1989.[1]

To explain these developments in any precise sense is not easy; several interrelated factors are involved and the relative weight to be attached to

---

[1] It may be noted that the sectors experiencing the greatest improvement in export perform-ance, e.g. chemicals, electrical engineering, mechanical engineering and scientific instruments, are also the sectors which perform two-thirds of the non-aerospace research and development carried out in UK manufacturing industry. See 'Manufacturing Industry in the Seventies: An Assessment of Import Penetration and Export Performance', *ET*, 1980. A useful account of some of the pitfalls of interpreting movements in these ratios is contained in C. Kennedy and A.P. Thirwall, 'Import Penetration, Export Performance and Harrod's Trade Multiplier', *OEP*, July 1979, pp. 303–23.

each is difficult to establish and may vary over time. At the most general level, there would seem to be two potential sources of the poor UK trade performance: an increasing lack of price competitiveness; and a failure to produce and market commodities of the right quality, in the face of rapidly changing technologies and world demand structures. Unfortunately, the precise role of these factors has proved impossible, as yet, to determine, although it is interesting to note that similar explanations of poor British competitive performance were employed at the end of the nineteenth century.[1]

3.2   Explanations of Trade Performance

Traditional trade theory explains patterns of international trade by reference to national differences in endowments of factors of production, a country exporting those commodities which use relatively intensively its abundant factors. While this may have some relevance to the explanation of exchanges of manufactured goods for raw materials between industrialized and developing countries, it is of less obvious relevance to the explanation of the dominant component of world trade, exchange of manufactures between industrialized nations. Indeed, the assumptions of traditional theory immediately invite a cautious interpretation of its content, for they specify homogeneous outputs of each industry, equal access to technical knowledge in all countries, and all factors of production of equal quality. Prima facie, they do not reflect the reality of modern industrial competition, i.e. conditions of imperfect competition with non-price factors being dominant in competitive performance.

A powerful indication of the weakness of traditional theory is provided by the phenomenon of intra-industry trade, the simultaneous importing and exporting of products of the same industry, which is estimated to comprise some 60% of trade between developed countries.[2] In part, of course, this phenomenon is a statistical aberration, reflecting the lack of detail within even the finest classification of industrial statistics. For example, within the steel industry, there are many qualities of steel each of which is a poor substitute for the other in many applications but which are treated statistically as if they were perfect substitutes. More fundamentally, it reflects the role of intra-industry product-differentiation as a key element in the competitive process.[3] It is no puzzle that the UK should simultaneously import and export whisky or automobiles of different brands, given the many

---

[1]   R. Hoffman, *Great Britain and the German Trade Rivalry 1875–1914* (Pennsylvania University Press, 1973), pp. 21–80.
[2]   D. Greenaway and C. Milner, 'On the Measurement of the Intra-Industry Trade', 1983, *EJ*, Vol. 93, pp. 900–8.
[3]   Inter-industry trade and other aspects of 'new' theories of trade patterns are discussed in D. Greenaway (ed.), *Current Issues in International Trade: Theory and Policy* (Macmillan, 1985).

grades of product which exist within these commodity groups, each defined by a unique set of characteristics. Design, technical sophistication, after-sales service, durability and reliability are easily recognized as elements which successfully differentiate products in the minds of consumers.

The major determinants of inter-industry trade relate to product differences rather than cost differences, and may be outlined as follows. First, there must exist a diversity of preferences for commodities of many different kinds within countries. Second, the domestic market is important to the initial development of a new commodity, which implies that the types of commodities produced in an economy reflect the pattern of domestic preferences. The same industry within different countries will then produce different product designs. Third, the existence of economies of scale in industrial production, including the spreading of overhead marketing and R & D expenses, induces firms to specialize within particular product niches. In general, specialization will be directed to those products in which home demand is greatest. Economies of scale and diversity of preferences then create the basis for intra-industry trade between industries organized in an imperfectly competitive fashion.

The conditions which generate intra-industry trade also make technological innovation an important element in trade performance. Economists have long recognized the connection between technical innovation, technology transfer and changes in the structure of foreign trade. Three factors are recognized as being of importance here: time-lags in the inter-country transfer of technology; differences in the national rate of diffusion of innovations; and differences in the rates of growth of national production capacity to exploit innovations.[1] From this perspective, a country's trade performance is determined by the rate at which it acquires and exploits new technologies relative to its major competitors. Moreover, as technologies mature, the inputs which are required for effective exploitation change significantly. A new technology requires major scientific and technical manpower inputs to compete effectively. But as it matures, production processes become standardized and the emphasis shifts to the exploitation of economies of scale and access to cheap labour.

Although the links between innovation and trade are difficult to measure, some pieces of evidence are suggestive.[2] First, if one divides UK trade according to the R & D intensity of the underlying industries, one finds that, for the last two decades, R & D-intensive industries consistently experienced a trade surplus, while other industries were in deficit.[3] Second, there

---

[1] The classic reference is M.V.Posner, 'International Trade and Technological Change', *OEP*, 1961, Vol. 13, pp. 323–41.
[2] For studies of individual industries, see for example E.Braun and S.McDonald, *Revolution in Miniature* (Cambridge, 1978); E.Tilton, *International Diffusion of Technology: The Case of Semi-conductors* (Brookings Institution, 1971), and B.A.Majumdar, *Innovations, Product Developments and Technology Transfers* (University Press of America, 1982).
[3] Business Monitor, QAID. High-technology industries are those with a ratio of R & D expenditures to value added greater than 3%.

is evidence to show that export success in the advanced industrialized nations is positively related to the resources devoted to R & D and to measures of inventive activity, e.g. patenting.[1]

These dynamic considerations can be reconciled with the factor endowment theory of trade, provided we interpret human capital skills and the state of technology as part of the endowment. However, unlike raw material endowments, human capital skills change over time, often rapidly as new knowledge is discovered and transmitted into the workforce by formal education and practical experience. Seen in this light, it is clear that long-term trade trends will be profoundly influenced by the level of education and training of the labour force and its ability to innovate and adapt to new technologies. These qualities are exceedingly difficult to measure in practice, and the exact ways in which they impinge on trade patterns are still not well understood.

Much of what we have said stresses the role of non-price factors in trade performance. Relative prices also play an important role even if they are not the overriding determining factor. The relation of prices to costs determines the financial base from which firms may engage in R & D, investment and marketing. Thus profit margins are a key determinant of the resources available for innovation and the relative dynamic performance of different national industries.[2] In addition, the export of modern industrial products typically involves a substantial initial investment: in market research, in the establishment of a shipping and distribution network, and in advertising the product in foreign markets. From a firm's point of view, these are 'sunk' costs. Once the firm is established in exporting to a foreign market it will not necessarily withdraw if an exchange-rate change renders its foreign sales unprofitable at existing foreign prices. First, in an era of floating exchange rates, the exchange rate change may be temporary and soon reversed. Second, once a firm withdraws from a foreign market, re-entering will again be costly. Often, therefore, a firm may decide to 'hang on' and wait for an improvement in market conditions such as an exchange-rate change could bring. The analogy is with the purchase of a financial option. The decision to enter or exist from a foreign market involves not only the concrete costs of entry or exit, but also the hidden costs of exercising the option to reverse the decision.

For these reasons, it may take very large changes in prices and profitability to induce firms to alter their exporting strategies. These arguments also give rise to the hypothesis of 'hysteresis': if an exchange-rate appreciation (say) is sufficiently large as to induce home firms to withdraw from foreign

---

[1]   For a review, see the valuable paper by C.Freeman, 'Technical Innovation and British Trade Performance', in F.Blackaby (ed.), *op. cit*. See also the study by K.Pavitt and L.Soete, Chapter 3 of K.Pavitt (ed.), *Technological Innovation and British Export Performance* (Macmillan, 1980).

[2]   For a discussion of these issues, see 'The Terms of Trade', *BEQB*, August 1987, pp. 371–9.

markets, merely reversing the appreciation will not reverse the trade balance as it will not be sufficient to pay the sunk costs of firms to re-establish themselves in foreign markets. This hypothesis is particularly relevant to considering the impact of the 1979–80 appreciation of sterling and the difficulty seemingly experienced in reversing the current account deficit of the late 1980s.[1]

Overall, therefore, the determinants of price competitiveness are complex, and include such factors as the structure of costs, the size and nature of different industries and the existence of economies of scale, labour productivity, the pricing policies of individual firms and movements in wages and interest rates. The hysteresis argument suggests that the relationship between price competitiveness *per se* and trade performance is also not a simple one. Moreover, it is likely that price competitiveness interacts with technological factors, with a deterioration in competitiveness resulting in a loss of markets, a slow rate of economic growth, and concomitant lack of resources to invest in new technologies. This, in turn, makes a country less competitive in other markets, thus exacerbating the problem further in a form of vicious circle. A country such as the UK has no option but to maintain its technological level close to 'world best practice'. As technologies mature, the centre of comparative advantage moves to low-real-wage economies, so an advanced country such as the UK can only maintain its comparative advantage by continuously shifting resources into production at the frontiers of technological change. Only thus can the UK expect to maintain its historically high living standards.

UK Trade and the EC: The effects of UK membership of the EC for trade in manufactures follow in part from the customs union aspects of the Community.

All tariffs on trade between the UK and other members were reduced to zero in 1977 when the UK adopted the final stages of the common external tariff (CET) on trade with non-Community countries. The discrimination which is now imposed against former Commonwealth countries (excluding signatories of the Lomé Convention)[2] and the associated loss of UK export preferences in the same countries must also be taken into account. Over the years 1963 to 1973, UK exports of manufactures to the EC increased at an

---

[1]   The hypothesis of hysteresis and the role of sunk costs in foreign trade were first studied by A.V.Dixit, 'Hysteresis, Import Penetration and Exchange Rate Pass Through', *QJE*, Vol. 104, No. 2, May 1989, pp. 205–27. A simplified account of Dixit's idea, as well as a more general review of pricing factors in international trade under floating exchange rates, is given by P.Krugman *Exchange Rate Instability*, (Cambridge, MIT Press, 1989), Chapter 2.

[2]   For additional details of the Lomé Convention, which grants tariff preference on exports to the EC of industrial products and some agricultural products from signatory developing countries, see C.H.Kirkpatrick, 'The Renegotiation of the Lomé Convention', *NWBQR*, May 1979, pp. 23–33.

average annual rate of 10.7%, while imports from the EC increased by 16.6%. Between 1973 and 1983, these average annual growth rates of trade in manufactures increased dramatically, with exports to the EC increasing by 21.1% and imports from the EC increasing by 19.1%. Since about 1987, the EC's share of UK merchandise trade has been more or less the same as the EC average share of trade with other member countries at between 50% and 55%.

As far as manufacturing trade performance is concerned, the most severe deterioration in the UK's balance of trade in manufactured goods has been with other EC countries. However, it would be simplistic to ascribe this deterioration to EC membership *per se*. As over 50% of the UK's visible trade is with other EC countries, it is inevitable that any fundamental deterioration in the UK's trade position would show up strongly in UK–EC trade, particularly as it is in this market that trade in manufactured goods is virtually free of restriction and therefore, in principle, most subject to forces of international competition. It is more likely that the deterioration in the UK's balance of manufactured trade with the EC is simply the most visible manifestation of the deeper-seated problems associated with price competitiveness and innovation discussed above.[1]

The EC generally forms a smaller but increasing share of the UK's trade in services, accounting for 29% of UK private-sector service credits and 40% of debits in 1990, the higher figure for debits being almost completely accounted for by UK residents' foreign travel within the EC. A major factor underlying the service position is the existence of various regulatory and other non-tariff barriers (discussed in section 3.3).

Such barriers are particularly evident in the financial services sector where the UK might be expected to have a comparative advantage over many of the other member countries. A major part of the Single European Market (SEM) programme involves the elimination through harmonization of the multifarious regulatory and non-tariff barriers to trade. It is recognized that financial services pose a special problem in this respect, and the June 1988 Capital Liberalization Directive aimed to liberalize all capital movements within the EC by June 1990, with special transitional arrangements for Greece, Ireland, Portugal and Spain. In principle the directive has the implication that a resident of one EC member country will have unrestricted access to banking services, stock exchanges, real estate and all financial services in other EC countries. However, the directive includes a safeguard clause similar to, but more circumscribed than, that in the original Treaty of Rome to allow individual countries to impose capital controls for up to six months to prevent disturbances to foreign-exchange markets and the balance of payments. Moreover, it is recognized that harmonization of

---

[1] For a detailed analysis of the impact of EC membership on UK manufacturing trade, see S. Dearon, 'EEC Membership and the United Kingdom's Trade in Manufactured Goods', *NWBQR*, February 1986.

regulatory rules for financial services is required prior to full implementation of the directive.

3.3 Trade Policy

Arguments for Free Trade and Protection: Trade policy is concerned, in the first instance, with the effects of tariffs and subsidies aimed at influencing the prices of exports and imports and thus the performance of exporting and import-competing industries. However, virtually any form of government intervention in the economy has some impact on the trading position. In this section we concentrate on policies which have as their primary purpose the influencing of international trade flows.

Even thus defined, trade policy is by no means confined to tariffs and subsidies on exports and imports but includes also import quotas, taxes and subsidies on domestic production, and taxes and subsidies on the use of labour and capital in different industries. Moreover, in recent years, government intervention in this area has become increasingly complex and ingenious. Subsidized export credit, differential treatment of foreign firms in bidding procedures for government contracts, the establishment of product quality standards which favour particular firms, and voluntary export restraints are all examples of differing forms of trade intervention aimed at securing a competitive advantage for particular groups of firms or industries. In general, most of these kinds of trade policy involve, to differing degrees, some element of protection for domestic industries.

The principles of comparative advantage suggest that interventions in the flow of trade are generally harmful both to the country imposing the intervention and, if several countries act or 'retaliate' in this way, to the world as a whole. The case for free trade is largely analogous to the case for *laissez-faire*. It enables each country to produce the goods in which it has a comparative cost advantage and thus to export products which it can produce relatively cheaply and import products which can be produced relatively cheaply elsewhere. Each individual country, and thus the world as a whole, benefits from this international specialization.

Nevertheless, countries have intervened in trade over the years in a wide variety of ways, the most common being the imposition of tariffs on imports. Under certain assumptions, an import tariff can be expected to raise real wages in the tariff-imposing country, even though national income, and therefore overall welfare, in that country will fall as a result.[1] More recently, arguments have been devised to show that individual countries can benefit

---

[1] This argument was originally set out by W.F.Stolper and P.A.Samuelson, 'Protection and Real Wages', *Review of Economic Studies*, Vol. 9, 1941, pp. 58–73. For a detailed study of arguments relating to the pros and cons of tariff protection, see W.M.Corden, *Trade Policy and Economic Welfare* (Oxford University Press, 1974).

from certain forms of protection.[1] These arguments stem from a recognition that most industries do not correspond to the perfectly competitive paradigm of the theory of comparative advantage. There are numerous examples of 'natural' monopolies or industries where economies of scale are such as to keep the number of firms in the industry relatively few in number. In these cases, firms in the industry typically earn more than normal profit, i.e. they receive an economic rent. Intuition and theory suggest that it may pay an individual country to protect a firm in such an industry so as to help secure a share in the worldwide economic rents to be earned in the industry.

A related argument is that certain industries create external economies in their operations, that is, their activities help reduce the costs of other firms. Knowledge-based high-technology industries are generally cited as examples of this phenomenon. 'Silicon Valley' and 'Route 128' computer firms are usually thought to benefit from their proximity to one another. Here, too, there is an argument for the protection of certain 'strategic' aspects of the activities of such industries which may be regarded as central to the operation of the industry as a whole but in which firms in the industry no longer enjoy a comparative advantage. Thus, local production of microchips is generally regarded as strategically important to American and European industry, even though other countries may well have a cost advantage in their production and thus, according to the theory of comparative advantage, should be the ones to specialize in their production.

Such strategic aspects of protection have been at the forefront of recent international discussions of trade policy. However, it should be emphasized that these strategic arguments rest on the idea that an individual country can gain from protection. It must be questioned whether such protection produces any worldwide benefits, or merely involves a transfer from one country to another.

Trade Policy in Practice: In the United Kingdom, tariff protection is circumscribed by UK membership of the EC and by membership of GATT. However, the influence of these bodies is different in that EC policy has concentrated on the removal of internal trade barriers to the extent that by 1977 industrial tariffs on intra-EC trade and EC trade with EFTA had been completely removed, but has equally acted as a trading block to maintain and, in some cases, expand the degree of protection afforded to EC-based activities against comparable activities located elsewhere, the prime example in this respect being the very high level of protection implicit in the CAP, discussed in more detail below.

In contrast, GATT is an international body founded in 1947 as a part of the international economic system which includes also the IMF and World Bank. By holding a succession of trade negotiations (called 'rounds'), GATT has succeeded over the years in bringing about an agreed, substantial

---

[1] For a comprehensive study of these arguments, see P.R.Krugman (ed.), *Strategic Trade Policy and the New International Economics* (MIT Press, 1986).

and worldwide reduction in the tariffs on industrial goods levied by all countries.[1] At the conclusion of the seventh (Tokyo) round of negotiations in 1979, the weighted average tariff on manufactured goods in the world's nine major industrial markets was reduced to about 4.7%. With the exception of some exemptions accorded to particular industries and, more generally, to developing-country imports of certain kinds of industrial products, it can be said that the world is now relatively free of industrial tariffs.

This does not, however, mean that there is no protection. First, agriculture remains highly protected, particularly by the EC, Japan and the USA. Second, textiles have repeatedly been exempt from the provisions of successive GATT agreements, exemptions which were formalized in the 1974 Multifibre Arrangement (MFA). Moreover, whilst the MFA in principle provided for the gradual liberalization of the textile trade, it has in practice ratified a relatively high level of protection and trade restraint for these industries, particularly in the industrial countries. Third, as tariffs have come down, a very wide range of non-tariff barriers of the kind mentioned above have been erected in their place, particularly on trade in services. The latest round of GATT – the Uruguay round – was scheduled to run from 1986 to end-1990 and had as its specific aim the freeing up of trade in these three problem areas. However, at the time of writing this chapter, the Uruguay round remains stalled, with numerous deadlines having been deferred, passed, and then reset.

It is not surprising that agreement on non-tariff barriers should prove elusive. Such barriers are easy to erect and defend as 'normal domestic practice' and, because each barrier is distinctive in certain ways, it will be exceedingly difficult to write an agreement which can cover any new devices which may be invented in the future. A good example of this problem is provided by the enforcement of domestic product quality standards. Such standards often have the clear effect of protecting domestic industries to the exclusion of cheaper import-substitutes and thus to the detriment of local consumers. However, quality standards often constitute an 'externality' in the production of goods. Consumers are invariably not equipped nor can they reasonably be equipped to determine if a product is of a certain quality. This provides a *prima facie* argument for official regulation in the provision and enforcement of quality standards. This means in practice that criticisms of one country's standards can easily appear arbitrary; it is not clear what basis can be used to assert that a particular standard is unjustifiably strict since it is put in place precisely to ensure that consumers obtain products of a particular quality.

Clearly this calls for some degree of international agreement on quality standards but this is a far more ambitious task than agreement on the level of a tariff. In fact, informal agreement on most of the matters before the GATT

---

[1] For a brief history of GATT and preliminary discussion of the current (Uruguay) round, see S.J.Anjaria, 'A new Round of Global Trade Negotiations', *FD*, 23:2, June 1986, pp.2–7.

was reached in 1991, but little progress was made on agriculture, with the USA, EC and Japan all calling for substantial cuts in each other's farm-support programmes while defending their own support policies, the main losers in this fiasco being the Cairns Group of agricultural producers,[1] more efficient third-world producers, and consumers worldwide who are compelled to pay unduly high prices for their food.

In considering the level of protection of an individual product, it must also be remembered that the actual tax or subsidy rate does not, on its own, measure the full extent of the protection which that product enjoys. In particular, import-competing goods which use imported inputs and raw materials can be protected in (at least) two ways: first, by the imposition of a tariff on imports of the product itself, but second, by a cut in the tariff or the imposition of a subsidy on imports of the inputs and raw materials used in its manufacture. Thus a logical tariff system needs to take account of the industrial structure of the economy. Protection of products which are widely used as intermediate inputs can easily result in negative protection (or 'dis-protection') of the wide range of goods for which the intermediate inputs are required.

The concept of 'effective protection' has been developed to measure the degree of protection afforded to an industry after allowing for tariffs and subsidies on intermediate inputs. Recognition of the industrial structure of an economy also gives rise to the principle of 'escalation', that is, that a rational tariff structure should involve increasing rates of tariff for goods which are relatively more highly processed, with the lowest tariff rates applying to commodities and raw materials.

Given our earlier discussion about the high degree of worldwide agricultural protection and relatively low degree of industrial protection, it will come as no surprise to learn that few countries have a rational tariff structure and the UK is no exception in this respect. The most recent study[2] of the tariff structure of the UK (for 1979) found some evidence of escalation overall. However, in 99 industry groups only 44 had an effective tariff rate in excess of the nominal tariff, while 53 had an effective tariff rate less than the nominal rate; the remaining two had equal nominal and effective rates. This means that for the 53 industries concerned, the nominal protection afforded by the tax on competing imports was partly or wholly offset by tariffs on intermediate inputs. The influence of agricultural protection was

---

[1] The fourteen countries of the Cairns group consist of Argentina, Australia, Brazil, Canada, Chile, Colombia, Fiji, Hungary, Indonesia, Malaysia, New Zealand, The Philippines, Thailand, and Uruguay. Together these countries account for some one-third of world farm trade, or about the same as the USA and EC combined. In general, these countries are more efficient producers and pay far lower levels of farm support than do the EC, Japan, or USA. The group was formed with the aim (*inter alia*) of achieving worldwide reductions in agricultural protection, particularly but not exclusively through the GATT.
[2] See D. Greenaway, 'Effective Tariff Protection in the United Kingdom', *BOUIES*, 50:3, 1988, pp. 311–24. The concept of the effective rate of protection was devised by W. M. Corden and is discussed in detail in W. M. Corden, *The Theory of Protection* (Oxford University Press, 1971).

particularly marked. Thus agriculture itself enjoyed a nominal tariff of 16.3% but an effective tariff of 47.3%. However, food-processing industries such as milk and meat slaughtering, while nominally enjoying a tariff of 7.5% and 5.8% respectively, actually experienced substantial disprotection through the high cost of their agricultural raw materials with effective tariff rates of −22.4% and −14.6% respectively, amounting to a net import subsidy.

These and similar figures highlight the underlying absurdity of a good deal of protection. In practice, protection is often granted to an industry on an ad hoc basis as the result of an industrial lobby aimed at protecting real wages in that industry. The overall effects of this protection, both direct and indirect, are rarely taken into account. The result is a system in which consumers pay higher prices than necessary for some products while industries, often only distantly connected to the original protective measures, are unable to compete in world markets because they too have to pay higher prices than necessary for their raw materials and other inputs.

The Common Agricultural Policy of the EC: The CAP system of agricultural price support has generally been reckoned to be the main source of costs imposed on the UK by EC membership. The original purpose of the CAP was to increase farm incomes, with the twin aims of preserving family farms and promoting rural industrialization. These goals can be achieved in different ways. Three are worth mentioning: direct income payments to farmers; producer price support through deficiency payments (the pre-entry UK system); and general price support by variable import and export taxes (the CAP). A detailed discussion of the relative merits of these schemes can be found elsewhere.[1] However, it is generally recognized that, on strict efficiency grounds, direct income payments are typically superior as they involve the smallest 'deadweight' loss.

In practice, governments throughout the world have intervened in agriculture with a variety of price support schemes. Under its pre-membership deficiency payments system, the UK imported and consumed foodstuffs at world prices and subsidized (less efficient) UK farmers out of general taxation. Under the CAP, a set of common EC farm prices is agreed annually. The prices of imports from non-EC countries are then brought up to EC prices by a system of variable import taxes. Likewise, EC food exports receive a variable subsidy.

The main economic differences between deficiency payments and the CAP are two in number. First, CAP taxes and subsidies impose a cost on more efficient non-EC producers. Second, EC consumers suffer a loss under the CAP through having to pay higher than world prices for their foodstuffs. Thus, as compared with deficiency payments, the CAP shifts the cost of price support from general taxation onto foreign producers and domestic

---

[1] See T. Josling, 'The Common Agricultural Policy of the European Economic Community', *Journal of Agricultural Economics*, May 1969, pp. 175–91.

consumers of foodstuffs. Given that the UK has a much smaller and mostly more efficient farm sector than other EC countries, it is easy to see why the UK should prefer a system of deficiency payments.

The cost of the CAP to the UK balance of payments and to EC consumers in general depends largely on the gap between EC prices and world market prices for foodstuffs, which varies over time. Since EC farm prices are set by an annual round of bargaining, they are far more stable over time than world prices.[1] Moreover, the EC bargaining process is such that it has proven much easier to raise intervention prices than to lower them. The fundamental fact is that, over more than two decades, EC intervention prices have almost always been above world market prices and often far above these prices.[2] The result has been substantial over-production of many commodities, much of which has had to be stockpiled, forming the notorious 'food mountains', the management of which imposes a further substantial burden on the Community.

Food stocks on this large scale are wasteful and absurd. The scale of intervention implied by the EC's farm policy is such that it has had a major impact not only on the EC's own budget but also on the overall structure of world trade. During the 1980s, expenditures on agriculture absorbed over 70% of the EC's total budget, and in 1987 Community expenditures were only kept within total revenues, thus avoiding a situation of technical bankruptcy, by postponing expenditures for price support until 1988. As far as world trade is concerned, the primary impact of EC food surpluses has been to depress world food prices, thus reducing production incentives and incomes in non-EC food-producing countries.[3] Many of these are poor developing countries which are dependent on a few key export crops, and have no resources to protect their own producers of these crops. Since 1980, the major industrial countries led by the EC have become substantial net food exporters, with both the former socialist bloc and the developing countries as a whole becoming net food importers.

It is sometimes argued that the CAP has contributed to an improvement in global 'food security' by increasing and stabilizing world food production levels. This is completely incorrect. The CAP has created food self-

---

[1] Agricultural price stability is not necessarily a desirable goal. See D.M.G.Newbury and J.E.Stiglitz, *The Theory of Commodity Price Stabilization* (Oxford University Press, 1981).
[2] In 1979–80, EC farm prices varied from 31% above the world level (sugar) to a staggering 311% above the world level (butter). Since 1980 the EC Commission has stopped publishing the information necessary to facilitate such comparisons. The administration of farm price support has been made particularly complicated because of the need to translate support prices into the different currencies of EC members. This has been achieved by the use of the so-called 'green currencies' which were discussed in detail in the 12th and earlier editions of this volume. See also C.Mackel, 'Green Money and the Common Agricultural Policy', *NWBR*, February 1978; and A.E.Buckwell *et al.*, *The Costs of the Common Agricultural Policy* (Croom Helm, 1982).
[3] For further discussion see M.J.Roarty, 'The Impact of the Common Agricultural Policy on Agricultural Trade and Development', *NWBQR*, February 1987, and J.Rosenblatt, T.Mayer, K.Bartholdy, D.Demekas, S.Gupta and L.Lipschitz, 'The Common Agricultural Policy of the European Community: Principle and Consequences', *IMF Occasional Paper* No.62, February 1988.

sufficiency in the EC, a very different concept from global food security. The low world prices resulting from the CAP have done substantial damage to the agriculture of developing countries and have contributed significantly to a decrease in global food security, reflected in the recurrence of famine conditions and malnutrition problems in these countries during the 1980s. It is true that the United States and Japan have also pursued protectionist policies towards their respective agricultures, but only in the EC has agricultural protection been pursued on such a scale. Overall, the record of events constitutes a damning indictment of EC agriculture policy, particularly over the last decade.

As long as the basic principles of the CAP are adhered to, the only options for reform are a sharp cut in EC support prices together with rules to link them more closely to subsequent changes in world food prices, and the imposition of limits on the amount of farm production which will receive support. Very little progress has been made in either direction. In general, the Community has been unable to agree on meaningful price cuts and has preferred instead, beginning in 1984, to rely on production quotas for sectors in surplus. Such quotas are only effective if backed up by sanctions against over-production. So far, few effective sanctions have been imposed. Following the budgetary crisis of 1987 the Council of Ministers agreed to a new package of farm and budgetary measures at the Brussels summit in February 1988. As far as agriculture is concerned, an overall ceiling was imposed on the growth in agricultural spending relative to the growth in the Community's GNP. However, it is not clear how the ceiling will be enforced. The 'Co-responsibility levy', a 3% tax on cereal production introduced in 1986, was extended to allow for a supplementary levy if production quotas are exceeded. For the first time, automatic price cuts were agreed for a range of products, notably cereals, when quotas are exceeded. In addition, a 'land set-aside' scheme was introduced to compensate farmers for withdrawing land from agricultural production. Finally, in a typically cosmetic 'reform', the cost of depreciating surplus farm stocks was transferred from the agriculture budget to the general budget of the Community.

While all but the last measure can be said to represent some progress on CAP reform, it is clear that until more vigorous action is taken, the CAP will continue to absorb a huge volume of resources in an extremely wasteful and damaging manner. Since the previous edition of this volume, little further progress has been made on CAP reform, with the EC unable to agree either on significant cuts in the level of support within the GATT or on any internal measure of structural reform to the support system as a whole.

The Single European Market (SEM): The SEM has its origins in proposals made by the President of the European Commission, Jacques Delors, when he took office in 1985, and set out in detail in June of that year.[1]

---

[1] 'Completing the Internal Market', White Paper from the Commission to the European Council, COM(85) 310 final, June 28 and 29, 1985.

The creation of a single European market was, of course, one of the central aims of the EC embodied in the Treaty of Rome. Internal tariffs on industrial goods were largely eliminated by 1977, but there remain numerous obstacles to trade within the community. First, in the industrial sector, individual countries have adopted numerous special arrangements to protect their own industries. Second, the agricultural sector remains subject to internal restrictions because of the complexities of the CAP. However, the June 1985 White Paper focused on other restrictions, notably non-tariff barriers of the kind highlighted in section 3.3. Four in particular were singled out. First are inter-country differences in technical regulations and quality standards. Second are frontier delays and administrative burdens imposed on goods in transit. Third are restrictions on competition for public-sector contracts, which in practice favour home-country firms. Fourth are restrictions on trade in services, particularly financial services, which inhibit firms from setting up in other EC countries.

The White Paper set out a comprehensive programme of liberalization measures (300 in all) which are required for completion of the SEM, with a timetable calling for full implementation by the end of 1992. The liberalization programme consists of three main components: the removal of physical barriers to movements of goods and people; the removal of technical barriers covering quality standards, public procurement, and regulation; and finally the removal of fiscal barriers.

These proposals would, if implemented, involve major changes in the organization of the EC economies. Differential technical and quality standards are pervasive throughout the EC. The Commission's proposals imply, for example, that goods produced to a certain standard in one EC country could not be denied importation by another EC member on grounds of different standards. Likewise, the college degrees and other professional qualifications earned in one EC country would be accepted for all recognized purposes in other EC countries. Fiscal harmonization is implied by the free movement of goods and services. VAT rates, in particular, differ widely within the Community. At present, EC countries impose border restrictions to prevent tax avoidance by limiting the importation of goods purchased tax paid in other EC countries. If border checks are abolished, such restrictions cannot be enforced and, in the absence of VAT harmonization, consumers will have an incentive to cross frontiers to purchase goods, especially high-value consumer durables, in the low-tax countries of the Community.

An analogy is often drawn with the United States where different states maintain different sales tax rates but, to prevent tax avoidance, differences in rates between contiguous states have to be relatively small – no more than about 5%. This is in contrast to the EC where VAT rates vary from zero on selected items in the UK up to 38% on various consumer durables in Italy. The Commission proposed a set of uniform rates for 1992, with the standard rate between 14–20% and a reduced rate for an agreed list of basic items of 4–9%. Member states would be free to choose their VAT rates within these bands. Comparable proposals were made for excise duties. These proposals highlight the reduction in the fiscal autonomy of individual states which is implicit in the move towards a single market. As yet, they have not proved acceptable to individual EC members.

Nevertheless, progress towards the SEM has been more rapid than would have appeared possible in 1985. Several reasons can be advanced for this. First, the Single European Act (SEA) ratified by member governments in 1985 and coming into effect on 1 July 1987 represented the most significant amendment so far to the Treaty of Rome. The SEA not only codifies the main principles of the SEM in the form of legislation passed in all member countries, but it also makes some significant changes to the decision-making procedures within the Council of Ministers, involving a reduction in the blocking powers of individual members and a greater reliance on majority voting. Moreover, about two-thirds of the measures proposed by the Commission for the SEM are covered by these new arrangements. Second, in addition to the activities of the Commission in promoting the SEM, the 1988 Brussels agreement, despite its unsatisfactory nature, nevertheless represented a measure of progress on budgetary and agricultural matters and enabled member states to turn their attention to the SEM. Third, the Commission produced a major study of the costs and benefits of the creation of the SEM (the Cecchini Report).[1] This argued that considerable benefits would flow from the completion of the internal market: between ECU 70bn and ECU 190bn of static welfare gains, equivalent to between $2\frac{1}{2}\%$ and $6\frac{1}{2}\%$ of the EC's 1988 GDP; an increase in the potential growth rate of the Community by about 1% p.a.; the creation of some 2 million additional jobs in the Community; and a fall in consumer prices of as much as 6%.

These considerations have given a considerable impetus to the move towards the SEM and it seems clear that the Community will increasingly enjoy a freer flow of goods, services, labour and capital than before, even though this will not necessarily all take place from 1992. However, it also seems likely that liberalization will be less than originally envisaged by the Commission. First, the economic arguments for liberalization are subject to important qualifications. In principle, it is clear that the standard arguments for freer trade are applicable to the SEM and benefits are likely to flow therefrom.[2]

---

[1] A version of the report for the general reader was published as P. Cecchini (ed.), *The European Challenge 1992: The Benefits of a Single Market* (Gower Press, 1988). A more technical report containing detailed economic analysis was published as 'The Economics of 1992: An Assessment of the Potential Economic Effects of Completing the Internal Market of the European Communities', in *European Economy*, No. 35, March 1988. Reports commissioned on individual sectors were published in a sixteen-volume series by the EC entitled *Research on the Cost of Non-Europe*. Finally, the May 1988 (No. 36) issue of *European Economy* was given over to a report on 'The Creation of a European Financial Area' which concentrated in particular on the implications of free movement of capital and financial services within the EC.

[2] A few independent studies have broadly confirmed the qualitative direction of the Cecchini Report's findings but not necessarily its quantitative estimates. See, for example, L. A. Winters, *Completing the European Internal Market*, CEPR Discussion Paper No. 222.

However, there are many areas in which unrestricted trade is recognized not to be the best option. Financial services are a case in point where some degree of regulation is desirable to ensure that consumers can make an informed choice among the services on offer, and also to help prevent or to minimize the costs of bankruptcy if the management of a financial institution is either incompetent or incurs excessive risks in its investment policies. The costs of inappropriate liberalization in such areas are difficult to measure but are nevertheless real, and the Commission's calculations do not take them into account. The second factor likely to slow progress towards the SEM is that EC governments have so far been reluctant to give up any degree of sovereignty over their national affairs and it is clear that full implementation of the SEM will involve a greater loss of national sovereignty in certain key areas than has hitherto been conceded. As yet it is too early to say how complete will be the implementation of the SEM, but it is already clear that movement towards the SEM has provided a major impetus to greater integration in the Community both in the private and the public sectors.

3.4 Britain and the EC Budget

Finally in the current account, we turn to transfers; the most important and certainly the most (politically) controversial item in this respect being those involving UK contributions to and receipts from the EC budget. The EC budget is financed from the 'own resources' of the Community, which consist of all import duties and agricultural levies from non-EC sources (less 10% to cover costs of collection and administration), plus a VAT contribution which in January 1986 was raised from the equivalent of a 1% to a 1.4% rate of VAT levied on a uniform basis in the Community. The contribution to own resources is known as the 'gross contribution', the 'net contribution' being the gross contribution less receipts from the budget in the form of regional aid, agricultural support and the like.

For the UK, the fundamental problem is that structural features of the economy mean that its net budget contribution will be large and positive for the foreseeable future. The fact that the UK is relatively dependent on food imports from (more efficient) non-EC (mainly Commonwealth) producers enhances her gross contribution, while the small size and greater efficiency of her agricultural sector mean that receipts from the agricultural funds are relatively small. At the same time, because CAP expenditures are so large relative to other expenditures, the UK cannot expect to receive significant compensating benefits from these other programmes.

Between 1980 and 1984, negotiations took place aimed at securing for the UK a special system of rebates. These culminated in agreement at the June 1984 Fontainebleau summit, which confirmed a series of cash rebates to the UK for the years 1980 to 1984. Since 1985 the UK has received annual cash rebates equivalent to 66% of the gap between UK VAT payments to the Community and EC expenditures in the UK, and these rebates will continue at least until a further increase in EC revenues, to 1.6% of member states' VAT income, is agreed. The UK's rebates are financed by other member states according to their relative shares of the EC's VAT income although, exceptionally, Germany contributes two-thirds of its share.

Although the Fontainebleau summit effectively settled the matter of the UK's budgetary contribution, the agreement to increase overall budgetary contributions was immediately overtaken by the inexorable rise in farm spending which produced the budgetary crisis of 1987. The February 1988 Brussels agreement called for the introduction of a 'fourth resource' for EC revenues with national contributions based on GDPs of member states. At the same time, a ceiling was placed on the size of the base used to calculate a country's VAT-related budget contribution. However, the major budgetary proposal involved a new formula for determining Community expenditures; these will now be subject to an overall ceiling of 1.2% of EC GDP. This will permit the budget to rise to an estimated ECU 52.7bn at 1988 prices in 1992 (equivalent to £34.2bn) compared with ECU 44.1bn in 1988, representing a 19.5% increase over the four years. In addition, it was agreed that 'structural funds' for general economic assistance to poorer regions of the EC would be sharply increased over the same period. However, the principal measure was a substantial increase in expenditures, the revenue burden of which will be borne largely by the new 'fourth resource'.

The main positive feature of these changes is a move towards the use of 'objective indicators' to guide the expenditure and revenue contributions of member states. On the debit side, there are still no real signs of effective expenditure control measures, and thus no clear mechanism, other than further tortuous ministerial meetings, to ensure that the new ceilings on expenditures including that for agriculture will not be breached.

The Brussels agreement also introduced five-year budget planning. Although this provides for greater stability and less frequent wrangling within the EC, it also helps to postpone reform measures. The EC Commission's budgetary proposals for 1992–7 announced in February 1992 call for an increase in the ceiling on Community spending from 1.2% of EC GDP to 1.35% or 1.4%. The share of spending on agriculture (excluding that shifted to the general budget) would fall from about 54% of the total in 1992 to about 47% in 1997, although total farm spending in ECU terms would still increase. The structural funds would be the main beneficiary of the budget increase.

These proposals offer little encouragement for the future. Effectively the EC appears content to let the share of farm spending in the budget decline gradually as the overall budget is increased. As the Community makes progress towards monetary integration, EC institutions will become increasingly important in determining overall fiscal policy, and the reforms of the budget and the budget process itself will become increasingly necessary if the EC is to avoid becoming entrenched in a cycle of patched-up last-minute deals which have increasingly characterized the American budget process in recent years. This would be a very poor model for the EC to follow.

4 THE CAPITAL ACCOUNT

4.1 Portfolio and Direct Investment

Influences on Overseas Investment: Recent data as well as longer-term trends in the capital account as a whole have already been presented in Tables 3.1 and 3.3. In this section, we examine in more detail the main influences on portfolio and direct investment and consider some of the possible costs and benefits of such investments.

From the viewpoint of individual investors the main forces governing overseas portfolio and direct investment are not likely to be qualitatively very different from those governing domestic investment, with the overriding factor in decisions to invest being the anticipated rate of return on the project or security relative to the cost of any funds which have to be borrowed to finance the investment and relative to the perceived riskiness of the investment. In this calculation, investors will obviously be comparing the prospective risks and returns of overseas investments with those of alternative domestic investment opportunities.

In practice, the calculation for overseas investment is more complex than that for domestic investment. Beginning with portfolio investment, investors do not only have to evaluate the prospects of the company in which they are investing but also, to some extent, the overall prospects for the particular foreign economy in which the company operates, especially for interest rates, as these are likely to affect the performance of the stock market on which the shares of the company are quoted, and this in turn will have an impact on the share price of the individual company itself. Movements in the exchange rate also affect the return on overseas investment, with a depreciation of sterling increasing the sterling rate of return of a foreign currency investment, and vice-versa. For direct investment the calculations are more complex still, as foreign countries typically impose different rules and regulations on company investment activities covering matters as diverse as taxation, quality control, employment standards, and information disclosure requirements.

All these factors impose both costs and benefits. Indeed, to a large extent, foreign direct investment is just one mechanism by which modern corporations seek to gain competitive advantages over their rivals by siting their production, administration and marketing activities in a combination of locations designed to take maximum advantage of differential tariffs, investment incentives, wage levels, and demand conditions for their products. Direct investment must also be considered in relation to exporting and foreign licensing of its products as just one of several ways by which a firm can extract maximum advantage from its knowledge and human capital base.[1]

---

[1] Cf. R.E.Caves, 'International Corporations: The Industrial Economics of Foreign Investment', *Economica*, Vol. 38, 1971, pp. 1–27.

Overseas investment may also be constrained by regulation, and UK overseas investment was strictly regulated by exchange controls until their abolition in 1979. Exchange-control abolition produced a clear and relatively unambiguous effect on portfolio investment. Outward portfolio investment, largely by financial institutions such as unit trusts and pension funds, rose steeply from £0.96bn in 1979 to £3.3bn in 1980 and it reached £22.1bn in 1986. Many fund managers reported that their activities corresponded to a once-for-all portfolio adjustment to bring overseas assets to the desired proportion in their portfolio following which the outflow would level off.[1] In fact, there was no sign of any such levelling off until 1987 when the gross outflow was dramatically reversed, with UK residents repatriating a net £7.26bn of portfolio investment. Since then, outward portfolio investment has fluctuated without any clear trend. To the extent that there was a substantially increased outflow following exchange-control abolition, it can be concluded that this policy was successful in helping to limit the oil effect on the sterling exchange rate and widening the ambit of profitable investment opportunities for UK residents.

The impact of exchange-control abolition on outward direct investment is harder to quantify because the practical effect of the controls in this area was less severe. The main implication of abolition is that firms face a wider range of financing options than before – they can either borrow from abroad or within the UK; or they can use retained earnings from abroad or from the UK. Outward direct investment actually fell from £5.9bn in 1979 to £4.9bn in 1980; it varied between £4.0bn and £9.0bn per annum between 1979 and 1985 before rising sharply after 1985, reaching a high of £21.5bn in 1989, and then falling to £11.7bn in 1990. It is probably reasonable to conclude that direct investment was stimulated by exchange-control abolition, but the exact magnitude of the stimulus must remain a matter for debate.

Other structural factors influencing the portfolio and direct investment position include North Sea oil, whose implications were considered in detail in section 1.5, and UK membership of the EC. The influence of EC membership on UK direct investment is again difficult to quantify with any precision. Of the total stock of UK direct investment assets in the mid-1970s, it has been estimated that 28% was located in Western Europe and 23% in North America, compared to 1962 figures of 13% in Western Europe and 23% in North America, suggesting a trend of increasing investment in Western Europe.[2] However, more recent balance-of-payments data show that during the ten years 1974–83 only 8% of total outward direct investment flows went to Western Europe, with 51% going to North America. In the seven years 1984–90, the rate of direct investment in Western Europe was stepped up to 20.7% of the total outward flow. Over this period, too, there was a marked

---

[1] See 'The Effects of Exchange Control Abolition on Capital Flows', *BEQB*, September 1981.
[2] For further details, see J.H.Dunning, 'The UK's International Direct Investment Position in the Mid-1970s', *LBR*, April 1978.

increase in European direct investment in the UK, with a total of £22.6bn of other EC countries' direct investment in the UK compared to £20.6bn of UK investment in the rest of the EC.

Any explanation for these flows must be very tentative in nature. One possibility is that a major motive for outward investment is for large firms to avoid tariffs and other import restrictions imposed by the host country. On this interpretation, the dismantling of such barriers within the EC largely obviated the need for UK firms to invest in other EC countries, and provided incentives for them to concentrate their foreign investment activities instead in non-EC markets where barriers to imports may be more important. The more recent surge in investment in the EC and by the EC in the UK could, in turn, be associated with the progressive dismantling of internal barriers in the EC in the formation of the SEM. However, these two explanations are, to some extent, in conflict with one another and the exact reasons must await more detailed analysis.

Costs and Benefits of Overseas Investment: Historically, foreign investment has been the subject of debate in the UK, one strand of thinking arguing that investment overseas has an adverse effect on the UK economy because it creates jobs in overseas countries rather than in the UK, while at the same time producing balance-of-payments pressures through the outflow of funds associated with the investment activity. While it is obviously correct that overseas investment helps create overseas jobs, it is far from being the case that this is the only effect of such investments or, as a result, that overseas investment harms the UK economy. In fact, to consider the full costs and benefits of overseas investment, it is necessary to take account of its overall effects both on the balance of payments and the domestic economy as well as of the opportunities open to domestic investors.

First, under a floating exchange rate, overseas investment by UK firms tends to depress the sterling exchange rate because of the outflow of funds which is implied. On the one hand, there are circumstances in which a relative depreciation of the exchange rate is desirable and cannot easily be brought about by other means. Indeed, as we saw in section 2.4, this was exactly the situation in the early 1980s when North Sea oil production and high oil prices were placing strong upward pressures on the currency. At that time, the strong portfolio outflow of funds was desirable as a way of relieving the upward pressure on the exchange rate. More generally, it can be argued that a steady flow of net overseas investment is a sensible method of keeping the exchange rate lower than would otherwise be the case and thus helps to maintain the price competitiveness of British exports and import-competing industries.

Second, it is often argued that foreign direct investment leads directly to a fall in exports and a rise in imports because output which could have been produced in the UK is now produced overseas. This argument presumes that the output could have been produced profitably in the UK, and in many instances, the structure of costs, availability of raw materials and other factors mean that this is not the case. If the project could not be carried out profitably in the UK, it is sensible for British firms to undertake the investment overseas because the profit will subsequently accrue to UK residents.

Third, in practice, foreign investment may well be complementary to exports rather than competitive with them. An overseas investment project may generate UK exports in the form of the plant and equipment needed to set up the project or in the form of exports of semi-finished goods required to run the plant.

Clearly these factors are complex, and quantifying them is not easy. Available evidence does indicate that on balance UK overseas investment does not adversely affect the UK economy.[1] More generally, the proposition that the UK should not invest overseas runs contrary to the principles of comparative advantage. If taken to extreme, the proposition could easily imply that the UK ought to attempt self-sufficiency in all areas of the economy – clearly an absurd and exceedingly wasteful proposal.

Ultimately, foreign investment should satisfy many of the same criteria as domestic investment, that is: it should be profitable. If UK firms cannot find profitable investment opportunities in the UK then, prima facie, if they can find such opportunities abroad they should exploit them. In this connection, an argument can reasonably be made that the restructuring associated with North Sea oil and oil-related industries combined with a high pound placed a severe squeeze on profit opportunities elsewhere in the UK and must have encouraged a relative outflow of funds.

Rough calculations of rates of return on domestic and overseas investment as well as on overseas investment in the UK are given in Table 3.7. We have already emphasized the variable quality of capital-account data and the change in recording procedures following exchange-control abolition which makes the pre-1979 figures conceptually different from the post-1979 figures. Thus the data in Table 3.7 can be regarded as no more than indicative in nature. These data suggest that the return on UK direct investment has been of a comparable magnitude to, and generally (and in the eighties, substantially) in excess of, the domestic earnings yield on UK equities, the appropriate benchmark for comparison. Likewise, portfolio investment has earned a rate broadly comparable to the UK dividend yield. For overseas investment in the UK, it is no surprise that portfolio investment earns a rather higher return than the dividend yield on equities, as a relatively high

---

[1]   The seminal study is by W.B.Reddaway, *The Effects of UK Direct Investment Overseas* (interviews and final report), Cambridge University Press, 1968. This study has been partially updated and the new results are summarized in D.Shepherd, 'Assessing the Consequences of Overseas Investment', *RBSR*, No. 152, December 1986. See also E.J.Pentecost, 'A Model of UK Non-Oil ICC's Direct Investment', *Bank of England Discussion Paper*, No. 30, November 1987.

TABLE 3.7

Rates of Return on Domestic and Overseas Assets, 1978–90

	1978	1981	1984	1987	1990
	Year average : % per annum				
Calculated Rates of Return[1]					
UK Direct Investment Overseas	13.18	16.32	13.54	13.27	13.73
UK Portfolio Investment Overseas	4.60	5.18	6.04	3.71	3.66
Overseas Direct Investment in the UK	14.22	17.81	16.88	13.90	7.75
Overseas Portfolio Investment in the UK	7.38	9.94	8.40	7.37	6.59
Market Rate of Return					
UK Equities: Earnings Yield	16.47	12.12	10.76	8.98	11.70
UK Equities: Dividend Yield	5.65	6.23	4.66	3.73	5.28
UK Government Bonus: Flat Yield on consols	11.92	12.99	10.15	9.31	10.84
	Year-end to year-end = % p.a.				
Depreciation (+)/Appreciation (−) of the pound	1.79	10.36	11.94	−9.54	8.95

Sources: Pink Book, ET.

[1] Calculated as the ratio of the current year flow of earnings (IPD account) to the stock of assets outstanding at the end of the previous year (Net External Assets Account).

proportion of such investment is in UK government bonds. It is, however, more surprising that overseas direct investment in the UK has (with the exception of 1990) earned a somewhat higher return than UK investment overseas, although this could be due to the fact that a substantial part of such investment has been in the relatively profitable North Sea oil industries. It could also reflect a possible under-recording of inward direct investment in recent years. Exchange-rate changes also affect the return on overseas investment and the generally downward movement in sterling since 1981 has served to increase the realized sterling rate of return on overseas investments over the long run because the sterling value of investments denominated in foreign currencies rises as the exchange rate depreciates, producing sterling gains for UK investors.

4.2   Other Capital Transactions

The remaining items in the capital account consist chiefly of two components. First, those involving bank loans and deposits, representing either the business of UK residents with overseas banks or, more commonly, the business of overseas residents with UK banks, and second, transactions (some of which are included in banking transactions) which are related to the finance of foreign trade.

Short-term capital movements have traditionally played an important role in the overall UK balance-of-payments situation. Some short-term capital movements reflect changes in the sterling balances which foreign governments and individuals have acquired as matters of commercial and financial convenience. (These correspond to line A10 in Table 3.1 on page 151: Foreign Authorities' sterling reserves.) The remainder reflect the role of

London as the major centre for the Eurocurrency, Eurobond and other international financial markets, with banks in the UK lending and borrowing extensively in dollars and other currencies. The development of the Eurocurrency markets since 1958 has meant the increasing integration of European and American capital and money markets.[1] The volume of deposits and the ease with which they may be switched between currencies have important implications for the stability of exchange rates and the conduct of national monetary policies.

The significance of short-term capital flows for the conduct of UK policy arises from their magnitude relative to the official reserves and from their volatility. It is convenient, though artificial, to divide these flows into two broad classes: speculative and non-speculative. The motive behind speculative capital flows is one of making a capital gain from anticipated movements in spot exchange rates or interest rates. A risk-neutral currency speculator would be indifferent between holding sterling- or dollar-denominated assets, for example, if the interest rate on sterling assets equalled the interest rate on dollar assets plus the anticipated depreciation of sterling relative to the dollar. (This is equivalent to uncovered interest parity.) If the anticipated sterling devaluation exceeds the sterling interest advantage, holders of sterling assets will switch their assets into dollars while UK importers will accelerate (lead) dollar payments for imports and UK exporters will try to delay (lag) dollar payments due from foreigners.

Non-speculative activities are undertaken to avoid the risk of capital gains or losses associated with exchange-rate movements, and typically involve simultaneous transactions in both spot and forward currency markets so that the risks associated with currency transactions may be shifted onto speculators.[2] In sum, short-term capital movements depend on a complex set of interactions between national interest rates, spot and forward exchange rates, and expectations of future changes in spot rates.

With floating exchange rates, the impact effect of a net capital flow falls directly upon the spot exchange rate: a capital outflow will tend to depreciate sterling, and an inflow to appreciate sterling. Moreover, any such change in the exchange rate acts upon the current account in the same way as a policy-induced parity change. Hence, a capital inflow which generates an appreciation also has the effect of discouraging exports, encouraging imports, and depressing the inflation rate. With a fixed exchange rate, a speculative outflow necessitates official intervention to maintain the exchange rate. This in turn leads to a loss of central bank reserves and, to the extent that sterilization is impossible, a reduction in the money supply, putting downward pressures on domestic prices and incomes.

---

[1] Eurocurrency deposits are bank deposits in currencies other than that of the country in which the bank in question is located. For the working and development of the Eurocurrency markets, consult R.B.Johnston, *The Economics of the Euro-Market* (Macmillan, 1983). See also 'Eurobanks and the Inter-Bank Market', *BEQB*, September 1981.
[2] For a more detailed treatment, see R.MacDonald, *op. cit.*

It should be clear, therefore, that large, sudden capital flows can provide difficult policy problems for economies both under floating and fixed exchange rates. Until 1979 the UK attempted to exert some direct influence over capital flows using exchange controls, but the history of the post-1945 era shows that these controls were almost completely ineffectual in preventing periodic short-term speculative outflows from and inflows to sterling (although the controls did restrain longer-term flows, as discussed in section 4.1). Following exchange control abolition in October 1979, the capital and money markets of the UK became fully integrated with those of the rest of the world, and the main weapon for influencing capital flows is now the manipulation of domestic interest rates. This has already been discussed in some detail in section 2.

By far the most significant structural elements influencing short-term capital movements for much of the 1970s and 1980s were the abrupt movements in oil prices and the associated changes in the lending capacity of OPEC nations. UK banks played an important role in the so-called 're-cycling of petro-currencies'. Thus, UK and other international banks borrowed OPEC funds in dollars, sterling and other currency denominations, and re-lent them, mainly to foreign governments and international companies. The global issues involved in recycling are summarized in section 5. The more immediate impact of recycling from the UK's point of view was that it produced a mushrooming in the foreign (and mostly foreign currency) business of UK banks.

The scale of this business is worth emphasizing. As of June 1991, the total of all countries' commercial bank foreign liabilities outstanding in all currencies reported to the IMF was US$6554bn. UK-based banks' share of this total was US$1072bn, or 16% (including foreign banks operating in the UK), compared with the USA's share of 1% and Japan's share of 13%. The exact figures fluctuate from month to month as exchange rates change, but these are broadly representative. Borrowing and lending abroad by commercial banks do not in and of themselves affect the balance of payments and the exchange rate except to the extent that they generate bank profits and to the extent that total borrowing and lending are not equal to one another. UK banks typically have a mismatch between their foreign assets and liabilities which is significantly larger (particularly in proportion to the share of the home economy) than is that of banks operating in the USA or Japan. Thus, in June 1991, UK banks' foreign liabilities exceeded their foreign assets by US$111bn, or 10% of foreign liabilities. Banks in the USA had net foreign liabilities of US$47bn, while banks in Japan had net foreign assets of US$14bn. Changes in net foreign liabilities may help to finance a balance-of-payments deficit but the size of the imbalance between assets and liabilities for the UK also creates the potential for disruptive flows across the foreign exchanges, if foreign residents withdraw short-term deposits from UK commercial banks.

5   THE INTERNATIONAL FINANCIAL SYSTEM

The International Monetary Fund: If the quarter-century from 1945 had one dominant characteristic in the international economic arena, it was the integration of national commodity and capital markets into a unified and rapidly growing system of world trade and investment. A key role in this process was played by the international financial rules established at the Bretton Woods conference of 1944, the supervisory institution of which is the International Monetary Fund (IMF).

The principal features of the Bretton Woods system were its emphasis on international co-operation and its creation of a system of fixed but adjustable exchange rates, the Par Value System, together with the provision of temporary and conditional balance-of-payments finance by the IMF to assist the adjustment process. Under the Par Value System the world as a whole, and industrial countries in particular, enjoyed a period of unprecedented expansion in trade and prosperity. Nevertheless, the system itself was subject to increasing strain, culminating in August 1971, when the US Government announced that the US dollar was no longer convertible into gold. In June 1972 the pound sterling was floated and, by April 1973, the exchange rates of all the major currencies were floating independently of their par values. Since then, the world has been operating a system of relatively flexible exchange rates.

Throughout the postwar era the IMF has remained at the centre of the international monetary system with its role being progressively modified following the abandonment of the par value system. During this process, the IMF has acquired a number of the functions of a putative world central bank but it would be a considerable exaggeration to claim that the IMF does actually act as a world central bank. Although the IMF's role of supervising par value adjustments disappeared after 1971, subsequent events proved that international co-operation on monetary and exchange-rate matters was, if anything, more important under flexible exchange rates than under the par value system, and the IMF was able to act as the forum through which international monetary co-operation could be co-ordinated. Thus, after a period of hiatus in the early seventies, the IMF has re-emerged as the central body in the international monetary system, albeit with a modified role as compared with the Bretton Woods era.

As of end-1991, the IMF consisted of 155 member countries including all the industrialized and developing nations of the world.[1] In addition, nearly all the former socialist bloc countries had either already attained membership (e.g. China) or were in the process of moving towards membership (e.g. the Commonwealth countries of the former Soviet Union). The basis for a good deal of Fund activity, including in particular country voting rights and amounts of IMF loans for which a country is eligible, is the quota of each

---

[1]   For full details on the IMF the reader should consult the annual 'Supplement on the Fund' published each September in the *IMF Survey*.

country in the Fund. This is expressed in Special Drawing Rights (SDRs), a composite currency discussed more fully below, and it constitutes the country's subscription to the IMF, the total of all subscriptions being equivalent to the capital of the IMF. Each country's quota must be subscribed 25% in SDRs and the remaining 75% in the member's own currency. The size of a country's quota is determined largely by an objective formula based on indicators such as population, GNP, and role in world trade, but also to some extent by a process of bargaining among member countries.

Quota sizes and formulae are reviewed every 5 years when the overall size of the IMF's capital is also reviewed. The last quinquennial review, which was adopted in May 1990, called for an overall 48% increase in quotas from SDR 91.1bn to SDR 135.2bn, and it proposed consideration of a third amendment to the IMF's articles to provide for the suspension of voting and other rights of members who do not fulfil their obligations under the articles, particularly in respect of the repayment of IMF borrowing. By end-December 1991 a majority of members had agreed to both proposals, but these members had existing quotas which amounted to less than the 85% of total IMF quotas required to make any of the proposed new quotas effective, and they excluded most notably the USA. Moreover, with the application for IMF membership of all the constituent countries of the former Soviet Union, it seems clear that the proposed quota increases will not be adequate to fund the IMF's prospective lending operations in the 1990s, and a further review of quotas may prove necessary ahead of the current schedule which calls for a review by March 1993.

There are three major aspects to the IMF's work, namely: the provision of an international reserve currency, the SDR; the provision of lending facilities to assist countries in balance-of-payments difficulties; and acting as a forum for debate on international monetary matters, with its concomitant mechanisms for surveillance of the international monetary policies pursued by member states.

Special Drawing Rights (SDRs):   SDRs are a composite international currency created in 1970, and analogous to but predating the ECU. The total allocation of SDRs is reviewed by the IMF on a regular but not a prescribed basis, and the allocation is increased as agreement is reached by IMF members on the need for an expansion in this particular source of supply of international liquidity. Thus far, there have been six SDR allocations totalling SDR 21.4bn, the most recent being in January 1981, since when a number of unsuccessful attempts have been made to reach agreement on a seventh allocation. Each country is assigned a net cumulative allocation of SDRs, in proportion to its allocation in the general account of the IMF, and can treat this allocation as 'owned reserves' to finance payments imbalances. A country in deficit, for example, may use its SDR quota to purchase needed foreign exchange from other countries.

The fundamental question surrounding the SDR has always been that of whether SDRs simply co-exist with other reserve assets, or whether they are destined to replace gold and foreign exchange, or both, as the reserve base of the system. In the initial arrangements, SDRs were effectively a gold substitute and carried a notional rate of interest on net holdings of 1.5%. Since the abandonment of the par-value system, however, the arrangements for SDRs have been progressively revised to extend the range of trans-actions for which they could be used. With effect from the Seventh General Increase in Quotas in 1980, members contributed 25% of their additional quota in SDRs and, from 1981, the SDR interest rate was set at an average of short-term interest rates in the financial centres of the five countries with the largest SDR holdings, and its valuation was based on a basket of the currencies of the same five countries. Finally, a multitude of developments have taken place, extending the right to hold SDRs to non-member organiz-ations and legalizing the use of SDRs for currency swaps and forward transactions.[1]

Despite these developments, SDRs have declined in importance as there has been no new allocation and, by November 1991, they accounted for only 3% of total world reserves (excluding gold). The main mechanism proposed for enhancing the role of the SDR is the introduction of a Substitution Account at the IMF, in which members would deposit currency reserves in return for SDRs. Thus far, however, little progress has been made with this idea.[2] Unless the Substitution Account or any similar idea is implemented, the SDR is likely to continue to play a relatively minor role in international monetary affairs other than as a convenient international unit of account. Indeed, in the last two decades, the growth in reserves has generated periodic fears of there being excess liquidity rather than a shortage. Judged by conventional criteria, these fears appear rather exaggerated. Thus, in the period 1979 to 1990 (the latest date for which comparable figures are available) world international reserves (valued in SDRs and excluding gold) increased at an average rate of 7.3% p.a. However, world imports grew at an average annual rate of 8% over the same period. As world reserves amounted to only 2.7 months of world imports in 1979, these (imperfect) data suggest that world reserves are, if anything, too low. Nevertheless, the failure of Fund members to agree on a new SDR allocation since 1981, despite the urging of the IMF itself, indicate that fears of excess liquidity and its role as a possible cause of world inflation are still uppermost in the minds of national governments, particularly in the major industrial countries.

IMF Lending Facilities: Lending facilities provide the framework within which the IMF provides assistance to countries in balance-of-payments deficit. Underlying this assistance is the fundamental principle of con-ditionality, which simply means that in providing assistance the IMF must be

---

1 IMF *Annual Report*, 1988. The total number of prescribed 'other holders' is currently 16.
2 Cf. 'The Proposed Substitution Account in the IMF', *MBR*, Winter 1979, and P.B.Kenen, 'The Analytics of a Substitution Account', *Banca Nazionale del Lavoro*, Quarterly Review, December 1981.

assured that countries are pursuing policies consistent with the provisions of the Fund's Articles of Agreement. These policies have often provoked controversy in borrowing countries for being unduly restrictive. However, it must be remembered that IMF assistance is intended primarily to be relatively short term, repayable within three to five years except as discussed below, and the elimination of a balance-of-payments deficit within this or any other period necessarily involves a cut in national expenditures relative to national income and hence some fall in the domestic standard of living.

As well as involving conditionality, Fund Lending is provided in tranches expressed as percentages of the size of a member's quota, which thus governs the amount of borrowing a country may have outstanding at any time. In the so-called 'reserve tranche', members are entitled to draw up to 25% of their quota automatically without incurring any conditionality. Further drawings incur different degrees of conditionality depending both on the amounts involved and the facility under which they are drawn. Under the Fund's credit tranche policies, members can borrow successive amounts in tranches of 25% of quota up to a cumulative maximum of 100% of quota. Countries may also borrow under the IMF's buffer stock facility which helps finance contributions to an approved international buffer stock, and under its Compensatory and Contingency Financing Facility (CCFF) which was expanded in 1988 to provide special assistance to countries pursuing Fund-supported programmes in addition to its previous function of providing loans to countries in compensation for shortfalls in export revenues and/or excesses in the cost of cereal imports.

Until 1971, these four arrangements constituted the entire range of Fund lending facilities. The collapse of the Bretton Woods system and advent of worldwide floating exchange rates did not, however, alleviate the need for IMF lending facilities. Indeed, balance-of-payments imbalances have become larger and more prolonged, thus necessitating additional temporary balance-of-payments financing. In response to these trends as well as to intensive arguments on the part of developing countries, a range of additional lending facilities aimed at providing greater sums of money as well as making it available over a longer period than 5 years, was developed. Arrangements which may be mentioned under this heading include the Oil Facility, set up to assist with adjustments after the 1973 oil price shock and since wound up; the Extended Fund Facility (EFF), and the Enlarged Access Policy (EAP), each of which has as its aim the provision of assistance for programmes of structural change with repayments being made over 10 years (EFF) or 7 years (EAP). In addition, the Structural Adjustment Facility and Enhanced Structural Adjustment Facility were created to provide, in conjunction with the World Bank, lending over a ten-year period to especially low-income countries to support programmes of balance-of-payments and structural adjustment, the distinguishing feature of these two facilities being that loans are made available on special concessional terms. Of equal importance has been the increased level of Fund quotas which raises the base on which assistance is given under the tranche policies and other facilities.

International Monetary Surveillance and Co-operation: Following a transitional period after the collapse of the par-value system, the IMF has been operating within the framework set in April 1978 by the Second Amendment to its Articles of Agreement.

The most fundamental element in the post-1978 framework is the amendment to Article 4 of the IMF Agreement. The main points of the amended Article are as follows:[1] (i) a general return to stable but adjustable par values can take place with the support of an 85% majority in the IMF; (ii) such par values may not be expressed in terms of gold or other currencies but can be expressed in terms of SDRs, the margins of fluctuation around par values remaining at +/- 2.25%; (iii) with the concurrence of the IMF, any country may abandon its par value and adopt a floating exchange rate; (iv) the exchange-rate management of a floating currency must be subject to IMF surveillance and must not be conducted so as to disadvantage other countries; (v) the agreed practices with respect to floating rates will operate until such time as a general return to par values is attained. In effect, these rules legitimize floating exchange rates within the framework of the IMF system and without any diminution of the powers of the IMF. A second aspect of the Second Amendment dealt with the relative positions of SDRs and gold. We have commented above on the attempts to enhance the reserve status of the SDR; the associated measures to demonetize gold were equally significant. In particular, the official price of gold was abolished and members were no longer allowed to use gold to make their general quota contributions. Furthermore, members were again allowed to trade in gold at free-market prices.

The reforms embodied in the Second Amendment left unresolved many of the practical issues concerned with the orderly management of flexible exchange rates. Since 1978, there have been large swings in nominal exchange rates, well in excess of those which might be predicted by reference to PPP, imperfect indicator though that may be. The IMF response to such volatility has been to emphasize the role of surveillance with the purpose of identifying unwelcome economic developments, including exchange-rate practices, which arise from inappropriate economic policies such as fiscal and monetary measures or exchange-market intervention. At the same time, under the auspices of the IMF, a number of ministerial committees have emerged to provide a basis for consultation and co-ordination at a more senior level than is possible at the regular meetings of the IMF's own executive board. Six such committees are now in existence, the oldest being

---

[1] The text of Article IV is contained in the 19 January 1976 issue of *IMF Survey*, pp. 20–1. Full details of the Revised Articles of Agreement may be found in *The Second Amendment to the Articles of Agreement of the International Monetary Fund*, Cmnd. 6705 (HMSO, 1977).

the Group of Ten formed in 1962 in connection with the establishment of the General Arrangements to Borrow (GAB) which provide a formal mechanism for the Fund to augment its resources through borrowing. The GAB have been used on nine occasions and were renewed most recently through December 1993. The Group of 24, formed in 1972, represents the developing countries in negotiations on international monetary matters. The interim and development committees were formed in 1974 to advise the Fund respectively on matters dealing with disturbances to the international monetary system, and on resource transfers to developing countries.

However, of most importance in recent years have probably been the Group of 5 (G-5) and the Group of 7 (G-7). The G-5 consists of the countries whose currencies constitute the SDR: France, Germany, Japan, the UK and the USA. Since an initial agreement in September 1985 (the so-called 'Plaza Agreement'), these countries' ministers have periodically agreed to engage in co-ordinated intervention, initially to reduce and subsequently to stabilize the value of the dollar. Of equal importance is the G-7, which consists of the G-5 together with Canada and Italy and whose heads of state have now evolved a regular pattern of annual 'economic summit' meetings. In the recent past, the G7 have co-ordinated a variety of actions including, in November 1991, a debt agreement with the successor countries to the Soviet Union.

While it may be true that greater co-ordination is desirable, it remains unclear how effective co-ordination has thus far been, as it has largely been confined to intervention policy. As we have seen, exchange rates are more fundamentally determined by monetary and fiscal policy than by intervention, and any attempt to stabilize exchange rates at a level inconsistent with underlying policies is likely to prove expensive and futile for central banks. In this connection, it is clear that the US budget deficit has been a major cause of relatively high US interest rates, which in turn have helped raise the value of the dollar. However, although the G-7 has had extensive discussions on national budgetary and interest-rate policy, very little positive active has yet emerged from these discussions.[1] In the near future, there seems to be little alternative to a regular round of consultations with the aim of minimizing excessive fluctuations in exchange rates. While the experience of the EMS has shown that greater stability of exchange rates is achievable, arguably this has been achieved as much through the willingness of (non-German) ERM members to align their economic policies to those of Germany as through any great increase in co-ordination, and it is not clear that the lessons of the EMS could be applied on a global scale.

---

[1]   For an evaluation of how the effectiveness of policy coordination depends on the underlying structure of the economy, see for example, R. van de Ploeg, 'International Interdependence and Policy Co-Ordination in Economics with Real and Nominal Wage Rigidity', Centre for Labour Economics Discussion Paper no. 986, September 1987.

World Debt and Bank Lending: We have already referred in section 4 above to the problem of recycling petro-currencies following the oil price shocks of 1973, 1979 and 1985–6. Recycling proved to have complex world-wide repercussions.[1] On the one hand the international financial system was initially able to absorb the massive international redistributions of income and wealth implied by the oil price shocks. On the other hand, it later became clear that the debt position that many less developed countries (LDCs) had built up in the wake of the oil price shocks was unsustainable, and the threat of default on large amounts of LDC debt raised the spectre of a possible collapse of the international banking system.

The pressures on the banks were clear enough. *De facto* they had taken on the job of recycling, of which arguably a greater share should have been borne more directly by international agencies such as the IMF. In the worldwide recessions which followed the 1973 and 1979 oil price increases, banks were only able to find profitable outlets for OPEC funds by lending increasingly large amounts to LDC governments, with the misplaced faith that governments do not default. However, oil-importing LDCs and, after 1986, some oil exporters were, in fact, borrowing short-term funds largely to finance a balance-of-payments deficit on current account. Debt repayments could only be made in the longer term if LDC current accounts moved into surplus and, by the mid-eighties, as it became clear that this would not occur for many years, a number of major borrowers, such as Mexico, Brazil and Poland, announced their inability to meet immediate obligations, including even interest payments on outstanding debts.

It now seems clear that the danger of a collapse in the international capital market has passed, although this has not been as a result of any one major policy initiative. A variety of initiatives have been proposed, notably the Baker initiative in October 1985 and the Brady proposals in March 1989. These and other proposals called for a variety of co-ordinated measures to ease the debt problems of LDCs, concentrating in particular on improving policy-making mechanisms in these countries, to restore confidence, and on the joint use of IMF, World Bank and private sources to increase the flow of resources to the LDCs.

In practice, such initiatives have been less effective than the spur of imminent default on commercial bank thinking on the one hand, and the threat of exclusion from world capital markets on the thinking of LDC policy-makers on the other. Thus, banks have agreed to a variety of rescheduling arrangements, such as the extensions of repayments, swaps of debt for equity and, beginning in 1987, banks with large exposures to third-world debt substantially increased their contingency reserves, thus effectively writing off a part of the debt. Among LDCs, there has been a greater recognition that external borrowing needs to be associated with viable investment projects and not merely used to underpin a balance-

---

[1] For a fuller account of recycling and the debt problem, see the twelfth edition of this volume.

of-payments deficit. Thus there has been a steady increase in the amount of borrowing from the IMF under stand-by arrangements, typically requiring some adjustments in economic policies, but also associated with a more substantial flow of resources from private and official lenders in the form of new lending and rescheduling of existing debt. Recent reschedulings have typically been characterized by the so-called 'menu' approach in which creditors and debtors are brought together under the auspices of the IMF or World Bank and offered a range of options for rescheduling.[1]

Although the prospects for the international financial system now appear much better than in the mid-1980s, it remains true that the IMF and other international agencies such as the World Bank can only act primarily as catalysts to provide a lending and a policy framework within which to exhort the governments of the industrial world to increase their own foreign assistance and, equally pertinently, to reform their trade practices which inhibit the expansion of many LDC economies, particularly in the agricultural sector. The comprehensive dismantling of the CAP would represent a significant contribution in this respect. In the absence of such reforms, the medium-term outlook for many LDCs remains very bleak, with the prospect of continuing low economic growth and a seemingly endless struggle to reduce high debt-service ratios.

The Reconstruction of Eastern Europe and the Soviet Union: Undoubtedly the major global political event of the last decade and, arguably, apart from the success of the EC, since the end of World War II, was the break-up of the socialist bloc countries of Eastern Europe and of the Soviet Union itself. In the late 1980s, democratic reform movements swept through Eastern Europe, and communist governments which had formerly enjoyed a monopoly of power were successively overthrown, in general by non-violent means. These events culminated in the reunification of Germany in October 1990, and the dissolution of the Soviet Union itself in November–December 1991 into 15 independent states, of which 12 formed a new Commonwealth with the aim of maintaining common arrangements and policies in certain areas such as trade and national defence. These developments raise an immense range of local and global political and economic issues. In this brief section we confine ourselves to noting the main international economic problems which follow from the break-up.

Economic developments played an important role in the break-up in that the system of central economic planning adopted by the socialist bloc failed to deliver a satisfactory growth in living standards for its people over the 45 years since the end of World War II. The central challenge for these countries now is to reform their economic systems to provide a higher rate of economic growth than in the past, with models for reform being sought from the Western capitalist systems based on free markets and the private ownership

---

[1]   See K.P. Regling, 'New Financing Approaches in the Debt Strategy', *FD*, March 1988.

of capital, but differing considerably among different countries in the ways in which these arrangements are applied within each sector of the economy.

Within each of these countries, the economic agenda consists of five main elements.

First is the reform of the price system so that prices more nearly reflect conditions of demand and supply and hence the relative scarcities of different products.

Second, the industrial structure has to be reformed to enable consumers and producers to respond to and benefit from the improved allocation of resources which will follow from a properly fluctuating price system. In general, this includes the break-up and privatization of (most) state enterprises. In principle, widespread state ownership of capital is not inconsistent with a properly functioning price system but in practice they have rarely co-existed successfully together.

Third, much of the capital stock in these countries is outdated and inefficient, and a massive investment programme is required to re-equip factories and to modernize infrastructure such as the transport system. The clearest indication of the scale of the problem is provided by the former East Germany which, on unification with the West, was effectively immediately integrated into a modern industrial economy. Industrial production in the East fell by 43% between July 1990 and February 1991 as obsolete factories were shut down, with the impact on the labour market being borne by a combination of increased unemployment, short-time working, and commuting or immigration to the West. This outcome was due in large part to the fact that, on unification, the currency of the former East Germany was converted into Western Deutschmarks at a rate of one-for-one, effectively endorsing a very large over-valuation of the East German currency.

Other eastern bloc countries have the option (which most have exercised) of a substantial devaluation of the currency to bring their exchange rates more into line with their true international purchasing power. A devaluation does not avoid a cut in living standards but, as suggested by the analysis in section 2, it can enable balance-of-payments adjustments to be made without the exceptionally large rise in unemployment and migration of labour that has taken place in East Germany.

The fourth element in economic reform is the adaptation of the monetary and financial systems to a free market economy, one of the most important measures under this head being an exchange rate change. Other measures include the determination of monetary and fiscal policies in the new environment.

The fifth element in reform is the redefinition of the role of the state. Clearly, this has ramifications going well beyond the economic sphere. However, even within the economic sphere the former socialist countries must still determine how far the state will continue to play an active role in the economy and within what framework. Thus, few western countries are willing to leave the provision of health, education, and social infrastructure such as roads and parks exclusively or even partly to the private sector, and judgements on these matters will also have to be made in the East.

We have already referred in section 2.5 to the implications of German unification for German interest rates – the sharp increase in demand for investment funds for the East tending to push rates upwards. Other former socialist countries will also require an infusion of investment funds, much of which will have to be borrowed from abroad thus increasing again possible stresses on the international financial system. Nevertheless there is a considerable advantage in borrowing from abroad for reconstruction, as such borrowing will provide the foreign currency which will be required to import much of the necessary machinery and equipment and will therefore help prevent an excessive devaluation of the domestic currency. With this in view, a new European Bank for Reconstruction and Development (EBRD) was launched in April 1991, with initial capital of ECU10bn. The Bank has the economic objective of channelling funds from the established industrial countries, particularly of the EC to the eastern countries, and the political objective of fostering democracy and market economies in these countries.

In conclusion, the transformation of the eastern economies represents a major task for the world's financial system in the next several years. However, it must not be forgotten that, by virtually every indicator, these countries are still considerably more prosperous than all but a handful of third world countries. It would be a considerable failure of the international community if, as appears possible, the problems of the east are allowed to push the far more severe problems of the third world 'south' off the international agenda in the years ahead.

4

Industry

Malcolm Sawyer

1   INTRODUCTION

This chapter is concerned with the production of goods and services. It considers the role of different types of industry (i.e. primary, secondary and tertiary), the scale and operation of firms and then in the second part the type of policies which governments have adopted towards firms and industries.

The purpose of the first part of this chapter is to describe some important features of the industrial landscape. The descriptions are written to bring out features which are regarded as important for the perspective of theories on how industrialized economies work. The first section considers the composition of output and employment across different sectors of the economy. The reasons for this consideration include the view that different sectors display quite different productivity trends and make substantially different contributions to exports and to the balance of trade. Thus a changing composition of output and employment would have implications for the growth of productivity and for the balance of trade. The second section considers the size of firms, the extent to which industries are dominated by a few firms and the operation of multinational enterprises. Economic theory suggests that industries with a large number of small firms (atomistic competition) will perform in ways which are different as compared with industries with a few large firms (oligopoly and monopoly). The growth of multinational enterprises raises another range of issues, from those of national sovereignty to the possible benefits of investment and technical innovation flowing from multinational enterprises.

2   COMPOSITION OF OUTPUT AND EMPLOYMENT

We begin by considering the composition of output and employment between different major sectors of the economy. Figure 4.1 provides some indication of the relative size of the three sectors (primary, secondary and tertiary) and some sub-sectors in 1970, 1980 and 1990.

The primary sector consists of industries which produce raw materials (e.g. minerals, crops), and encompasses agriculture, forestry and fishing (which for brevity will be hereafter referred to as agriculture), and the extraction of minerals and oil. The historic trend has been that of decline of

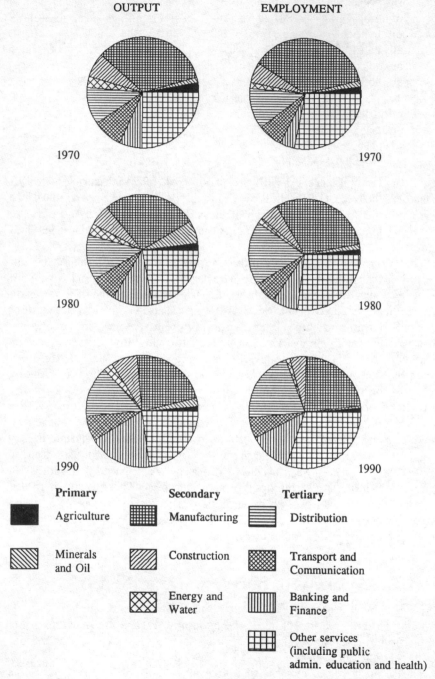

Figure 4.1　Sector Composition of Output and Employment 1970, 1980 and 1990
(*Source*: Calculated from the *United Kingdom National Accounts* (The Blue Book 1981, 1991).)

the primary sector. For example, in Britain, agriculture accounted for 36 per cent of employment in 1801, declining to 22 per cent by 1851, and then to 9 per cent by the turn of the century. In this century, there has been a further virtually continuous decline to under $1\frac{1}{2}$ per cent by 1990. This decline can be seen as still continuing in agriculture despite its already low share : from 1970 to 1990 the share of agriculture in total production was halved from 3.0 per cent to 1.5 per cent. The extraction of minerals and oils has similarly generally declined, with employment in coal mining falling from nearly three-quarters of a million in the late 1940s to well under 50,000 in the early 1990s. This general trend was temporarily reversed in the eighties with the exploitation of North Sea oil, giving rise to a substantial increase in the share of mineral and oil extraction in total output in the early eighties (as can be seen in the figures for 1980 in Figure 4.1) but with a subsequent decline by 1990.

The secondary sector consists of industries which process raw materials, and covers manufacturing, construction and energy production (gas and electricity). This sector is quite often referred to as industry, and statistics on industrial production ('production' industries) relate to the secondary sector plus mining but minus construction. In the early stages of economic development, the secondary sector grows rapidly, with the primary sector declining in relative importance. Employment in the secondary sector ('industry') peaked at 46 per cent in 1966. The decline in the importance of the secondary sector has generally been referred to as deindustrialization, though sometimes that term is used to refer only to decline in the manufacturing sector.

The tertiary sector covers the distribution of goods and the production of services and is now the predominant provider of employment (and to a lesser degree of output). From Figure 4.1 it can be seen that over the twenty years up to 1990 the share of output accounted for by the tertiary sector rose by twelve percentage points to reach just over 63 per cent by 1990. The growth in this sector's share of employment has been even faster, and one reason for the faster growth of the employment share as compared with the output is that much of the employment growth in the tertiary sector has been in part-time jobs.

2.1   Deindustrialization

The general decline in the importance of manufacturing and the secondary sector is often described as deindustrialization. The term deindustrialization does not have a precise meaning and a number of different interpretations have been used. However, the main distinctions to be made are :

(a)   a decline in the absolute employment level
(b)   a decline in the share of employment

(c)   a decline in the share of output
(d)   a decline in the absolute level of output in the industrial sector (or often just in manufacturing).

For Britain, the absolute level of employment in both manufacturing and 'industry' peaked in 1966, and has been generally declining since then. The share of manufacturing employment peaked rather earlier in the mid-fifties at 36 per cent in 1955, and stayed close to that level until 1966 (when it was 35 per cent) but then declined significantly to reach 30 per cent by 1980 and $22\frac{1}{2}$ per cent in 1990. The share of output accounted for by manufacturing has declined substantially in the past 20 years (cf. Figure 4.1). There has been little tendency for the absolute level of manufacturing output to grow and it did not regain its 1973 level until 1988.

These trends for British industry raise the question whether they are of any significance. It is argued by some that they are an inevitable accompaniment of economic development and growth. As the agricultural sector declined (especially in terms of employment) with the growth of the secondary sector, so now the secondary sector (especially manufacturing) declines as the composition of demand shifts away (in relative terms) from goods to services. In recent years, the advent of North Sea oil (and gas) would contribute to this trend (though as North Sea oil declines in importance this aspect would be expected to operate in reverse). North Sea oil affects the size of the secondary sector in two ways. First, it is obviously the case that if one sub-sector (here North Sea oil) grows rapidly then other sectors will thereby decline in relative importance. Second, North Sea oil tends to raise the sterling exchange rate (cf. Chapter 3, pp. 186–189), which makes British exports more expensive (and imports cheaper). Since (as will be seen below) the secondary sector is much more heavily involved in international trade than the tertiary sector, the exchange rate is likely to have a greater impact on the secondary sector than on the tertiary sector.

The argument that the decline in the secondary sector arises from the virtually inevitable shift of demand from the goods produced by that sector to the services of the tertiary sector can be examined in (at least) two ways. The first is to make some international comparisons. The argument here would be that if the decline in the secondary sector is inevitable, then it would be expected to afflict most if not all developed economies. Whereas, in relative terms, manufacturing employment peaked in UK in 1955, it peaked rather later in most other countries, for example in 1970 in Germany. However, over the decade to 1983, the share of employment accounted for by manufacturing declined in virtually all advanced capitalist economies.[1,2]

The second way is to consider the composition of demand rather than of

[1]   The information in these paragraphs is taken from R.E. Rowthorn and J. Wells, *De-Industrialization and Foreign Trade* (Cambridge University Press, 1987).
[2]   Of nineteen countries on which Rowthorn and Wells report, the share of manufacturing employment rose in only three small economies (Finland, Iceland and New Zealand).

supply. The share of manufacturing output may decline for a variety of reasons. It may be, as suggested above, that the (relative) demand for manufactured products declines whilst the (relative) demand for services increases. There are, however, at least two other reasons. First, (as will be seen below) productivity tends to increase faster in manufacturing than elsewhere in the economy. This would mean that (relative) employment would tend to decline in manufacturing as employment would grow more slowly (or decline more rapidly) in manufacturing than elsewhere for any given growth of output. Further, the relative price of manufactured products would be expected to decline to reflect the faster growth of labour productivity. The share of manufactured products is given by $p_M \cdot M/(p_M \cdot M + p_R \cdot R)$, where p_M is price of manufactured products and p_R are other prices, and the output of manufactured products is M and of other goods and services R. The fall in the relative price of manufactured products (p_M/p_R) would, *ceteris paribus*, lead to a fall in the share of manufactured products.[1]

Second, the data used refer to the domestic output of manufactured goods. The domestic demand for manufactured goods is split between domestic and foreign supply, and domestic output supplies both domestic demand and exports. Thus it is possible that a (relative) decline in the output of manufactured goods represents a combination of a shift in the composition of demand away from British-made goods to foreign-made goods, and a failure of British manufactured industry to meet the demand. The move from a surplus to a deficit on international trade in manufactures, discussed below, would be consistent with this view.

Whilst many countries have experienced a decline in the relative importance of manufacturing, the British experience of a failure of manufacturing output to grow to any significant extent since 1973 is unusual. Over the period 1973–90, the growth of manufacturing net output averaged −0.4 per cent per annum, compared with a rate of 3.0 per cent in the period 1960 to 1973. In contrast, the growth of manufacturing output in the OECD area averaged 2.7 per cent over the period 1973–90 (much lower than the average rate of 6.1 per cent over the period 1960–73).[2]

Concern over the size of the British manufacturing sector has arisen in two particular ways. The first relates to the rate of productivity growth in the secondary sector compared with the rate elsewhere in the economy (which is dominated by growth of productivity in the tertiary sector). The basic argument is that production in many service industries is labour-intensive and the substitution of capital equipment for labour and technological change would be difficult to implement. Thus service industries would tend to display low (or even zero) rates of growth of productivity. In contrast, manufacturing and other production industries can benefit from technological change, from the exploitation of economies of scale and from

---

[1] For further discussion and evidence, see Rowthorn and Wells, *op. cit.*, Appendix 3.
[2] Calculated from OECD, *Historical Statistics 1960–87* and OECD, *Indicators of Industrial Activity 1991/4*.

% of GDP

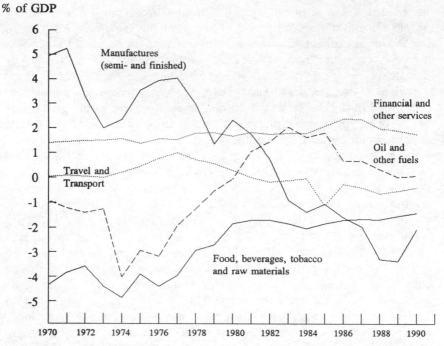

Figure 4.2 Net Trade Balance (expressed as percentages of GDP) by Type of Commodity, 1970–90

(*Source*: Calculated from the *United Kingdom Balance of Payments* (The CSO Pink Book).)

the substitution of capital equipment for labour. All of these features aid productivity growth.

Some relevant statistics are given in Table 4.1. These clearly indicate that distribution, hotels, repairs and catering have a productivity record much below those of the other sectors. It could be expected that these industries are ones in which the arguments of the previous section relating to the service sector would particularly apply. Thus as the relative size of the service sector increases, it would be expected that the average growth rate of productivity would decline. This may be an inevitable consequence of a change in the composition of demand away from manufactured goods towards services.

The second concern arises from the international trade implications,[1] and some of these can be seen by reference to Figure 4.2 and Table 4.2. Figure 4.2 traces the net balance of trade (exports minus imports) for a number of categories measured relative to GDP since 1970. The position shown in Figure 4.2 for the 1970s is indicative of the general experience of Britain up to that time. Deficits on food, basic materials and oil were offset by surpluses on manufactured goods and services (of which financial services are an important element). In the period since 1970 there has been a general

---

[1] For a full discussion see House of Lords, *Report from the Select Committee on Overseas Trade*, HL 238 (HMSO, 1985).

TABLE 4.1

Productivity Statistics: Trend Growth of Output per (full-time equivalent) Person (annual rates: percentages)

	1971–85	*1979–85*
All industries and services	1.79	2.38
Manufacturing	2.19	4.73
Distribution, hotels, repairs and catering	−0.03	0.82
Transport	1.72	3.05
Communications	3.47	3.44
Banking, finance and insurance	2.57	2.81

Source: D.G.Mayes, 'Does Manufacturing Matter?', *NIER*, no. 122, November 1987 (based on unpublished work by A. Murfin).

tendency for a decline in the deficit on food, beverages, tobacco and basic materials. The impact of the quadrupling of the price of oil in late 1973 on the oil deficit can be clearly seen as can that of the exploitation of North Sea oil and gas, which meant that during the 1980s Britain gained a balance of trade surplus on oil, although it had virtually disappeared by 1990. The emergence of a deficit on travel and transport is a reflection of, *inter alia*, the growth of overseas holidays and the decline of the British merchant navy. There has been some upward trend in the surplus on trade in financial and other services.

The importance of the manufacturing sector arises, in part, from its significance in terms of international trade, which is reflected in Table 4.2. It can be seen that manufactures accounted (in 1990) for nearly 62 per cent of exports but also nearly 64 per cent of imports. Thus the significance of manufacturing is much larger in international trade than it is in national output. Since it is likely, given climatic and geological conditions, that Britain will remain a net importer of primary products then it would follow that to achieve a balance on the current account Britain would have to run a surplus on the combined manufactured goods and invisible items account.

However, the main concern has been over the emergence of a deficit on trade in manufactures in 1983 which, as the House of Lords Select Committee on Overseas Trade noted, was the first year in which Britain had run a deficit on trade in manufactured goods.[1] In the years up to and including 1989 the deficit on manufactured goods widened year by year, though it did diminish in 1990 and 1991 under the impact of recession.

The optimistic interpretation of this deterioration of the manufacturing net balance is that it is the other side of the coin of the emergence of a net surplus on oil. Insofar as foreign trade has to be in balance, then the surplus on one part of the trade account will have to be balanced by deficits elsewhere.[2] On this basis, a trade surplus on manufactured goods will

[1] House of Lords, *ibid*.
[2] As the United States experience during the 1980s has shown, it may be possible to run a trade deficit for many years with an inflow of capital required to balance the trade deficit.

TABLE 4.2

International Trade Statistics

	1980	1985	1990
Exports			
Share (%) of:			
Food, beverage & tobacco	5.2	4.8	5.2
Basic materials	2.4	2.2	1.7
Oil	10.2	16.4	5.8
Semi-manufactures	22.1	19.5	21.5
Finished manufactures	33.6	31.6	40.2
Services	24.7	23.7	23.9
Imports			
Share (%) of:			
Food, beverage & tobacco	9.6	8.8	7.9
Basic materials	6.1	5.1	3.7
Oil	11.4	10.4	5.1
Semi-manufactures	21.8	20.6	21.4
Finished manufactures	29.4	36.1	42.4
Services	20.5	17.7	18.2
Net balance (£m) in:			
Food, beverage & tobacco	−2,282	−3,723	−4,620
Basic materials	−2,010	−2,842	−3,280
Oil	−138	+6,406	+384
Semi-manufactures	+1,335	−417	−2,690
Finished manufactures	+4,093	−3,348	−8,750
Services	+3,653	+6,687	+5,201
Goods & services	+1,357	+3,342	−13,475
Current account balance (£m)	+2,843	+2,878	−14,380

Source: Calculated from *United Kingdom Balance of Payments 1991* (The CSO Pink Book).
Notes: Services include financial services and tourism. Figures in first two parts do not sum to 100 per cent because of rounding and from the omission of a category not classified. Net balance is positive if exports exceed imports, negative otherwise. Total balance also includes the net balance of a not classified category. Current account balance also includes transfers, net receipts of interest, dividends and profits.

re-emerge as production of oil declines. This will come about through some adjustment of the exchange rate and by the movement of resources back into manufacturing industry as they are released from oil production.

The pessimistic interpretation is that there is a fundamental weakness in British manufacturing such that it is unable to compete successfully in international markets. It can be noted that the net deficit in manufactures is not simply the obverse of a surplus on oil in that a substantial deficit on the current account has been evident since 1987, reaching a peak in 1989 at over £20 billion, though falling to £14 billion in 1990 and to under £6 billion in 1991 with the onset of recession in mid-1990.

Figure 4.3 provides some information on relative living standards (as measured by GDP per capita) since 1970 for a range of industrialized countries. For each year, the OECD average is taken as 100. These figures refer to purchasing power parity exchange rate calculations. This means that differences in the level of prices between countries have been taken into account.[1] The figures underlying Figure 4.3 suggest that Britain's living standards have remained at around the same level *relative* to those in the rest of the OECD area.

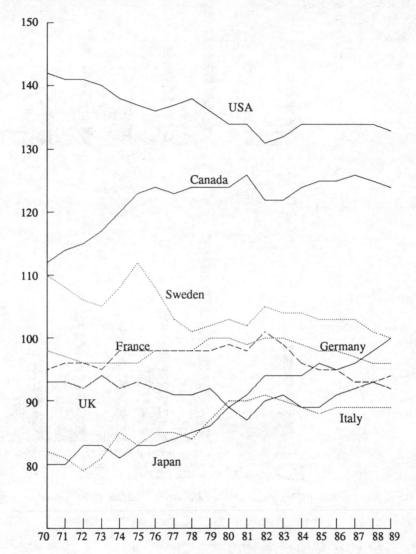

Figure 4.3   Comparison of International Living Standards, 1970–89. GDP per head in purchasing power parity terms (OECD average = 100)
(*Source*: OECD *National Accounts 1960–1989*.)
(*Note*: Germany refers to West Germany before reunification.)

---

[1]   It can be seen from Figure 4.3 that the GDP per head in Japan in 1989 on the purchasing power parity basis was below the OECD average and was around 75 per cent of the USA level. Whilst prior to 1987 there was a substantial gap between Japan and the USA in GDP per head terms when actual exchange rates are used, this was reversed in 1987; and in 1989 Japan's GDP per head at actual exchange rates was about 10 per cent above that of the USA.

Total factor productivity

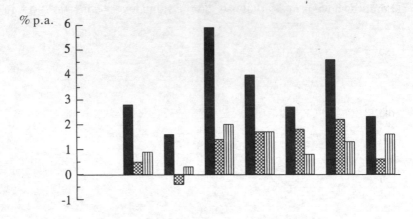

Labour Productivity

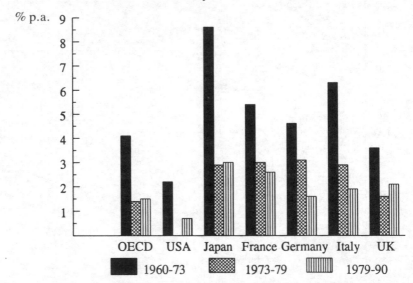

Figure 4.4 Productivity Trends in Selected Countries (Business sector, compound annual growth rates).
(*Source:* OECD *Economic Outlook*, December 1991, Table 48.)
(*Notes:* Total factor productivity is real gross value added at factor cost divided by total factor inputs. Labour productivity is real gross value added divided by private sector employment including self-employed.)

Since the failure of the British economy to match the growth performance of other industrialized countries became apparent in the early 1960s, successive governments have tried a wide range of economic and industrial policies to seek to reverse the trend. Figure 4.4 provides some information which may help our discussion. The data displayed there indicate that UK productivity growth (whether in terms of labour or total factor) fell between the period 1960–73 and the period 1973–9 and then rose in the period 1979–90 but did not regain the rate of the earlier period.

3   FIRM SIZE AND INDUSTRIAL CONCENTRATION

Casual observation of the British economy reveals an enormous range in the size of firms, from one-person businesses through to firms employing over 20,000 people. Some idea of the range of size of firms can be seen from Table 4.3, which relates to manufacturing industries only. Firms employing less than 200 workers have sometimes been defined as small firms. On that definition, around 147,000 small firms employed nearly two million workers in 1989, accounting for over 40 per cent of total employment in manufacturing. At the other end of the scale, 41 firms each employing over 5,000 workers accounted for nearly 9 per cent of employment.

Over the past decade or so there appears to have been a substantial growth in the number of small firms (though some of that increase arises through improved data collection).[1] The figures in Table 4.3 indicate a substantial increase in the share of employment in manufacturing accounted for by firms employing less than 200 rising from 28 per cent in 1978 to over 40 per cent in 1989. But the rise in the share of output is not so marked and amongst manufacturing firms employing less than 100 whilst the share of employment rose from 17.5 per cent to 24.3 per cent in the period 1979 to 1988, their share of output rose from 14.6 per cent to 18.6 per cent.[2]

It would be expected that the typical size of firms in an industry would be strongly influenced by the cost conditions under which that industry operates. When there are substantial economies of scale, then it would be expected that there would be a few large firms (since small firms would be at a significant cost disadvantage *vis-à-vis* large firms). Conversely, when there are diseconomies of scale, then a predominance of small firms would be expected.

The growth in the importance of small firms in the past two decades reverses previous trends and appears to have occurred in many other industrialized economies.[3]

On one interpretation the trends mark a significant break with the past and offer the opportunity of harnessing new flexible technologies in a

---

[1]   For further discussion, see P. Dunne and A. Hughes, 'The Changing Structure of Competitive Industry in the 1980s', in C. Driver and P. Dunne (eds.), *Structural Change in the UK Economy* (Cambridge University Press, 1992).
[2]   Source: Dunne and Hughes, *ibid.*, Table 4.6.
[3]   For further discussion see, for example, W. Sengenberger, J. Loverman and M. Piore, *The Re-emergence of Small Enterprises* (International Institute for Labour Studies, ILO, 1990).

TABLE 4.3

Size Distribution of Enterprises in Manufacturing Industries, 1978 and 1989

Size of enterprises (employees)	1978		1989	
	Number of enterprises	Share of employment (%)	Number of enterprises	Share of employment (%)
1–99	84 518	22.8	142 905	28.3
100–199	2 650	5.5	4 140	11.7
200–499	1 578	7.3	3 019	18.7
500–999	619	6.5	943	13.0
1 000–4 999	590	18.8	536	19.7
over 5 000	179	44.6	41	8.7

Note: The increase in the number of small businesses between 1978 and 1989 indicated here is inflated through a change in 1984 in the way in which the register of firms for which information was sought was compiled.

Size distribution of UK firms

Employment range	Cumulative share of total firms (%)		Cumulative share of employment (%)	
	1979	1986	1979	1986
1–2	61.4	63.9	6.6	9.7
3–5	79.2	83.1	12.4	18.6
6–10	89.1	90.7	19.1	25.8
11–19	95.2	96.4	26.7	35.9
20–49	97.8	98.2	33.6	42.6
50–99	98.7	99.0	38.9	49.5
99–199	99.5	99.5	49.1	59.4
200–499	99.8	99.8	57.3	71.3
500–999	99.9	100.0	64.7	81.8
over 1 000	100.0	100.0	100.0	100.0

Sources: Calculated from *Census of Production*, 1978, 1989; G. Bannock and M. Daly 'Size distribution of UK firms', *Employment Gazette*, May 1990.

more decentralised and small scale system of industrial production, a 'second industrial divide' marking a break away from the mass production industrial culture . . . Other interpretations stress the persistence if not increased dominance of large-scale producers, the impact of their risk-spreading vertical disintegration in creating a small business sector dependent upon their needs and objectives . . . [1]

The theory of perfect competition assumes a large number of firms each of which is a price-taker and free entry into the industry concerned. The profit-maximization condition under perfect competition is the equality between price and marginal cost. The theory of monopoly refers to

---

[1] Quote is from Dunne and Hughes, *op. cit.*; for further discussion see Sengenberger *et al.*, *ibid*.

an industry dominated by one firm where there are substantial difficulties facing new entrants into the industry. The profit-maximising condition here is marginal revenue equal to marginal cost, which can be re-
written as:

$$p \cdot (1 - 1/e) = m.c.$$

where p is price, e the elasticity of demand and $m.c.$ marginal cost.[1] This
yields a price of $p = (e/e - 1) \cdot m.c.$, which implies that price would be higher
(relative to marginal cost) under a situation of monopoly than under
a situation of perfect competition. We return later to this comparison
of perfect competition and monopoly with a discussion of its policy
implications. For our purposes here it is sufficient to note that this view
suggests that the structure of an industry is of some significance. The
structure of an industry would include the number of firms in an industry, the
inequality of size amongst those firms, and the ease or difficulty of entry into
the industry.

One purpose of measuring industrial concentration is to have some idea of
where along the spectrum between perfect competition and monopoly an
industry lies. A low level of concentration would indicate the atomistic
competition end of the spectrum and a high level the monopoly end. There
are numerous measures of industrial concentration which can be used.[2] The
simplest, and the one which is used here, is the n-firm concentration ratio.
This is the share of the largest n firms in the industry concerned. The value of
n is generally determined by data availability rather than any indication from
economic theory. In the case of Table 4.4 below, the value of n is five. The
share of the largest n firms can be measured in a variety of ways, e.g. in terms
of sales, employment, capital stock. Since the concentration ratio is intended to reflect market power within a product market, the use of sales
would appear the 'natural' variable to use, but once again data availability
often forces the choice.

Concentration can be reported at both the industry (or market) level[3] and
at the aggregate level. The discussion above linking concentration measures
to the perfect competition/monopoly spectrum would suggest that the industry (market) level would be the appropriate one. But a large firm typically
operates in a range of industries, which may enable it to co-ordinate decisions across a range of industries. Concern over the centralization of
decision-making in an economy (e.g. over prices, investment, employment)
leads to an interest in aggregate concentration measures.

---

[1] The profit-maximization condition is marginal revenue equal to marginal cost. The marginal
revenue, $\Delta(pq)/\Delta q$ where Δ signifies a small change, which can be expanded as $p + \Delta p \cdot q/\Delta q$.
This can be written as $p \cdot (1 + \Delta p \cdot q/\Delta q \cdot p)$ which is equal to $p \cdot (1 - 1/e)$. Hence $p \cdot (1 - 1/e) =$
$m.c.$
[2] For further discussion of measures of concentration, see L. Hannah and J. Kay, *Concentration in Modern Industry* (Macmillan, 1977) and M. Sawyer, *The Economics of Industries and
Firms* (Routledge, 1985) Chapter 3.
[3] In the text the terms 'market' and 'industry' are used interchangeably.

TABLE 4.4

Distribution of Five-Firm Concentration Ratios, Manufacturing Industries, 1989

Concentration ratio in range (%)	Number of industries	Share of employment
0–10	4	9.1
10–20	18	30.2
20–30	18	16.1
30–40	17	14.7
40–50	13	12.5
50–60	11	6.2
60–70	10	2.0
70–80	4	6.7
80–90	3	0.8
90–100	4	1.6

Weighted averages for 102 industries
Share of largest five firms (ranked by employment):
   Employment   31.9 per cent
   Sales   40.8 per cent
   Net Output   39.0 per cent

Source: Calculated from Business Statistics Office, *Census of Production,
1989* (HMSO).

Table 4.4 provides some statistics on the level of concentration in manufacturing industries in 1989. In view of the increasing importance of the
tertiary sector it is regrettable that recent statistics are not available for that
sector also. The statistics given refer to the group level (sometimes referred
to as the 3-digit level). On this basis, the manufacturing sector has 102
groups or industries. Even so, these industries may be too broad for our
purposes and contain a number of separate markets (industries). For
example, one of these industries is soap and toilet preparations, which
covers products such as soaps, soap powder, shampoos, toothpaste, etc. It
could reasonably be argued that a lower level of aggregation would be more
appropriate so that, for example, the market for soaps would be treated
separately from that of toothpaste.

The lower part of Table 4.4 indicates that on average in 1989 the largest
five firms in an industry (when ranked in terms of employment) accounted
for 31.9 per cent of employment, and 40.8 per cent of sales. These averages
mask considerable variations between industries. In the seven separately
identified industries falling within the timber and wooden furniture sector,
the largest five firms account, on average, for 15 per cent of employment,
whilst in the four metal manufacturing the largest five firms average a share
of 63 per cent. The spread of concentration ratios is also indicated in Table
4.4, which shows that there were four industries accounting together for 9
per cent of employment in which the five-firm concentration ratio was below
10 per cent. At the other end of the scale, there were seven industries (with

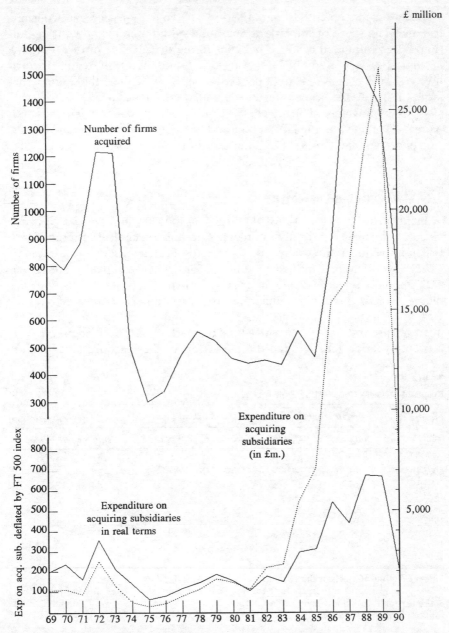

Figure 4.5 Merger Activity in UK, 1969–90.
(*Source: Business Monitor*, M7, *CSO Bulletin, Financial Statistics.*)

2.4 per cent of employment) in which the largest five firms employed over 80 per cent of the industry workforce.

The level of concentration has generally risen during the first seventy years of this century but appears to have levelled off in the past twenty years.

This can be conveniently summarised by the course of aggregate concentration.[1] The share of the largest one hundred firms in manufacturing net output was estimated to be 16 per cent in the first decade of this century, around 22–4 per cent in the inter-war period, and then rose steadily from a level of 22 per cent in 1949 to 41 per cent in 1968. Since then, the share of the largest 100 firms has been rather steady, and was 37 per cent in 1989 (with the share of employment at 30 per cent).[2] For the whole economy, Hughes and Kumar[3] estimate that the largest hundred companies accounted for 24.7 per cent of employment in 1968, 24.5 per cent in 1975 and 25.1 per cent in 1980.

3.1   Acquisitions and Mergers

A major route by which the structure of an industry and the size of firms change is by acquisitions and mergers. There is a technical difference between an acquisition (where one firm takes over another) and a merger (where two or more firms fuse together to form a new company), but in line with common usage we do not make any distinction between acquisition and merger below. Figure 4.5 illustrates the variation in merger activity in Britain over the past twenty years. The number of firms acquired has averaged around 700 a year, with a total of nearly 15,000 firms acquired over a twenty-year period. Around three-quarters of these acquisitions involve

TABLE 4.5

Proposed Mergers Classified by Type (per cent)

Year	Horizontal		Vertical		Diversified	
	Number	Value	Number	Value	Number	Value
1970/4	73	65	5	4	23	27
1975/8	65	67	9	8	26	25
1979/82	61	68	6	3	34	30
1983/4	67	76	4	1	29	23
1985/6	64	58	3	3	35	40
1987	67	80	3	1	30	19
1988	58	45	1	1	41	54
1989	60	44	2	3	37	53
1990	75	81	5	3	20	16

Source: Annual Reports of the Director-General of Fair Trading.
Note: 'The allocation of mergers to these three categories involves an element of judgement and this should be kept in mind when interpreting these figures' (Review of Monopolies and Mergers Policy, *A Consultative Document*, Cmnd. 7198 (HMSO, 1978)).

[1] The trends on industrial concentration are summarized in M.Sawyer, *op. cit.*, Chapter 3; for discussion of concentration outside of manufacturing see S.Aaronovitch and M.Sawyer, *Big Business* (Macmillan, 1975).
[2] There are complications arising from some (rather slight) changes in the definition of the manufacturing sector and from nationalization and privatization of firms. The figures in the text refer to private firms only.
[3] A.Hughes and M.Kumar, 'Recent Trends in Aggregate Concentration in the United Kingdom Economy: Revised Estimates', *CJE*, vol. 8 (1984).

the purchase of independent companies, whilst the remainder involve the sale of subsidiaries by one company to another.

Expenditure on acquisitions fluctuates substantially. The number of firms acquired in the most active acquisition year is around three times the number in the least active year. But the variation in terms of the expenditure is much greater. For example, even after deflating for variations in share prices, expenditure on acquiring subsidiaries in 1988 was nearly ten times the value in 1975.

The early years of the period (1968–72) witnessed a merger boom which was larger than any previous merger boom, but this was followed by a decade during which merger activity was rather subdued. This could be seen as a response to a general disenchantment with the benefits of mergers.[1] However, there was a dramatic upswing in merger activity beginning in 1985 and continuing up to the time of writing. The scale of merger activity over the four years 1985–9 well surpassed the levels reached in the last merger boom of 1968–72.

The scale of merger activity can be gauged by comparing expenditure on acquiring subsidiaries with total investment in fixed capital assets (plant, machinery and buildings). For example, amongst relatively large companies, expenditure on acquiring subsidiaries in 1988 was equivalent to 35 per cent of the expenditure on fixed assets.[2] The relevance of this comparison is twofold. First, the figures for total investment provide an appropriate benchmark and put the large numbers involved in merger activity into perspective. Second, and more important, the comparison draws attention to the use to which firms put their investment resources. Whereas investment in plant and equipment and so on represents the creation of new resources and an addition to the productive potential of the economy, expenditure on acquisitions does not add to productive capacity but rather represents a change of ownership of existing assets.

The direction of merger activity is indicated to some extent by the figures in Table 4.5, which refer to the proposed mergers considered by the Office of Fair Trading as part of mergers policy (see below). These figures refer to relatively large potential mergers, and most large firms are already diversified. A merger is regarded as horizontal if the two (or more) firms involved are operating in the same industrial sector, whereas it would be regarded as vertical if the firms were in a purchaser/supplier relationship with each other. The diversified merger category covers remaining cases. There is no

---

[1] The disenchantment was perhaps a reaction to the claims for the benefits of mergers made during the merger boom of 1968–72. The alleged advantages of mergers (and the resulting larger scale of firms) lay behind the establishment of the Industrial Reorganisation Corporation mentioned below. The disenchantment was aided by academic work such as G.Meeks, *Disappointing Marriage: A Study of Gains from Merger* (Cambridge University Press, 1977), which strongly suggested that mergers did not on average raise profitability and efficiency. For a survey of recent work see J.Fairburn and J.Kay (eds.), *Mergers and Merger Policy*, especially Chapter 1.

[2] The source of data is Business Monitor MA3, *Company Finance* (HMSO).

discernible trend in the figures shown in Table 4.5, with horizontal mergers accounting for two-thirds or more of mergers, and vertical mergers being rather unimportant.

3.2   Multinational Enterprises

Most large firms operating in Britain are multinational enterprises (MNEs). In the minority of cases, the firm is owned by foreigners and most of its activities take place outside the United Kingdom. In the other cases, the firm is mainly owned by UK nationals with the larger part of its activities based in Britain. Amongst the largest 100 manufacturing firms (based on net output) in Britain 20 are foreign-owned, but the vast majority of the remaining largest 100 firms operate internationally.[1]

In manufacturing in 1989 of nearly 140,000 enterprises, 1,356 were foreign-owned, but they accounted for nearly 15 per cent of employment, and produced 21.5 per cent of net output. Of the foreign enterprises 347 were EC-owned (18.4 per cent of employment) and 1,009 non-EC (81.6 per cent), of which 633 were US-owned (54.6 per cent) and 86 Japanese (3.8 per cent, and 2.8 per cent of net output).[2]

Foreign-owned companies are not evenly spread across all sectors of the economy. They tend to be sparsely represented in what could be considered the less dynamic sectors of manufacturing industry. Foreign-owned companies account for less than 5 per cent of employment in metal manufacturing, manufacture of other transport equipment, textile industries, manufacture of leather and leather goods, footwear and clothing industries and timber and wooden furniture industries. The sectors where foreign-owned companies account for more than 15 per cent of employment are the chemical industry, metal manufacture, mechanical engineering, manufacture of office machinery and data processing equipment, electrical and electronic engineering, manufacture of motor vehicles and parts thereof, instrument engineering and processing of rubber and plastics. Employment in foreign-owned manufacturing companies is proportionately greater in the South-East, West Midlands, Wales and Scotland than in the other regions.

The significance of MNEs regardless of nationality in the British economy can be gauged by some other measures.[3] Production abroad by British-based MNEs has been estimated as equivalent to nearly 130 per cent of exports and 36 per cent of GDP in period 1980–8. These figures put the UK towards the top end of the scale of involvement with MNEs (especially relative to GDP where amongst ten countries for which figures are available

---

[1]   For some estimates see K.Cowling and R.Sugden, *Transnational Monopoly Capitalism* (Wheatsheaf Books, 1987).
[2]   Source of information in this and the next paragraph is Business Statistics Office, *Census of Production, 1989* (HMSO).
[3]   The source of information in this paragraph is Grazia Ietto-Gillies, *International Production: Trends, Theories, Effects* (Polity Press, 1992).

the UK figure is only exceeded by that for the Netherlands). Much international trade is essentially a movement of goods between one branch of a MNE and another branch: of UK exports in 1981 30 per cent consisted of such movement within a MNE of which 16 per cent was with UK-origin ones. Over the period 1980–7, outward direct investment from the UK was equivalent to 14.1 per cent of gross domestic fixed capital formation, and inward direct investment was 6.7 per cent.

The arrival of a MNE is often welcomed by the host government. The establishment of a multinational enterprise will generally involve new investment and the creation of employment.[1] Further, multinational enterprises may bring new technology. However, in order to attract multinational enterprises, governments (national and local) often offer substantial investment subsidies, tax exemptions and the like. The competition between countries and regions of countries tends to lead to a bidding up of the subsidies offered to MNEs, with obvious benefit to the MNEs concerned. Further, decisions on employment, production etc. are then taken by people based well outside the country concerned. A feature of many MNEs is that they are willing and able to move production from one country to another which would mean that inward investment made in response to the offer of subsidies etc. may move out in response to subsidies elsewhere.

4   INTRODUCTION TO INDUSTRIAL POLICIES

We now turn to some consideration of industrial policies. These policies can range from changing the form of ownership of a firm or industry (i.e. nationalization and privatization), the encouragement or discouragement of mergers through to legislation governing the relationship between firms (e.g. limiting collusion between firms). There are many other policies which influence the behaviour and perforance of firms and industries. For example, macroeconomic policies influence the general economic environment within which firms operate, and the price, employment and investment decisions of firms are likely to be strongly influenced by macroeconomic conditions. Further, taxation and subsidy policies are often designed to influence what firms do. But macroeconomic and taxation policies are discussed elsewhere in this book, so that discussion here is restricted to industrial policy, by which we mean policies designed to change the behaviour and performance of specific firms and industries.

The appropriate role of the State in industrial matters has always been a matter of controversy, and the sharp differences between the role of the State as viewed by the Labour government of 1974–9 and as viewed by the

---

[1]   This would not be the case when the multinational enterprise arrives through the acquisition of an established domestic firm. The employment creation effect may be overstated, insofar as employment elsewhere in the economy is displaced.

current Conservative government illustrate that controversy. At the risk of over-simplification, it may be useful to consider three broadly defined views on the role of the State in connection with the operation of firms and industries. These can be labelled the market failure approach, the Austrian school, and the developmental State view. The first of these has been the dominant view amongst economists, whilst the second has had considerable influence on the policies of the current government. The third view has not had as much influence in Britain as in countries such as Japan and France, but some elements of this view can be seen as reflected in policies pursued particularly by the Labour governments of 1964/70 and of 1974/9.

4.1   The Market Failure Approach

The market failure approach has two basic elements. The first is the proposition that a system of perfect competition would, under certain assumptions, generate a desirable (Pareto-optimal) outcome.[1] The second is that when some of those assumptions are not (or cannot be) met, then there is a role for government. This role may be to try to bring about the conditions of perfect competition (e.g. by increasing the number of firms in an industry); or it may be to alleviate the consequences of the impossibility of achieving perfect competition. The discussion now turns to an elaboration of these ideas, along with some examples.

It is convenient to consider an industry in which production takes place subject to constant costs so that average costs and marginal costs are equal. This assumption allows a simplification of the analysis without losing anything of importance for this discussion. With constant costs, the unit costs in

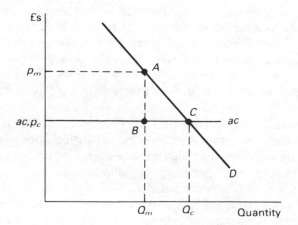

Figure 4.6   Monopoly Welfare Loss

---

[1]   A Pareto-optimal outcome is one from which it is not possible to make some people better off without making others worse off.

an industry are not affected by the number of firms in that industry, and hence the average (and marginal) cost curve can be drawn as a horizontal line without reference to the number of firms. This has been done in Figure 4.6, where the average cost curve is labelled as *ac*. The demand curve facing the industry is drawn as *D*. If the industry was perfectly competitive, then each firm would equate price with marginal cost (as a condition of profit maximization) and the normal profit requirement would be that price (average revenue) equal average cost. The output produced, with price equal to marginal cost, would be Q_c.

The outcome of price equal to marginal cost is seen to have some desirable features. The demand curve for a product indicates how much consumers are willing to pay per unit for different quantities. It is intended to represent the consumers' marginal evaluation of the product as the scale of output varies. The marginal cost is the incremental cost of production. In a fully employed economy, greater production of one good requires less production of some other goods. Assuming that the marginal costs of production reflect the opportunity cost of reducing production elsewhere, then the marginal cost is equal to the consumers' evaluation of the forgone alternative production. When consumers value the product under consideration more than the alternative, then price exceeds marginal cost, and economic welfare can be increased by shifting resources into its production. This would continue up to the point where price is equal to marginal cost. This argument forms the basis of the idea that perfect competition would generate a desirable outcome, since price would then equal marginal cost.

A situation of monopoly can also be represented in Figure 4.6. The profit-maximizing position of a monopolist is the equality of marginal revenue and marginal cost, and this would yield an output of Q_m and a price of p_m. It can be readily seen that price is higher and output lower under monopoly than under perfect competition (when both face the same cost and demand conditions). The loss to consumers of the higher price under monopoly is given (approximately) by the area p_mACBp_c. The basis of this approximation is as follows. Consider a consumer who would have been willing to pay an amount p_a for the good in question. At a competitive price this consumer would gain to the extent of $p_a - p_c$ as the excess of the value of the good to that consumer over the price which is paid. As the price is raised from the competitive level to the monopoly level, a range of consumers withdraw from purchase of this good, and their individual loss is the excess of the price they would have been prepared to pay over the competitive price. This excess summed over all the relevant individuals gives the area p_mACBp_c. This welfare loss can be divided into the rectangle p_mABp_c and the triangle *ABC*. The former is the monopoly profits (excess of price over average cost times output), and represents a transfer from consumers to producers (as compared with perfect competition). Subtracting this transfer, it is the triangle *ABC* which represents the net welfare loss of monopoly (again as compared with perfect competition).

The estimates of the size of monopoly welfare loss have ranged from the trivially small to the substantial.[1] The original estimate made by Harberger[2] for the American economy in 1929 was that the loss was less than $^{1}/_{10}$ per cent of GDP, and a number of studies arrived at estimates of a similar order of magnitude. However, some recent estimates have placed the losses at a much more significant level. For example, Cowling and Mueller[3] estimate the welfare loss from monopoly in the range 3–7 per cent of gross corporate product for the United Kingdom in the mid-sixties.[4]

The implication that the welfare costs of monopoly are (or could be) substantial (as compared with perfect competition) underlies many ideas on anti-monopoly policies. At a minimum, it suggests that situations of monopoly require some monitoring. British monopoly policy is discussed below, but two points should be noted here. First, our discussion has concerned the extreme cases of monopoly and perfect competition, whereas most industries in reality lie somewhere between the two. Monopoly policy in practice is not concerned with firms which are complete monopolists (in the sense of being the only supplier) since there are virtually no firms in such a position but rather with firms which have a considerable market share (in the British case a share of more than 25 per cent). Second, the only aspect of performance which has been considered has been pricing (and the consequences for output). There are many other dimensions of performance (e.g. technical progress, advertising) which are important, and in which monopolies and oligopolies may have advantages over atomistic competition. An oligopolist with a reasonably secure market position and a flow of profits may be in a better position to finance and undertake research than a competitive firm in an insecure position with only a competitive level of profits. Research and development (and production in general) may be subject to some economies of scale providing further advantages for an oligopolistic structure over a competitive one.

The idea that perfect competition has certain desirable properties and the related idea that price should equal marginal cost for an optimal outcome relies on a range of restrictive assumptions, and some of those are now briefly considered. First, the equality achieved by perfectly competitive firms would be between price and marginal *private* cost, whereas the welfare requirement would be for an equality between price and marginal *social* cost. The difference between private and social costs arises from the

---

[1]   For survey of monopoly welfare loss and its estimation, see M. Sawyer, *op. cit.*, Chapter 14.
[2]   A. C. Harberger, 'Monopoly and Resource Allocation', *AER*, vol. 44 (1954).
[3]   K. Cowling and D. Mueller, 'The Social Costs of Monopoly Power', *EJ*, vol. 88 (1978).
[4]   There are a number of reasons for the differences in the orders of magnitude of the estimates of Cowling and Mueller (and others) from those of Harberger (and others). Cowling and Mueller assume joint profit maximization and estimate the elasticity of demand from the observed price-cost margin by applying a formula similar to that given in the footnote on page 249 above. Harberger assumed a unit elasticity of demand in all markets. A further major difference arises from the estimation of the competitive level of prices. Harberger used the average rate of profit, with the consequence that some actual prices were below the calculated competitive level. Cowling and Mueller used an estimate of the opportunity cost of capital.

existence of externalities. The pollution from a factory is suffered by many people, and some or all of the costs of pollution are borne by people other than the firm which generates the pollution.[1] An extra traveller on a crowded road imposes further congestion on other travellers. Although further discussion of this point falls outside the range of this chapter, it can be seen that the difference between private and social costs would lead to policy suggestions of imposing taxes and subsidies to remove (or at least reduce) the difference between private and social costs.

Second, there is the presumption of full employment of workers and machinery in the economy. The withdrawal of resources from the industry under consideration is assumed to lead to the use of those resources elsewhere in the economy. Thus re-deployment rather than unemployment of resources (including labour) is assumed.

Third, consumers (and indeed firms as well) are assumed to be well informed on the quality of the product which they are buying as well as the price which they are paying. But for many products, their quality can only be judged by use. It may not be possible to judge the safety of a product (e.g. an electrical good) or to know the conditions under which a product was produced (e.g. whether food has been hygienically made). When a product malfunctions and requires repair, most of us are not technically equipped to judge what repairs are necessary (and that applies whether we are thinking of cars or of ourselves). Prices may be quoted in a misleading manner (e.g. the price offered compared with some notional recommended price). Much consumer protection legislation is devoted to imposing minimum standards on products. Codes of practice have been negotiated with a range of industries. The Consumer Protection Act 1987 makes it an offence to give misleading price indications. Thus, much public policy is designed to overcome problems arising from difficulties which consumers face in acquiring necessary information to judge quality and price.

Fourth, unit costs are assumed to be constant (as in our example) or to increase as the scale of production rises. In other words, production is assumed to involve constant or increasing costs. However, in some industries production involves decreasing costs. Industries such as railways, gas and electricity, which have often been labelled 'natural monopolies', are seen as operating subject to decreasing costs. It would, for example, be wasteful of resources to have two railway lines linking city A with city B unless there was sufficient traffic to warrant both of them.

In a situation of decreasing costs, marginal costs are below average costs and so marginal cost pricing is not viable in the sense that price would be less than average costs and losses would result. Further, perfect competition would not be viable in such a situation for the largest firm would have the lowest costs and be able to undercut its rivals. This would enable the largest

---

[1] This would depend on the nature of the laws governing pollution; e.g. whether those who suffer from pollution can seek legal redress from the polluter.

firm to expand further, operate subject to even lower costs and eventually reach a monopoly position.

The dilemma which this presents is clear. Technical efficiency would require a single firm, but one firm would possess monopoly power. There have been a range of policy responses to this dilemma. In Britain as in many other countries (the USA being the notable exception), the 'natural monopolies' of public utilities (postal service, telephone, gas, electricity, water, railways, television and radio) have until recently been under public ownership.

The second response, followed in the USA and now for the newly privatized 'natural monopolies' in Britain, has been to subject the firms to regulatory control, especially of prices and profits. Some of the difficulties of regulation are considered below.[1]

The third response, which has been developed in the past decade or so, argues that the number of firms in an industry is largely irrelevant, and that attention should be directed to the ease of entry into and exit from an industry. This line of argument has been associated with the theory of *contestable markets*, though it can also be linked with the Austrian approach discussed below. The general argument can be illustrated by reference to Figure 4.6. The implicit assumption in arriving at the conclusion that a monopolist would charge a price of p_m was that its position was not threatened by the prospect of other firms being able to enter the industry. The entry of other firms into the industry would increase total output and reduce prices and profits. The existence of substantial monopoly profits would provide a strong incentive for other firms to seek to enter the industry concerned.

Baumol and his co-workers[2] define a market as perfectly contestable if there are no barriers to entry or to exit. The absence of barriers to entry would mean that any new entrant could compete with the existing firms without any handicap. The absence of barriers to exit would mean that there are no financial or other penalties for leaving an industry. This would mean, for example, that any equipment which was used in that industry could be readily resold for use elsewhere. The relevance of the ease of exit is that firms considering entry into an industry are not put off by the difficulties of leaving the industry. This leads to the possibility of 'hit-and-run' entry; that is a firm entering an industry briefly, forcing down prices and then leaving the industry. Baumol and others argue that under conditions of free entry and exit an incumbent firm (even with a monopoly position) would not dare to raise price above the competitive level. For if the firm were to do so, then

[1]   For an extensive discussion of regulation and its difficulties, see M. Waterson, *Regulation of the Firm and Natural Monopoly* (Blackwell, Oxford, 1988).
[2]   W. J. Baumol, 'Contestable Markets: An Uprising in the Theory of Industrial Structure', *AER*, vol. 72 (1982), and W. J. Baumol, J. Panzar and R. D. Willig, *Contestable Markets and the Theory of Industrial Structure* (Harcourt Brace Jovanovich, New York). For further discussion see M. Sawyer, *op. cit.*, pp. 250–2.

other firms would immediately enter (seeking the available profits) and that would force down prices.

The policy implications of this line of argument are clear, namely that regard should be paid to entry and exit conditions and not to monopoly positions *per se*. A monopolist which seeks to secure its position by raising entry and exit barriers would be condemned.

The final response considered has operated to some degree in commercial television and radio, where the government has begun to auction off the right to operate in a particular market.[1] In the case of commercial television, a franchise to operate has been granted to a single company in each of the television regions, though the granting of the franchise has been based on company plans for programme quality, range of programmes etc. The basis of this response can again be illustrated by reference to Figure 4.6. A monopolist would gain profits of $p_m ABp_c$, and a firm would be prepared to pay up to that amount for the right to have the monopoly position. If several firms compete for the right to be the monopolist, then the price paid for that right would be bid up to the level of the monopolist profits. When the price is bid up to that level, in effect the monopoly profits are gained by the firm with the licence but paid over to the government. There would still be some loss of consumer welfare as compared with the atomistic competition case, though with decreasing costs (which underpin the 'natural monopoly' case) atomistic competition would not be viable for the reasons explained above.

4.2   The Austrian School

The view of competition which is embedded in the traditional approach is that of the static equilibrium of atomistic competition with a large number of small firms. In contrast the Austrian approach views competition as a dynamic process taking place against a background of change and un-certainty. The existence of profits, particularly high profits, is seen as an indicator that the firms concerned are particularly efficient both in terms of productive efficiency and of producing goods which consumers wish to buy. In particular, high profits are not seen as associated with market power, though there may be an association between high market shares and profits. But the link is not from high market share indicating monopoly to high profits, but rather that above-average efficiency generates a high market share and large profits.

The prospect of high profits is seen as the necessary inducement for firms to introduce new ideas, products and techniques and to pursue efficiency. A firm which is particularly successful will indeed earn high profits. However,

---

[1]   See, for example, Home Office, *Broadcasting in the 90s: Competition, Choice and Quality*, Cmnd. 517 (HMSO, 1988).

high profits are seen as always under threat from the entry of other firms. A firm with high profits may be able to maintain those profits, but only if it can remain more efficient than its rivals (potential as well as actual). It is the threat of new entry into an industry which keeps the incumbent firms on their toes. This leads to an emphasis on the importance of entry conditions into an industry, rather than the number of firms in the industry. One firm in an industry may appear to be in a situation of monopoly, but if there are a number of firms ready to enter that industry if the existing firm allows its prices to rise above their level of costs then the incumbent firm is highly constrained in its pricing.

In the analysis of monopoly welfare loss, it was implicitly assumed that the excess profits arose from the possession of monopoly power. In contrast, the Austrian approach would argue that the profits were temporary and are the necessary spur to innovation and efficiency. Thus Littlechild[1] considers that an innovating monopolist 'generates a social gain given by his own entrepreneurial profit plus the consumer surplus'.

Another important element of the Austrian approach is the importance of property rights and of the entrepreneur. If the entrepreneur is to seek after profits, then (s)he must have the claim to the profits generated, and hence, it is argued, the property rights to the profits must be assigned to the entrepreneur. The single entrepreneur is seen to be willing to take risks, to strive for lower costs etc., because (s)he will be the beneficiary of any resulting profits. In an organization with a large number of owners, the link between effort and profits is much diluted. The essential difficulty of nationalised industries, workers' co-operatives and also of large manager-controlled corporations is seen to be that ownership is dispersed.[2]

These lines of argument can be seen to have influenced the policies of the present government. The stress on property rights, with a strongly implied preference for private ownership over public ownership, is reflected in the privatisation programme discussed below. The emphasis on competition as a process and the focus on conditions of entry into an industry rather than the number of incumbent firms have influenced monopolies and mergers policies.

4.3   Developmental State

A quite different view of the appropriate roles of private firms, markets and the State is given by a set of ideas which we include under the heading of the developmental state. The 'market failure' approach discussed above focuses on government intervention when markets in some sense fail, and could also be described in a number of respects as the regulatory view of the state (e.g.

---

[1] S.Littlechild, 'Misleading Calculations of the Social Cost of Monopoly Power', *EJ*, vol. 91 (1981).
[2] There may be cases such as mutual organizations like building societies where the ownership of the assets of the organization may be very difficult to define.

regulating monopolies). The developmental state view is seen as complementary with the regulatory view.[1]

Marquand[2] argues that 'the state has played a central part in economic development in virtually all industrial societies, with the possible exception of early nineteenth century Britain. Even in Britain, moreover, the state played an important facilitating role' in passing a variety of Acts of Parliament which allowed for example the building of the railways and the necessary infrastructure.

There are numerous examples of the developmental state in the post-war era, and here three (Japan, France and Italy) are briefly discussed to indicate the type of policies which a developmental state may follow.

The economic success of Japan in the last four decades is well known. Whilst Japan has operated a market economy, there has been much government influence on the direction of development of the economy. Much of this was undertaken through the Ministry of International Trade and Industry (MITI). The essential objective of industrial policy was to move Japan from a relatively backward economy specializing in labour-intensive products to an advanced industrial power. This meant moving the economy away from the production of goods and services in which it had a comparative advantage to the production of industrial products (initially products such as ships, steel, and later cars and computers). It involved targeting certain key sectors of the economy for development. A barrage of policy devices was used to protect the key sectors and to ensure their development. These included

> the extensive use, narrow targeting and timely revision of tax incentives; the use of indicative plans to set goals and guidelines for the entire economy; the creation of numerous, formal and continuously operating forums for exchanging views, reviewing policies, obtaining feedback and resolving differences; the assignment of some government functions to various private and semi-private associations . . . ; an extensive reliance on public corporations, particularly of the mixed public-private variety, to implement policy in high-risk or otherwise refractory area; the creation and use by the government of an unconsolidated 'investment budget' . . . ; the orientation of anti-trust policy to developmental and international competitive goals rather than strictly to the maintenance of domestic competition; government-conducted or government-sponsored research and development (the computer industry); and the use of the government's licensing and approval authority to achieve developmental goals.[3]

---

[1] This distinction is drawn by R.Dore, 'Industrial Policy and How the Japanese Do It', *Catalyst*, Spring 1986, and K.Cowling, 'An Industrial Strategy for Britain: the Nature and Role of Planning', *IRAE*, vol. 1 (1987).
[2] D.Marquand, *The Unprincipled Society* (Fontana Press, 1988).
[3] Chalmers Johnson, *MITI and the Japanese Miracle: The Growth of Industrial Policy, 1925–1975* (Stanford University Press, Stanford, 1982).

The route initially followed in France was the use of national plans (which influenced the National Plan drawn up for the UK in the mid-sixties). One feature of the French approach was that the plan 'is at one and the same time comprehensive and passive. The plan provides a coordinating structure plus information flows but the planners are left in a peripheral position in relation to crucial strategic decisions . . .'.[1]

One of the intentions of such a national plan is that it presents a consistent economic scenario against which individual firms can make their investment and other decisions. Investment decisions are geared to future growth prospects, and one intention of 'indicative planning' is that firms share common expectations about those growth prospects. There is an element of expectations becoming self-fulfilling: the expectation of fast growth becomes translated into a high level of investment which then enables the growth to occur. Another aspect of 'indicative planning' is the identification of constraints on economic growth and the direction of resources to overcome those constraints.

French governments have generally pursued policies of support for 'national champions' in certain strategic, high-technology industries. Assistance has been provided to such industries on a highly selective basis, and can range from provision of subsidies, protection from foreign competition and the use of public procurement programmes etc.

State holding companies in Italy (particularly the Institute for Industrial Reconstruction, IRI) have been important instruments in industrial development. The development of an Italian steel industry and telecommunications industry came largely from the initiative of IRI. There has been a heavy involvement of the public sector in trading activities, and these have included partial ownership of trading companies. In recent years, there has been an emphasis on the promotion of investment, research and innovation through subsidies and other incentives.

The general idea of the developmental state is that the private market will not produce the best possible outcome. It identifies a range of ways by which state intervention can operate to improve the operation of markets. Some industrial policies pursued in Britain over the past thirty years can be seen as influenced by that general idea. The creation of the National Plan in the mid-sixties was to some degree based on the French experience. Similarly, the original idea of the National Enterprise Board was strongly influenced by the Italian experience with state holding companies.[2]

5   COMPETITION POLICY: AN INTRODUCTION

From 1948 onwards, British governments have operated with a varying degree of vigour, evolving competition policies. It is convenient for

[1] Cowling, *op. cit.*
[2] See, for example, S. Holland, *The State as Entrepreneur* (Weidenfeld and Nicolson, 1971).

purposes of discussion to divide these policies into five different types. The first to emerge was monopoly policy (starting from the 1948 Monopoly and Restrictive Practices Act), which originally covered restrictive practices as well. The restrictive practices policy was separated from monopoly policy with the passage of the Restrictive Trade Practices Act 1956. Some control over mergers and acquisitions was added in 1965, and the Office of Fair Trading (OFT), created in 1973, is heavily involved in the administration of competition policy. The impact of EC membership for competition policy is considered in section 10.

5.1 Monopoly Policy

The previous discussion suggested that a situation of monopoly offered some advantages over a comparable situation of perfect competition but also some disadvantages. A situation of monopoly provides the monopolist with substantial market power. This power could be used to raise prices and lower output (as compared with a situation with more firms). It may enable more research and development to be undertaken and economies of scale to be exploited. In addition, though, the monopolist can in effect take the monopoly profits by allowing costs to rise above those technically necessary.

Monopoly policy since 1973 has had the following structure. A firm (or group of firms acting in concert) can be referred to the Monopolies and Mergers Commission (MMC hereafter) for investigation when its market share is thought to exceed 25 per cent. Thus the statutory definition of monopoly is a market share of 25 per cent. The MMC are required to first investigate whether the firm (or firms) concerned do indeed have a market share of 25 per cent. The major part of their work is to investigate whether the actions and performance of the monopolist have been in the public interest. The public interest is not precisely defined and its interpretation has indeed varied. However, successive Acts since 1948 have indicated that regard should be paid, *inter alia*, to efficient production and distribution, a balanced distribution of industry and employment within the United Kingdom, increase of efficiency and the encouragement of new enterprise. The only change of significance has been the explicit mention of the desirability of competition *per se* in the Fair Trading Act of 1973.

British monopoly policy operates on a discretionary basis. The Secretary of State for Trade and Industry has discretion over whether a firm (or group of firms believed to be acting together) are referred to the MMC for investigation. In practice, there are many firms with market shares of over 25 per cent which have not been referred for investigation. Further, the MMC has considerable discretion over the interpretation of the public interest. There is no explicit build-up of case law.

In its reports the MMC gives its judgement and usually makes recommendations for changes in the firm's behaviour, though the implementation of any such recommendations is in the hands of the Secretary of State for Trade and Industry. In the overwhelming majority of cases, the MMC has made some criticisms of the practices of the firms under investigation. Predominant in terms of number of times reported amongst the practices which have been condemned are restriction of sale of competitors' goods, price notification agreements, monopoly pricing and profits and discriminatory pricing.[1] Most of the practices found to be against the public interest were aspects of behaviour which either operated to make life more difficult for (actual or potential) competitors without benefiting consumers through the supply of 'better' products or the charging of lower prices. These types of behaviour include supplying a retail outlet only if that outlet agreed not to sell competitors' goods and the favouring of some firms at the expense of others by discriminatory pricing. Excessive profits and prices have generally been condemned, particularly when reinforced by entry barriers and restrictions on competition. In the past few years, increasing attention has been given by the MMC to the effect which an existing monopoly or oligopoly position has on competition and on the possibility of new entry into the industry concerned. The majority of those recent MMC reports on monopoly situations which have found activities as against the public interest have included the restriction of competition amongst the activities against the public interest.

In none of their reports did the MMC condemn a monopoly position as such and recommend structural change. The nearest the MMC came to recommending structural change was in the case of roadside advertising services.[2] Ten companies had set up and owned a company called British Posters Ltd, and the MMC made the recommendation, which was carried out, that this company be disbanded. In March 1989, the MMC recommended that brewers be limited to the ownership of 2,000 public houses, and six brewers operated more than this number (with Bass operating the most at 7,100).[3] However, after negotiations between the Department of Trade and Industry and the brewers, an order was made requiring those brewers with more than 2,000 tied public houses to release a half of the number in excess of 2,000.

5.2   Merger Policy

Since 1965, a proposed merger which would create or enhance a monopoly position or which involves the acquisition of assets above a specified size, is

[1] For a summary of practices found against public interest, see *Review of Monopolies and Mergers Policy, A Consultative Document*, Cmnd. 7198 (HMSO, 1978).
[2] Monopolies and Mergers Commission, *Roadside Advertising Services: A Report on the Supply in the UK of Roadside Advertising Services* (HMSO, HC 365, 1981).
[3] Monopolies and Mergers Commission, *The Supply of Beer* (HMSO, 1989).

evaluated by the government. The definition of a monopoly position is that used in the monopoly policy, i.e. a market share of more than 25 per cent. The size requirement for a merger to be evaluated was initially set at £5m, raised to £15m in 1980 and further raised to £30m in mid-1984. The initial evaluation of a proposed merger is made by a panel of civil servants (the Mergers Panel), who consider whether there should be a referral of the merger to the MMC for further investigation. The final decision on referral is made by the Secretary of State for Trade and Industry, with advice from the Director-General of Fair Trading (DGFT). A firm contemplating a merger can seek confidential guidance from the OFT on its likely attitude to the proposed merger. The bidding firm can also respond to such guidance by designing the takeover bid in such a way as to reduce the chances of referral of the merger to the MMC. For example, a firm may seek to acquire another but state its intention to re-sell part of the firm acquired to avoid the creation of a monopoly position. Any investigation by the MMC is normally expected to be completed within six months, during which time the takeover bid usually lapses (under the conditions of the Stock Exchange Takeover Code). The changes in merger policy arising from the move to a European Single Market are considered below in section 10.

The thrust of the current policy has been described by the then Secretary of State for Trade and Industry (Norman Tebbit) in July 1984 in the following terms. 'I regard mergers policy as an important part of the government's general policy of promoting competition within the economy in the interests of the customer and of efficiency and hence of growth and jobs. Accordingly my policy has been and will continue to be to make references primarily on competition grounds.' The report of this speech continues by saying that '[i]n evaluating the competitive situation in individual cases Mr Tebbit said he would have regard to the international context: to the extent of competition in the home market from non-UK sources; and to the competitive position of UK companies in overseas markets'.[1] Some other aspects of the public interest continue to be taken into account but a recently added consideration is any state-owned company involvement (e.g. a foreign nationalized firm).

The limited impact of merger policy is evident from the proportion of proposed mergers investigated by the MMC. During the period 1965 to 1978, about $2\frac{1}{2}$ per cent of proposed mergers covered by the Fair Trading Act were referred to the MMC for more detailed consideration, with the remainder allowed to proceed. In the period 1979 to 1990, 2,918 mergers fell within the scope of the legislation, of which 108 potential mergers were referred to the MMC, amounting to nearly $3\frac{3}{4}$ per cent of total.[2] In the period 1979–90 of the 108 mergers referred to the MMC, 34 were declared against the public

---

[1] The quote in the text is taken from a speech by the then Trade and Industry Secretary, Norman Tebbit, as reported in *British Business*, 13 July 1984, p. 381.
[2] There were a number of instances when a single company was subject to more than one takeover proposal.

interest, 52 were declared as not against the public interest, and 22 were abandoned by the firms involved before the MMC reported and the referral was withdrawn.[1]

5.3   Restrictive Practices

Restrictive practices cover matters such as agreement between firms over prices to be charged, over sharing out a market (e.g. agreeing that each geographical area be supplied by only one firm) etc. The major legislation on restrictive practices dates from 1956. There are two notable contrasts between the policy on restrictive practices and policy on monopolies and mergers. The first is that the body which is charged with the operation of the restrictive practices legislation is part of the judiciary, namely the Restrictive Practices Court (hereafter RPC). This means that there is a build up of case law on restrictive practices, in contrast to the situation with monopolies and mergers policy. The second is that there is a presumption in the legislation that restrictive practices are against the public interest unless proved otherwise (whereas the merger legislation has the presumption in favour of mergers). This presumption against restrictive practices has been reinforced by the way in which the RPC has interpreted the legislation. There are eight 'gateways' through which a restrictive practice can pass in order to continue.[2]

Initially the restrictive practices legislation covered only goods, but was extended to cover services in 1976. The application of the restrictive practices legislation to the operation of the Stock Exchange led eventually to the reorganization of the Stock Exchange in October 1986 in the 'Big Bang' (see Chapter 2). The restrictive practices operated by the Stock Exchange were referred to the RPC but the matter was taken out of their hands by the government. An Act of Parliament was enacted to exempt the Stock Exchange from the restrictive practices legislation in exchange for a number of concessions by the London Stock Exchange, the most important of which was the scrapping of minimum commission rates.

Resale price maintenance (RPM) is one type of restrictive practice which is separately dealt with under the Resale Prices Act 1976. RPM operates when a supplier makes it a condition of supply of goods to retailers that the retailers charge consumers at least some minimum price. Under the Act, such a condition is generally illegal. This legislation contains the presumption against RPM, with the possibility of exemptions being granted by the RPC. Although RPM has declined substantially, firms may resort to practices such as stating recommended prices which can have similar effects. The Office of Fair Trading receives around 35 complaints a year to the effect that

---

[1]   The corresponding figures for the period 1965 to 1978 were 14 declared against the public interest, 14 not against the public interest and 15 abandoned before a report was made.
[2]   These gateways included the defence that removal of the restrictive practice would cause unemployment, lead to public injury or a fall in exports.

producers are imposing conditions on the minimum price to be charged by retailers or wholesalers. In the past few years, investigation of these complaints has led to a few firms (around four to five a year) being required to give undertakings to desist from imposing minimum prices to be charged as a condition of supply.

5.4   Consumer Protection

Some other limitations on the activities of firms come from legislation relating to consumer protection, much of which is enforced by the DGFT and by Trading Standards Officers. The DGFT has a duty to collect and assess information on commercial activities, so that trading practices which may affect consumers' interests may be discovered. The DGFT has sought to draw up codes of practice in a range of industries (covering, for example, direct selling, double glazing, motor trade and credit) and can set in motion procedures which can lead to the banning of specified trade practices. Under the Fair Trading Act 1973, the DGFT can seek assurances on future good conduct when traders persistently disregard their obligations under the law in a manner detrimental to consumers, and if such assurances are not given or given and then broken the DGFT can bring proceedings to obtain a court order (breach of which may result in action for contempt of court). In the 18 years up to 1990, the DGFT had sought assurances, court undertakings and orders in connection with 720 traders, with the five sectors of car & motoring, electrical, home improvements, mail order and carpets & furniture accounting for 535 of these cases.

Another area of regulation and consumer protection which is overseen by the Office of Fair Trading is credit licensing. However, that aspect as well as the regulation of financial markets in general has already been discussed in Chapter 2. Under the Control of Misleading Advertisements Regulations 1988, the Office of Fair Trading can take action (including court orders) to limit such advertisements and dealt with nearly 600 complaints under this heading in 1990.

6   STRUCTURAL REORGANIZATION

The policies on monopolies, mergers and restrictive practices can have impacts on industrial structure, even if those impacts are to prevent change occurring as would be the case with mergers policy. Whilst the present Conservative government has sought to withdraw from direct intervention in industrial structure and behaviour, this represents a significant change from previous practice. This section briefly reviews the structural reorganization policies which have been pursued. It should be noted first that a number of industries (e.g. coal-mining, steel, railways), which appear to be in long-term decline in most industrialized countries, have been under public ownership in Britain. The contraction of these industries has then been largely in the hands of government. In some cases (e.g. steel) there were many companies involved in the industry at the time of nationalization, but the privatization of these industries has resulted in only one company in each industry (British Steel) being returned to the private sector.

The major agency designed to promote general structural change was the Industrial Reorganization Corporation (hereafter IRC) which came into existence in December 1966, its operation effectively ending four years later. The IRC operated mainly through the promotion of mergers, and its aims have been summarized as 'threefold. First, they aimed to increase productivity by improving the logical structure of industry ... Secondly, they aimed to promote (or at least not harm) regional development. Thirdly, they aimed at retaining company control in the UK'.[1] In contrast to the philosophy underlying existing merger policy (and industrial policy more generally) the IRC was based on the view that market forces were inadequate. McClelland[2] stated that one of the propositions

> on which the case for the IRC rests is that market forces would not have cured these structural inadequacies quickly enough. In theory, where there are economies of scale to be exploited, or where one company's management is inadequate, the stock market provides a mechanism whereby a takeover bid will occur. In practice, the mechanism is often ineffective. Shareholders are inadequately informed, directors have vested interests; having regard to the risks for any particular party, finance may not be forthcoming.

The IRC sought to use a combination of persuasion and money (to help finance takeover bids) to encourage mergers.

The National Enterprise Board formally existed from 1975 until 1981, though its effective role was ended in 1979. Although it had been conceived originally as part of a considerable extension of public ownership and government intervention, it actually performed two rather different roles. The first one, which involved the bulk of its funds, was to act as a holding company for the government stake in companies such as British Leyland and Rolls Royce, which had come into public ownership through government rescue of large companies in danger of going bankrupt. The second role was that of filling a gap in the capital market through the provision of finance to firms involved in areas of advanced technology and to medium-sized firms to foster regional development.[3]

---

[1] A. Graham, 'Industrial Policy', in W. Beckerman (ed.), *The Labour Government's Economic Record* (Duckworth, 1972).
[2] W. G. McClelland, 'The Industrial Reorganisation Corporation 1966–71: An Experimental Prod', *TBR*, no. 94 (1972).
[3] For further discussion see M. Sawyer, 'Industrial Policy', in M. Artis and D. Cobham (eds), *Labour's Economic Policies, 1974–1979* (Manchester University Press, 1991).

6.1   Policies towards Small Businesses

The present government has placed considerable emphasis on the promotion and formation of small businesses. There is no precise definition of small business, and the promotion of small business is often undertaken on the grounds that today's successful small business is tomorrow's large business. Following the Bolton Committee,[1] independent businesses employing less than 200 people have been regarded as small businesses, though many would regard that size limit as too high especially when applied outside the manufacturing sector.

The Enterprise Allowance Scheme (EAS) began in 1982 to encourage the formation of new businesses by the unemployed. The amount paid as an allowance can now be varied, previously having been £40 a week, with the payment being made for a year with recipients required to provide at least £1000 in start-up capital (which can be borrowed). Up to 1990/1 it was claimed that over 566,000 unemployed had been helped to become self-employed.[2] Estimates based on the earlier years of the scheme estimated that of every 100 aided under the EAS, 57 are still operating after 3 years, and those surviving firms provide a further 65 jobs. The survival rate six months after the end of the period for which the allowance has been paid was 73 per cent in 1990–1.[3] The estimation of the effect of any policy designed to create or protect employment is fraught with difficulties. The policy may appear to help the creation of jobs which would have been created anyway. Further, the jobs created may be at the expense of jobs elsewhere in the economy. The establishment of a new business will to some degree attract custom from existing firms. The Department of Employment assumes that half of the EAS businesses displace existing business, but admit that there is no firm statistical basis for this estimate.

The Small Firm Loan Guarantee Scheme is designed to fill a perceived gap in the availability of finance for small and medium sized firms. Application for finance is made direct to a bank which is responsible for the appraisal of the scheme, but subject to final approval by the Department of Employment. In the case of default on the loan, the bank can call on the guarantee provided (on a proportion of the loan) by the Department of Employment. The borrower is charged an interest rate premium (over that which would be charged by the bank). In 1990/1 new loans to a total of £86 million were made to over 3,400 applicants, and the failure rate three years after loan was made was running at 32 per cent.

---

[1] *Report of the Committee of Inquiry on Small Firms*, Cmnd. 4811 (HMSO, 1971), often referred to as the Bolton Committee Report after the name of chair of the committee.
[2] Source: *The Government's Expenditure Plans 1992–1993 to 1994–1995, Department of Employment*, Cmnd. 1906 (HMSO, 1992); see also National Audit Office, Department of Employment/Training Commission: *Assistance to Small Firms*, HC 655 (HMSO, 1988).
[3] Source: *The Government's Expenditure Plans 1992–1993 to 1994–1995, Department of Employment*, Cmnd. 1906 (HMSO, 1992).

The Business Expansion Scheme (BES) provides tax relief on money invested in business (with a limit of £500,000 on the total amount invested in a single company within a year). The intention of this scheme is to encourage the supply of venture capital and the financing of relatively small firms.

The figures in Table 4.3 above suggest significant recent growth in the number of small businesses in manufacturing industries. The number of self-employed has grown from around 2 million in 1980 to just over 3 million in 1991. How far these changes are a result of the types of policies described above and how far a result of changing market and technological conditions is a matter of considerable debate.

6.2   Informal Planning

The present government has displayed considerable hostility towards any idea of planning and government intervention. There had, however, been a variety of attempts during the sixties and seventies to have government involvement in the co-ordination of economic activity. The establishment of the National Economic Development Council (NEDC) in 1962 as a tripartite body representing employers, trade unions and government, supported by a permanent staff, was the first major move. The NEDC continued in existence until 1992, but it played little role over the last decade. The general idea behind the establishment of the NEDC was to build a consensus between the various parties involved on the problems facing the British economy. The establishment of EDCs covering individual industries was intended to provide a forum within which impediments to faster growth could be identified and overcome.

The industrial strategy[1] pursued by the 1974–9 Labour government sought to build on this structure. The first stage of that strategy was to analyse difficulties facing particular sectors and search for ways of overcoming those difficulties. Some sectors of the economy were viewed as particularly important for future success, and the idea behind the strategy was to identify and then aid those sectors which were important and potentially successful. Sector Working Parties (SWPs) were tripartite bodies involving government, business and trade unions established to aid the implementation of the strategy. A major problem which this approach faces is that of the implementation of the remedies for the difficulties identified, for the tripartite bodies did not have powers of implementation.

The Industry Act 1972 provided powers for government to provide selective financial assistance to industry. An example of such assistance was the wool textile scheme which was designed to encourage new investment and the rationalization of existing capacity. This Act was used by the industrial strategy to finance sectoral schemes such as the provision of assistance for investment. Fifteen sectoral schemes were supported under section 7 of the

---

[1]   *An Approach to Industrial Strategy*, Cmnd. 6315 (HMSO, 1975).

1972 Industry Act as part of the industrial strategy, and the government estimated that these had led to the creation of 150,000 new jobs and the protection of 90,000 others,[1] though the point made above on the difficulties of the estimation of impact of such policies on jobs would also apply here.

7   PRIVATIZATION

The major programme of nationalization in the post-war period was undertaken by the Labour Governments of 1945–51. During that period, industries such as coal-mining, railways, part of road haulage (later de-nationalized), gas, electricity and the Bank of England were nationalised. Nationalization in the sixties and seventies was concentrated on industries in long-term decline (such as steel, shipbuilding and aerospace). Individual firms such as British Leyland and part of Rolls-Royce came into public ownership more by accident than design as a response by the government to the threat of the extinction through bankruptcy of those firms.

The general trend in the direction of nationalization has been sharply broken over the past decade. Whilst there was some limited sale of nationalized firms during the period of Conservative Government in 1970–4, these were restricted to the sale of a travel agency (Thomas Cook) and state-owned public houses in the Carlisle area. During the period of the Conservative governments from 1979 onwards, privatization, which started off in a rather low-key way, has grown in importance particularly since 1984.

The term 'privatization' has been used to cover a number of different policies. It is convenient to distinguish three policies which have sometimes been included under the heading of privatization.[2] The first type of policy is the sale of assets which the government had previously owned, and this would constitute the narrow definition of privatization (and the sense in which the term will be used below). In some cases, as in the first stages of the privatization programme, the assets sold were largely those which had been relatively recently acquired by the government and often as part of a rescue programme. This part of privatization was largely a selling off of those assets which had been acquired by the National Enterprise Board under the preceding Labour government. In other cases (notably the sale of part of British Telecom), the privatization involved the sale of firms which had been nationalized for long periods of time.

---

[1] *Trade and Industry*, 24.11.1978, p. 383.
[2] For further discussion of privatization see, e.g., Symposium on Privatization and After, *FSt*, vol. 5 (1984); J. Kay and A. Silberston, 'The New Industrial Policy – Privatisation and Competition', *MBR*, Spring 1984 (1984); J. Kay and D. Thompson, 'Privatisation: A Policy in Search of a Rationale', *EJ*, vol. 96 (1986); J. Vickers and G. Yarrow, *Privatization: An Economic Analysis* (M.I.T. Press, 1988). For a more critical approach, see B. Fine, 'Scaling the Commanding Heights of Public Enterprise Economics', *CJE*, vol. 14 (1990).

TABLE 4.6

Proceeds from the Sale of Public Assets (£bn at 1989/90 prices)

1979/80	0.8	1980/81	0.4	1981/82	0.8	1982/83	0.7
1983/84	1.6	1984/85	2.7	1985/86	3.4	1986/87	5.4
1987/88	5.9	1988/89	7.5	1989/90	4.2	1991/92	4.9 (est.)

Source: Public Expenditure Analyses to 1993/94, Cmnd. 1520 (HMSO).

The second type of policy, often labelled 'contracting-out', is the provision to public bodies (government departments, nationalized industries, publicly owned hospital and schools) of certain goods and services by private firms, which had previously been provided by the public bodies themselves. Public bodies have always purchased goods and services from the private sector, and this policy of 'contracting-out' aims to increase the extent to which that is done. An example of 'contracting-out' is the use of private contract cleaning firms by hospitals instead of the hospitals hiring their own cleaning staff.

The third type of policy included under this heading does not necessarily involve any change of ownership that would be implied by the term privatization and could be more accurately labelled de-regulation or liberalization. This policy involves the removal of some of the restrictions on

TABLE 4.7

Main Asset Sales by British Government, 1979–91

Sale of Shares
Amersham International
Associated British Ports
British Aerospace
British Airports Authority
British Airways
British Gas
British Steel
British Telecom
Britoil
Cable and Wireless
Enterprise Oil
Jaguar Cars
Electricity companies and Regional electricity boards
Rolls-Royce
Regional water companies (12 in number)

Other Sales
Royal Ordnance and Rover Cars to British Aerospace
Sealink sold to British Ferries
National Freight sold to consortium of managers, employees and company pensioners
National Bus Company (sold as 72 separate companies)
Girobank sold to Alliance and Leicester Building Society
British Shipbuilders (warship yards)
Sales of minority shareholdings in British Sugar, British Petroleum, ICL, Ferranti and
  British Technology Group
Sales of property etc. of Crown Agents Holdings, Forestry Commission, New Town
  Development Corporation

which firms can provide certain types of goods or services (for example, limits on companies which are able to provide local bus services). The link between privatization and de-regulation is that the firms eligible to provide the goods and services have often been publicly owned.

The scale of the privatization programme in terms of the receipts from sales is indicated in Table 4.6. It can be seen that in the early 1980s, the receipts from privatization were relatively modest, but rose in 1984–5 with the first part of the proceeds from the sale of British Telecom. From 1986–7 onwards, the proceeds from privatization have been around £5 billion, and are projected around that level for the next few years, though the figure will inevitably drop as few nationalized industries remain which could be sold. Since the sale of assets is counted as negative public expenditure, these sales were useful for a government committed to the reduction of public expenditure and of the budget deficit. The scope of the privatization programme is also indicated in Table 4.7, which provides a list of the main asset sales.

The setting of the issue price of the shares in the to-be-privatized firms presents a dilemma.[1] The government wishes to secure proceeds from the sale which are as great as possible but at the same time wishes to ensure that the sale is successful. The spread of share ownership amongst individuals has also been one of the aims of the Conservative governments,[2] and this points in the direction of a lower price (to encourage sales). Indeed, the observation that the shares of privatized firms have traded immediately after privatization at levels above the issue price suggests that the issue price has been set too low.[3] The privatized public utilities have been sold with their monopoly position largely intact. This would be expected to lead to higher profits and a higher market valuation as compared with the break-up of the

---

[1]   In a number of cases (e.g. sale of the Rover group to British Aerospace), shares were not offered to the public and the company was sold as a going concern to another company. In such cases, the considerations in the text do not apply.

[2]   The proportion of shares owned directly by individuals has tended to decline throughout the postwar period, whilst ownership by financial institutions (mainly banks, unit trusts, pension funds and insurance companies) has tended to rise. This has continued during the 1980s, with the proportion of shares held by individuals declining from 30.4 per cent at the end of 1981 to 23.4 per cent by the end of 1989 (figures taken from CSO, *Share Register Survey Report*, HMSO, 1991).

In privatized companies at the end of 1989, individuals owned 18.4 per cent and financial institutions 49.0 per cent, with central government retaining 19.2 per cent. One effect of the privatization programme appears to have been to increase the number of shareholders; estimates vary but from something of the order of 5–7 per cent of the adult population to around 20 per cent. However, the impact here of privatization appears to be of shareholders with a small holding of shares in one or two companies.

[3]   For some details see Vickers and Yarrow, *op. cit.*, pp. 173–80. Their Table 7.1 (covering sales up to the end of 1987) indicates that where the sale was at a set price (rather than by tender offer) the gross proceeds to the government were £16,782m. The estimated under-valuation on these sales is £3,517m (using the share price at the end of the first day of trading for these estimates, i.e. over 20 per cent of the gross proceeds).

public utilities into competing firms. Thus, striving for a higher price for the firm conflicts with the aim of increased competition.

There has not yet been a full evaluation of the effect of privatization in the UK. Our discussion considers, first, the theoretical issues and then refers to the general evidence on comparisons between the performance of private and public sector companies.

In the first phase of privatization, the companies which were privatized were mainly companies which had been in competition with private-sector companies even when nationalized. Some of this privatization was the sale of assets which had been acquired by the National Enterprise Board under the preceding Labour government. In the second phase the focus shifted to the sale of public utilities, beginning with British Telecom, continuing with British Gas, and then electricity and water companies.

The issues raised by privatization are rather different for the sale of companies in competition with others and for the sale of public utilities. The managers of a company operate under a variety of constraints, but two sets of constraints are generally emphasized by economic analysis. The first is that which derives from the nature of the market in which the firm operates. It is generally argued that the more competition the less discretion the managers have and the greater the pressure to strive for maximum profits. The second arises from the capital market and relates to takeovers. The argument is that if the current management fail to make the best use of the assets at their disposal, then the company is likely to become the target of a hostile takeover bid. Others will see that they can put the assets to more profitable use and launch a takeover bid. Suppose that on the basis of the existing management and the expected profits and dividends the stock market values firm A at V_a. Further, suppose that another company (or set of potential owners) believe that the value of firm A would be V_b, then they would be prepared to pay up to V_b for firm A. In order to be successful, a takeover bid has to offer a price substantially above the existing stock market valuation; and premia of 20–30 per cent are common. There are also significant costs associated with launching a takeover bid (e.g. cost of advice from merchant bank, press advertising campaign directed to shareholders of target company).

It is debatable whether most takeovers are of the hostile form which this line of argument would indicate, and also whether the effect of takeovers is to raise the efficiency and profitability of the assets acquired (see p. 253, fn 1). In the case of a number of privatized firms, the government has retained a so-called golden share which prevents a takeover (for example, a 'special share' in Rolls-Royce would enable the Secretary of State for Trade and Industry to limit foreign and individual ownership, which in effect blocks a takeover). In the case of British Telecom, the government initially retained a 49 per cent stake, subsequently reduced to 25 per cent. A merger may not come to fruition because of an adverse judgement by the MMC, and it is arguable whether a government would be prepared to allow the acquisition of companies such as, say, British Gas or British Telecom especially if the acquiring firm were foreign.[1] It can also be noted that all mergers between water companies with gross assets of more than £30 million must be referred to the MMC.

The nature of the market in which a firm operates is generally seen to place constraints on what the firm can and cannot do. It is, of course, usually argued that a firm in a monopoly position has much more freedom of manoeuvre than a firm in a situation of atomistic competition. Many firms which have been privatized, such as the Rover Group, Jaguar, National Freight Corporation, etc. were operating in competition with many other firms even when nationalized. The act of privatization has not changed the nature of the market in which they operate.

When public utilities have been privatized with their monopoly position largely intact, then their activities have been subject to regulation. The major regulatory authorities are the Office of Gas Supply (OFGAS), of Telecommunications (OFTEL), of Water (OFWAT) and of Electricity Regulation (OFFER) with possible referral of the monopoly situation to the MMC.

The regulation has three aspects to which attention is drawn here. The first relates to price. In the case of gas, prices for domestic consumers are allowed to change to fully reflect changes in the cost of gas, whereas any rise in non-gas costs can only be reflected in price to the extent of 2 per cent below the rise in the retail price index (RPI). Similarly, the price of an index of BT's services is limited to a rise of 6 per cent below the rise in the RPI, but since this applies to an index of all services the price of some services can be increased much more. The formulae for the water companies has been described as RPI + K, where the K varies between the companies and between years, and has been set to the year 2000. This formula generally allows price rises faster than inflation to permit the companies to generate investment funds. A further restriction on the water companies is that half of the proceeds of land disposals must be used for price reductions. This approach involves certain difficulties. The public utilities have little incentive to keep price increases below the limit set. The limitation of price increases to 2 or 3 per cent below the rate of increase of the RPI is presumably based on an assumption about the rate of productivity increase which can be achieved. But that productivity increase is likely to vary over time and to depend on investment decisions made by the utility. There is also the difficulty for the regulatory authority of securing the relevant information. This is illustrated by the following quotation from the Director-General of Gas Supply:[2]

---

[1]   The Kuwait Investment Office (owned by the Kuwait government) built up a stake of 20 per cent in the oil company BP following the sale of the final British government stake in BP (which at one time had been 49 per cent). This was referred to the MMC, and the KIO was required to reduce its stake substantially.
[2]   Quote from the *Report of the Director-General of Gas Supply 1987*, HC 293 (HMSO, 1988).

Condition 3 of the authorization stipulates that, at the time of any change in its published tariffs, British Gas must provide OFGAS with a written forecast of the maximum average price per therm, together with its components, for the year in which the change is to take effect and the following year. These forecasts should contain sufficient information as to the assumptions underlying the forecasts to enable the Director-General to be reasonably satisfied that the forecasts have been properly prepared on a consistent basis. Initially British Gas refused to provide sufficient information for the Director-General to be so satisfied. This resulted in OFGAS giving notice in August that it proposed to make an order under section 28 of the Gas Act requiring B.G. to produce the necessary information.

Eventually information was provided and undertakings were given that information would be provided in future.

The second aspect concerns the general control over the possible use of monopoly power in other areas than those covered immediately above. This has largely related so far to the prices charged for the supply of gas or telephone services other than those subject to regulatory control. British Gas was referred to the MMC over pricing and supply of gas to contract customers (broadly speaking non-domestic customers). The MMC concluded that

> [w]e have found extensive discrimination by BG in the pricing and supply of gas to contract customers. We believe that this is attributable to the existence of the monopoly situation and operates or may be expected to operate against the public interest. First, BG's policy of price discrimination imposes higher costs on customers less well placed to use alternative fuels or to obtain such fuels on favourable terms. . . . Second, BG's policy of relating prices to those of alternatives available to each customer places it in a position selectively to undercut potential competing gas suppliers. This may be expected to deter new entrants and to inhibit the development of competition in this market. Third, the lack of transparency in pricing creates uncertainty in the minds of customers about future gas prices and renders more risky the business environment in which they operate.[1]

The third aspect relates to a range of unprofitable activities which the public utility is obliged or expected to undertake. This would include, for example, the provision of public call-boxes in remote areas.

The difficulties which confront the regulatory agency include obtaining the information necessary to perform their function (as indicated above). This may be exacerbated by the relatively small number of staff which they have, 30 in the case of OFGAS and 117 in the case of OFTEL. A problem

---

[1] Monopolies and Mergers Commission, *Gas*, Cmnd. 500 (HMSO, 1988).

which has been identified from American experience is that of 'agency capture'. This simply means that the personal contacts and interchange of personnel between the regulatory agency and the regulated firm as well as deliberate attempts by the regulated firm can lead the agency to act in the interests of the firm it is formally charged to regulate.

We turn now to the empirical question of whether ownership and control does make any difference to the efficiency of a firm. Making comparisons between the performance and efficiency of private and public sector companies is not a straightforward exercise. There are some general difficulties in making useful comparisons between companies which are in different situations (here of private or public ownership). There may be reasons why the firms are in different situations and those reasons can influence the comparisons. For example, a company may be in the public sector because it failed under private ownership but was judged to be too important to be allowed to go bankrupt. In such a case, a poor performance by a company under public ownership may not be due to the fact that it is in the public sector; rather, it is in the public sector because it is a poor performance company. Comparisons between public sector companies and private sector ones are also complicated by differences in the objectives of the two type of companies. Public sector companies may be required to maintain unprofitable services, be encouraged to maintain employment (particularly in periods of substantial unemployment) and be limited in their range of activities (e.g. British Rail is largely restricted to operating a railway service and is not permitted to diversify into other forms of transport).

Millward and Parker[1] conducted a wide-ranging survey on the available evidence, and indicate the extensive difficulties in making comparisons between privately owned and publicly owned firms. They conclude that 'while the results are rather mixed, there is some evidence that competition does reduce the costs of public firms and regulation raises the costs of private firms. Neither finding is inconsistent with the finding about the effects of "ownership" on costs – namely that, . . . there is no general indication that private firms are more cost efficient than public firms.'

Ferguson[2] summarized 15 comparisons of public and private sector efficiency. Eight of these refer to American electricity generation with the following conclusions. Two studies report no difference between the sectors, three report the public enterprise as more efficient and one reports private firms more efficient. One study finds both types of firm with costs $2\frac{1}{2}$ per cent above the competitive level, and the final study reports that private firms sell wholesale electricity at higher prices and buy in at lower prices (than public sector firms). The results of the other seven studies (covering water, rail and airlines) are similar in tone.

---

[1] R.Millward and D.M.Parker, 'Public and Private Enterprise: Comparative Behaviour and Relative Efficiency', in R.Millward *et al.*, *Public Sector Economics* (Longmans, 1983).
[2] P.Ferguson, *Industrial Economics: Issues and Perspectives* (Macmillan, 1988).

Yarrow[1] concludes that

> ... private sector monitoring [i.e. private ownership] is more efficient
> where the relevant firm faces strong competition and other forms of
> product and factor market failure are relatively unimportant. ... The
> evidence on comparative performance in cases where product and
> factor markets inefficiencies are substantive is much less clear cut,
> Indeed, in examples such as electricity supply it tends to point in the
> other direction, towards better performance by public firms.

Contracting-out by the public sector has particularly affected local authorities and the health service.[2] In the near future, local authorities will be
compelled to seek competing tenders (i.e. bids from private companies as
well as estimates from their own workforce) for refuse collection, street and
building cleaning, vehicle and ground maintenance etc. Thus contracting-
out can be viewed as a move from a monopoly supply situation (e.g. where a
local authority always employed its own workforce for, say, refuse collection) to one of some competition (with a number of firms bidding for the
contract).

One survey has concluded 'that in areas such as refuse collection and
cleansing services, the available evidence points to privately owned firms
being cheaper on average than the municipal operations by a significant
amount'.[3] This conclusion is based mainly on American experience, though
some limited British evidence points in the same direction. A study of
competitive tendering in refuse collection[4] in Britain estimated that costs
under private contracting for refuse collection were 22 per cent below those
with local authority provision. However, in those cases where refuse collection had been put out to tender but the tender had been won by the local
authority refuse department, costs were also lower; in this case to the extent
of 17 per cent. The same group of authors[5] finds rather similar results for
hospital domestic services, namely private contracting of such services
resulted in a cost reduction of 34 per cent and of in-house provision after
competitive tendering of 22 per cent. However, there was some evidence of
private contractors offering unsustainably low prices ('loss-leaders') to
secure entry into this market. These studies would be consistent with the
view that it is competition rather than the form of ownership which is
relevant for efficiency.

A lower cost service is not necessarily more efficient than a higher cost
one, in that the lower costs may have been achieved by the payment of lower

[1]   G. Yarrow, 'Privatization in Theory and Practice', *EP*, 1986.
[2]   For extensive discussion see K. Ascher, *The Politics of Privatisation: Contracting-out Public Services* (Macmillan, 1987).
[3]   M. Waterson, *op. cit.*
[4]   S. Domberger, S. A. Meadowcroft and D. J. Thompson, 'Competitive Tendering and Efficiency: The Case of Refuse Collection', *FSt*, vol. 7 (1986).
[5]   S. Domberger, S. A. Meadowcroft and D. J. Thompson, 'The Impact of Competitive Tendering and the Costs of Hospital Domestic Services', *FSt*, vol. 8 (1987).

wages and by a lower quality service. In particular, the British studies referred to above do not make much allowance for possible lower quality and wages.[1]

Liberalization and de-regulation has not followed a uniform pattern. There have been some areas of de-regulation and liberalization. One area of increased regulation has been that of financial services, as discussed in Chapter 2. During the 1980s there has been, partly under the impact of changing technology, some liberalization in the telecommunications area. This has included, for example, the abolition of British Telecom's exclusive right to supply customer telephone apparatus (though the equipment has to be approved by the British Approvals Board for Telecommunications or the Secretary of State for Trade and Industry). The Secretary of State can also license firms other than British Telecom to run a telecommunications system. Mercury (a subsidiary of the recently privatized Cable and Wireless) has been granted such a licence. The effectiveness of Mercury in competing with British Telecom depends on the terms on which their network is connected in with the British Telecom network (since the vast majority of telephones are in that network). OFTEL has ruled that there must be full interconnection between the two networks.[2]

The Road Traffic Act 1930 brought in the regulation of bus services. Quality was regulated, by, for example, the setting of standards for vehicles and for drivers and this continues. The quantity of bus services was also regulated with licences required to be able to operate a particular route. These restrictions were lifted for inter-city bus services in 1980 and for most other bus services in 1986. One study on the deregulation of the inter-city services[3] found that prices of express bus services initially fell dramatically with many prices dropping to half their previous level. Prior to 1980, the right to operate many of the most important inter-city routes was held by the publicly owned National Bus Company. Those companies who had previously provided contract coach services provided a ready source of new entrants, helping to generate the substantial price fall. However, the National Bus Company was able to reassert its dominant position in a few years. Prices have since risen, and in many cases prices of express services have returned to close to their level (in real terms, that is relative to the retail price index) prior to deregulation. This study found that there were some gains in efficiency following deregulation.

The government argued that for local bus services, deregulation would bring reductions in unit costs of up to 30 per cent and viewed the market as 'highly contestable' (cf. p. 260 above).[4] Several changes took place

---

[1] For some critical comments on one of these studies see J. Gurley and J. Grahl, 'Competition and Efficiency in Refuse Collection: A Critical Comment', *FSt*, vol. 9 (1988).
[2] For further discussion see Vickers and Yarrow, *op. cit.*, Chapter 8.
[3] S. A. Jaffer and D. J. Thompson, 'Deregulating Express Coaches: A Reassessment', *FSt*, vol. 8 (1987).
[4] Department of Transport, *Buses*, Cmnd. 9300 (HMSO, 1984).

simultaneously including deregulation, compulsory competitive tendering of subsidized services, privatization and subsidy reduction.[1] Unit costs do appear to have fallen,[2] with some effect coming from falling fuel costs and from extending vehicle life but most from a combination of productivity gains and lower wages. A number of studies[3] have concluded that the bus market does not approach being perfectly contestable and issues of monopoly remain. Further, 'local bus markets have remained highly monopolised after deregulation. Active competition is relatively rare, and is probably now well past its peak'.[4] Whilst unit costs fell, there was also a decline in bus usage; where there was competition average waiting times fell but with uncertainty over timetables and lack of co-ordination of arrival of buses. One study[5] which sought to bring together the various effects concluded that competitive tendering (which operated in London) worked better than deregulation, and there were net gains from the changes in London and metropolitan areas but net losses in the shire counties and in Scotland.

8   PUBLIC ENTERPRISES

The nationalized industries contributed 9 per cent of GDP in 1979, and under the impact of privatization this figure had declined to 3 per cent in 1990. In 1990 these industries employed around 660,000. These figures refer only to public corporations and hence exclude ownership in other types of companies. Privatization has been more extensive in connection with those forms of state ownership.

The three main forms of public ownership in Britain have been:

(i)   the public corporation, which is a corporate body established by statute and free to manage its own affairs without detailed Parliamentary control;

(ii) sole or majority state shareholding in an otherwise conventional commercial company;

(iii) organization of an industry as a department of state under the direct control of a government minister. The Post Office was the only significant example of this approach, but was turned into a public corporation in 1969.

---

[1]   The special issue of *Journal of Transport Economics and Policy*, vol. 24, 1990, on bus deregulation contains detailed analysis of the various effects.

[2]   P.M.Heseltine and D.T.Silcock, 'The Effects of Bus Deregulation on Costs', *Journal of Transport Economics and Policy*, vol. 24, 1990.

[3]   For a summary see A.Evans, 'Competition and the Structure of Local Bus Markets', *Journal of Transport Economics and Policy*, vol. 24, 1990.

[4]   A.Evans, *ibid*.

[5]   P.R.White, 'Bus Deregulation: a Welfare Balance Sheet', *Journal of Transport Economics and Policy*, vol. 24, 1990.

The framework within which the public corporations operate has been subject to a number of changes in the post-war period. During the first phase the public corporations were largely required to break even on average. This requirement did not encourage efficiency. The 1961 White Paper[1] introduced financial targets for public corporations, with target rates of return specified for each industry but varying between industries depending on factors such as demand conditions and the degree to which the corporation was required to provide unprofitable services. The 1967 White Paper[2] brought in a number of innovations. These included:

(i)   the setting of prices to reflect long-run marginal costs;
(ii) subjecting investment to a test discount rate (initially set at 8 per cent, later increased to 10 per cent);
(iii) identifying and seeking government funding for any non-commercial activities (e.g. rural train services).

In addition, it was determined that industries would continue to be required to meet a financial target.

The 1978 White Paper[3] signalled a substantial downgrading of the linking of price with marginal cost. It also led to the framework of control which is currently in use. This framework has a number of elements. Strategic objectives are agreed by the relevant government department with each industry and these provide the framework within which the financial controls and industrial planning procedures are set. Investment is usually required to secure a 5 per cent rate of return in real terms (i.e. after allowing for inflation) before taxes and interest payments. In some industries, public enterprise may have little discretion over prices through competition with other firms. In those industries where nationalized industries do have discretion, 'the financial targets will determine the level of prices in the light of general objectives, their control of costs and the need to cover the continuing cost of supply including an adequate return on capital'.[4] Financial targets were set usually for three years ahead. These limits in effect cover the cash flow (difference between revenue and the sum of current and capital expenditures) of the public corporations, which means that there is an additional constraint which largely bites on the investment programme of the public corporations. These EFLs may be negative (which means that the public corporation concerned is required to make a net contribution to the Exchequer), or positive. The government's concern with the public sector

---

[1] *Financial and Economic Obligations of the Nationalised Industries*, Cmnd. 1337 (HMSO, 1961).
[2] *Nationalised Industries: A Review of Economic and Financial Objectives*, Cmnd. 3437 (HMSO, 1967).
[3] *The Nationalised Industries*, Cmnd. 7131 (HMSO, 1978).
[4] *The Government's Expenditure Plans 1988/9–1990/1*, Cmnd. 288 (HMSO, 1988).

TABLE 4.8

Statistics Relating to Research and Development Expenditure

	Expenditure on Research and Development as % of GDP		Defence R & D as % of Government-financed R & D
	1983	1989	1990
United Kingdom	2.3	2.25	44.8
France	2.1	2.34	37.0[a]
Germany	2.5	2.88	13.5
Italy	1.0	1.25	10.3[a]
Japan	2.4	2.98	n.a.
Sweden	2.6	2.76	23.6
United States	2.7	2.82	62.6

Composition of Government-financed Research and Development Expenditure, 1989/90 (%)

	Civil	Defence	Total
Basic	36.5	0.	20.0
Strategic	31.6	1.6	18.1
Specific	23.7	16.6	20.5
Experimental	8.2	81.8	41.5

Sources: Cabinet Office, *Annual Review of Government Funded Research and Development* (HMSO, 1991); OECD, *Main Science and Technology Indicators, 1991/2.*
[a] Figures refer to 1989.

borrowing requirement (of which the EFLs are part) has given the EFLs particular importance.

Since 1980, public bodies have been subject to efficiency investigations by the MMC. These investigations have covered a wide range of issues including costs, productivity, service quality, pricing and investment policies. The referrals of public bodies to the MMC on this basis have averaged around three a year.

The recent productivity performance of currently nationalized industries represents a substantial improvement over the performance during the seventies, and has outperformed many other sectors. Over the decade 1979/80 to 1989/90, output per employee in the currently nationalized industries grew at an average annual rate of 4.4 per cent, compared with an average of 4.1 per cent in the manufacturing sector and 1.9 per cent in the whole economy.[1,2]

[1] Source of figures is Trade and Industry, *Expenditure Plans 1991/92 to 1993/94*, Cmnd. 1504.
[2] For figures for earlier periods which suggest that labour and total factor productivities grew faster in the nationalized industries than in manufacturing, see R.Millward, 'The Nationalised Industries', in M.Artis and D.Cobham (eds.), *Labour's Economic Policies 1974–79* (Manchester University Press, 1991). Millward also argues that the performance of British public utilities relative to those in other countries improved following nationalization in the 1940s.

9 TECHNOLOGY AND RESEARCH AND DEVELOPMENT

Expenditure on research and development (R & D) in Britain amounts to around 2¼ per cent of GDP. The statistics in the first half of Table 4.8 allow some comparisons with other industrialized economies. It can be seen that expenditure in Britain is, relative to GDP, somewhat less than in most of the other countries included in the table with Italy as the exception. It can also be seen that whilst R & D expenditure has not risen relative to GDP in Britain, it has done so in many other industrialized economies.

Around half of R & D is financed by private industry (50.4 per cent in 1989) with 36.5 per cent financed by government, 3.2 per cent by other national sources (e.g. charities) and the remaining 9.9 per cent financed from abroad (e.g. by multinational enterprises). Business performs 65.9 per cent of the research and development, with 15.4 per cent undertaken in higher education institutions, 14.5 per cent in the government sector and the remaining 4.2 per cent in non-profit organizations.[1] The involvement of government in the financing of research and development in most industrialized countries is also apparent from Table 4.8. However, the USA and the UK stand out as having particularly high proportions of research and development in areas which are related to defence.

The division of research and development expenditure into four categories in Table 4.8 is based on the following distinctions. Basic research is that undertaken primarily to acquire knowledge and with no specific application in mind, whereas strategic research is undertaken with eventual practical application in mind even though these cannot be clearly specified. Specific research is that which is directed primarily towards identified practical aims or objectives; finally experimental research is systematic work drawing on existing knowledge to produce new products, processes, etc.

The three approaches to industrial policy suggested above can be applied to the case of research and technology. The 'market failure' approach has to be extended to introduce research and development. Research has a number of key features. First, research is the exploration of the unknown so that calculations on the benefits and costs of an avenue of research are particularly difficult to make. This uncertainty may militate against firms undertaking research with firms tending to opt for less risky ventures. There are often very long lags between the start of a research programme and the commercial implementation of the fruits of that programme. The combination of uncertainty and long lead times is seen to discourage research and also the provision of finance for research programmes. There may be a transfer of knowledge generated by research programmes so that despite the patent laws firms other than the one undertaking the research benefit from the discoveries made. This line of argument suggests that there will be a systematic tendency for there to be under-investment in research and

---

[1] Source of data, OECD, *Main Science and Technology Indicators, 1991/2.*

development. This is reflected in estimates that the rate of return on research and development is much higher than rates of return on other investment projects.[1]

Second, research is not homogeneous; a crude division would be, on the one hand, between basic and strategic research as defined above and, on the other, applied research and development. The former could be seen as research undertaken in the pursuit of knowledge without any thought of commercial or other application, whereas the latter is undertaken for commercial reasons. However, the basic research of one era provides the platform for applied research of the next era. For example, those scientists who discovered the principles of electricity could be seen as undertaking basic research whereas those who have used those principles to develop, say, washing machines are engaged in applied research. The distinction between basic and applied is of course not a hard and fast one, though useful for our discussion. Basic research is particularly prone to the difficulties identified above, namely uncertainty of outcome and long lead times. Yet such research is necessary for future progress. Further, the output from basic research should be spread as quickly as possible so that it can be drawn into applied research.

Third, knowledge is costly to produce, but once it has been produced it can be spread at very low cost. This sets up the following conflict. An individual will only undertake costly research if the benefits will eventually exceed the estimated costs (of course mistakes are often made). From that perspective, the individual can be encouraged to undertake research by being able to reap the gains. But once the discovery has been made, it would appear beneficial for that knowledge to be passed on to others (since it can be spread at virtually zero marginal cost); in which case the discoverer would not benefit. The patent laws have been seen as an attempt to strike a balance by giving inventors certain rights over the use of their invention for a specific period (generally 16 years in the United Kingdom). The patent holder can be compelled to grant licences for the use of the invention if the patentee is abusing the monopoly position granted by, for example, not working the invention commercially.

The Austrian school draw on the work of Schumpeter particularly.[2] Schumpeter argued that a (temporary) monopoly position often arose out of a successful research programme and the discovery of new products. Hence monopoly profits were often the return to previous research and development, though in turn these profits provide a source of funds for further investment in research and development. But these high profits do not last

---

[1] One estimate puts the social rate of return at 56 per cent on research and development as compared with a private rate of return of 25 per cent, both of which would be above the rate of return on investment in general: see E. Mansfield, 'Measuring the Social and Private Rates of Return on Innovation', in *Economic Effects of Space and Other Advanced Technologies* (Strasbourg, Council of Europe, 1980).
[2] See, for example, J. Schumpeter, *Capitalism, Socialism and Democracy* (Allen and Unwin, 1954).

for ever for there is a 'perennial gale of creative destruction' which threatens the monopolist's position. The prospect of profits provides the spur to undertake research and development, but competition from others (e.g. development of close substitutes) will eat away at those profits. Thus there is an interplay between a temporary monopoly position (arising from successful innovation) and the background of competition. Schumpeter suggested that the benefits of (temporary) monopoly were to aid the pace of research and development and to more than offset the short-run costs of monopoly in terms of higher price and lower output, as suggested in Figure 4.6.

Another element of the Austrian approach (as indicated above) would be the view that '[f]irms themselves are best able to assess their own markets and to balance the commercial risks and rewards of financing R & D and innovation. The Government should not take on responsibilities which are principally those of industry'.[1]

The developmental state perspective would to some degree draw on the arguments outlined to the effect that the private market will systematically under-invest in research and development. It would further note that competition between firms and between countries in the late twentieth century often takes the form of technical innovation rather than price. This general view is reflected in the argument that '[t]he Government has ... a general responsibility to support science and technology because this is fundamental to the social and economic well-being of the country'.[2]

The present government has generally sought to reduce industrial subsidies and assistance, both in terms of selective assistance (much of which went to aerospace, shipbuilding, coal, steel and vehicle industries) and regional and general industrial support. The overall budget for trade and industry has virtually been halved in real terms during the 1980s, and within that budget there has been a relative shift towards scientific and technological assistance. However, the government's view of its own policy is that 'innovation policy should be focused primarily on the circumstances when research is necessary before commercial applications can be developed, or where the benefits of the research are likely to be widespread, and on technology transfer'.[3]

There are a large number of government programmes which can be placed under the heading of the encouragement and support of industrial research and development. Most of them, however, account for only very small sums of public expenditure. The bulk of public expenditure in this area (as can be seen from Table 4.8) relates to research in defence-related industries. It has also been estimated[4] that around 30 per cent of Britain's highly qualified

---

[1] Department of Trade and Industry, *DTI – the Department for Enterprise*, Cmnd. 278 (HMSO, 1988).
[2] *House of Lords Report of Select Committee on Science and Technology*, HL 20 (HMSO, 1986).
[3] Department of Trade and Industry, *op. cit.*
[4] M.Kaldor, M.Sharp and W.Walker, 'Industrial Competitiveness and Britain's Defence', *LBR*, no. 162 (October 1986).

scientists and engineers are employed in the defence sector. One particular difficulty which arises here is that the secrecy which surrounds defence-related work limits the spread of knowledge arising from this type of research work. The industrial spin-offs benefiting other sectors of industry are then likely to be limited. It has been argued that 'technological spin-offs from the military sector, while obviously tangible, are generally few and far between and thus represent a poor return on R & D compared to equivalent civilian outlays. This is partly because Britain's particularly tight security laws inhibit the flow of knowledge from military laboratories, but it stems as much from the qualitative difference between military and civilian technology'.[1]

The Civil Aircraft Research and Demonstration Programme (CARAD) is 'part of a national aircraft research effort conducted by industry, government, research establishments, higher education institutes and other agencies. Its objective is to help key sectors of UK aircraft and aerospace industry maintain the technological base needed to compete effectively in world markets.'[2] Much of the research is carried out at the Royal Aerospace Establishment involving public expenditure of nearly £30 million in 1989/90.

In non-defence areas, existing government support of research and development can be conveniently placed under two headings. The first heading is that of collaborative project support. The major programme here has been the ALVEY project which was designed 'to stimulate [information technology] research through a programme of collaborative pre-competitive projects fitting into the strategies developed for the key technologies of intelligent knowledge based system (IKBS), the man/machine interface (MMI), software engineering, very large scale integration (VLSI) and computing architectures.'[3] Government funding provided £300 million out of a total of £350 million. 'UK government policy now puts greater emphasis on support for IT R & D through ESPRIT II.'[4]

The LINK initiative aims to 'encourage pre-competitive research and ensure rapid take-up of research ideas by bringing together industrial and academic workers at the earliest stage of development of new technologies'[5] with the government financing up to half of the cost of each programme. Over the five years ending in 1993 it is estimated that £210 million will be provided by government. The areas covered include biotechnology, advanced materials and electronics. The Advanced Technology Programmes (ATPs) are also designed to encourage pre-competitive research by industrial companies in new technologies such as computer-aided engineering, high temperature superconductivity.

The EUREKA project was a French-inspired agreement, adopted by 18

1 M.Kaldor *et al.*, *ibid*.
2 Quote is from *Trade and Industry Expenditure Plans 1991–92 to 1993–94* (HMSO, 1991).
3 J.Shepherd, 'Industrial Support Policies', *NIER*, no. 122, November 1987.
4 Quote is from OECD, *Science and Technology Policy Review and Outlook 1991*.
5 Quote is from OECD, *op. cit.*

EC and EFTA nations and the EC Commission in November 1985. It seeks to encourage industry-led collaborative projects in advanced technologies leading to innovative products, processes or services. There is no central fund, and each government is responsible for the financial support of its own firms. The British participation is described as designed to 'improve the competitiveness of British firms in world markets in civil applications of new technologies by encouraging European industrial and technological market-led collaboration in R & D'.[1] The extent of government support is 50 per cent of the costs of applied research projects and up to 25 per cent of the costs of development projects. By 1991 there were some 470 EUREKA projects which had been agreed of which British participants were involved in 115 of which 37 were UK-led.[2]

SMART (Small Firms Merit Award for Research and Technology) is a competition for small firms (50 employees or less) with 180 awards made in 1990 from 1,420 applications. The prize from the competition was a 75 per cent grant (up to £37,500) for a feasibility study lasting up to a year, with further grants for some of the prize-winners. The intention is to encourage the development of high risk projects and the start-up of high-technology firms, and the competition looks for the best novel ideas, particularly in biotechnology, information technology, advanced materials technology and advanced manufacturing technology.

The second heading covers technology transfer, consultancy, advice and awareness programmes. Technology transfer initiatives provide access for small and medium-sized enterprises to new ideas. These initiatives include Advanced Information Technology (with a £12 million programme over 3 years) and Materials Matter (£2.5 million over 3 years) which provides information on modern engineering materials and their processing methods. Other programmes range from the provision of IT equipment in schools through to business and technical advisory services (BTAS). They are mainly linked to micro-electronics and information technology.

10 EUROPEAN COMMUNITY AND INDUSTRIAL POLICIES

Britain has been a member of the European Community since 1973, and that membership has had a number of effects on British industry and the conduct of industrial policy. The composition of international trade has moved towards the EC and hence away from the more traditional markets such as those of the British Commonwealth. By 1990 53 per cent of British trade was with other European Community countries. In this section we discuss two aspects of the impact of EC membership on British industry. The first part concerns the impact of the Treaty of Rome, which established the EC, on

---

[1] J.Shepherd, *op. cit.*
[2] Source here is OECD, *op. cit.*

industrial policies. The second part considers some of the consequences of the proposed establishment of a 'single market' by the end of 1992.

The EC has operated (under Articles 85 and 86 of the Treaty of Rome of 1957) a monopoly and mergers policy to which British firms have in principle been subject. The relevant parts of the Treaty of Rome are Articles 85 (dealing with cartels and restrictive trade practices) and 86 (monopoly). These articles refer to inter-state trade, which would appear to exclude any cartels or monopolies affecting only within-country trade, but agreements and actions which serve to limit imports from one EC country to another would be covered by these articles.

The implementation of competition policy is in the hands of the European Commission with cases which appear to break Articles 85 or 86 being taken to the European Court of Justice. There is a similarity with British policy in the area of cartels and restrictive practices in that there is a presumption that they are against the public interest with the possibility of exemptions being granted. Article 85 covers agreements, decisions and concerted practices which may affect trade between member states and which have the effect of restricting or distorting competition. The article specifically mentions agreement and practices which fix prices, limit production, share out markets between firms or which charge discriminatory prices. In practice, the Court and Commission have placed a 'tough' interpretation on Article 85. However, the implementation of the article is subject to a *de minimis* rule under which agreements involving firms with a combined market share below 5 per cent or with a combined annual turnover below 50 billion ECU (around £30m) are excluded from consideration. Firms do not have to register any restrictive trade agreements, but may notify the Commission of agreements. There is an incentive to notify an agreement 'since if they do not do so there can be no question of their agreement being exempted' and if 'the agreement is duly notified it enjoys a provisional or temporary validity'.[1]

Article 86 deals with the abuse of market dominance rather than with monopoly *per se*, and with those abuses which affect trade between member states. In the Article, particular abuses mentioned are:

(a) directly or indirectly imposing unfair purchase or selling prices or other unfair trading conditions;

(b) limiting production, markets or technical development to the prejudice of consumers;

(c) applying dissimilar conditions to equivalent transactions with other trading parties, thereby placing them at a competitive disadvantage;

(d) making the conclusion of contracts subject to acceptance by the other parties of supplementary obligations which, by their nature or

---

[1] D. Swann, *The Economics of the Common Market* (Penguin Books) 6th edition.

according to commercial usage, have no connection with the subject of such contracts.[1]

The Treaty of Rome does not define dominance but the Court has looked at both market share and actions before arriving at a view as to whether there is dominance in a particular case. A market share as low as 40 per cent has been used as partial evidence of dominance. There is the problem of finding an appropriate definition of the market, and this problem is exacerbated in the EC context since the question arises as to whether the appropriate market area is the whole of the EC or is one particular country or region.

Mergers are not explicitly covered by the Treaty of Rome, and indeed there has been debate over whether mergers were covered. However, the European Court has ruled that Article 86 does cover mergers, partly on the grounds that Article 85 (on restrictive practices) could be side-stepped by firms merging (rather than operating illegal agreements amongst themselves). However, there has not actually been a formal decision of the Court prohibiting a merger. Since late 1990, the European Commission has had jurisdiction over 'concentrations with a Community dimension', which are those where 'the aggregate world-wide turnover of all parties concerned is more than ECU 5 billion; *and* the aggregate Community-wide turnover of each of at least two of the parties concerned is more than ECU 250 million; *unless* each of the parties achieves more than two thirds of its aggregate Community-wide turnover within one and the same Member State'.[2] National authorities may *not* apply their own competition laws to these mergers except in very limited circumstances.

The conduct of industrial policy (particularly in the realm of subsidies) has probably been more affected by the rules limiting national governments providing 'unfair' advantages to their own firms. Articles 92 to 94 of the Treaty of Rome restrict state aid to firms. The range of state aid which is covered has been defined to be constituted by not only grants 'but also by loans on more favourable terms than are available on the market, guarantees, tax concessions, relief of social security contributions, and by the State putting up new capital for enterprises in circumstances in or on terms which a private investor would not do so'.[3] Part of Article 92 makes State aid which distorts (or threatens to distort) competition by favouring some firms or industries in so far as trade between member countries is affected. Article 93 leads to State aid being kept under constant review, with member countries having to report plans on State aid.[4] The rules have impinged on British government policy in terms of the extent of financial assistance offered. Further, the terms governing the sale by the government of the

---

[1] Quote is from Article 86 of the Treaty of Rome.
[2] Quote is from Office of Fair Trading, *Mergers* (HMSO, 1991).
[3] Commission of the European Communities, *Fourteenth Report on Competition Policy* (Office for Official Publications of the European Communities, Brussels, 1985).
[4] For further details, see D. Swann, *op. cit*.

Rover Group to British Aerospace were similarly influenced by the European Commission.[1]

The effect of British membership of the EC on British industry and industrial policy has been much greater in the last few years and is likely to be much greater in the next few years than it has been in the first decade and a half. This will be a consequence of the Single Market, sometimes referred to by the year at the end of which it is intended to have full implementation, namely 1992. There are three particular aspects of the single market in the EC context to which attention should be drawn. First, there is the removal of customs barriers affecting the movement of goods between one member country and another (which will mean the disappearance of duty-free shopping on journeys between member countries). Second, each member country sets product standards for specific goods and services sold within its borders. These product standards may be of a general form (e.g. that a good be of 'merchantable quality') but also of a specific form. There are, for example, laws governing the required contents of different types of food, laws on the pollution levels from cars, etc. Third, government (central and local) of each member country often favours the purchase of goods and services produced within its borders or by its firms.

TABLE 4.9

Estimated Benefits of a Single Market in the EC

	ECU (billions)	% GDP
Gains from removing barriers affecting trade	8–9	0.2–0.3
Gains from removal of barriers affecting overall production	57–71	2.0–2.4
Gains from exploiting economies of scale more fully	61	2.1
Gains from intensified competition reducing inefficiencies and monopoly profits	46	1.6
Total (for seven member states)	127–187	4.3–6.4
Total for all 12 member states	164–258	4.3–6.4
Central estimate	216	

Source: P. Cecchini, *The European Challenge 1992: The Benefits of a Single Market* (Wildwood House, 1988).

Notes: Monetary value of benefits expressed in billions of European Currency Units (ECU) in 1985 prices. 1 ECU was equal to about 70p at the time of writing.

There is overlap between categories of gains from exploiting economies of scale and gains from intensified competition: it is assumed that the range for these two categories combined is 62–107 billion ECUs.

The detailed studies were mainly undertaken for seven member states which were Belgium, France, Germany, Italy, Luxembourg, Netherlands and United Kingdom, and the estimated gains for seven member states refer to these countries. These seven states account for 88% of total EC GDP. The figures for twelve member states assume the same proportionate gain in the additional five states as in the seven for whom the calculations were made.

---

[1]   Although it was described as a sale, the terms of the transfer of ownership of the Rover Group from the government to British Aerospace (BAe) was more like a gift. The government sold the Rover Group to BAe for £150m. However, the government offered £800m to write off the company's debts, which was subsequently reduced to £547m at the insistence of the European Commission.

The intention of the single market is that each of these three impediments to inter-country trade should be eliminated. However, these impediments to trade will still apply (and indeed may be intensified) in regard to trade between member countries and non-member countries. Further, transport costs, differences in national tastes and so on, will obviously still remain and there will also be differences in VAT rates, etc., though there is pressure for the 'harmonization' of these tax rates.

The 'official' estimate of the effect of removing these impediments to trade between member countries (the first two items in Table 4.9) is for a gain amounting to around $2\frac{1}{2}$ per cent of GDP. There are two points to note on these estimates. First, a reduction in employment is counted as a gain since it is a reduction in costs. Thus, the reduction in employment of customs officers is viewed as a reduction in costs (largely in this case costs incurred by governments) and hence counted as a gain. But this assumes (implicitly) that customs officers find employment elsewhere in the economy. If, in contrast, they remain unemployed (or whilst the customs officers find employment they replace others) then the gain is zero or may be negative (when the customs officer values being employed).

Second, national and local governments will be unable to express preference in their procurement policies for goods and services which have been domestically produced. There appears a gain on public expenditure in that governments now must purchase at the lowest price (from a Community-based supplier) rather than from domestically based suppliers. Thus, governments will not be able to use their purchasing power to help stimulate local employment nor to encourage technical advance through their procurement policies.

The impact of these changes on prices, output and technical efficiency has been described as follows:

> highlights of the 1992 picture include a substantial gain for consumers (consumer surplus) as prices drop and product choice and quality increase under the impact of open competition. Producers face a more mixed outlook. In the short term, profits (particularly those resulting from monopoly and protected positions) may be squeezed. But in the longer run, business as a whole is expected to respond to the new competitive climate by making various adjustments – e.g. scaling up production ('economies of scale of production'), gaining experience of how to produce more efficiently ('economies of scale of learning' or 'learning curve effects'), eliminating management inefficiencies ('X-inefficiency' to the economist), and by improved capacity to innovate. Gains from these and other adjustment, when netted out, lead to an increase in the community's 'net economic welfare'.[1]

---

[1] P. Cecchini, *The European Challenge 1992: The Benefits of a Single Market* (Wildwood House, 1988).

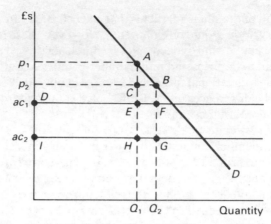

Figure 4.7   The Impact of Lower Unit Costs on Welfare

The estimated impact of these changes in economic welfare is given by the third and fourth items in Table 4.9. These estimates are clearly substantial, and in total suggest an increase of around 6 per cent in the GDP of the EC countries. Our discussion of these estimates has two parts. The first is to indicate the nature of these estimates, and the second is to suggest that there are reasons for thinking that the benefits will not be as large as indicated (with particular reference to the UK).

The basis of the estimates of the gains of the single market can be seen by reference to Figure 4.7. The existing price is taken as p_1, at which Q_1 is purchased, and the average costs of production are ac_1. After the formation of the single market, the price is assumed to fall on the basis that there will be an increase in effective competition. Customs barriers and other impediments to trade have the effect of providing some protection for firms in their domestic market, and this allows price to be somewhat higher than otherwise. Price is also assumed to fall because costs fall (as indicated in the quote above and for reasons to be discussed below). The overall effect on price is represented by a fall in price from p_1 to p_2. Following the line of argument given above (pp. 256–7), the gain in economic welfare to consumers stemming from the lower price (and the related increase in quantity consumed), is p_1ABp_2, of which p_1ACp_2 represents a reduction in profits, leaving ABC as the net gain from lower prices.

The reduction in costs is argued to arise from the combination of three sources. The first is the further exploitation of economies of scale (decreasing unit costs). This assumes that firms are currently prevented from fully exploiting available economies of scale through an inability to sell the resulting output. A firm may find that the average cost of producing 50,000 units would be £10 and of producing 100,000 units would be £9. But if the market for its output is only 50,000 units then it clearly would not be worthwhile to fully exploit the available economies of scale. However, if another market now becomes available in which a further 50,000 can be sold, then it would be worthwhile to expand productive capacity to meet that extra demand at a lower unit cost. The basis of this argument is further discussed below.

The second source of cost reduction is to be found in 'learning curve effects'. The general notion here is that as experience of a particular production process builds up, ways of improving the production process are gradually discovered and put into effect. There has been debate over whether experience is better measured by the amount of (cumulative) output produced or by the length of time during which the process has been used. In the cumulative output case, it is usually argued that many of the learning or experience effects can be summarised by an equation of the form $\log UC = a + b \log Q$, where UC is the unit cost (of output produced to date) and Q the cumulative output; b is expected to be negative. A value of $b = -0.32$ for example would indicate that for each doubling of output, unit costs decline by 20 per cent.[1]

The third source of cost reduction is the decrease of X- (or technical) inefficiency.[2] The general idea here is that firms often operate with some technical inefficiency (though economists often assume technical efficiency), and that an increase in effective competition will force firms to operate in a more efficient manner.

These three effects are represented in Figure 4.7 by a reduction in the average cost curve from ac_1 to ac_2.[3] The profits in the industry are initially p_1AED and become p_2BGI. The change in profits is thus $DFGI + CBFE - p_1ACp_2$. The last term has already been discussed above. Of the change in profits, the area $DEHI$ corresponds to lower costs on the initial output.

These estimates of the gains from a single market have been subject to a number of challenges, some of which we now briefly discuss. It can be seen by reference to Table 4.9 that the gains from economies of scale are estimated as just over 2 per cent of GDP, providing around two-fifths of the estimated gains. It should first be noted that the estimation of economies of scale is fraught with difficulties.[4] Further, policies such as those pursued by the IRC during the sixties were strongly influenced by the notion that British firms were 'too small', and the resulting larger firms were not noticeably successful.

The concentration of production which is associated with the exploitation of economies of scale involves costs which are often omitted from the calculations. On average, the distance between the point of production and

---

[1] See Review of Monopoly and Mergers Policy, *op. cit.*
[2] The term X-inefficiency comes from H. Leibenstein, 'Allocative Efficiency vs. X-efficiency', *AER*, vol. 56 (1966).
[3] Economies of scale would mean, of course, declining unit costs, whereas Figure 4.7 assumes constant unit costs. Drawing in declining unit costs would complicate the figure and the analysis. However, Figure 4.7 can be interpreted as saying that the industry in question could have operated on a cost curve lower than ac_1 before (reflecting economies of scale) but did not do so since the resulting output could not be sold.
[4] For further discussion, see M. Sawyer, *op. cit.*, Chapter 4.

the eventual sale is increased, thereby raising transport costs. It is also argued that industrial relations become more fraught in large factories. For these and other reasons, firms may not wish to build factories of the size indicated by studies of economies of scale.

The exploitation of economies of scale will usually involve the emergence of a smaller number of large firms at the level of the EC. This would involve some firms going out of business, with the remaining firms able to expand and satisfy the demand previously met by the firms which have now disappeared. The exact effect of this on competition is difficult to estimate. On the one hand, there is seen to be more competition arising from the reduction of trade barriers; but on the other hand, the number of firms gradually declines. If the latter effect is significant and as a consequence effective competition declines it would be expected that prices would rise, thereby offsetting some of the gains of the single market.

Some sectors, particularly those which have been protected from international competition (e.g. through public procurement policies) are likely to be much more affected by the completion of the Single Market than others. A report[1] from the Commission of European Communities suggests that 40 sectors out of 120 considered would be most affected by the Single Market, and these sectors fell into four groups, namely high-tech public-procurement markets, traditional public-procurement and regulated markets, sectors facing competition for the Newly Industrialized Countries (NICs) and sectors with moderate non-tariff barriers. In the first case, European firms were felt to suffer a productivity disadvantage as compared with American and Japanese firms. In the second case there were degrees of government support for 'national champions', whilst for the fourth there were a variety of technical, administrative or fiscal barriers to trade. For the UK, the high-tech public-procurement markets were estimated to account for 7 per cent of manufacturing employment, the traditional public-procurement and regulated markets for $3\frac{1}{2}$ per cent, sectors facing competition from NICs for 4 per cent and sectors with moderate non-tariff barriers for 35 per cent. Hence the sensitive sectors (as the report described them) form around half of manufacturing.

The concentration of production also raises the question of the geographical location of that production. There will be a further tendency for production to be located towards the geographical centre of the EC area. Further, since richer consumers have a higher level of demand, it would be expected that production would tend to move towards the more prosperous regions of the EC. Some have spoken of a 'golden triangle' within the EC with apexes of (approximately) London, Hamburg and Milan. Movement of industry towards the geographical centre and towards the richer areas would mean a movement away from most of the regions of the United Kingdom (with the exception of London and the South-East).

---

[1]   European Economy, *Social Europe* (1990).

SUGGESTIONS FOR FURTHER READING

General Texts on Industrial Economics

R.Clarke, *Industrial Economics* (Blackwell, 1985)
D.Hay and D.Morris, *Industrial Economics, Theory and Evidence* (Oxford University Press, 1979)
M.Sawyer, *The Economics of Industries and Firms* (second edition, Croom Helm, 1985)

Recent Developments

C.Mayer, 'Recent Developments in Industrial Economics and their Implications for Policy, *OREP*, vol. 1 (1985)

Manufacturing Sector and Foreign Trade

R.E.Rowthorn and J.Wells, *De-Industrialization and Foreign Trade* (Cambridge University Press, 1987)
House of Lords, *Report from the Select Committee on Overseas Trade*, HL 238 (HMSO 1985)

Competition Policy

D.Hay and J.Vickers, 'The Reform of U.K. Competition Policy', *NIER*, no. 125, August 1988

Privatization and Regulation

J.Vickers and G.Yarrow, *Privatization: An Economic Analysis* (M.I.T. Press, 1988)
K.Ascher, *The Politics of Privatization: Contracting-out Public Services* (Macmillan, 1987)
M.Waterson, *Regulation of the Firm and Natural Monopoly* (Blackwell, 1988)

Research and Development

Symposium on Technical Progress, *OREP*, vol. 4, no. 4 (1988)

Single Market and 1992

P.Cecchini, *The European Challenge 1992: The Benefits of a Single Market* (Wildwood House, 1988).

5

Labour

Geraint Johnes and Jim Taylor

Introduction

The unsettled nature of the British labour market over the last two decades has led to spectacular swings in unemployment. In 1974, unemployment in the UK stood at just under 0.6 million. By 1979 this had risen to 1.2 million. The rise continued until 1986, when unemployment peaked at 3.2 million. The total then fell to 1.7 million in 1990 before rising once more above 2.5 million during the current recession.

High unemployment affects some households profoundly and others not at all. It causes great human misery, and is an inequitable and generally inefficient means of riding a slump in economic activity. This being so, economists have focused on the labour market's apparent imperfections in an effort to improve its functioning. The tasks of explaining the market's failure and of devising means to improve its performance are challenging. This makes the study of the labour market especially exciting and rewarding.

We begin this chapter with a description of the British labour force, paying special attention to the rapid changes in its composition since the Second World War. We then study the incidence and causes of unemployment. Regional disparities and employment policies are given particular attention. The next section of the chapter is devoted to a consideration of wages. We examine the factors underlying income differences between individuals and discuss the system of social security benefits which provides an income to those who are disadvantaged in the labour market. Finally, we take a look at industrial relations.

1   EMPLOYMENT

1.1   The Labour Force

One of the most striking changes in the UK labour market over the past two decades is the increasing relative importance of female workers. Between 1971 and 1990, the number of females in the UK's civilian labour force increased by over 40%, from 8.9 million to 12.6 million, while the number of males in the workforce barely changed. The growth of the UK's workforce by 3.8 million during 1971–90 was therefore due almost entirely to more females taking jobs. The growing importance of females in the labour force

TABLE 5.1

The Civilian Labour Force in the United Kingdom by Sex, 1971–90

Year	Civilian labour force (millions)			% of total	
	Males	Females	Total	Males	Females
1971	15.9	8.9	24.8	64.1	35.9
1981	16.1	10.4	26.5	60.8	39.2
1990	16.0	12.6	28.6	56.0	44.0

Sources: British Labour Statistics Yearbook, 1973; Regional Trends 21, 1991.

is vividly demonstrated in Table 5.1, which shows that females increased their share of the workforce from under 36% in 1971 to 44% in 1990.

The increasing importance of females in the workforce is also reflected by the long-run trend in the female activity rate, which is the percentage of females of working age who either have a job or are seeking one. As can be seen from Figure 5.1, the female activity rate rose from under 44% in 1971 to over 53% in 1991 and is expected to rise still further during the next decade. In contrast to this, the activity rate for males has moved in the opposite direction, from over 80% in 1971 to under 75% in 1991. The gap between male and female activity rates has therefore narrowed remarkably quickly during the past two decades. These statistics indicate very clearly the increasing dependence of the UK economy on female workers relative to male workers.

The stark contrast in the long-run trends in activity rates between males and females raises an interesting and important question: why has the male activity rate declined whilst the female rate has been increasing? Before searching for answers to this question, it is important to realize that the long-run trend in the activity rate has differed considerably according to age group. This is true for both males and females (see Table 5.2). The activity

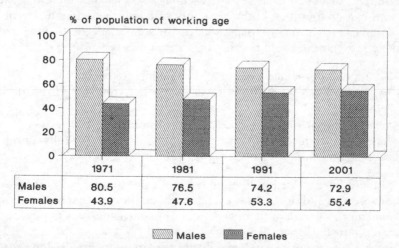

	1971	1981	1991	2001
Males	80.5	76.5	74.2	72.9
Females	43.9	47.6	53.3	55.4

Figure 5.1 Economic Activity Rates for Males and Females in Great Britain, 1971–2001
(*Source:* Table 5.1)

TABLE 5.2

Economic Activity Rates in Great Britain : by Age and Sex

Age group	Males				Females			
	1971	*1981*	*1991**	*2001**	*1971*	*1981*	*1991**	*2001**
16–19	69.4	72.4	75.5	74.6	65.0	70.4	74.3	70.4
20–24	87.7	85.1	87.1	82.6	60.2	68.8	74.9	77.4
25–44	95.4	95.7	94.3	93.9	52.4	61.7	73.9	79.4
45–59(45–54)	94.8	93.0	83.0	87.5	62.0	68.0	72.7	73.4
60–64(55–59)	82.9	69.3	54.5	51.5	50.9	53.4	54.3	54.9
65+(60+)	19.2	10.3	8.0	5.4	12.4	8.3	7.7	6.6
All	80.5	76.5	74.2	72.5	43.9	47.6	53.3	55.1

Source: Social Trends, 1991 and 1992.
Notes:
( ) = females.
* = projected.

rate for males aged 16–19, for example, has actually increased rather than fallen as was the case for males in most other age groups. The most dramatic fall in the male activity rate occurred in the 60–64 age group; it fell from 82.9% in 1971 to 56.4% in 1988 in this group. Since this accounts for a substantial proportion of the fall in the overall male activity rate, it can be inferred that earlier retirement has been a major cause of the falling long-run trend in the male activity rate.

As far as the female activity rate is concerned, the long-run trend has been upwards for all age groups below 60. The upward trend has been particularly steep for females in the 25–44 age group, increasing from 52.4% in 1971 to 73.9% in 1991. Substantial increases have also occurred in other age groups. The reasons for this long-run upward trend in the female activity rate are still the subject of debate, but recent research suggests that plausible explanations can be found on both the supply side and the demand side of the labour market. The main explanations on the supply side are that the female activity rate has increased because of:

– a reduction in sexual discrimination against females
– a change in social attitudes towards mothers returning to work after childbirth
– the rapid growth of nurseries and playschools
– and the introduction of household products such as the fully-automatic washing machine, the microwave oven and frozen food

All these have helped to liberate females (and some males!) from domestic chores. In addition, it may even have been the case that husbands have become more tolerant of their wives working, particularly as family income has been boosted as a consequence.

There are three primary demand-side explanations for the long-run increase in female economic activity. Firstly, very high levels of labour

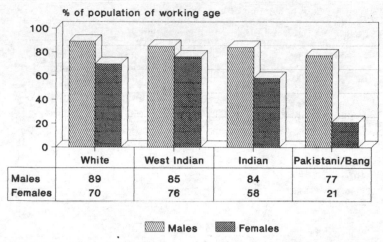

% of population of working age

	White	West Indian	Indian	Pakistani/Bang
Males	89	85	84	77
Females	70	76	58	21

Males Females

Figure 5.2 Economic Activity Rates by Ethnic Group in Great Britain, 1989
(*Source: ST* 21, 1991)

demand for over three decades following the Second World War led employers to search for additional workers. Secondly, a rising real wage has increased the opportunity cost of not working in paid employment, thereby inducing more women to take a job. Thirdly, in their search for cheaper labour, employers have provided more opportunities for short-time working and this has been found to be particularly popular among married women. Research in recent years has tended to support these various explanations of the long-run upward trend in the female activity rate (Briscoe and Wilson, 1992).

Differences in economic activity rates occur not only between males and females, and between different age groups, but also between people with different ethnic backgrounds. This is particularly true for females. The *Labour Force Survey*, for example, shows that the percentage of females of working age who are economically active is lower for Indian females and very low for Pakistani/Bangladeshi females in the UK compared to white and West Indian females (see Figure 5.2). Differences in male activity rates between ethnic groups are considerably smaller than is the case for females. These differences are probably partly due to differences in custom and practice between ethnic groups, especially among older people, though racial discrimination is also likely to play a part. It will be interesting to see by how much the economic activity rates for different ethnic groups converge over the next decade as the younger generation from ethnic minorities enters the workforce.

Finally, international comparisons indicate that the UK has higher activity rates for both males and females than her European partners (see Figure 5.3). It seems likely that any convergence of activity rates within the EC will occur as a result of increases in female activity rates in other countries and not by any decrease in the UK.

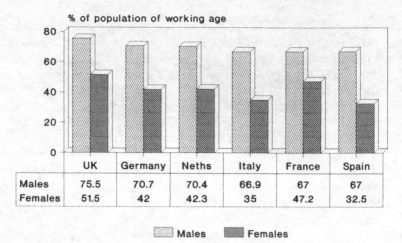

Figure 5.3   Economic Activity Rates in Selected EC Countries, 1988
(*Source: ST* 21, 1991)

1.2   Long-Run Trends in Employment: Industrial and Regional Aspects

The UK's industrial base has undergone radical re-structuring since the 1970s. Four of the most prominent structural changes are discussed in this section.

The first is the shift in jobs between the main industrial sectors. By far the most striking change is the loss of two and a half million jobs in the manufacturing sector during 1971–90. Employment in manufacturing industries shrank from 8.2 million in 1971 to 5.5 million in 1990 (see Table 5.3). While this de-industrialization was happening, industries in the service sector were expanding rapidly. Employment in banking, finance and insurance, for example, doubled during 1971–90, providing an additional 1.6

TABLE 5.3

Employment in the United Kingdom by Industry

Industrial Sector	Employment in thousands				% change	
	1971	1980	1990	2000	1971–80	1980–90
Agriculture, forestry, fishing	770	670	600	490	−13.0	−10.4
Energy and water	800	720	450	370	−10.0	−37.5
Manufacturing	8 190	7 070	5 460	4 430	−13.7	−22.8
Construction	1 550	1 620	1 810	1 830	4.5	11.7
Distribution, hotels, repairs	4 430	4 990	5 660	5 720	12.6	13.4
Transport and communications	1 630	1 600	1 570	1 420	−1.8	−1.9
Banking, finance, insurance	1 490	1 860	3 140	3 220	24.8	68.8
Public admin and defence	1 810	1 900	1 800	1 980	5.0	−5.3
Education and health	2 370	2 980	3 290	3 950	25.7	10.4
Other services	1 390	1 820	2 580	3 330	30.9	41.8
All industries	24 430	25 230	26 360	26 740	3.3	4.5

Source: Employment Gazette.
Note: The forecasts for the year 2000 were obtained from Cambridge Econometrics.

million jobs in the process. The growth of banking, finance and insurance was particularly rapid during the 1980s as the government's deregulation of the financial sector introduced more competition into the UK's financial markets (see Chapter 2). Coupled with a worldwide growth of financial activity, these reforms helped London to become an even more important player in world financial markets, thus benefiting the financial services sector. The sharp fall in employment in London's financial sector during 1990–1, however, suggests that the growth of the 1980s was over-optimistic. Other service industries which have expanded rapidly include education, business services and retailing. These changes demonstrate just how quickly industrial re-structuring has been occurring in the UK.

The second major structural change which has occurred in the UK labour market during the 1980s is the rapid growth in the number of self-employed workers. Between 1981 and 1990, the number of self-employed workers increased by over a million, from 2.1 to 3.4 million. By 1990, nearly 15% of UK workers were self-employed, compared to only 8% in the mid-1970s. This increase in self-employment occurred across a wide range of industries, the largest increases being in the construction and service sectors.

The third prominent structural change in the UK labour force in the 1980s has been the shift in employment in favour of females. The most rapidly declining industries have been dominated by males while the most rapidly expanding industries have been dominated by females. The high concentration of females in clerical occupations and the low concentration in craft occupations (see Figure 5.4) provides some indication of the reason why employment growth has been much stronger for females than for males during the 1980s. Moreover, many of the new jobs coming on stream in the later 1980s have been part-time rather than full-time, and this has suited

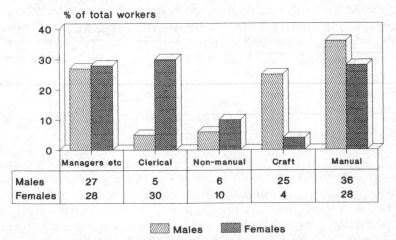

	Managers etc	Clerical	Non-manual	Craft	Manual
Males	27	5	6	25	36
Females	28	30	10	4	28

Males   Females

Figure 5.4   Distribution of Workers between Broad Occupational Categories, 1989
(*Source: ST* 21, 1991)

TABLE 5.4

Employment in the Regions of the United Kingdom: Long-Term Trends

Region	Numbers employed in thousands			% of total UK employment		
	1971	1980	1990	1971	1980	1990
South East	8,000	8,250	8,860	32.7	32.7	33.6
East Anglia	700	820	980	2.9	3.2	3.7
South West	1,690	1,840	2,130	6.9	7.3	8.1
East Midlands	1,560	1,700	1,800	6.4	6.7	6.8
West Midlands	2,380	2,370	2,400	9.7	9.4	9.1
Yorkshire/Humberside	2,100	2,140	2,200	8.6	8.5	8.3
North West	2,880	2,860	2,740	11.8	11.3	10.4
North	1,290	1,280	1,240	5.3	5.1	4.7
Wales	1,090	1,120	1,180	4.5	4.4	4.5
Scotland	2,160	2,270	2,240	8.8	9.0	8.5
Northern Ireland	580	610	600	2.4	2.4	2.3
United Kingdom	24,430	25,240	26,360	100	100	100

Source: Regional Trends, 21, 1991.

many married women with families. It is not therefore surprising to find that male employment failed to grow during the 1980s while female employment expanded by around 2 million.

The major shifts in employment which have been occurring between industries have been accompanied by less dramatic, though still substantial shifts in employment between regions. This shift in jobs between regions is the fourth major structural change which has occurred during the 1980s. Since 1971 the three southern regions of the UK have increased their share of total employment from 42.5% to 45.4% (see Table 5.4). The structural changes in the industrial distribution of employment and the regional shifts in employment are not, of course, unrelated. The most severe job losses since the early 1970s have been in traditional industries such as shipbuilding, textiles and heavy engineering, all of which have been relatively more important in the northern than in the southern regions. The structural decline of the older staple industries is only part of the story, however, since jobs in private services have expanded more rapidly in the South than in the North.

1.3 Hours Worked

Average weekly hours worked in the UK have been on a steady downward trend since the mid-1950s. For male manual workers, average hours worked have fallen from around 48 hours per week in the early 1950s to 45 hours per week in 1990 (see Figure 5.5). For females, hours worked fell sharply from the mid-1950s to the late 1960s but have been very stable since the early 1970s. The long-run downward trend in hours worked seems to have halted for females, at least for the time being. The almost continuous downward trend in hours worked for male workers reflects an increasing preference for leisure as real income increases. Thus, although an increase in real wages may be expected to induce workers to work longer hours, this has apparently been more than offset by an increase in the desire for more leisure as income increases. Leisure is more useful if income is high enough to enjoy it.

A further interesting feature of the hours worked time-series shown in Figure 5.5 is that it fluctuates pro-cyclically. This means that the number of hours worked increases when the economy is in a boom phase of the economic cycle (as in 1955, 1964, 1973, 1979 and 1988) and decreases during slumps. The effect of the 1979–81 depression on the hours worked by males is particularly well marked; weekly hours worked fell from 46.2 in 1979 to 44.2 in 1981 and then to 43.9 in 1983 before eventually rising strongly as the economy grew rapidly in the mid-1980s. The 1990–2 slump is having a similar effect on the hours worked by males as the slump in the early 1980s. The 1980s slump and subsequent boom had a much greater effect on male hours than on female hours. This was probably a result of the far greater impact of the slump on the male-dominated manufacturing sector than on the service sector, which is more 'female intensive' in its use of labour.

International comparisons of hours worked provide some very interesting contrasts. Figure 5.6 shows that weekly hours worked by males are up to seven hours greater in the UK compared to some of our EC partners. The opposite is the case for female workers, who work fewer hours per week on average than in other EC countries. This is probably because part-time work is more common in the UK than in other European countries. (See section 6.5 below for a discussion of the prospects for 'convergence' in working conditions between the UK and its EC partners.)

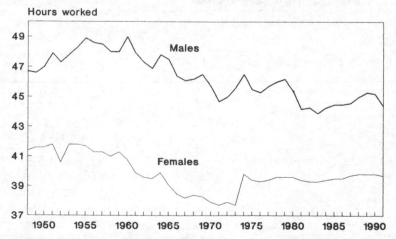

Figure 5.5 Average Weekly Hours Worked by UK Manual Workers, 1948–91
(*Sources: EG: British Labour Statistics, Historical Abstract*)

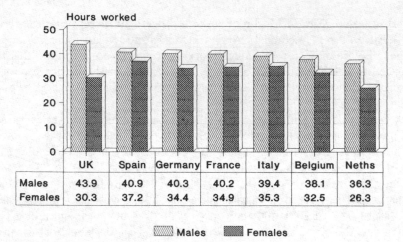

	UK	Spain	Germany	France	Italy	Belgium	Neths
Males	43.9	40.9	40.3	40.2	39.4	38.1	36.3
Females	30.3	37.2	34.4	34.9	35.3	32.5	26.3

Males   Females

Figure 5.6   Average Weekly Hours Worked in Selected EC Countries, 1988
(*Source: ST* 21, 1991)

2.   UNEMPLOYMENT

2.1   Labour Market Stocks and Flows

Unemployment in the UK increased dramatically in the 1980s compared to the golden age of low unemployment in the 1950s and 1960s when unemployment fluctuated around 2%. Figure 5.7 shows male unemployment rising to a peak of nearly 13% in 1986 while female unemployment rose to over 8%. This section examines the causes of unemployment.

To understand the causes of unemployment, it is useful to begin by examining the relationship between labour market stocks and flows. Basically, there are three primary stocks: the stock of employed workers, the

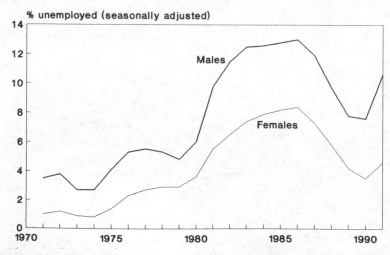

Figure 5.7   Male and Female Unemployment Rates in the United Kingdom, 1971–91
(*Source: EG*, April 1989, January 1992)

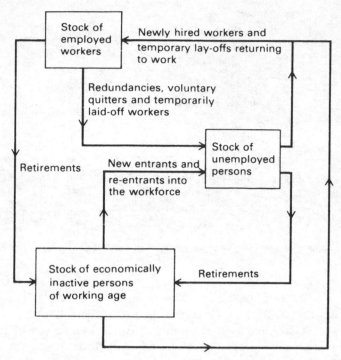

Figure 5.8   Labour Market Stocks and Flows

stock of unemployed and the stock of those who are not economically active. As Figure 5.8 shows, the stock of economically inactive persons includes those people of working age who are not in the working population (e.g. students, mothers with young children and those who are sick or retired). Each of these three stocks is connected to the other two by means of flows of persons between them. The unemployment stock, for example, is connected to the employment stock because redundant workers flow from the employment stock to the unemployment stock; and also because unemployed people who get jobs flow in the opposite direction. The reasons why unemployed workers leave their job are evident from Table 5.5, which shows that only about one-third of males (and one-fifth of females) leave their job because they are made redundant or are dismissed. Almost one in three females leave their job for family reasons.

It should be clear that the unemployment stock will increase whenever the inflow into the stock exceeds the outflow from it, as happens during recessions when firms are releasing more workers than they are taking on. The relationship between inflows into the unemployment stock and outflows from it is shown in Figure 5.9 for the period 1983–91. Two observations can be made about these inflows and outflows. Firstly, the inflows into and out of the unemployment stock are of a similar order of magnitude; and they tend to rise and fall together. Secondly, since the flows are very large in relation to the stock, it takes only small differences between the inflow and the outflow

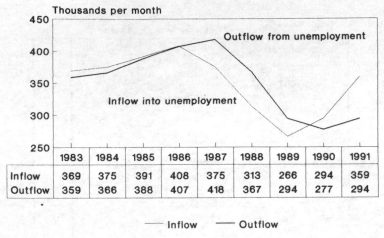

Thousands per month	1983	1984	1985	1986	1987	1988	1989	1990	1991
Inflow	369	375	391	408	375	313	266	294	359
Outflow	359	366	388	407	418	367	294	277	294

—— Inflow   —— Outflow

Figure 5.9   Inflow into and Outflow from the Stock of Unemployed in the United Kingdom
(*Source: EG*)

to cause a substantial change in the unemployment stock. The outflow exceeded the inflow, for example, during 1986–9 with the result that the unemployment stock fell by over a million (from 3.1 million to 1.8 million). Exactly the opposite occurred during 1990–2, with the result that the unemployment stock increased by over a million.

An analysis of the flows into and out of the unemployment stock raises crucially important questions about the factors which determine the probability that a person will become unemployed. Some people never experience unemployment throughout their working lives while others find themselves unemployed for several years; and of those who do become unemployed, some are able to find a job very quickly while others are less fortunate. The question therefore arises whether certain types of people are more likely to become unemployed than others; and if a person does become unemployed, what factors affect the speed at which they are able to get a job?

TABLE 5.5

Reason for Leaving Last Job by Sex: Spring 1990 (Unemployed persons 16 and over) (%)

Main reason for leaving last job (less than 3 years ago)	Males	Females
Redundancy/dismissed	35.5	20.8
Temporary job ended	17.2	13.3
Resigned	10.9	10.8
Health or retirement	10.1	6.7
Family/personal reasons	5.5	31.5
Other reasons	20.8	16.9
All reasons	100.0	100.0

Source: Employment Gazette, May 1991, p. 289.

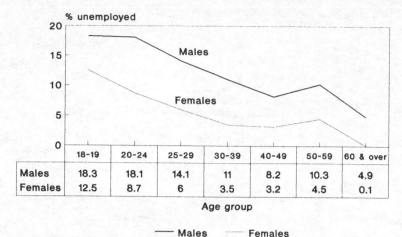

	18-19	20-24	25-29	30-39	40-49	50-59	60 & over
Males	18.3	18.1	14.1	11	8.2	10.3	4.9
Females	12.5	8.7	6	3.5	3.2	4.5	0.1

Age group

—— Males ---- Females

Figure 5.10   Unemployment Rate by Age Group, October 1991
(*Source: EG*)

The Likelihood of Becoming Unemployed: The chances that anyone will become unemployed are strongly influenced by demographic and socio-economic factors. These include a person's age, sex, geographical location, qualifications, skills and the general economic health of the economy. In addition, the likelihood of leaving the unemployment stock is closely related to the length of time a person has been unemployed.

The effect of a person's sex and age on their unemployment experience is shown in Figure 5.10, which shows that males have a much higher prob-ability of joining the unemployment stock than females. This is the case across all age groups without exception. It is also evident from Figure 5.10 that the unemployment rate is generally higher for younger workers than for older workers. This is only to be expected since younger workers are generally more mobile between jobs than older workers, who are often reluctant to move because of the loss of seniority rights which they have built up with their existing employer. Younger, less experienced workers are also more likely to be made redundant when firms are reducing their employ-ment levels.

One of the reasons for the lower unemployment rates recorded for females is that a substantial proportion of females who become unemployed are not recorded in the unemployment figures. This is a consequence of the lack of eligibility for unemployment benefit of many married women who are seeking work. This drawback of the official unemployment data (to be discussed further in the next section) is at least partly overcome by infor-mation obtained in the annual *Labour Force Survey*, which indicates a much narrower gap between male and female unemployment rates than the un-employment data based upon those claiming unemployment benefit.

Another factor which affects the probability of a person becoming unemployed is ethnic origin. Figure 5.11 shows that whites have much lower unemployment rates than those of either West Indian or Pakistani/

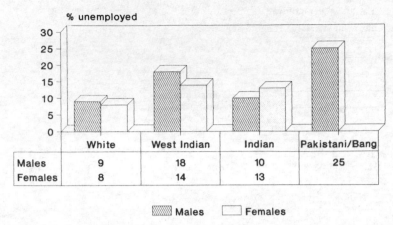

	White	West Indian	Indian	Pakistani/Bang
Males	9	18	10	25
Females	8	14	13	

▨ Males ☐ Females

Figure 5.11 Unemployment Rate by Ethnic Origin in the United Kingdom, 1989
(*Note:* Sample too small for Pakistani/Bangladeshi females.) (*Source: ST* 21, 1991)

Bangladeshi origins. The generally higher unemployment rates for non-whites probably results from a combination of factors, such as racial discrimination and less marketable average skill levels.

Age, sex and ethnic origin are not the only factors which affect the probability of becoming unemployed. A person's educational background, qualifications and skills also exert a substantial influence. In addition to enhancing a worker's value to employers, more highly educated and better qualified workers can expect to be more mobile and therefore have a wider range of job opportunities available to them. This is confirmed by Table 5.6: unemployment rates in 1990 varied from 2% for males with higher educational qualifications to 13% for males with no qualifications. For those males whose highest qualification was A-level or equivalent, the unemployment rate of nearly 5% was over twice as high as those with a higher qualification but was well below those with lower qualifications. A similar result is obtained for females.

Further evidence that the likelihood of becoming unemployed is related to qualifications is indicated by a survey of nearly 8,000 UK graduates undertaken in 1986/87. This survey provides information about their

TABLE 5.6

Unemployment Rates in Great Britain by Highest Qualification Attained: Spring Each Year

	% unemployed					
	Males			Females		
Highest qualification attained	1984	1988	1990	1984	1988	1990
Higher qualifications	3.6	2.7	2.1	6.8	4.0	3.2
A-level or equivalent	8.2	6.1	4.9	10.6	7.5	6.2
O-level or equivalent	11.2	7.2	5.7	10.6	7.8	5.7
CSE below grade 1	18.6	11.8	8.4	18.9	12.6	8.1
No qualification	18.2	15.4	12.8	13.4	11.0	8.7

Source: Employment Gazette, April 1989, p. 193 and May 1991, p. 299.

TABLE 5.7

Unemployment Rates of UK Graduates: by Degree Class

Degree class	% unemployed 6 months after graduation	6 years after graduation
First	4.2	2.9
Upper second	8.4	2.4
Undivided second	8.8	3.6
Lower second	12.1	3.1
Third	16.1	5.3
Other type	9.0	2.1
All classes	10.1	2.9

Source: National Survey of 1980 Graduates and Diplomates (1987), ESRC Data Archive.
Note: 'Other type' includes pass degrees and ordinary degrees.

employment status at two points in time: six months after their graduation (in 1980) and again six years later (in 1986). The results given in Table 5.7 show that the unemployment rate of graduates increases as the class of degree falls. The unemployment rate for those with third-class degrees, for example, was 16.1% compared to an unemployment rate of only 4.2% for those with a first-class degree. The situation six years after graduation, however, suggests that the effect of degree class on the likelihood of becoming unemployed wears off over time, though the rate is still highest for those with a third-class degree.

Finally, a person's occupation affects the probability of becoming unemployed. This relates to both the qualifications possessed by individuals as well as the particular industry to which they are attached. The impact of a person's occupation on the likelihood of becoming unemployed is shown in Table 5.8, which indicates that manual workers are more likely to become unemployed than non-manual workers. As might be expected, managerial and professional workers are less likely to join the ranks of the unemployed than any other occupational group. The very high unemployment rate for labourers indicates the advantage of acquiring a skill.

TABLE 5.8

Unemployment Rates in Great Britain by Occupation and Sex: Spring 1990

Occupation	Males (%)	Females (%)
Non-manual		
Managerial and professional	2.2	2.3
Clerical and related	4.3	3.4
Other non-manual occupations	4.7	5.7
Manual		
Craft and similar occupations	4.9	7.4
General labourers	17.0	—
Other manual occupations	7.7	5.8

Source: Employment Gazette, May 1991, p. 293.
Note: These unemployment rates refer to the previous occupation of those whose last job was less than 3 years ago.

TABLE 5.9

Duration of Unemployment in Great Britain by Sex: Spring 1990

Duration	Males (%)	Females (%)
Under 3 months	28.1	41.3
3–6 months	14.8	19.1
6–12 months	14.6	17.5
12–24 months	12.8	9.9
24–36 months	6.4	4.3
Over 3 years	23.3	7.9
All	100.0	100.0

Source: Employment Gazette, May 1991, p. 294.

The Likelihood of Leaving the Stock of Unemployed: We have shown that the likelihood of *becoming unemployed* varies considerably between different types of people. The same is true for those in the unemployment stock: the likelihood of *leaving* the unemployment stock can be shown to vary according to age, sex, location and the length of time for which a person has been unemployed.

Young workers, for example, are far more likely to leave the unemployment stock quickly after joining it than are older workers. This is probably because employers generally have a preference for younger workers and because younger workers are often less choosy about their choice of job than older workers, who are more likely to be set in their ways and more reluctant to try new types of work.

A further factor which affects a person's likelihood of leaving the unemployment stock is the length of time a person has been unemployed. It becomes increasingly difficult to get out of the unemployment stock the longer a person has been in it. There are two reasons for this. First, as the duration of unemployment increases, the unemployed become discouraged and consequently search for a job with less enthusiasm. They may even run out of local firms to search! Second, employers are more reluctant to hire those who have been unemployed for long periods compared to those who have been unemployed for only a short time. This is partly because employers believe that the long-term unemployed are in some sense inferior; their job applications have already been rejected by other employers, perhaps several times. The long-term unemployed are also less attractive to employers because their skills deteriorate as the duration of their unemployment increases. It is not simply that the unemployed lose their skills but rather that the appearance of new products and new processes require those in jobs to learn new skills. Those in work are constantly up-dating their skills with the result that the skill gap between the employed and the unemployed widens as the time spent in the unemployment stock increases. The consequence of an increase in the duration of unemployment is therefore an increasing mismatch between the skills required by employers and the skills offered by the unemployed.

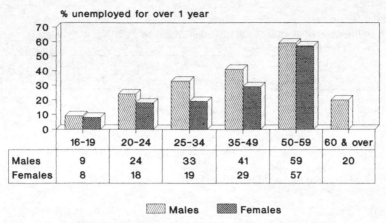

% unemployed for over 1 year

	16-19	20-24	25-34	35-49	50-59	60 & over
Males	9	24	33	41	59	20
Females	8	18	19	29	57	

▨ Males   ▩ Females

Figure 5.12   Long-term Unemployment in the United Kingdom by Age and Sex, 1990
(*Note:* Females over 60 excluded due to small sample size.) (*Source: ST* 21, 1991)

The distinction between short-term unemployment and long-term unemployment is an important one since it is long-term unemployment which is generally regarded as being in most urgent need of attention by policy-makers. As might be expected, long-term unemployment is more prevalent among some groups of workers than among others. Males, for example, are more likely to be unemployed for long periods than are females once they join the unemployment stock (see Table 5.9); and older persons are more likely to be unemployed for long periods than are younger persons (see Figure 5.12). One reason why younger persons are able to get out of the unemployment stock more quickly is their greater mobility and greater flexibility in the eyes of employers.

2.2   Some Problems in Measuring Unemployment

The official unemployment count includes only those who are successfully claiming unemployment benefit. It therefore excludes all those seeking work but who are *not* claiming unemployment benefit.

The official UK definition of unemployment should be compared with the international definition, which defines a person as being unemployed if that person is not in work but is available for work and has looked for work in the last four months. In the Spring of 1990, the UK's *Labour Force Survey* estimated that there were 1.95 million people unemployed compared to the official count of only 1.61 million. This suggests that the official unemployment count understates true unemployment in the UK by around 20%. The main reason for this underestimation of true unemployment is that a large proportion of married women who are seeking a return to the labour force are not entitled to unemployment benefit. This is indicated by Table 5.10, which shows that 60% of married women who are seeking work give 'looking after family or home' as their current status.

TABLE 5.10

Status of Unemployed Persons before Seeking Work by Sex: Great Britain, Spring 1990
(Unemployed persons 16 and over)

Status before seeking work	Males	Married females	Non-married females
Working	70.5	33.5	38.2
In full-time education or training	16.4	1.7	25.0
Looking after family or home	2.5	59.8	26.4
Other (sick, disabled, not looking for work)	10.6	5.0	10.4
All	100.0	100.0	100.0

Source: Employment Gazette, May 1991, p. 290.

Estimates of unemployment therefore vary substantially according to how the unemployed are counted. The official definition of unemployment has changed several times during the 1980s. According to the Department of Employment, these changes have led to a substantial reduction in the unemployment total. At the 1980s unemployment peak (in 1986) the measured unemployment total stood at around half a million below the level which would have occurred if the changes had not been made. Two changes which were estimated to have reduced unemployment (by 190,000 and 162,000 respectively) are, first, the replacement of the old method of counting all those registered as unemployed at jobcentres by the count based on benefit claimants only; and second, the effective lowering of the early retirement age for men to sixty by replacing unemployment benefit by income support. A more recent change in the method of counting the unemployed is the removal of all 16–17-year-olds from the unemployment count following the withdrawal of their entitlement to unemployment benefit in October 1988. This reduced the unemployment count by over 50,000 – once again by changing the unemployment benefit rules.

Less obvious and less quantifiable changes have occurred in recent years which have affected the unemployment count. Firstly, unemployment benefit offices have tightened up the 'availability for work' tests in order to discourage those claimants who are not genuinely seeking work. The 1988 Social Security Act specifies that a person has to be 'actively seeking work' in order to be eligible for unemployment benefit. This means that they will be expected to be applying for job vacancies and to be registered with a job agency. In addition, to maintain their entitlement to benefits, those unemployed for over three months have to accept any available job in the area regardless of the person's previous work experience or wage. Secondly, the number of workers on government employment and training programmes has reduced the unemployment total substantially since without access to such programmes many more would be in the unemployment stock.

On the other hand, it has been argued that a substantial number of unemployed persons are not interested in finding a job because they are supplementing their unemployment benefit by working in the black economy. This view is supported by a Department of Employment Survey of 2,700 unemployed people in London in 1988 which concluded 'that a significant minority of the capital's 280,000 unemployed were claiming benefit while working in the black economy' (*Financial Times*, 13 October 1988).

Nevertheless, on balance, it seems likely that the current method of measuring unemployment in the UK seriously underestimates the economist's definition of unemployment.

2.3   International Comparisons of Unemployment

Between 1948 and 1968, the annual unemployment rate in the UK averaged 1.8% and never rose above 2.6%. The following two decades witnessed a remarkable change, especially during the 1980s when a new dimension was added to the post-war history of UK unemployment. The unemployment rate rose from 2% in 1974 to 4% in 1979. This was followed by a sustained increase to over 11% in 1986, when more than three million people were recorded as claiming unemployment benefit; and about a million others were unemployed but not entitled to benefit and so were not recorded in the unemployment total.

The UK was not alone, however, in experiencing high unemployment during the 1980s, as can be seen from Figure 5.13. With the exception of Japan, all of the major industrialized nations experienced substantial increases in their unemployment rates in the early 1980s. Closer inspection of these long-run trends reveals two substantial upward shifts in the unemployment rate, the first in 1974 and the second in the early 1980s. The fact that these two upward shifts in unemployment were so widespread across the world's major trading nations suggests the existence of a common cause. Both cases were marked by a sharp decline in world trade as a direct result of concerted international action to deal with two serious and related economic problems. Firstly, the sharp and unprecedented increase in the price of oil in 1973/74 from three dollars to ten dollars per barrel had serious adverse effects on the balance of payments of the major industrialized nations, all of which relied heavily on imported oil. This oil price increase also provided an unwelcome impetus to inflation, which was already increasing in these countries. In order to rectify their balance of payments deficits on current account and to deal with the threat of inflation, these nations deflated their economies by operating more restrictive fiscal and monetary policies. Similar policies were introduced in the aftermath of the increase in oil prices in 1979/80, this time from 13 dollars to 29 dollars per barrel.

An interesting question which is posed by the long-term unemployment trends in Figure 5.13 is why Japan has managed to keep its unemployment rate so low during the 1980s compared to most other industrialized nations. The answer to this question helps to throw some light on the high levels of unemployment experienced by the UK and other European countries

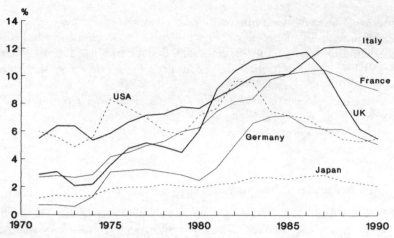

Figure 5.13 Unemployment Rates in Selected Countries 1971–90
(*Source: OECD Economic Outlook*, July 1991)

during the 1980s, since one of the reasons for the low unemployment rate in Japan is that wages there are far more flexible during recessions than they are in Western European labour markets.

It has been argued that wages are more flexible in Japan because large firms offer lifetime employment for their employees but in return the annual earnings of workers are closely tied to the firm's profitability. In Japan, wages contain a large bonus element which is directly related to profitability. When profits fall, the bonus payment falls and so therefore does a worker's annual earnings. The lifetime employment system, which flourishes in Japan's major companies, actually *requires* wage flexibility. This system allows a great deal of wage flexibility without workers feeling that their status has been eroded by the wage cuts which are necessary in periods of low profitability if employment is to be maintained. In addition, it has been shown that there is a high level of wage flexibility in the highly competitive small firms sector, which is very large in Japan. Japanese workers therefore appear to place a much higher value on employment security than on wage targets compared to Western European workers. Given the fact that output fluctuates as much in Japan as in Europe, it is clear that the willingness to take wage cuts in Japan helps to keep its unemployment rate at very low levels.

Another reason why Japanese unemployment rates are generally low compared to Western Europe is that many workers who lose their jobs are not recorded as unemployed. Many part-time workers, such as housewives and older semi-retired workers, simply disappear from the labour force when they lose their jobs during recessions. This discrepancy between 'true' unemployment and 'official' unemployment is not peculiar to Japan, though it may well be substantially larger in that country compared to Western Europe.

2.4   Long-Run Unemployment Trends in the UK

The Natural Rate of Unemployment: The underlying long-run trend in UK unemployment has risen strongly during the post-war period. Some researchers have argued that this upward trend is the result of an increase in the *natural rate of unemployment*, which is defined as the unemployment rate which exists when the labour market is in equilibrium (i.e. when the demand for labour equals the supply of labour). Labour market equilibrium only exists when the actual rate of unemployment equals its natural rate.

This concept of a natural rate of unemployment can be extended to allow for the persistent increase in wages and prices by defining it as the unemployment rate that is consistent with a constant rate of inflation. If unemployment is below its natural rate, inflation will rise; if unemployment is above its natural rate, inflation will fall; only if unemployment is at its natural rate will inflation remain constant. This special rate of unemployment is often referred to as the non-accelerating inflation rate of unemployment – or NAIRU for short. The fairly steady inflation rate of around 5% in the UK during 1983–7 suggests that the UK unemployment rate was at its NAIRU level during this period. The sharp fall in unemployment during 1986–90, followed by an increase in the rate of inflation (from 3.4% in 1986 to 9.5% in 1990), indicates that unemployment fell below its NAIRU level at the end of the 1980s.

More recently the natural rate of unemployment has been defined not only in terms of a stable inflation rate but also in terms of the balance of trade. Unemployment is said to be at its equilibrium level only if there is stable inflation and a balance of trade equal to zero at the same time. This is a far more restricted view of the equilibrium unemployment rate. Layard, Nickell and Jackman (1991) have recently undertaken very detailed research on the UK unemployment rate and are able to provide estimates of the natural rate of unemployment from the mid-1950s through until 1990. Table 5.11 allows us to compare the actual unemployment rate with their estimates of the natural unemployment rate. These results show that the actual unemployment rate and the natural unemployment rate were approximately equal during 1956–73, but that the natural rate rose sharply during the 1970s, from 3.6% to 7.3%. Since the actual rate was less than the natural rate during 1974–80, it is not surprising to find that this was associated with a period of high inflation. The early part of the 1980s witnessed exactly the opposite: the actual rate rose above the natural rate and inflation fell steadily until the late 1980s. The rapid fall in unemployment during 1987–90 then reversed the situation yet again.

2.5   The Causes of Unemployment

The detailed research into UK unemployment undertaken by Layard, Nickell and Jackman (1991) identifies seven major causes. These are as follows:

TABLE 5.11

Actual Unemployment and the Natural Rate of Unemployment in the UK, 1956-90 (yearly average)

	Actual rate of unemployment	*Estimated natural rate of unemployment*
1956–59	2.2	2.2
1960–68	2.6	2.5
1969–73	3.4	3.6
1974–80	5.2	7.3
1981–87	11.1	8.7
1988–90	7.3	8.7

Source: Layard, Nickell and Jackman (1991).

(i) Demand Factors: Substantial fluctuations in unemployment around its natural rate have been caused by variations in the *aggregate* demand for goods and services. A fall in aggregate demand, for example, can originate from contractionary fiscal or monetary policies as well as from a fall in world trade due to an international recession. The sharp increase in interest rates from $7\frac{1}{2}\%$ to 15% during 1988–9 in order to reduce inflationary pressures provides an excellent example of a contractionary monetary policy which resulted in a sharp increase in the UK unemployment rate.

(ii) Trade Union Power: An increase in trade union power can cause unemployment to increase by forcing wages up beyond the level warranted by increases in labour productivity. This is sometimes referred to as 'classical' unemployment since it is caused by the real wage being pushed above its market clearing level.

(iii) Employment Taxes: Firms have to pay national insurance contributions for every worker they employ (provided they earn more than a certain amount per week). Any increase in this tax on employment can be expected to reduce the demand for labour since it raises labour costs for the employer.

(iv) Mismatch Unemployment: Unemployment occurs when there is a mismatch between the demand for labour and the supply of labour. The unemployed may have the required skills to fill a job vacancy but may not be located in the same geographical labour market area as the vacancy. There is a *geographical* mismatch in this case. Likewise, job vacancies and unemployment may occur within the same geographical labour market but the unemployed may not have the required skills to fill those vacancies. There is a *skill* mismatch in this case. Both a geographical mismatch and a skill mismatch can, of course, occur simultaneously. Mismatch unemployment is more likely to occur during periods of severe structural change, as in the early 1980s when the collapse of many manufacturing industries led to the loss of predominantly male jobs, many of which were located in the northern and western parts of the UK. At the same time as male manufacturing jobs were being lost in the North, new jobs were being created in the South – but mainly in the service sector and mainly for females. These structural changes in UK industry during the 1980s led to a serious mismatch between labour demand and labour supply.

(v) Unemployment Benefit: Unemployment benefit may alter the level of unemployment in two ways. First, an increase in unemployment benefit (or other income support measures) relative to earnings available from work will induce some workers to become unemployed (Minford, 1983). Alternatively an increase in benefits will encourage those who become unemployed (perhaps through no fault of their own) to spend more time unemployed than they would have done if benefits had been lower.

Second, substantial changes have been made, especially during the 1980s, to the rules governing the payment of unemployment benefit. An example of this is the Restart Programme (introduced in 1986), which requires all those unemployed for over six months to attend a Restart interview, the primary intention of which is to provide special guidance for the long-term unemployed. A further aim, however, is to encourage the long-term unemployed to seek out and accept job offers more readily. This approach was strengthened in 1989 by withdrawing unemployment benefit from anyone who refused to accept a 'reasonable' job offer, even if this means accepting lower pay than in the person's previous job. Another recent change to the unemployment benefit rules is the raising of the waiting period, for those who quit their job voluntarily, from six weeks to thirteen weeks before becoming entitled to unemployment benefit. Changes in the eligibility rules could have substantial effects on the level of unemployment.

(vi) Incomes Policy: Successive governments from 1961 through until the end of the 1970s tried to reduce inflation by using various methods of restraining pay increases. These ranged from gentle persuasion to statutory controls on wage increases. Although incomes policies do not seem to have had much success in holding down inflation (except temporarily), there is less evidence available about their effect on unemployment. The main aim was to reduce the unemployment rate which is consistent with non-accelerating inflation (i.e. the NAIRU). Most research suggests that incomes policies have had little effect on both inflation *and* the unemployment rate.

(vii) Import Prices: A sharp increase in import prices, as happened in 1973/74 when oil prices surged, can result in higher unemployment if workers respond by demanding higher nominal (money) wages in order to maintain their real wage. This happened in the mid-1970s when the UK labour force was unwilling to adjust to the new terms of trade which had been imposed on the industrialized world by oil exporters (through OPEC). Real wages had to fall if competitiveness was to be maintained and workers were not willing to accept this new fact of life. The consequence was a loss of competitiveness and a deterioration in the performance of Britain's export industries.

To what extent have these various factors contributed to the huge increase in unemployment which has occurred in the UK since the 1950s and 1960s, when the unemployment rate fluctuated around 2% ? As far as the underlying natural rate of unemployment is concerned, three factors have played a predominating role:

(1) there has been a continuing increase in the mismatch between labour demand and labour supply, especially during the 1980s;
(2) trade union power resulted in higher wage inflation and hence more deflationary policies, especially during the 1970s;
(3) a rise in import prices led to wage push and a consequent reduction in competitiveness, especially in the 1970s and 1980s.

As far as short-run fluctuations in unemployment are concerned, the predominating influence has undoubtedly been the level of demand. The early 1980s and early 1990s provide two striking examples of how the government itself can cause unemployment to increase. The 1980–2 recession was a direct consequence of a contractionary monetary and fiscal policy that was designed to bring inflation down (which it succeeded in doing at the cost of raising unemployment to historically record levels). More recently, unemployment has risen sharply during 1990–2 as a direct result of another period of tight monetary control (i.e. high interest rates).

One commonly held view about the causes of unemployment has not yet been mentioned. It is widely believed that unemployment is caused by the replacement of workers by machines. New technology destroys jobs through the replacement of labour-intensive production methods by capital-intensive methods. But historical experience does not support the view that new technology leads to a loss of jobs *nationally*. It needs to be remembered that there is no reason to expect the *total* demand for labour to fall when labour-saving techniques are introduced into particular sectors of the economy. Indeed, new technology permits more to be produced with the same inputs. It also provides opportunities to supply entirely new products, therefore creating new markets. Technical change is necessary if firms and industries are to remain competitive in world markets. Firms and industries which are reluctant to keep pace with new technology are unlikely to stay in business for long.

3   REGIONAL UNEMPLOYMENT PROBLEMS AND POLICIES

3.1   Regional Unemployment Disparities

Regional differences in unemployment have changed dramatically during the past two decades (see Figure 5.14). The early 1980s witnessed the widest regional differences in unemployment since the 1930s. The reason for this North–South divide is not hard to find. Job losses in the manufacturing sector were severe in *all* regions, but the South was able to offset the loss of manufacturing jobs with an increase in service sector jobs (see Tables 5.12 and 5.13).

The North–South unemployment gap did not begin to narrow until the southern regions ran into severe labour shortages in 1989–90. Then came the 1990–2 recession with a vengeance. Past experience suggested that the northern regions would again be hit the hardest. Surprisingly, this failed to happen. It was the southern regions which suffered the immediate impact of the 1990–2 recession with the result that unemployment in the South rose far quicker than in the North. For once, history was not repeating itself. The explanation for this totally unexpected impact of the recession to the

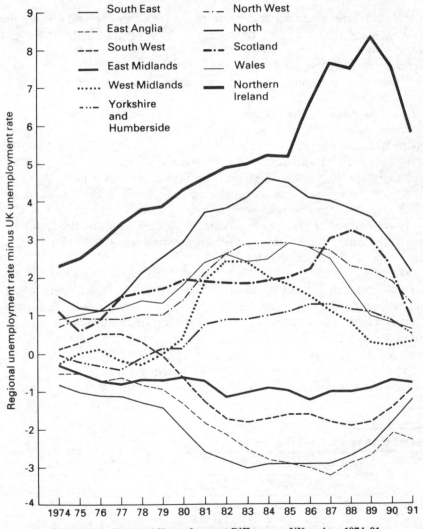

Figure 5.14   Regional Unemployment Differences: UK regions 1974–91
(*Source: DEG*)

TABLE 5.12

Changes in Employment by Broad Sector, 1971–91 (in thousands)

	Manufacturing		Non-manufacturing		Total	
	1971–80	1980–91	1971–80	1980–91	1971–80	1980–91
North[1]	−700	−1192	852	877	152	−315
South[2]	−404	−776	1060	1488	656	712

Source: Regional Trends 26, 1991.
Notes:
[1] North = West Midlands, Yorkshire and Humberside, North West, North, Wales, Scotland and Northern Ireland.
[2] South = South East, East Anglia, South West and East Midlands.

detriment of the southern regions is to be found in the collapse of the housing market. Just as the rapid rise in house prices had encouraged house-owners in the South to spend more during the late 1980s due to their increased wealth, the rapid fall in house prices in the South during 1990–2 had exactly the opposite effect. House-owners reduced their spending as their wealth fell.

It is important not to become obsessed with the North–South divide. Unemployment black spots exist in *all* parts of the UK – even in regions where the unemployment rate is relatively low. In the South West, for example, Cornwall's unemployment rate is higher than the rate in all UK regions except for Northern Ireland. The wide disparities in unemployment rates within each UK region can be seen in Table 5.14. These spatial differences in unemployment become even greater as smaller and smaller areas are compared. The inner city areas, for example, usually have the highest unemployment rates, and suburban areas and small towns tend to have lower unemployment rates.

One of the striking features of the 1990–2 recession is that regional unemployment disparities continued to narrow. But this narrowing of unemployment disparities is unlikely to continue into the mid-1990s for two reasons. Firstly, past experience strongly suggests that unemployment rates in the South will fall faster than unemployment rates in the North as the economy moves into the next expansionary phase of the economic cycle. Secondly, and more important over the longer term, the process of increasing economic integration within the European Community is expected

TABLE 5.13

Percentage Changes in Employment by Broad Sector, 1971–91

	Manufacturing		Non-manufacturing		Total	
	1971–80	1980–91	1971–80	1980–91	1971–80	1980–91
North[1]	−15.0	−30.0	10.8	10.1	1.2	−2.4
South[2]	−11.5	−25.0	12.6	15.7	5.5	5.6

Notes: See Table 5.12.

to aggravate regional unemployment disparities. The intention to eliminate all barriers to trade, labour mobility and capital mobility within the EC is likely to have a substantial impact upon the geographical allocation of resources throughout the Community during the 1990s.

The actual impact of the removal of internal barriers in the EC on regional economic disparities will depend upon several factors. Firstly, regions on the geographical periphery of the EC are likely to be at a locational disadvantage compared to regions nearer the Bonn–Paris–London triangle. The heavy concentration of purchasing power in the core regions of the EC will act as a magnet for mobile capital, especially labour-intensive service sector activities. Secondly, the industry mix is more favourable to economic restructuring in some regions than in others. The South East, for example, has an industry mix which is better able than other UK regions to respond to the sectoral restructuring that will occur as a consequence of the '1992 process'. This is because it is more dependent than other UK regions upon industries which are likely to be favourably affected by the increasing economic integration between the member states of the European Community (Begg, 1990). Thirdly, the higher quality of the economic infrastructure in the core regions of the EC makes these regions more attractive to mobile capital than the peripheral areas. This applies not only to fixed capital assets, such as transport networks, but also to human capital. The educational qualifications and skills of the workforce tend to be of higher quality in the core regions, partly because of higher living standards in these areas and partly because of the inflow of more highly-educated and highly-skilled workers from the peripheral regions. Although these advantages of the core EC regions will be partly offset by lower labour costs and lower land costs in the peripheral areas, there is nevertheless a strong presumption that it is the core regions which will benefit the most from further integration. This expectation is clearly reflected by the decision of the European Council of Ministers to double the funds available (between 1989 and 1993) for assisting those regions likely to be adversely affected by the single market.

Regional economic disparities in the EC will be further aggravated by the steady progression towards full economic and monetary union (EMU). The adoption of a single currency throughout the EC, for example, will mean that individual nations will no longer be able to use currency devaluation to offset any inflationary tendencies which originate within their own borders. It will no longer be possible to devalue the pound in response to higher inflation rates in Britain compared to our major competitors. Wage bargaining will *have* to become more responsive to market circumstances if high levels of unemployment are to be avoided. Full economic and monetary union will impose severe penalties on any country (and hence regions within countries) which refuse to take into account the effects of wage increases on the competitiveness of the products they produce. Moreover, the adoption of a single currency will impose severe limits on the independence of individual member states to determine their own fiscal policies. The regional

TABLE 5.14

Unemployment Rates in the Counties of Great Britain, December 1991

SOUTH EAST		WEST MIDLANDS		NORTH	
Bedfordshire	7.9	Hereford and Worcester	7.4	Cleveland	12.7
Berkshire	5.7	Shropshire	7.1	Cumbria	6.4
Buckinghamshire	6.4	Staffordshire	8.0	Durham	10.6
East Sussex	9.6	Warwickshire	7.0	Northumberland	9.6
Essex	8.8	West Midlands Conurbation	11.3	Tyne and Wear	12.1
Hampshire	7.5				
Hertfordshire	6.8	EAST MIDLANDS		WALES	
Isle of Wight	11.0	Derbyshire	8.7	Clwyd	7.9
Kent	8.6	Leicestershire	7.2	Dyfed	9.2
Oxfordshire	5.6	Lincolnshire	8.1	Gwent	9.6
Surrey	n.a.	Northamptonshire	7.1	Gwynedd	10.5
West Sussex	5.7	Nottinghamshire	9.6	Mid-Glamorgan	12.0
Greater London	9.2			Powys	5.2
		YORKS AND HUMBERSIDE		South Glamorgan	8.9
EAST ANGLIA		Humberside	9.7	West Glamorgan	9.7
Cambridgeshire	6.6	North Yorkshire	5.5		
Norfolk	7.4	South Yorkshire	12.1	SCOTLAND	
Suffolk	6.0	West Yorkshire	8.7	Borders	6.0
				Central	9.3
SOUTH WEST		NORTH WEST		Dumfries and Galloway	7.7
Avon	8.6	Cheshire	7.5	Fife	10.4
Cornwall	12.3	Lancashire	8.0	Grampian	4.0
Devon	9.3	Greater Manchester	9.8	Highland	8.9
Dorset	8.9	Merseyside	14.7	Lothian	7.7
Gloucestershire	6.6			Strathclyde	11.4
Somerset	7.4			Tayside	8.2
Wiltshire	6.8			Orkney Islands	4.8
				Shetland Islands	3.0
				Western Islands	13.6

Source: Employment Gazette.
Note: Figures are not given for Surrey.

consequences of the progression towards greater economic and monetary union therefore need to be carefully monitored.

3.2   Regional Policy

Economic theory tells us that regional disparities in unemployment would disappear if markets were efficient. Areas of high unemployment should experience a fall in wages relative to areas of low unemployment. These wage disparities would then have two effects: workers would migrate from low wage areas to high wage areas; and firms would migrate in the opposite direction. In addition, the lower wages would make existing firms in high unemployment areas more competitive, thereby raising the demand for the area's products and hence employment.

Reality is more complicated. Wages do respond to geographical variations in unemployment and workers do move from high unemployment to low unemployment areas. But the adjustment process is far too slow to make a significant dent in regional unemployment disparities. This market failure occurs for two main reasons. Firstly, wages fail to respond to regional differences in unemployment. This is partly because wages are often set at national level, particularly in the public sector and particularly in firms which have plants in several locations. In addition, there has been an increasing tendency for wages to be determined according to the profitability of individual parts of firms, irrespective of local labour market conditions. High unemployment in local labour markets therefore tends to have very little impact on the determination of wages in highly profitable plants (Walsh and Brown, 1990).

Since wages do not respond sensitively to regional disparities in unemployment, the reduction of these disparities depends upon the extent to which the unemployed are willing to move to areas where jobs are available, and the extent to which firms are willing to move to areas where labour is available (i.e. high unemployment areas). This brings us to the second reason why regional disparities in unemployment persist for generations: there are severe constraints on labour and capital mobility. The unemployed are immobile because:

- the financial costs of moving from one area to another are high
- a substantial proportion of the unemployed live in subsidized accommodation and are reluctant to move since the standard of their accommodation may fall
- the profitability of getting a job in another area may be low (especially for the unemployed)
- the psychological costs of moving to another area may be very high (due to loss of friends and family).

Similar arguments apply to firms. They exhibit a strong preference for the certainty of their present location rather than the uncertainty and disruption costs which result from a move to another region. This geographical inertia is particularly powerful in small firms since they normally have close ties with other firms in their own locality.

Although there have been attempts to reduce the barriers to labour migration in order to encourage unemployed workers to move from areas of high unemployment to areas where jobs are available, these policies have not made any significant impression on regional unemployment disparities. Successive governments have tried to reduce regional unemployment disparities by creating jobs in areas of high unemployment through various forms of regional policy (Taylor, 1991). These are as follows:

(i) Encouraging Inward Investment into High Unemployment Areas: The first serious attempt to induce industry to move from areas of low unemployment to areas of high unemployment was made in the immediate aftermath of World War II, when strict controls were imposed on the location of industry. Location controls remained the main instrument for directing industry to the assisted areas until the 1960s, when investment and then labour subsidies were used on a substantial scale. The primary purpose of this carrot and stick policy was to achieve a better geographical match between labour demand and labour supply so that unemployment could be reduced in areas of high unemployment while simultaneously reducing inflationary pressures in the labour-scarce South East.

Detailed statistical research into the effect of location controls and financial incentives indicates that these policy instruments succeeded in creating many thousands of jobs in assisted areas. However, these earlier policies had several flaws. Firstly, much of the expenditure on automatic investment incentives (i.e. the Regional Development Grant) went to capital-intensive projects and this led to reductions in employment in some cases. Secondly, investment incentives were directed, in the main, at the manufacturing sector even though employment in this sector has been declining since the late 1960s. Until the mid-1980s, little attention was paid to the potential importance of the service sector as a generator of jobs. Thirdly, investment grants were often paid to firms which would have invested in the assisted areas even without these grants. This deadweight spending appears to have been particularly substantial in capital-intensive industries such as chemicals and steel. Fourthly, controls on the location of industry were heavily criticized, in spite of research findings which indicated that this policy instrument was very effective in diverting industry from the South East to the assisted areas in the 1960s and 1970s. These location controls were abandoned in 1982 since policymakers believed that they were having an adverse effect upon national investment. A more likely reason is that policymakers viewed these location controls as too restrictive and not consistent with a market-oriented political ideology.

These are forceful criticisms. But they should not go unchallenged. Firstly, the apparently high cost of the investment subsidies per job created is misleading since the direct jobs created in the plant receiving the subsidy are typically only a proportion of the total jobs created. Extra jobs are created in other industries in the same locality due to increased household expenditure on locally produced goods and services. In addition, there may be induced investment effects in related industries. A further problem with the cost per job estimates is that they refer to the gross Exchequer costs, which are likely to exceed the net costs to the Exchequer. To calculate the net costs to the Exchequer, it is necessary to deduct from the gross costs any reduction in government spending (e.g. due to lower unemployment benefit payments) and any increase in tax revenues accruing from higher employment and higher household expenditure. Secondly, it needs to be realized that investments which save existing jobs are just as valuable as investments which create entirely new jobs. Jobs saved should be counted alongside jobs created in the cost per job calculation. Thirdly, investment subsidies help to maintain and enhance an area's competitiveness since new plant and machinery will incorporate the latest technology. Raising an area's technological capability will improve its image and make a more attractive location for further inward investment.

(ii) Stimulating Indigenous Growth: The second strategic approach to reducing regional economic inequalities is to get the assisted areas to create their own growth rather than relying on inward investment. This is exactly what happened in the 1980s as traditional redistribution of industry policy was downgraded and as policies were introduced to encourage local firms to invest in their own localities.

The switch towards an indigenous growth policy was bolstered by the increasingly popular view that Britain's economic future depended very largely upon the success of small and medium-sized enterprises. Policies were introduced to stimulate new firm formation as well as encouraging the expansion of small firms. The Loan Guarantee Scheme, for example, was introduced to encourage the banking sector to lend more freely to new and small businesses while the Business Expansion Scheme was designed to attract small scale investors to buy equity in small firms by offering tax incentives. Neither of these schemes has been very successful, however, in generating jobs in the assisted areas.

The importance of small firms in generating new jobs is clear from Table 5.15. This shows that firms with under 10 workers created over half a million additional jobs in the late 1980s – nearly half of all the additional jobs created even though this sector employed under one fifth of all workers. The small firm sector was therefore very important in providing additional jobs when the UK economy was booming in the late 1980s.

Relying on small firms to create new jobs in areas of high unemployment, however, faces two serious drawbacks. Firstly, small firms as a group are extremely vulnerable during recessions. Jobs gained in boom times may therefore be just as easily lost in times of economic slump. Secondly, the growth of small firms has been far faster in the southern, more prosperous, regions than in the northern regions (see Figure 5.15). The economic environment has been far more favourable for new and small firms in the South

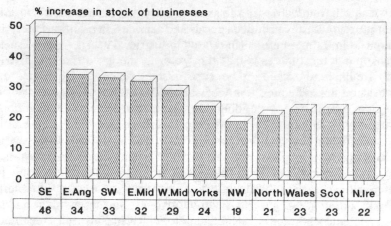

Figure 5.15   The Formation of New Businesses in UK Regions, 1980–90
(*Note:* New businesses are those firms which register as eligible for VAT.)
(*Source:* Daly (1991).)

than in the North. It is not therefore surprising to find that the South has benefited far more than the North from the government's small firms policy. If anything, the government's small firms policy has led to a widening of regional economic disparities rather than a narrowing (Storey and Johnson, 1988).

(iii) Improving the Economic Infrastructure: The third main arm of regional policy is public investment in the infrastructure of depressed areas. It is vitally important to improve both the physical infrastructure and the socio-economic fabric of the assisted areas. Investment in the physical infrastructure ranges from rejuvenating derelict sites (such as the Albert Dock scheme in Liverpool) to improving transport networks, housing stock, educational facilities, recreational amenities and the physical environment more generally. Improving the physical environment acts as an important signal to the private sector since it demonstrates the government's

TABLE 5.15

Contribution of Small Firms to Employment Growth, 1987-89

Size band (employees)	Net increase in unemployment (thousands)	Share of total net increase in unemployment (%)	Share of 1987 employment (%)
1–9	523	46.4	18.9
10–49	168	14.9	22.4
50–99	84	7.5	8.0
100–499	123	11.0	13.8
500–999	55	4.8	3.7
1000 & over	175	15.4	33.4
Total	1127	100	100

Source: Daly (1991).

commitment to reviving depressed areas and acts as a confidence booster for private sector investors. This is the main principle, for example, underlying urban regeneration schemes which are aimed at levering private sector investment into inner city areas. Public investment in the physical infrastructure also makes depressed areas better places in which to live and work, thus helping these areas to retain and attract a highly-skilled workforce.

Public investment is also needed to upgrade the skills of workers in depressed areas. The absence of growth industries and the higher incidence of long-term unemployment in northern regions (see Figure 5.14) has had a detrimental effect on workforce skills, thus reducing the attractiveness of these regions to employers. In addition, depressed areas suffer from the out-migration of their most highly educated workers to regions which offer better career prospects. Considerably more public investment is needed in further education and in training if skill levels in depressed areas are to be raised significantly.

4   EMPLOYMENT POLICIES

Employment policies are targeted specifically on the unemployed. They are designed to get people out of unemployment and into a job. Since the vast majority of those who become unemployed are able to get back into employment quickly, employment policies are aimed primarily at the long-term unemployed.

The three main types of employment policy are:

- training programmes for the unemployed
- employment subsidies to firms willing to employ the long-term unemployed
- the provision of jobs in the public sector (as an employer of last resort).

Employment subsidies and employment in the public sector are normally regarded as being inferior to training programmes. They have come under fire for three main reasons. Firstly, employment subsidies result in a 'deadweight' loss in so far as some of those who get jobs would have got them anyway, in which case the subsidy is wasted. Secondly, firms will substitute subsidized workers for unsubsidized workers. There is no net gain in employment in this case. Thirdly, firms which take on extra workers in order to receive the subsidy may displace employment in firms which do not do so since they may take work from these latter firms. The net increase in employment may therefore be small. But all these criticisms assume that the overall level of demand in the economy is fixed. The whole process of retraining and getting the long-term unemployed back into jobs is designed to increase the productive capacity of the economy, thereby allowing the aggregate demand for goods and services to be raised. The national level of output and employment should be greater as a result of such policies.

Current employment policy in the UK is based upon the following programmes.

TABLE 5.16

Percentage of 16–18-year-olds in Full-Time and Part-Time Education and Training

	Full-time	*Full-time and part-time*
UK	35	69
France	66	74
Germany	47	90
Japan	77	80
USA	79	80

Source: *Statistical Bulletin*, Department of Education, January 1990.
Note: UK and Japan (1988), Germany (1987), France and USA (1986).

4.1 Restart

Restart was introduced in 1986. It requires anyone drawing unemployment benefit for over six months to see a Restart counsellor. The job of the counsellor is to identify possible routes back into employment. These include:

– encouraging the unemployed to search more intensively for a job
– joining a Job Club in order to gain experience of making job applications and contacting employers
– placing a person on a government-financed training scheme
– finding a person a temporary job subsidized by a government grant.

How effective has Restart been? Immediately after its introduction in 1986, unemployment fell very rapidly and continued to do so through until 1990. But this was largely due to a rapid expansion in the level of economic activity throughout the UK economy. Restart may have helped, however, by encouraging the long-term unemployed to search more actively for a job just at the right time. One of the less desirable consequences of Restart is that many unemployed persons have had to take low paid jobs rather than improving their skills. Restart may therefore have done little to raise the skill level of the workforce.

4.2 Employment Training

The UK has a poor record on training its workforce compared to France, Germany and the USA. This is illustrated by the very low proportion of 16–18-year-olds in either full-time or part-time education or training in the UK (see Table 5.16). The importance of improving the skills of the workforce became very apparent in 1988/89 when the UK economy faced severe shortages of skilled labour when the overall unemployment rate was still around 6% (very high compared to what it had been in the first three postwar decades).

The Employment Training (ET) programme, introduced in 1988, was seen as a method of relieving skill shortages and reducing unemployment simultaneously. The aim of ET was 'to train the workers without jobs for the

TABLE 5.17

Outcomes of Two Training Programmes: Employment Training (ET) and Youth Training (YT) in Great Britain, 1990–1

Programme	% proceeding to a job	% proceeding to further training	% gaining qualifications
Employment Training (ET)	36	–	28
Youth Training	57	16	38

Source: *Labour Market Quarterly Report*, Department of Employment, Sheffield, February 1992.

jobs without workers'. Training places were made available for around 300,000 and were reserved for those who had been unemployed for over six months. One of the criticisms levelled against ET is that the training period of six months is far too short. It is also argued that the training programme should include a much larger element of direct work experience.

It is not therefore surprising that the ET programme has faced major problems. Firstly, many trainees have been unable to find a suitable job (to match their newly-acquired skills) after completing their training. In 1990/91, for example, only about one in three persons who participated in the ET programme proceeded to a job (see Table 5.17). Secondly, the scheme has had a very high drop-out rate. According to Layard and Philpott (1991), only 43% of those who join the ET programme actually complete it. The success of the ET programme depends very heavily upon the growth of the national economy. Training workers for non-existent jobs will help to reduce unemployment only in so far as it takes the unemployed out of the unemployment stock during the period of training. A steady and sustained growth of the national economy is the best guarantee of jobs for the unemployed. Thirdly, less than one in three of those leaving the ET programme gained a qualification.

The national training programme in the UK is now run by a system of Training and Enterprise Councils (TECs), which are based upon areas with a working population of around 250,000 and each TEC has a budget of about £20 million per year. In addition to providing training schemes for the unemployed and for school leavers, the 82 TECs in England and Wales (and the 22 Local Enterprise Councils in Scotland) will administer various business enterprise schemes such as the Enterprise Allowance, the Small Firms Service and the Business Growth Training Scheme. The TECs are expected to supplement the money they receive from the government by selling their services to local employers who require training schemes for their workers. They have faced a tough task, however, in the early 1990s since firms have generally been unwilling to take on trainees due to the recession.

4.3 Youth Training

Youth Training (YT) is by far the largest of the employment and training programmes. This is because a place on YT is guaranteed for all those leaving school at sixteen and is now the norm for those not proceeding to further education. The two-year training programme is widely supported by employers because of the large element of government subsidy which it provides.

How successful is the YT programme in getting youths into jobs and in improving the skills of those who participate in the scheme? During 1990–1, nearly 75% of youths proceeded to a job or to further training on completion of their YT scheme and just under 40% gained a qualification. Questions therefore need to be asked about why over 25% of youths completing YT do not proceed to a job or to further training, and why over 60% fail to gain a qualification. These outcomes indicate that much still needs to be done to the YT programme to make it more effective in raising the skill level of the workforce.

4.4   Employment Action

The sudden onset of an unexpectedly severe recession in 1990 led to one of the most severe increases in unemployment since the early 1930s. Policy-makers responded by introducing a new temporary work programme – Employment Action. The aim of this programme is not to train workers directly but to provide work experience by placing workers in full-time jobs for six months. As with the Employment Training programme, anyone on the Employment Action scheme receives unemployment benefit plus £10 per week. Critics of Employment Action argue that it is just another 'cheap labour scheme' – the main criticism levelled against the Community Pro-gramme during 1983–8 – and will provide only temporary relief for the unemployed. Moreover, only 60,000 places per year are to be made avail-able, a small fraction of the total number unemployed.

4.5   Enterprise Allowance

The Enterprise Allowance is intended to induce unemployed people to create their own business. It was motivated by the enterprise culture of the Thatcher era and was intended to contribute to the growth of small firms which were regarded as crucial to the UK's future prosperity. Anyone unemployed for over two months who has an initial capital of £1000 can obtain a grant of £40 a week for one year if they become self-employed. This scheme, introduced in 1982, contributed considerably to the rapid expan-sion of self-employment in the UK during the 1980s. Although the En-terprise Allowance has attracted up to 80,000 unemployed people onto the scheme every year, it has been estimated that half of these would have become self-employed even if the scheme had not been available (Layard and Philpott, 1991). The effect of the Enterprise Allowance on unemploy-ment is therefore likely to have been relatively small. Whether it has helped to create a more entrepreneurial culture in the UK has still to be seen.

4.6   Employment Policy: Lessons from Abroad?

Can the UK learn from the employment policies of other countries? Layard and Philpott (1991) argue strongly in favour of Sweden's employment policy, where unemployment has been extremely low compared to other industrialized countries.

The principle underlying Sweden's employment policy is that everyone has the right to work. The policy focuses on making the unemployed employable and this is achieved through a three-pronged strategy:

– training
– efficient job placement services
– work experience schemes.

A further important factor in Sweden's employment policy is that no one can receive unemployment benefit for more than fourteen months. The up-side of this maximum duration of benefits is that all persons are guaranteed a job (often in the public sector) if they have been unemployed for fourteen months.

What could be done to the UK's employment policy to make it as effective as the Swedish policy in keeping unemployment down? One way forward would be to place greater emphasis on improving the quality of training. Training courses should lead to a recognized qualification and should include direct work experience, organized through the Training and Enterprise Councils (TECs) which would receive the necessary funding for an expanded programme from the government. Employers in each TEC area would have a major role in determining the training programme and in return they would guarantee employment for a proportion of those completing the programme. The public sector would employ the remainder for, say, six months in order to allow trainees to build up a solid work record. Since the highest unemployment rates are in the most depressed areas, it should not be too difficult to create socially worthwhile jobs in the public sector.

This policy would cost money. But it has been estimated that the benefits to the economy would far exceed the costs over the medium term. It should not be forgotten that reducing unemployment actually saves the government money since expenditure on unemployment and related benefits will fall when unemployment falls. In addition, the government's revenue will increase since an increase in employment will raise income tax revenue, national insurance contributions and value added tax as national spending increases.

5   INCOME AND EARNINGS

In this section the distributions of income and earnings are discussed. Various explanations of the distribution of income between households and the pattern of earnings between workers are examined. This leads to a consideration of the factors which influence earnings. These are seen to

TABLE 5.18

Composition of UK Personal Incomes, 1990

Source	%
Pay	59
Income from self-employment	10
Rents, dividends and interest	9
Private pensions, annuities, etc	9
Social security benefits	11
Other current transfers	2

Source: Social Trends 22, 1992, table 5.2

include occupation, industry, gender, ethnic origin and family background. Finally the structure of the social security system is discussed.

5.1 Distribution of Income

Table 5.18 shows the composition of UK personal incomes in 1990. Pay makes up around three-fifths of total personal income. This proportion varies inversely with unemployment. If the unemployment rate rises over time, then the contribution of pay to total personal income tends to fall; meanwhile the contribution of social security benefit rises.

The distribution of household incomes in 1988 is shown in Table 5.19. The spread of original income is very wide indeed – many of the bottom fifth have zero income and rely on benefits. A combination of a progressive income tax system and a programme of social security benefits ensures that the final income distribution is much narrower. Nevertheless the average net income of households in the top fifth of the distribution is well over four times that of households in the bottom fifth.

In choosing the appropriate spread of the final distribution by making decisions on tax and benefit policy, the government faces a tricky balancing act. Too narrow a spread reduces the incentive for workers to supply their labour, especially in difficult or dangerous occupations; it would therefore impair the efficiency of the economy. The other side of the coin is that too

TABLE 5.19

Distribution and Redistribution of Household Income, 1988

	Original income		Final income	
	Average per household (£s)	*% of total*	*Average per household (£s)*	*% of total*
Bottom fifth	1 210	2	4 880	9
Next fifth	4 440	7	6 570	12
Middle fifth	10 750	17	9 700	18
Next fifth	16 260	26	12 360	23
Top fifth	29 170	47	20 700	38
All households	12 360	100	10 830	100

Source: Social Trends 22, 1992, Table 5.16.

wide a spread of the final income distribution might be unacceptable because of the inequity this would imply. A suitable balance between efficiency and fairness must therefore be struck; what is deemed suitable here implies a value judgement, and this is an issue which in large measure defines the difference between political parties of the right and left.

Comparison of the 1988 data on income distribution with corresponding data for 1986 suggests that the distribution narrowed somewhat between these two years. The ratio of average final incomes of households in the top fifth to those in the middle fifth fell from 246% to 213%. Meanwhile, the share of the top 40% of households in original income has fallen from 78% to 73%, while that of the bottom 40% has risen from 6 to 9%. This narrowing of the income distribution is in marked contrast to the widening which was observed in the early part of the last decade; that widening was itself a reversal of an earlier trend towards more equal incomes.

Many of the households in the top quintiles receive part of their income in the form of a return on their stock of wealth. The return from investments in housing or shares is an example of this. In 1989, the most wealthy 10% of the population owned 53% of marketable wealth. Total marketable wealth was estimated to be £1578 billion at this time, about three times the value of the UK's Gross Domestic Product.

5.2   Distribution of Earnings

Since it is impossible to earn a negative amount, and since there is virtually no upper limit on how high incomes can rise, it should not be surprising to find that the distribution of earnings is highly skewed. Moreover, the provision of a system of welfare payments to those in need guarantees (in all but the most extreme cases) a strictly positive lower limit to income. As a consequence, there exists a bunching of workers who earn amounts just above the benefit level. While many workers earn more than this, few earn less.

The distribution of earnings in April 1991 is shown in Table 5.20. The distribution is not symmetric; most workers receive earnings which are below the average, while a few receive very high earnings indeed (thus pulling the average up). This skew in the earnings distribution is highlighted by the fact that 10% of the male workforce earn less than three-fifths of median earnings. Meanwhile the top 10% of earners receive more than one-and-three-quarter times the median earnings. So it appears that those on high earnings enjoy a position which is further away from the median than do those on low earnings. Table 5.20 also shows the distribution of earnings in 1980 and 1987. The widening of the earnings distribution over this whole time period is very marked; there has been a steady drop in all figures below the median over time while a steady rise in the figures above the median can be observed. It is tempting to conclude that the rich have been getting richer while the poor have been getting (relatively) poorer since

TABLE 5.20
Distribution of Earnings

	Median earnings per week (£s)	Earnings as a % of median			
		lowest decile	lower quartile	upper quartile	highest decile
1980					
Men	113	66	81	127	162
Women	72	69	82	126	163
1987					
Men	198	60	76	133	177
Women	133	64	78	134	171
1991					
Men	278	58	75	136	183
Women	196	62	77	139	181

Source: New Earnings Survey.
Note: Exactly 10%, 25%, 50%, 75% and 90% of workers respectively earn less than the lowest decile, lower quartile, median, upper quartile and highest decile.

1980. However these are highly aggregated data, and without more detailed information it is impossible to ascertain whether the individuals receiving below median earnings in 1980 are the same people as those earning below median earnings in 1991.

One reason underlying the skew of the distribution of earnings has already been mentioned – the existence of a lower bound, but no upper bound, on earnings. Several other reasons have been advanced to explain this skew, though, and we now turn to a consideration of these.

The first explanation concerns the productivity enhancing effects of training. Unless training and education are undertaken *purely* for enjoyment, investment by workers in their own human capital raises their productivity. In a market which has at least some of the hallmarks of competition, general training and education must therefore lead to increased earnings. Now suppose, as seems to be the case, that workers with more innate ability invest more heavily than others in training and education (perhaps because they alone pass entrance qualifications). In this instance, earnings at the top end of the ability distribution will be boosted more by education and training than those at the bottom end. Even though the distribution of innate abilities might be unskewed, the distribution of productivity still has a positive skew.

Second, a division of the labour market into two sectors – union and non-union – might lead to a positive skew in the earnings distribution. If unions push up the wage in the union sector, employment in that sector will be reduced and workers will be displaced into the non-union sector where wages are pushed down. This leaves a relatively large number of workers in low-wage non-union jobs, while a smaller group occupy comparatively well-paid jobs in the union sector.

Third, it is important to note that earnings and productivity are determined by a whole host of factors, some of which may themselves have skewed distributions. This being so, it is sensible to proceed by investigating the determinants of earnings. If relatively few workers are employed where – other things being equal – the forces of demand and supply generate high wages, then the positive skew of the earnings distribution is easily explained.

5.3   The Determinants of Wage Structure: Occupation, Industry and Region

(1) Wage Structure by Occupation: Suppose all workers are alike and compete in a single labour market which operates perfectly. In such a world, workers engaging in unpleasant tasks would have to be compensated to the extent that they would be indifferent between their present job and more enjoyable but less well-paid jobs. The rate of return to all occupations would be equal. This idea, introduced into economics by Adam Smith, is known as the principle of compensating wage differentials.

Compensating wage differentials are to a large extent observed in the world in which we live. Workers can expect wage bonuses in return for working unsocial hours. Workers employed in a dangerous environment can expect to earn higher wages than they would receive in a safer situation.

Reasons other than compensating wage differentials also help to explain the spread of earnings between occupations. First, consider the exceptionally high wages earned by some sports players, actors, musicians, and other entertainers. In general these workers supply non-rival goods. Many people can attend a sports event, film, play, or concert at the same time, and so the productivity of such workers is very high even though the individual tickets may be relatively inexpensive. This means that high wages can be paid to artists of this kind – they earn a large amount of economic rent by exploiting the scarcity value of their talent. This rent allows them to earn sums over and above what is needed to induce them to stay in their present occupation; for instance, top soccer stars can earn a wage which more than compensates them for bruises, broken bones, short careers and the pressures of being in the public eye. Where economic rents are earned, the labour market is imperfect because the uneven distribution of talent across individuals impedes freedom of entry into high-wage occupations.

Second, there may be other reasons which prevent competition in the labour market from being perfect. A world where unions bargain with large firms or even with employers' associations is far removed from the standard textbook model of demand and supply. Indeed there is little consensus amongst economists about the manner in which bargaining between unions and firms take place, despite a plethora of theories with such grandiose titles as the monopoly union model, the efficient bargains model, and the right-to-manage model. Often, minimum standards of performance are required of employees, either by the firm (which wishes to guarantee a standard of service) or by the unions (which may seek to limit the supply of labour in an attempt to boost wages). While such activities are not necessarily without merit, they do hinder free competition in the labour market. Likewise,

TABLE 5.21

Average Gross Earnings by Occupation, Full-time Adult Men and Women, April 1991

	Men		Women	
	weekly (£)	*hourly* (p)	*weekly* (£)	*hourly* (p)
Non-manual:				
Managers and administrators	448	1 159	294	745
Professional occupations	428	1 163	336	1 047
Technical occupations etc.	375	931	278	743
Clerical, secretarial	237	587	196	525
Personal, protective service	272	643	173	449
Sales	275	678	170	438
Manual:				
Craft and related occupations	273	604	159	398
Plant, machine operatives	255	549	166	403
Other	219	480	149	376
All non-manual	376	956	237	636
All manual	253	554	159	395
All occupations	319	757	222	589

Source: New Earnings Survey.

contracts made between firms and their workers typically restrict wage movements for the duration of the agreement (usually 12 months in the UK). Welfare benefits set a floor below which earnings cannot normally fall; minimum wage legislation can have a similar effect. In large organizations, wages are often determined by internal politics, and, where the career path of workers within the firm is clearly defined, wages for some jobs may be set without reference to a worker's earnings potential outside the firm.

The spread of average earnings across occupations is very wide. In 1991 the average ranged from £3.45 per hour for kitchen porters to £18.92 for company financial managers. The salary of this latter group reflects the relatively limited supply of talent in this field, and also compensates workers for the long training periods required for this type of work. The highest paid manual workers were face-trained coalworkers, who earned an average of £8.93 per hour. Such workers are compensated for the unpleasant and dangerous environment in which they work. Average earnings defined across broad occupational categories are reported in Table 5.21. As can be seen from the table, non-manual workers tend to be paid more than manual workers. Once again, this reflects the tendency for those employed in non-manual jobs to have forgone earnings in favour of education and training at an earlier stage in their lives.

The imperfections of the labour market receive a lot of attention in the economics literature. This being so it is easy to forget that – considering the difficulty of the task – the labour market usually performs rather well in allocating jobs to a mass of uncoordinated workers. During the late 1980s many employers complained of a shortage of engineers. Between April 1990 and April 1991, average gross weekly earnings of engineers and technologists rose by some 11%; this compares with an average across all occupations of 8%, and an average across all non-manual occupations of just 6%. It would appear, then, that relative earnings do indeed move in the direction required to clear the market within specific occupations.

To some extent it is inevitable that inter-occupational differences in earnings are the result of differences in the characteristics of the workforce rather than differences in the nature of the job itself. To illustrate this, it is instructive to compare nurses and judges. Pay differences may, to some extent, be due to differences in the job specifications, but it should be borne in mind that differences in the average age, experience, years of education and sex composition of employees in each occupation can influence average earnings too. Using 1973 data, Shah (1983) has estimated that even if all these factors were constant across occupations, judges would, on average, still earn a salary some 70% higher than that of nurses. This reflects, in part, a strong job preference on the part of nurses.

More recently, Blanchflower and Oswald (1989) found that between 1983 and 1986 non-manual workers earned 19% more per hour than manual workers. This estimate is based on a detailed statistical analysis in which such factors as personal characteristics, educational background, region of residence, industry within which they work, are all held constant across workers. In other words, even if occupational choice were the only respect in which workers differed, non-manual workers would still be paid 19% more per hour than manual workers. Since the total differential is close to 50%, we may conclude that personal characteristics, education and so on are all very important determinants of earnings.

(2) Wage Structure by Region: As can be seen in Table 5.22, wages vary substantially across the regions of the UK. Wages are highest in the South East and lowest in the South West. The relatively low wages observed in the latter region are due in large measure to its industrial structure. It is rather surprising to observe that the North and North West are – besides the South East – the highest wage regions; these were, in mid-1991, the two regions with the highest rates of unemployment. Where wages are high labour demand is relatively low; but the sources of friction in the labour market which prevent the real wage from falling rapidly in these high unemployment regions are difficult to identify.

Much of the inter-regional variation in wages discussed above is likely to be due to differences in the industry mix or occupation mix of regions. For example, the relatively high-wage financial sector is strongly represented in the South East. In 1991, 17.3% of all employees in this region were employed in financial services compared with just 12.0% for Great Britain as a whole.

Blanchflower and Oswald find that, even correcting for industry mix and for other factors, hourly wages outside the South East were, for 23-year-old workers in 1981, typically between 4 and 8% lower than in the South East. In Greater London, wages were, on average, 11% higher than in the South

TABLE 5.22
Earnings by Region in Great Britain, Full-Time Manual Men, April 1991

	Pence per hour	Relative to South East
South East	557.9	100
East Anglia	536.8	96
South West	522.7	94
West Midlands	542.7	97
East Midlands	536.2	96
Yorkshire & Humberside	535.8	96
North West	550.1	99
North	551.2	99
Wales	532.4	95
Scotland	532.8	96

Source: New Earnings Survey.

East as a whole, other things being equal. Higher property prices and the considerable costs of travelling long distances to work go a long way towards explaining these disparities.

Although average wages in the South East are higher than in any of the remaining nine regions of Britain, only two regions – East Anglia and the South West – can be said to have a particularly adverse industry mix. Even in these cases the impact on the average wage is very small (about 1%).

5.4   The Determinants of Wage Structure: Worker Characteristics

Many personal characteristics have a role to play in determining an individual's earnings. These include gender, race, family composition, employment history, union membership, health and education. In this section we deal with each in turn.

Gender: In mid-1991, 48% of all employees in employment in Great Britain were females. (If part-time women are excluded from the calculation, the proportion of female employees in employment falls to 34%.) Despite their obvious importance in the labour force, it remains the case that women are paid, on average, substantially less than men. In 1991, women were 2.75 times more likely than men to be earning less than £3.40 per hour. This is largely, but by no means solely, the consequence of differences in the type of work that men and women do. A glance at Table 5.21 shows that even within each broad occupational class, male earnings are well above those of females.

A number of reasons explain gender differences in earnings. First, women tend to be less strongly committed to membership of the labour force than do men. Counter-examples abound, of course, but it remains the case that a large proportion of women drop out of the labour force to have children and then return to work some years later. In the case of graduates, for example, some 28% of women leave the labour force for family reasons within five years of joining it (Dolton, 1992). Now work experience is a characteristic which carries a high reward in the labour market. Experience keeps individuals up to date with new techniques and maintains familiarity with the ways of the workplace. On average, earnings of both men and women rise by about 3% per year (in real terms) when they are in work. Earnings potential drops by some 3%, however, for every year a woman is out of the labour force. This means that older women who have returned to work after ten years raising a family can expect to earn just under half as much as a man whose career has not been interrupted in this way.

Second, labour turnover amongst women tends to be higher than is the case amongst men. This is partly due to the weak labour force attachment of women referred to earlier. In December 1989 the engagement rate for males in manufacturing was 1.4% per month and the leaving rate was 1.6%; the corresponding figures for women were 2.0% and 2.9% respectively. This relatively high turnover carries penalties for firms employing many women. Turnover costs firms money; persistently heavy recruitment caused by high turnover rates means that firms must employ a relatively large number of personnel management staff. The costs of this may be passed on to women in the form of lower wages. Furthermore, where labour turnover is high there is little incentive for the firm to use training programmes to invest in the human capital of its workers. Consequently, women tend to be trained to a lesser extent than their male counterparts.

A third reason why female earnings are relatively low is because of geographically isolated labour markets. Employers in remote areas enjoy a degree of monopsony power over female workers where the latter cannot move to find work because their husbands are tied to a job.

Since 1976, the Equal Pay Act (passed in 1970) has required that women performing similar tasks to men, or performing work of equal value to that of men, must be treated equally to men. The Sex Discrimination Act of 1975 requires that men and women should be guaranteed equality of opportunity. As can be seen from Table 5.23, these Acts had an immediate impact on the minimum rates of pay set in collective agreements (column 1). The effect of the Acts on hourly earnings is not so easy to assess, however. Certainly female earnings have risen relative to male earnings since the implementation of these two Acts. While full-time women earned, on average, 64% of male hourly earnings in 1970, this proportion rose to 73% in 1976 and has remained near that level ever since. But it is not possible unambiguously to attribute this improvement to the introduction of legislation without first considering some alternative explanations.

First, demand factors might explain the change. The demand for female workers might have risen during the mid-1970s, thereby pushing wages up. However, a short-run cyclical upswing is not sufficient to explain the figures of Table 5.23 because the hourly earnings ratio remained at historically high levels despite the recessions of the early 1980s and early 1990s. (The persistence of relatively high female earnings into the late 1980s also casts doubt on the theory that the rise in the female : male earnings ratio was due to the

TABLE 5.23

Relative Female/Male Pay and Employment (%)

	Full-time workers			Part-time females, full-time males	
	Hourly wage rates (W_f/W_m)	Hourly earnings (W_f/W_m)	Employ-ment (F/M)	Hourly earnings (W_f/W_m)	Employment (F/M)
1970	83	64	40	—	—
1973	87	64	41	51	10
1976	100	73	42	59	11
1980	100	71	46	58	12
1984	100	73	47	58	12
1987	100	73	49	56	12
1991	100	78	55	58	13

Sources: Tzannatos and Zabalza (1984) and authors' own calculations from the *New Earnings Survey*.
Note: W_f is wage or earnings of females; W_m is wage or earnings of males; F and M are, respectively, employment of females and males. Data for part-time workers are expressed as full-time equivalents. The hourly wage data refer to the weighted average of minimum rates of manual workers laid down in collective agreements.

partially flat-rate incomes policies of the 1970s. Were this the case, the removal of these policies in 1978 should have allowed the relativities to settle back to their equilibrium values over the subsequent ten years.) It is possible that the increase in the demand for female labour was not purely cyclical, and that women's pay rose in response to changes in the industrial composition of demand; hence women might have moved from low-wage to high-wage sectors of industry. Nevertheless, in all sectors of the economy bar one (Public Administration) the relative pay of females rose over the decade 1970–80.

The second alternative explanation is that female labour supply might have declined over the 1970s, thereby forcing female wages up. As can be seen from column 3 of Table 5.23, however, the ratio of female employment to male employment has been rising steadily over the last quarter century. On the basis of labour supply movements, the differential in pay between men and women should have increased, whereas in fact – as we have seen – it fell suddenly and substantially during the 1970s.

In the absence of any convincing alternative, it seems fair to conclude that the Equal Pay Act has contributed to the narrowing of gender differentials in rates of pay. It is clear from Table 5.21 that much more remains to be achieved. Female hourly earnings are still well below those of men. This remains the case even if education, experience, hours of work, industry mix and other variables are held constant across the sexes. Blanchflower and Oswald (1989) estimate that 23-year-old women in 1981 earned 23% less per hour than their male counterparts, other things being equal. Dolton *et al.* (1990) estimate the male:female earnings differential for university graduates six years after completing their courses, and find that the pay gap varies from subject to subject; for most subjects the differential is 10-15%, but for engineering it is 25%. These estimates are based on all things other than gender being equal. It seems then that women remain unable to climb as high up the career ladder as men. Since education and experience have been controlled for, this indicates that some degree of discrimination remains.

Race: Non-whites, like women, suffer from discrimination in the labour market. Blackaby (1986) has estimated that in 1975, other things being equal, non-white males earned approximately 9% less than white males. This estimate holds constant such important determinants of earnings as education, experience, family composition and unemployment history. To the extent that racial discrimination adversely affects employment opportunities among the ethnic minorities, this figure will be an underestimate.

A substantial part of the racial wage gap is due to the fact that non-whites find it difficult to enter occupations which have high wages. The 1982 Policy Studies Institute (PSI) Survey reveals that there is a concentration of ethnic minorities in manual jobs, particularly in semi-skilled and unskilled occupations. Sixteen per cent of the employed white work force, for example, fell into the semi-skilled and unskilled categories compared to 40% for non-whites (Brown, 1984). This is partly the consequence of ethnic differences in qualifications. Workers of West Indian origin, for example, are less highly qualified in terms of both academic and vocational training than are their white counterparts. Asian workers are a less homogeneous group, and they tend to fall into one of two extremes. On the one hand there are the highly educated, and on the other hand there is a large group which has received very little formal education. While on average Asians have better academic qualifications than either West Indians or whites, they have benefited relatively little from vocational training. Johnes and Taylor (1989), however, show that non-white graduates earned as much as white graduates, on average, after six years in the job market.

In all regions, white males earn more than non-white males, and the gap is especially pronounced in the North West and the East Midlands. Overall, the gap in England and Wales amounts to 17%. Comparing this with Blackaby's 9% estimate, it can be deduced that about one-half of the total gap between the earnings of whites and non-whites in Britain is due to such factors as education and occupation; this has obvious implications for education policy. The other half is due to pure discrimination.

Education: It is not at all surprising to find that education has a positive influence on an individual's earnings capability. After all, if this were not the case, it would be unlikely that people would sacrifice years of earnings in order to acquire post-compulsory education.

After controlling for other determinants of earnings, Blanchflower and Oswald (1989) compare the earnings of 23-year-old workers in 1981 who have no educational qualifications with those who do. As might be expected, it is broadly the case that more education leads to higher earnings. Those workers who have between one and four O-level passes (good GCSE grades) earn an average premium of around 5% per hour. Those with five or more O-level passes earn a premium of 9% per hour. A worker with two or more A-levels earns, on average, 14% more per hour than one with no qualifications, and the premium rises to 18% for those with degrees.

These figures may not seem very high at first sight, but it should be remembered that they are based on the assumption that all other determinants of earnings are held constant across all workers. To the extent that highly educated workers tend to enter relatively well-paid occupations, tend to have good promotion prospects and stable employment histories, the above estimates understate the true differential between the earnings of highly educated workers and others. The usefulness of the estimates lies in the fact that they indicate the extent to which an improvement in education alone (without changes in occupation, etc.) can raise earnings.

Family Composition: Married male workers tend to earn more than single males, other things being equal. One reason for this is that the responsibility and expense of a family imposes the discipline of a stable work habit. This has two effects: first, a worker might work harder in order to earn more, and second, men (in particular) will become more attractive to firms upon marriage and will therefore be in a position to move to higher-paying jobs. The most rigorous recent work on this topic has been that of Dolton *et al.* (1990) who analyse the 1986 salaries of workers who graduated from universities, polytechnics and colleges of higher education in 1980. They find that marriage raises male earnings by around 3% on average, other things being equal. The impact on male earnings of child rearing is negligible. For women the results are somewhat different. For women who continue to work after marriage, earnings typically fall by around 6%. If they have children, their earnings may fall on average by a further 7% per child.

Other Determinants of Earnings: Amongst 23-year-olds in 1981, the following variables were amongst the most important determinants of earnings, other things being equal. First, union membership raised the hourly wage by 7%. (The union mark-up on wages will be discussed at greater length in section 4.)

Second, those who work unsocial hours are paid a premium of 11% on average. It is clear that leisure is worth more to people at certain times of the day than at others. If workers must be on duty during the evening or at night, they cannot enjoy various leisure activities, such as a night out at the theatre, movies or pub; moreover the amount of time they can spend with their families is reduced. Such a reduction in the utility of their leisure must be compensated for in the form of higher wages.

Third, if a worker has a history of unemployment experience, his or her wage is, on average, likely to be 5% lower than it would otherwise be. As has already been mentioned, experience of work raises earnings potential whereas periods out of work lead to a depreciation of human capital and hence productivity. A history of unemployment also – rightly or wrongly – sends signals to an employer about a worker's motivation, aptitude and tenacity.

Fourth, workers who are employed in jobs which are part of a well-established career structure earn a premium of 8%. Such workers might be regarded as members of the 'primary' workforce. Firms which fill vacancies in senior positions exclusively from within the ranks of their own workforce will be keen to hold on to their best workers. Consequently, wages tend to be higher where a promotion ladder exists.

Fifth, registered disabled people earn, on average, 28% less than other workers. This may in part be the result of inevitable constraints on the type of tasks which they perform and the efficiency with which they can carry out their duties at work. Although the earnings of disabled people are lower than the earnings of people in good health, the difference in their incomes need not be so great since many of these workers will qualify for disability benefit.

Finally, an increase in local unemployment rates puts downward pressure on average earnings, other things being equal. In areas of high unemployment, the supply of labour is plentiful in relation to demand, and so firms are able to bid down the wage. There is, however, considerable evidence to suggest that this effect tapers off at levels of unemployment above 10%.

5.5   Changes in Earnings Over Time

Figure 5.16 shows the rate of growth of hourly earnings of male manual workers. In 1980, a short burst of inflation occurred which was largely stimulated by an oil price rise, an increase in the rate of value-added tax, and

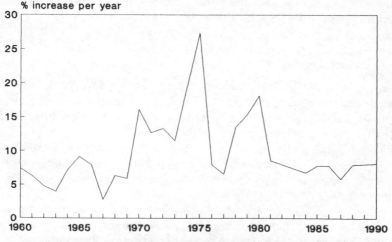

Figure 5.16   Earnings Growth of Male Manual Workers 1960–90
(*Sources:* Layard and Nickell (1986); *EG*)

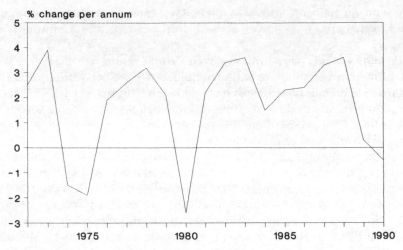

Figure 5.17   Annual Rate of Growth of Output per Person Employed, 1972–90
(Source: MDS)

the award of large public sector pay increases. Since then the rate of growth of earnings has slowed down considerably and has, over the last four years, stabilized at around 8% per year.

Labour productivity (output per person employed) rose rapidly in the early and mid-1980s, but the rate of improvement slowed subsequently, until in the early 1990s productivity was falling. This is shown in Figure 5.17. The rise in productivity during the early 1980s was caused partly by a shake-out of labour during the recession and partly by changes in industrial structure. The productivity improvement during these years is particularly noteworthy in view of the fact that it occurred during a period of low investment: the average annual rate of growth of capital stock in manufacturing was only 0.75% over the period 1980–5. This compares with 2.3% during 1973–9 and 1.1% during 1986–90.

5.6   Social Security

Having considered the determinants of earnings, we now consider another important component of total personal income, namely social security. The system of social security in the UK underwent radical reform in 1988. This resulted in a much simpler system which has eradicated numerous problems which had plagued its predecessor. Inevitably, however, virtually any change in the rules of entitlement to social security produces losers as well as gainers. In consequence, the 1988 reforms generated a considerable amount of controversy.

The system of welfare payments comprises numerous types of benefit. These include child benefit, unemployment benefit, statutory sick pay, invalidity benefit, and the flat-rate retirement pension. In addition to these, three main types of benefit exist, all of which are income-related; these constitute the main innovations of the 1988 reforms. Each of these three will now be discussed in turn.

(1) Housing Benefit: Housing Benefit entitles families on low incomes and with little wealth to claim up to 100 per cent of their rent. For social security purposes, a 'family' corresponds to the unit which is liable for income tax. No assistance is provided with mortgage interest payments for those who are buying their own homes. Such individuals may, however, be able to claim financial help under the Income Support scheme. Housing Benefit cannot be paid if the applicant's stock of capital (savings) exceeds £16,000. Initially, housing benefit was also available to provide claimants with help in meeting local tax burdens – up to 80% of a household's rates bill could be claimed in this way. When the rates were replaced by the community charge (poll tax), a new community charge benefit was set up to fulfil this role.

The Housing Benefit Scheme uses a taper system to ensure that as net incomes rises entitlement to support declines gradually. Up to a critical level of net income (which depends on family composition) the applicant is entitled to maximum support levels as indicated above. If net income exceeds the critical level, then assistance with rent is reduced by 65% of the difference. Thus a claimant with an annual net income of £3,500 receives £1.50 per week less in Housing Benefit than does a similar claimant with a net income below the critical level of £3,380 per annum.

(2) Family Credit: Family Credit is available to low-income families in full-time work who have children. Claimants receive an adult credit plus an additional credit for each child. The size of these credits depends on the age of the children. No Family Credit is payable if the claimant's stock of capital exceeds £8,000. As is the case with Housing Benefit, a taper system operates to ensure that Family Credit entitlements are reduced gradually as net income rises. The critical level of net income in this case is £3,463 per annum for the tax year 1992–3. As net income rises above this level, Family Credit payments are reduced by 70 per cent of the excess.

(3) Income Support: Income Support replaced Supplementary Benefit in 1988. This is available to low-income families not in full-time work. For the purposes of social security, full-time work implies a working week of 24 hours or more. Income Support is not payable if savings exceed £8,000. Claimants receive a personal allowance which rises with the number of dependants. Families with children, single parents, the old, sick and disabled are entitled to premiums in addition to their personal allowances. Claimants who are unemployed may also be entitled to unemployment benefit, which in the tax year 1992–3 amounts to £43.10 per week.

All the benefits discussed above together make up an intricate patchwork of welfare payments. Because of inflation, rates of benefit vary from one tax year to the next. Changes are announced towards the end of October each year (see, for example, Department of Social Security Press Release 91/147, 21 October 1991). Moreover, minor modifications are made to the system on a regular basis in response to the rapidly changing needs of society; a recent example is the addition of the community charge benefit. The cumulative effect of such tinkering is to increase the complexity of the system. Past experience suggests that as the system becomes more complicated, more anomalies occur. One such anomaly is the poverty trap. This arises where a worker loses more in tax paid and benefits forgone than he gains in pay by working an extra hour per week. The 1988 reforms were designed to remove poverty traps from the benefits system. They were largely successful in doing so. But marginal tax rates (taking account of benefits forgone) paid by the poor are still close to 100%.

Until 1988, one-off payments could be made to claimants facing exceptional needs. Major household items such as furniture and general maintenance could be financed in this way. This provided a necessary safety net, but also represented a disincentive to work. In addition, the scheme was vulnerable to abuse, and the costs of administration were high. For these reasons the system of one-off payments has been replaced by the Social Fund. The Social Fund provides a system of loans to claimants with a stock of savings of under £500. These loans are awarded at the discretion of local officers and are normally repayable at a rate of 15% of weekly benefit over a maximum period of 18 months. It is intended that the Social Fund should eventually be self-financing.

The amounts spent on various social security schemes and the number of recipients are shown in Table 5.24. As can be seen, these benefits comprise a major component of total government expenditure. The total budget of the Department of Social Security in 1991–2, at £61.3 billion, represents 28% of all government expenditure, and is more than twice as high as that of the other large departments, such as Health or Defence. It is inevitable that expenditure on social security rises during a recession, as unemployment and shorter working hours increase the number of claimants and reduce the gap between incomes and the tapering triggers. Thus the social security system potentially acts as a useful automatic stabilizer – as the economy moves into a slump, government spending automatically increases; this added injection into the circular flow of income puts a brake on the downward spiral of economic activity.

6 TRADE UNIONS, INDUSTRIAL RELATIONS AND EUROPEAN SOCIAL POLICY

6.1 Trade Unions

Trade union membership in the UK has been declining since 1979, when nearly 13.29 million workers were members. At the end of 1989 there were 10.04 million union members, and this represents a fall of 24% in ten years.

TABLE 5.24

Major Social Security Benefits; Public Expenditure and Estimated Number of Recipients, 1989–90

	Expenditure (£ million)	Recipients (thousands)
Housing Benefit	3 804	3 905
Family Credit	425	305
Income Support	7 675	4 155
Retirement Pensions	20 697	9 795
Child Benefit	4 537	12 000
Unemployment Benefit	733	375
Invalidity Benefit	3 837	1 190
Statutory Sick Pay	949	360
Social Fund	130	1 525

Source: Social Trends 22, 1992, tables 5.8 and 5.9.

This is the most dramatic fall in union membership since the 1930s and warrants more detailed investigation.

The first possible explanation for the decline of union membership is that workers leave unions on becoming unemployed. Unemployment rose by 462,000 over the years in question, and so it is hardly surprising that fewer workers should now be members of unions. Unemployment can only be a partial answer, though, since the fall in membership of 3.17 million has been greater than the rise in unemployment. It is possible that unemployment has a further *indirect* effect on union membership, since unions may become unattractive to workers during times of recession if it is believed that they serve to price workers out of jobs.

A second reason for the fall in the number of union members is that there has been a change in the structure of industry. Declining industries tend to be more heavily unionized than growing industries, so overall union density falls over time. Tables 5.25 and 5.26 show union density (that is, union membership as a percentage of the workforce) by industry and by region. While the inter-regional variation in actual union density is substantial, a large amount of the difference between regions can be explained by differences in industrial structure; those regions with a heavy concentration of older and highly unionized industries predictably enough have high union densities. The region-specific union densities which would obtain if all regions had the same industry mix as the country as a whole are reported in the second column of Table 5.26. It is easily seen that the union densities thus adjusted for industry mix are much less divergent than the unadjusted figures. Nevertheless, the northern regions still have the highest union densities even after allowing for inter-regional differences in industrial structure.

A third possibility is that a change in the sex mix of employees in employment explains the collapse of union membership. If women are less likely to join unions than are men, then the change in membership may be due to the increase in the female participation rate. This is not likely to be a major factor, however, since in 1989 women represented 33% of all union

TABLE 5.25

Trade Union Membership by Industry

Industry in which most members are deemed to be employed	Membership (thousand)	Density (%)
Agriculture, forestry, fishing	34	13
Coal, gas, electricity, water	424	76
Chemicals, metals (extraction and manufacture)	371	48
Engineering	1 002	41
Other manufacturing	863	39
Construction	351	30
Distribution, retail trades	640	15
Transport and communication	899	62
Financial services	595	25
Health, education, administration	3 319	52
Total	8 498	39

Sources: Employment Gazette, Labour Force Survey.

members and 35% of full-time employees in employment; the propensity of full-time women to join unions is therefore not much different from that of men.

A further factor which might explain the fall in union membership is political climate. Carruth and Disney (1988) find that, other things being equal, union density is around 2.5 percentage points lower when a Conservative government is in power than at other times.

Finally, it has been suggested that industrial relations legislation introduced in the 1980s contributed substantially to the decline in trade union membership (Freeman and Pelletier, 1990). Several important reforms have been introduced over the last twelve years. Amongst other things, these reforms emphasize the right of the individual union member not to participate in collective action, and in the eyes of many workers this has reduced the influence of the unions in bargaining; if the influence of unions

TABLE 5.26

Union Density by GB Region in 1984, adjusted for Industrial Structure

Region	Actual density (%)	Density adjusted for industrial structure (%)
East Anglia	40	54
Greater London	47	54
Rest of South East	43	58
South West	55	57
East Midlands	61	58
Scotland	63	61
West Midlands	65	60
Yorkshire & Humberside	67	59
Wales	71	58
North West	71	59
North	72	60

Source: Employment Gazette, May 1988.

diminishes, then so does their attractiveness to the potential membership. The legal changes will be discussed in more detail at a later stage.

The fall in union density is continuing – in 1990 density was 38%, and this compares with 39% a year earlier. Despite this, the influence of unions on bargaining remains wide. The proportion of employees in employment whose pay was affected by collective agreements in 1985 was 64%. Amongst manual male workers, only 29% are not covered by some kind of collective agreement. Thus union coverage is much greater than union density.

One aspect of union–firm relations which has received particular attention is the closed shop. A closed shop occurs when union membership becomes a condition of employment. It can take one of two forms. The first is the pre-entry closed shop, which is rather rare, and which requires a worker to be a union member before he or she can be hired. More common is the post-entry closed shop, in which a worker must join the union upon recruitment. While the closed shop is often regarded as anti-libertarian, it should be borne in mind that it usually only comes into being where union density is already high. Firms have often welcomed the more structured format of industrial relations which the closed shop offers. Finally, in the absence of a closed shop, unions are often frustrated by the ability of non-members to enjoy the benefits gained by the sacrifices of union members; this implies that – owing to such 'free riding' – unions suffer from being under-resourced where a closed shop does not exist.

It has been estimated (Millward and Stevens, 1986) that closed shops covered about 3.6 million workers – that is, about one-fifth of all employees – in 1984. Between 1980 and 1984 the proportion of manual workers covered by closed-shop agreements fell from 40% to 30%, and so it would appear that the closed shop is rapidly becoming less common. The legislation of the early 1980s may have precipitated this decline: since 1980 no new closed shops could be introduced without a ballot, and since 1984 existing closed-shop agreements have been subject to ratification by ballot. Individuals with strong personal convictions have, since 1980, been granted legal protection against dismissal for non-union membership in a closed shop.

Throughout most of the present century there has been a steady fall in the number of unions. This continued through the 1980s. At the end of 1989 there were 348 known unions in the UK. This is down from nearly 500 in 1975. Many of these are very small, with less than 100 members. These tiny unions include the Society of Shuttlemakers (around 40 members) and the London Society of Tie Cutters (which had 84 members in 1977). At the other extreme, 23 unions in 1989 had at least 100,000 members. These include the Transport and General Workers' Union (1,270,776 members in 1989) and the Amalgamated Engineering Union (741,647 members). Just over a quarter of all unions are affiliated to the Trades Union Congress (TUC), but since most of the large unions are affiliated, the TUC represents some 88% of all union members.

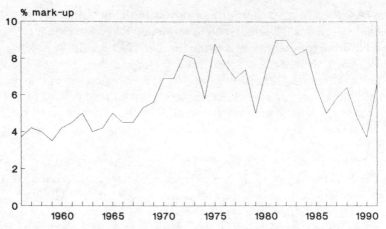

Figure 5.18   Estimated Mark-up of Union over Non-Union Wages, 1956–91
(*Source:* Layard and Nickell (1986) and authors' own estimates using
New Earnings Survey data for 48 industries)

6.2   The Union Mark-up

Much recent research has focused on the magnitude of the union :non-union wage differential. This is the difference which two workers would expect to obtain between their rates of pay if they were identical to one another in every respect except union membership. It is, of course, to be expected that union members will receive greater remuneration than non-members since a major aim of unions is to secure higher wages for their members, and if they failed in this task many members might consider withdrawing their financial support from their union.

Estimates of the union mark-up are provided in Figure 5.18. It is clear that until the early 1980s, the trend in this differential had been upward. The sharp rise in the mark-up between 1979 and 1981 coincided with the sudden increase in unemployment. While this might be interpreted as confirmation of the argument that an increase in trade union power during 1979–81 helped to raise the unemployment rate, it should be noted that a rise in the mark-up could just as easily be a consequence as a cause of the rise in the number of jobless. Union members who were made unemployed around 1980 will have raised the supply of labour in the non-union sector thereby reducing the wages in that sector relative to the union sector ; this in itself will have caused the mark-up to increase.

Since 1982, the mark-up has declined once more. Although the differential has varied somewhat from year to year, it remains well below the high levels which obtained in the early 1980s. This is due partly to cyclical factors, partly to the decline in union membership, and partly to the effects of union legislation.

The mark-up varies across occupations. Blanchflower (1984) finds a mark-up of around 10 per cent for semi-skilled workers in 1980, but his estimate of the differential for skilled workers does not significantly differ from zero. Stewart (1991) also finds a larger differential for semi-skilled than for skilled workers, and disaggregates his results by union status. Hence, for semi-skilled workers, he finds that in the absence of a closed shop the mark-up is 6% on average; in a post-entry closed shop it is 9%; and in a pre-entry closed shop the average differential is 19%. The mark-up also varies considerably across industries. The estimates reproduced in Table 5.27 indicate that it varied from 2% (electrical engineering) to 18% (shipbuilding) in 1975.

It should be noted that the estimates given above understate the true influence of unions. This is because they refer to the difference in wage that an individual could expect if that individual *alone* changed his or her union membership status; the estimates assume that overall union density is given. A more comprehensive picture of union impact may be obtained by comparing the wages of union members whose wages are determined by collective bargaining with those of non-members whose wages are *not* determined by union–firm agreements, simultaneously controlling for variation in other factors which determine earnings. Such an exercise has been conducted by Blackaby *et al.* (1991), who find a differential of 22% between the wages of covered unionists and those of uncovered non-unionists in 1983.

The extent of the union mark-up is likely to be determined by a number of factors. Beenstock and Whitbread (1988) argue that the differential rises if union density and the real value of unemployment benefit increase. Moreover, they find that the mark-up is some five percentage points lower under a Labour government than under a Conservative government. This last observation implies that unions respond more to government calls for wage restraint when Labour is in office. There is, however, no evidence to suggest that incomes policies influence the extent of the mark-up.

Time-series estimates of the union mark-up similar to those reported

TABLE 5.27
Estimates of the Union: Non-Union Wage Differential by Industry, 1975

Industry	Mark up (%)
Shipbuilding and marine engineering	18.2
Paper, printing and publishing	11.4
Other manufacturing industries	10.9
Metal goods not elsewhere specified	10.7
Clothing and footwear	10.1
Chemicals and allied industries	9.6
Vehicles	9.6
Timber and furniture	9.1
Instrument engineering	8.6
Food, drink and tobacco	6.6
Textiles	6.6
Metal manufacture	5.4
Mechanical engineering	4.1
Bricks, pottery, glass, cement	2.4
Electrical engineering	2.0

Source: Stewart (1983).

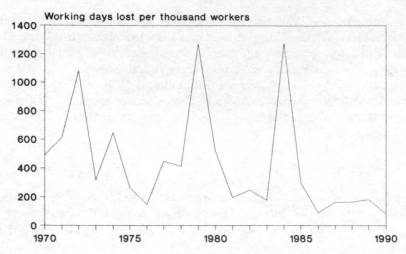

Figure 5.19   Working Days Lost in the UK through Industrial Stoppages, 1970–90
(*Source: EG*)

above have been used by Layard and Nickell (1986) in an attempt to explain the growth in unemployment between the late 1970s and the early 1980s. Although unemployment rose by seven percentage points over this period, only 0.8 percentage points can be attributed to the growth of the union: non-union wage differential.

6.3   Strikes

An important weapon in the armoury of trade unions is the ability to take industrial action. Of the forms which such action can take, strikes generate the most animated debate. Despite the publicity which they attract, strikes are quite rare. A time series of the number of working days lost per thousand workers through strike action in Britain is shown in Figure 5.19. There has, in recent years, been a considerable fall in strike activity. But even in 1979 – the year of the 'winter of discontent' – the average worker lost little more than a single day through industrial stoppage over the whole year.

The evidence therefore shows that strikes are uncommon events. Yet it is somewhat curious that they happen at all. During a strike, the strikers suffer a loss of earnings and the firm suffers output losses. It seems that everyone concerned is made worse off by the action, and, that being so, it seems a very peculiar kind of action to take. However, there are some possible explanations, and it is to these that we now turn.

First, we live in a world of imperfect information. Firms and unions are typically unaware of each other's true preferences. In particular, they do not usually know how hard a bargain they can drive. Inevitably in such situations the negotiating parties will sometimes push too hard and an impasse occurs. In such a situation a strike can serve to convey information to both parties about the strength of each other's resolution. Put simply, the strike has a positive economic value – it removes uncertainty; the stoppage is the price that must be paid for the failure of the negotiators to remove the uncertainty by other means.

Second, there may be externalities associated with strike action which mean that (although their actions cause an immediate loss of utility) the parties to the dispute may ultimately benefit. In this respect, strikes are like wars or martyrdom. In all cases suffering is volunteered, presumably because the parties concerned believe that a wider good will come of their suffering. For instance, a martyr might believe that his or her death will lead others to follow a cause. Likewise, by striking, a union striking at one firm might demonstrate to employers throughout the economy the current level of militancy. This could strengthen the hand of other unions in negotiations. Of course, the striking union would require a *quid pro quo* from these third parties. This might take the form of tacit agreements that the burden of striking is spread across unions over time.

Third, a firm which is making losses in the short term may wish to engineer a strike in order to reduce these losses. It may do this by making offers which the union is sure to reject. The firm can then share its savings from the strike with the union, in the form of an improved wage deal, once the strike is over.

The development of empirical work on strikes has been largely independent of theoretical research. Nevertheless, much is now known about the environment within which strikes are relatively likely to take place. Useful recent studies of strike incidence include Blanchflower and Cubbin (1986) and Ingram *et al.* (1991). The first significant determinant of strike activity is the size of the bargaining group. Strike incidence rises as the bargaining group increases in size. This suggests that strikes are more likely to occur in larger establishments than in smaller ones. Furthermore, strikes are more likely in multi-establishment firms than in single plant firms.

Second, unionization affects strike proneness in a number of ways. The co-existence of a number of unions at an establishment serves to raise the strike propensity, owing to inter-union competition; this takes the form of demarcation disputes between unions and a desire on the part of each union to convince workers of its own effectiveness. In addition, the presence of a large number of unions complicates negotiations with the employer and makes it difficult to resolve disputes peacefully. Manual bargaining groups are more strike prone than non-manual or mixed groups, and the presence of manual shop stewards also raises the propensity to strike.

Third, the adoption of payments by results schemes raises the probability of a strike occurring. Such schemes lead to uncertainty concerning remuneration levels and this can cause frustration on the part of the workforce.

Fourth, there is a high degree of persistence in industrial action: the probability of a strike occurring this year is higher than elsewhere at an establishment where a dispute occurred last year, other things being equal. This persistence leads to a distinct pattern of strike activity across industries and regions – some are more strike prone than others (see Table 5.28). In particular, timber products, vehicles and engineering are often affected by

TABLE 5.28

Percentage of Bargaining Groups Experiencing Strikes, by Region and by Industry, 1979–89

Region or Industry	% of groups experiencing strike	Mean strike duration days
South East	3.1	9.7
South West	1.3	4.5
East Anglia	1.6	33.0
East Midlands	1.8	15.6
West Midlands	2.2	7.4
North West	3.7	11.6
Yorkshire & Humberside	2.2	15.1
North	1.5	16.4
Wales	1.7	11.6
Scotland	3.4	32.3
Food, drink, tobacco	2.4	11.2
Coal, petroleum products	2.0	52.0
Chemicals	1.5	15.1
Metal manufacture	1.9	36.6
Mechanical engineering	3.0	11.4
Instrument engineering	3.2	9.4
Electrical engineering	4.5	7.1
Shipbuilding	0.0	0.0
Vehicles	4.5	9.6
Miscellaneous metal goods	2.5	10.6
Textiles	1.2	11.2
Leather goods	1.9	2.0
Clothing and footwear	0.0	0.0
Refractories	1.9	11.6
Timber	3.7	4.4
Paper, printing, publishing	1.7	10.8
Other manufacturing	2.3	11.5

Source: Ingram *et al*. (1991).

strike action, and the North West region of England has suffered from a high incidence of industrial disputes. The high average strike durations recorded here for coal and petroleum products and metal manufacture are heavily influenced by the prolonged strikes in the coal and steel industries during the early and mid-1980s.

Fifth, there is some evidence to suggest an association between strike activity and macroeconomic conditions. In particular, when unemployment is high strike activity is relatively low, other things being equal; at such times, firms' profits are generally squeezed so that there is relatively little surplus over which workers and firms can bargain. Further, strike activity appears to be greater during times of high inflation than in other periods. Expectations of high inflation are built into union wage bids, and this can lead to impasse in negotiations. The negative relationship between strike activity and unemployment, and the positive link between strike propensity and inflation together suggest that strike activity is pro-cyclical.

It is instructive to study the pattern of strike duration. Figure 5.20 shows the manner in which the probability of a strike ending on a given day varies with the length of the strike hitherto. In statistical terminology this is known

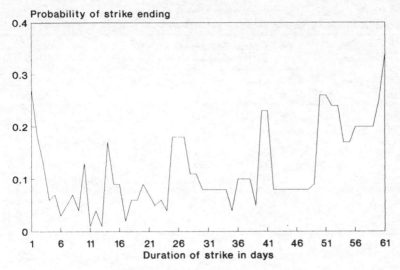

Figure 5.20   The Hazard Rate for Strikes
(*Source:* Ingram *et al.* (1991).)

as the hazard rate for strikes. It is easily seen that the hazard is high for
strikes of very short duration; indeed over a quarter of all strikes are
over after only a day. Once a strike has lasted more than a couple of days,
though, the probability of it ending on any given day is much reduced. The
hazard then slowly rises, but there are some very marked blips in the series.
The timing of these blips is likely to be affected by the periodic meeting of
negotiators; the hazard rate is higher than trend at 10 days, 2 weeks, and
about 4 weeks, 6 weeks and 7 weeks after the commencement of the strike.

It is worth noting at this stage that a strike is by no means the only form of
industrial action which unions can take. The commonest forms of non-strike
action are the go-slow or work to rule and the overtime ban (see Table 5.29).
In general these alternative forms of action are more commonly used than
strikes, but they are still rare. The incidence of industrial action declined
towards the end of the 1980s. This goes against the pro-cyclical pattern
referred to earlier and may be due in part to the effects of industrial relations
legislation. Another possible explanation is that union morale was still,
during the late 1980s, dented after the long and damaging miners' strike of
1984–5.

6.4   Industrial Relations

The nature of British industrial relations has changed markedly over the last
twelve years, largely as a consequence of changes in legislation. The
Employment Acts of 1980, 1982, 1988 and 1990, together with the Trade
Union Act of 1984, have fundamentally altered the balance of power

TABLE 5.29
Industrial Action in Manufacturing Industries, 1979–89

Year	strike	go-slow work to rule	overtime ban	other	any	Mean strike duration (days)
		% of bargaining groups undertaking the following forms of action				
1979–80	4.6	3.4	5.2	1.2	9.3	21.3
1980–81	2.7	2.3	4.7	0.9	7.7	10.8
1981–82	2.7	2.5	4.8	0.4	7.3	10.9
1982–83	2.6	1.9	4.4	0.5	6.8	8.9
1983–84	4.0	3.4	7.3	1.4	10.3	12.9
1984–85	1.5	1.6	3.8	0.1	5.3	12.2
1985–86	2.8	1.6	5.4	0.1	6.7	7.2
1986–87	1.6	1.7	4.3	0.2	5.3	8.9
1987–88	2.3	0.6	2.9	0.2	4.0	8.2
1988–89	0.8	0.8	2.1	0.3	2.4	12.6

Source: Ingram *et al.* (1991).

between employers and trade unions. This being so, it is important to consider the current state of the law as it affects employee relations in the UK.

Pay bargaining in Britain traditionally takes place at national level. National unions negotiate with large employers or (especially in the past) with associations of employers in order to set a wage which historically has been allowed to vary little from area to area. In recent years, many employers have adopted apparently freer practices, notably in allowing special consideration for workers in the South East, where labour is scarce and housing is expensive. Walsh and Brown (1991) observe, however, that this response has been piecemeal, and does not constitute a new enthusiasm for the principle of region-specific pay awards based on local labour market conditions. In general, both free competition and the existence of employers' organizations serve to equalize the rates of remuneration across firms. This means that the main sources of inter-regional variation in wage rates in Britain have traditionally been small firms and differences in industry mix.

It is usual for unions and employers to bargain over pay deals which are of twelve months in duration. There are exceptions to this rule, of course, and these exceptions have in recent years been getting more common, especially in cases where bargains have been late in being struck. Moreover, many issues which do not (directly) concern pay (such as tea breaks, working hours, overtime rates) are negotiated much less frequently than once a year.

In cases of impasse between a union and an employer, both sides may, at any stage in the negotiation process, agree to take the dispute to arbitration. In such cases, the parties normally agree beforehand that the arbiter's decision will be binding. A strike, if one occurs, therefore normally precedes arbitration in the UK. The conditions under which a strike can legally take place have changed significantly over the last twelve years; these changes are discussed later in this section. Since the *Simmons* v. *Hoover* case of 1977, the law has regarded a strike as constituting a breach of contract on the part of the union. Employers may therefore dismiss striking workers and can employ alternative labour for the duration of the strike. Within a period of three months the employer may not selectively re-employ workers who have been dismissed in this way (unless the strike is unendorsed by the union) – either all sacked workers must be re-employed or none. If the employer breaks this rule then unfair dismissal charges may be made. After the period of three months has expired, however, the employer may legally engage in the selective re-employment of dismissed workers. The dismissal of workers by a firm is similar in effect to a lock-out, though in the latter instance even non-strikers are prevented from working during the period of the dispute. In the UK, lock-outs are included in the data on industrial stoppages; no separate data are collected.

Another important aspect of industrial relations is that of employee participation. In the UK, this form of industrial democracy is not legally required, but various tax incentives have been introduced in order to encourage firms to set up share ownership schemes and profit-related pay. Since 1982 firms employing over 250 workers have been required by law to report annually to the authorities on progress made in the field of employee participation; this, of course, represents only the mildest form of encouragement. In view of all this, it is hardly surprising that worker participation has not been widely adopted in the UK. The available evidence suggests that the economic effects of such schemes are limited in any case – they have an insignificant impact on employment and remuneration levels, profitability and investment. They do, however, appear to improve productivity (Blanchflower, 1991).

We saw earlier that the proportion of the labour force covered by closed shops declined markedly during the early 1980s. One reason for this was the changed legal status of closed shops in Britain. After the introduction of the 1980 Employment Act, new closed shops could only be created after a ballot of the workforce, and workers who did not wish to join the union were given protection against dismissal or discrimination. These provisions were extended to existing closed shops in 1984. In 1988, the post-entry closed shop was effectively outlawed, since individuals are now protected against dismissal for non-union membership in all circumstances. Finally, in 1990 it became illegal for employers to discriminate between union and non-union members in hiring – that is, the pre-entry closed shop became illegal.

The effective abolition of closed shops is an example of legal changes which have increased the voice of individual workers at the expense of the collective voice of the unions. Another example concerns the provision in the 1988 Act which ensures that a union cannot discipline individual members who choose not to participate in a strike or other dispute which has been legitimized by majority vote. Clearly this change in the law weakens the hand of the union during a dispute.

At the same time, the circumstances in which a union can call a strike have been changed by law. Since 1984, a secret ballot of members must be conducted before a strike can take place; any strike which occurs otherwise can be stopped by the employer concerned by appeal to the courts. Since 1988 individual union members have the right to restrain the union from striking prior to conducting a secret ballot. In 1991, a Green Paper was published which argued in favour of changing the law once more; this would require postal ballots (rather than secret ballots at the workplace), and would require a union to give a week's notice in advance of any strike action.

Before 1980, trade unions had no legal entity. That meant that the unions enjoyed immunity from civil law action. In 1982 these immunities were withdrawn. (The individual immunity of trade union officials acting in their capacities as representatives of the union had been withdrawn two years earlier.) The effect of withdrawing these immunities on the ability of the unions to perform their traditional role has been dramatic. Once the unions had a legal entity, it became possible for a union to be sued for damages when acting unlawfully. This inevitably put union funds at risk through court orders and sequestrations. As an example of the impact of such changes, it is instructive to consider the National Union of Seamen – this union merged with the National Union of Railwaymen largely as a result of the crippling legal penalties of a dispute at P&O Ferries.

The scope of union strike activity has also been reduced by recent changes. After 1980, employers could restrain secondary action; this severely limited the ability of a union to picket or boycott a firm which supplied inputs (say) to the employer directly involved in a dispute. Moreover a code of practice was introduced which aimed to limit the number of pickets operating at the premises of the firm directly involved. In 1990, it became illegal to engage in any form of secondary action.

The changes listed above have contributed to a weakening of the unions' position in bargaining. They have been credited for the decline in union membership, the decrease in strike activity, and the increasingly positive perception of unions' contribution to the economy in the eyes of the public. Whether these are truly the effects of legislation remains to be seen. As we saw earlier, there are many reasons why the number of trade unionists has declined; the popularity of the strike as an industrial weapon declined partly as a result of the protracted miners' dispute of 1984–5; and the popular acclaim more recently enjoyed by the unions might simply be the consequence of a period of inactivity caused by factors other than legal changes.

6.5   The Social Chapter of the Maastricht Treaty

At Maastricht in December 1991, a summit meeting of leaders of the member states of the European Community (EC) reached agreement on the future development of the Community. The discussions which led to the signing of the Treaty of Maastricht included debate on the Social Chapter, the provisions of which will have widespread implications for the conduct of labour market policy in Europe. This is likely to remain true despite the outcome of the Danish referendum, which cast doubt on the ratification of the Treaty. The Social Chapter is based upon the earlier Social Charter, which was adopted as a solemn declaration by eleven states in 1989. Eleven states subscribed also to the Social Chapter. The twelfth state, in both cases, was the UK. Although the UK is not committed to the pursuit of these EC social policies, it is nonetheless important to examine the thrust of the Social Chapter in some detail. Competition in the labour market between the UK, on the one hand, and the rest of the EC, on the other, will ensure that (in the long run) many of the social policies adopted by the UK will converge on those pursued elsewhere in the Community.

The eleven states intend to co-ordinate numerous aspects of social and labour market policy. Workers will have freedom of movement between member states; within any state they will have exactly the same rights to work as the natives of that state. Minimum reference criteria concerning holiday entitlements, overtime, length of the working week, and pay are to be developed and observed. Equality of labour market opportunities across the sexes will be guaranteed. Means of promoting worker participation and consultation in industry will be encouraged. The welfare payment systems of the member states will converge over time on a common set of objectives; the elderly will be guaranteed pensions; the disabled will receive help in the form of transport assistance and training facilities. The freedom of workers to join or not to join a trade union will be guaranteed, and unions' right to strike will be protected. The normal minimum age of entry to the labour market will be set at 16 years, and young workers will be assured access to training opportunities. Indeed, vocational training will be available throughout individuals' working lives. Schemes designed to promote health, protection and safety at work will be encouraged.

The principle of subsidiarity – that the EC should involve itself only in matters with which it can deal more effectively than the governments of individual states – is enshrined in the Social Chapter. This might, in practice, limit the ability of the Community to enforce legislation in the social sphere. Nevertheless, two issues in particular have been of concern to the UK government in discussions about the Social Chapter. These are the minimum wage and the maximum length of the working week.

Basic economic theory suggests that, other things being equal, the introduction of a minimum wage designed to raise the remuneration of those on very low pay would reduce the demand for labour. Therefore unemployment would rise. The justification for the introduction of a minimum wage policy rests, therefore, on a value judgement: is the relief from poverty brought about by raising the wage of some workers sufficient to offset the unemployment forced upon others? The reader's opinion on this issue inevitably depends both upon the extent to which poverty is eased by the proposed policy and on the extent by which unemployment would rise. Unfortunately there is little clear-cut evidence on either issue. Minford and Ashton (1991) use the Liverpool macroeconomic model to estimate that

TABLE 5.30
Average Weekly Hours Worked per Person Employed

State	Hours
Belgium	38.5
Denmark	35.7
France	39.2
Germany	39.1
Greece	43.7
Ireland	43.2
Italy	39.8
Luxembourg	40.1
Netherlands	33.2
Portugal	43.8
Spain	41.2
United Kingdom	38.9

Source: European Economy, **50**, December 1991, p. 135.

introducing a minimum wage at 50% of average male earnings would raise the wages of the low paid by some 8%. However, it would also raise unemployment by 500,000. These figures may be compared with those obtained by Gregg (1990), who uses the National Institute model to estimate the effect of the introduction of a similar minimum wage. He finds that, five years after the introduction of the policy, average real earnings across the economy would, as a result of the wage floor, be nearly 2% higher than they otherwise would have been. Meanwhile, unemployment would be increased by some 60,000. So while commentators agree that unemployment would rise in response to the imposition of a minimum wage, the estimates are a long way apart from each other.

If Minford and Ashton's estimates are reasonably accurate, many neutral observers will consider that the price, in terms of jobs, of the minimum wage policy is too high. The same observers might, however, be in favour of introducing a minimum wage if Gregg's estimates are closer to the mark.

The average length of the working week in various EC states is reported in Table 5.30. As can be seen, the variation across member states is quite marked, and the UK has the fourth shortest average working week of the twelve states. The table does not provide information about the spread of working weeks within each state; if the variation between workers is greater in the UK than elsewhere, then any regulation concerning maximum length of working week could still affect the UK more severely than other member states.

The shape of UK social and labour market policy in the next few years will clearly differ somewhat from that of our European partners. But the pressures for convergence will be strong. The differences may make the UK more attractive to investors than otherwise would have been the case, but at the same time the rest of the EC will become more attractive to mobile labour. Both these effects will tend in the longer term to make working conditions more homogeneous than at present throughout the EC. Whether the UK eventually subscribes to the Social Chapter or not, developments in the rest of the EC will have a substantial impact on British labour market conditions.

REFERENCES

Beenstock, M. and Whitbread, C. (1988) 'Explaining changes in the union mark-up for male manual workers in Great Britain, 1953–83', *British Journal of Industrial Relations*, **26**, 327–38.

Begg, I. (1990) 'The Single European Market and the UK Regions', *Cambridge Regional Economic Review*, Department of Land Economy and PA Cambridge Economic Consultants, Cambridge.

Blackaby, D.H. (1986) 'An analysis of the male racial earnings differential in the UK', *Applied Economics*, **18**, 1233–42.

Blackaby, D.H., Murphy, P.D. and Sloane, P.J. (1991) 'Union membership, collective bargaining coverage and the trade union mark-up for Britain', *Economics Letters*, **36**, 203–8.

Blanchflower, D.G. (1984) 'Union relative wage effects', *British Journal of Industrial Relations*, **22**, 311–32.

Blanchflower, D.G. (1991) 'The economic effects of profit sharing in Great Britain', *International Journal of Manpower*, **12**(1), 3–9.

Blanchflower, D. G. and Cubbin, J. (1986) 'Strike propensities at the British workplace', *Oxford Bulletin of Economics and Statistics*, **48**, 19–40.

Blanchflower, D. G. and Oswald, A. J. (1989) 'The wage curve', Centre for Labour Economics Discussion Paper 340, London School of Economics; summary version published (1990) *Scandinavian Journal of Economics*, **92**, 215–35.

Brown, C. (1984) *Black and White Britain: the Third PSI Survey* (Heinemann, London).

Carruth, A. and Disney, R. (1988) 'Where have two million trade union members gone?', *Economica*, **55**, 1–20.

Daly, M. (1991) 'VAT registrations and deregistrations in 1990', *Employment Gazette*, November, 579–88.

Dolton, P.J. (1992) 'The early careers of 1980 graduates: work histories, job tenure, career mobility and occupational choice', Department of Employment, London.

Freeman, R. and Pelletier, J. (1990) 'The impact of industrial relations legislation on British union density', *British Journal of Industrial Relations*, **28**, 141–64.

Gregg, P. (1990) 'A national minimum wage', *National Institute Economic Review*, **134**, 60–3.

Ingram, P., Metcalf, D. and Wadsworth, J. (1991) 'Strike incidence and duration in British manufacturing industry in the 1980s', Centre for Economic Performance Discussion Paper 48, London School of Economics.

Johnes, G. and Taylor, J. (1989) 'Ethnic minorities in the graduate labour market', *New Community*, **15**, 527–36.

Layard, P.R.G. and Nickell, S.J. (1986) 'Unemployment in Britain', *Economica*, **53**, S121–S169.

Millward, N. and Stevens, M. (1986) *British Workplace Industrial Relations, 1980–84* (Gower, Aldershot).

Minford, P. (1983) *Unemployment: Cause and Cure* (Basil Blackwell, Oxford).

Minford, A.P.L. and Ashton, P. (1991) 'Effects in the UK of EC wage proposals in the Social Charter', *International Journal of Manpower*, **12**(2), 20–3.

Shah, A. (1983) 'Professional earnings in the UK', *Economica*, **50**, 451–62.

Stewart, M. (1983) 'Relative earnings and individual union membership in the UK', *Economica*, **50**, 111–25.

Stewart, M.B. (1991) 'Union wage differentials in the face of changes in the economic and legal environment', *Economica*, **58**, 155–72.

Taylor, J. (1991) *Reviving the Regions*, Fabian Society Pamphlet 551, London.

Tzannatos, Z. and Zabalza, A. (1984) 'The anatomy of the rise of British female relative wages in the 1970s', *British Journal of Industrial Relations*, **22**, 177–94.

Walsh, J. and Brown, W. (1991) 'Regional earnings and pay flexibility', in Bowen, A. and Mayhew, K. (eds.) *Reducing Regional Inequalities* (Kogan Page, London).

Statistical Appendix

TABLE A-1

UK GROSS DOMESTIC PRODUCT, EXPENDITURE (at 1985 prices), 1980–91 (£m)

Year	Consumers' Expenditure Total	Of which, Durables	General Government Final Consumption	Gross Domestic Capital Formation Total	Of which, Dwellings	Value of Physical Increase in Stocks and Work in Progress	Exports of Goods and Services	Total Final Expenditure at Market Prices[2]	Imports of Goods and Services	Adjustment to Factor Cost[1]	Gross Domestic Product at Factor Cost[2]
1980	195 825	15 417	70 872	53 416	12 379	−3 371	88 726	405 285	80 781	45 305	279 232
1981	196 011	15 707	71 086	48 298	10 247	−3 200	88 064	399 644	78 522	44 246	276 868
1982	197 980	16 504	71 672	50 915	10 899	−1 281	88 798	407 791	82 348	44 895	280 553
1983	206 932	19 448	73 089	53 476	12 247	1 357	90 589	425 443	87 709	46 355	291 379
1984	210 254	19 253	73 792	58 034	12 550	1 084	96 525	439 689	96 394	48 347	294 948
1985	217 618	20 251	73 805	60 353	11 854	821	102 208	454 805	98 866	49 367	306 572
1986	231 172	22 023	75 106	61 813	12 901	737	107 052	475 880	105 662	52 312	317 906
1987	243 279	23 894	76 034	67 753	13 475	1 158	113 094	501 318	113 916	55 539	332 179
1988	261 330	27 114	76 486	76 648	15 117	4 031	113 150	531 645	127 964	58 312	345 918
1989	270 575	29 363	77 182	81 845	14 565	2 668	117 929	550 199	137 389	59 974	353 420
1990	272 823	27 742	79 574	79 901	12 631	−399	123 773	555 672	138 795	60 542	356 848
1991	268 202	25 731	81 462	71 706	11 268	−2 925	124 658	543 103	134 774	59 981	348 356

Sources: BB, 1991; *ET,* April 1992.
Notes:
[1] This represents taxes on expenditure less subsidies valued at constant prices.
[2] Expenditure estimate: for years up to and including 1982, totals may differ from the sum of their components.

TABLE A-2

UK PRICES, EARNINGS AND PRODUCTIVITY, 1980–91: Index Numbers (1985=100)

Year	Retail Prices (all items)	Average Earnings (whole economy)[1]	Average Earnings (manufacturing)[1]	Average Earnings (services)[1]	Wages and Salaries per unit of output (whole economy)	Wages and Salaries per unit of output (manufacturing)	Output per Person Employed (whole economy)	Output per Person-Hour Worked (manufacturing)
	1	2	3	4	5	6	7	8
1980	70.7	65.0	61.5	66.1	75.9	80.1	87.0	78.5
1981	79.1	73.3	69.6	75.4	83.3	87.5	88.9	82.3
1982	85.9	80.2	77.4	81.3	87.3	91.3	92.6	86.7
1983	89.8	87.0	84.4	88.4	90.6	91.7	96.5	93.4
1984	94.3	92.2	91.7	94.0	94.8	94.5	97.6	97.5
1985	100.0	100.0	100.0	100.0	100.0	100.0	100.0	100.0
1986	103.4	107.9	107.7	107.7	105.2	104.0	103.2	103.8
1987	107.7	116.3	116.3	116.0	110.2	105.9	106.3	109.4
1988	113.0	126.4	126.2	126.2	118.4	108.6	107.2	115.3
1989	121.8	137.9	137.2	137.4	129.8	113.6	106.9	120.2
1990	133.3	151.3	150.1	150.7	142.5	123.4	107.3	121.6
1991	141.1	163.4	162.4	162.2	153.4	133.5	107.7	123.1

Sources: ET(AS), 1991; *ET*, April 1992.

Note:
[1] The samples on which the average earnings indices are calculated were changed in 1988. The figures shown for 1989–91 have been obtained by rescaling the 1988-based values for these years by the ratio of the 1985 to 1988 based indices for which overlapping values are available for one year (1988).

TABLE A-3

UK PERSONAL INCOME, EXPENDITURE AND SAVING, 1980–91 (£m, current prices)

| | *PERSONAL INCOME BEFORE TAX* | | | | | | |
Year	*Wages and Salaries and Forces Pay*	*Employers' Contributions*	*Current Grants from Public Authorities*	*Other Personal Income*	*Total[1]*	*UK Taxes on Income (Payments)*	*Social Security Contributions*
	1	*2*	*3*	*4*	*5*	*6*	*7*
1980	119 149	18 634	25 524	38 659	201 966	25 683	13 939
1981	128 037	21 700	31 242	42 840	223 819	28 949	15 916
1982	136 462	22 376	36 584	47 680	243 102	31 366	18 095
1983	145 737	24 110	39 856	52 598	262 301	33 180	20 780
1984	155 544	25 339	43 020	57 471	281 374	34 736	22 322
1985	169 214	26 494	46 813	62 519	305 040	37 774	24 210
1986	183 917	27 812	50 984	69 760	332 473	40 805	26 165
1987	200 143	29 389	52 494	76 738	358 764	43 386	28 645
1988	223 250	32 107	54 087	89 284	398 728	48 290	32 108
1989	248 537	35 048	56 793	101 255	441 633	53 517	33 025
1990	275 344	38 713	61 917	115 011	490 985	61 869	34 776
1991	289 791	41 074	71 701	118 914	521 480	63 857	36 837

Sources: ET, April 1992; *BB*, 1991.

Notes:

[1] Before providing for depreciation and stock appreciation.

[2] Before providing for depreciation, stock appreciation and additions to tax reserves.
   Column 5 = 1 + 2 + 3 + 4.
   Column 9 = 5 − 6 − 7 − 8.
   Column 12 = 13 − 10.
   Column 14 = 9 − 13.

[3] Includes Community Charge payments.

Other Current Deductions[3]	Total Personal Disposable Income[2]	CONSUMERS' EXPENDITURE				PERSONAL SAVINGS		
		Durable Goods		Other				
		Amount (£m)	As % of PDI	Amount (£m)	Total	Amount (£m)[2]	As % PDI	Year
8	9	10	11	12	13	14	15	
1 308	161 036	13 495	8.4	126 113	139 608	21 428	13.3	1980
1 234	177 720	13 942	7.8	141 470	155 412	22 308	12.6	1981
1 387	192 254	15 439	8.0	155 211	170 650	21 604	11.2	1982
1 413	206 928	18 250	8.8	168 778	187 028	19 900	9.6	1983
1 498	222 818	18 636	8.4	180 789	199 425	23 393	10.5	1984
1 684	241 372	20 251	8.4	197 367	217 618	23 754	9.8	1985
1 909	263 594	22 880	8.7	218 425	241 275	22 319	8.5	1986
2 128	284 608	26 269	9.2	238 611	264 880	19 728	6.9	1987
2 347	315 983	31 934	10.1	266 862	298 796	17 187	5.4	1988
3 060	352 031	35 838	10.2	291 548	327 386	24 645	7.0	1989
11 235	383 105	34 990	9.1	313 538	348 528	34 577	9.0	1990
10 757	410 029	33 610	8.2	334 481	368 091	41 938	10.2	1991

TABLE A-4

UK POPULATION, WORKING POPULATION, UNEMPLOYMENT AND VACANICES, 1980–91 (thousands)

Year	Total Population (mid-year estimate)	Workforce[1]	Workforce in employment[2]	Unemployed[3]	Unemployment Rate (%)[4]	Vacancies at Jobcentres[5]
	1	2	3	4	5	6
1980	56 330	26 759	25 301	1 298.3	4.8	134.2
1981	56 352	26 697	24 323	2 123.2	7.9	91.1
1982	56 306	26 610	23 889	2 522.8	9.5	113.9
1983	56 347	26 633	23 611	2 776.9	10.4	137.3
1984	56 460	27 309	24 226	2 901.4	10.7	150.2
1985	56 618	27 743	24 530	3 027.9	10.9	162.1
1986	56 736	27 877	24 559	3 097.9	11.1	188.8
1987	56 930	28 077	25 084	2 806.5	10.0	235.4
1988	57 065	28 347	25 922	2 274.9	8.1	248.7
1989	57 236	28 486	26 693	1 784.4	6.3	219.5
1990	57 411	28 509	26 889	1 661.7	5.8	173.7
1991	n.a.	28 476	26 172	2 227.1	8.1	118.0

Sources: ET, April 1992; *ET(AS)*, 1992; *EG*, April 1992.
Notes:
[1] The workforce is the sum of those in employment (including self-employed), the unemployed (claimants), the armed forces and participants in work-related government training programmes. Mid-year figures.
[2] Employees in employment, self-employed, armed forces, those on work-related government training programmes and the unemployed (claimants).
[3] Annual average of seasonally adjusted figures pertaining to claimants aged 18 or over. Wider definitions are inconsistent through time. See *EG*, December 1988.
[4] Unemployment as per cent of workforce.
[5] Average of monthly figures.

TABLE A-5

UK GENERAL GOVERNMENT: CURRENT ACCOUNT, 1980–1990, £m

	1980	1981	1982	1983	1984	1985	1986	1987	1988	1989	1990
CURRENT RECEIPTS											
Taxes on income	31 002	36 134	40 282	43 344	46 655	51 643	52 239	55 702	61 852	70 275	77 262
Taxes on expenditure	36 474	42 465	46 467	49 500	52 576	56 592	62 947	69 074	76 511	80 925	79 067
Social security contributions	13 939	15 916	18 095	20 780	22 322	24 210	26 165	28 642	32 108	33 025	34 775
Community Charge	–	–	–	–	–	–	–	–	–	619	8 811
Gross trading surplus[1]	180	236	216	50	–117	265	155	–75	–32	199	17
Rent etc.[2]	4 251	4 715	4 857	4 836	5 373	5 510	4 101	4 347	4 117	3 902	4 202
Interest and dividends, etc.	3 955	4 456	5 292	5 097	5 129	6 242	5 890	6 020	6 243	7 073	6 489
Miscellaneous current transfers	169	177	187	222	217	229	266	363	394	431	504
Imputed charge for consumption of non-trading capital	1 748	1 948	2 017	2 081	2 187	2 372	2 583	2 804	3 110	3 448	3 693
Total	91 718	106 047	117 413	125 910	134 342	147 063	154 346	166 877	184 303	199 897	214 820
CURRENT EXPENDITURE											
Current expenditure on goods and services	47 192	53 426	58 346	63 706	67 573	71 433	76 798	82 545	88 619	95 581	105 802
Non-trading capital consumption	1 748	1 948	2 017	2 081	2 187	2 372	2 583	2 804	3 110	3 448	3 693
Subsidies	5 719	6 369	5 811	6 269	7 537	7 225	6 187	6 173	5 940	5 692	6 217
Current grants to personal sector	25 524	31 242	36 584	39 856	43 020	46 813	50 984	52 494	54 087	56 793	61 983
Current grants paid abroad (net)	1 780	1 607	1 789	1 930	2 099	3 427	2 233	3 277	3 248	4 278	4 635
Debt interest	10 888	12 719	13 952	14 208	15 777	17 483	17 164	17 999	18 169	18 706	18 544
Total current expenditure	92 851	107 311	118 499	128 050	138 193	148 753	155 949	165 292	173 173	184 498	200 874
Balance: current surplus	–1 133	–1 264	–1 086	–2 140	–3 851	–1 690	–1 603	1 585	11 130	15 399	13 946
Total	91 718	106 047	117 413	125 910	134 342	147 063	154 346	166 877	184 303	199 897	214 820

Source: BB, 1991.

Notes:

1 Before providing for depreciation

2 Includes royalties and licence fees on oil and gas production

TABLE A-6

UK MONETARY AGGREGATES, PUBLIC SECTOR BORROWING REQUIREMENT (£m), INTEREST RATES AND EXCHANGE RATES, 1980–91

Year	The Wide Monetary Base M0[1,2]	M4[1,3]	Public Sector Borrowing Requirement	Yield on UK Treasury bills (%)	Gilts[4] (%)	Dollar Exchange Rate ($/£)[5]	Sterling Effective Exchange Rate[6]
	1	2	3	4	5	6	7
1980	11 647	114 133	11 786	13.58	13.78	2.3281	117.7
1981	11 923	137 817	10 507	15 39	14.74	2.0254	119.0
1982	12 298	154 794	4 868	9.96	12.88	1.7489	113.7
1983	13 035	174 302	11 574	9.04	10.80	1.5158	105.3
1984	13 777	199 203	10 300	9.33	10.69	1.3364	100.6
1985	14 288	225 066	7 445	11.49	10.62	1.2976	100.0
1986	15 025	261 211	2 499	10.94	9.87	1.4672	91.5
1987	15 661	302 809	−1 434	8.38	9.47	1.6392	90.1
1988	16 867	355 174	−11 868	12.91	9.36	1.7796	95.5
1989	17 827	422 891	−9 276	15.02	9.58	1.6383	92.6
1990	18 340	474 396	−2 132	13.50	11.08	1.7864	91.3
1991	18 859	501 890	7 651	10.45	9.92	1.7865	91.7

Sources: ET(AS), 1992; FS, April 1992.

Sources: ET(AS), 1992; *FS*, April 1992.
Notes:

1 Figures quoted are for the seasonally adjusted level as at the end of the last quarter of each year (average of Wednesday figures in December for M0).

2 The monetary base consists of notes and coins together with bankers' operational balances at the Bank of England.

3 M4 is a wide aggregate consisting of M3 together with deposits held at building societies (less building societies' holdings of notes and coin and bank deposits).

4 The yield on long-dated (20-year) British Government bonds.

5 Average of daily Telegraphic Transfer rates in London.

6 As calculated by the IMF; indexed on 1985 = 100. A decline in the index indicates an overall depreciation of sterling.

TABLE A-7

UK BALANCE OF PAYMENTS, 1980–91

CURRENT ACCCOUNT[1]

| Year | Visible Trade | | | Invisibles (balance) | | | | |
	Exports (f.o.b.)	Imports (f.o.b.)	Visible Balance	Services	Interest Profits and Dividends	Transfer	Total Invisible Balance	Current Balance
	1	2	3	4	5	6	7	8
1980	47 149	45 792	1 357	3 653	−182	−1 984	1 487	2 843
1981	50 668	46 416	3 252	3 792	1 251	−1 547	3 496	6 748
1982	55 331	53 421	1 910	3 022	1 460	−1 741	2 741	4 649
1983	60 700	62 237	−1 537	4 064	2 831	−1 593	5 302	3 765
1984	70 265	75 601	−5 336	4 519	4 357	−1 730	7 146	1 811
1985	77 991	81 336	−3 345	6 687	2 646	−3 111	6 222	2 878
1986	72 627	82 186	−9 559	6 808	5 096	−2 157	9 747	187
1987	79 153	90 735	−11 582	6 745	4 078	−3 400	7 423	−4 159
1988	80 346	101 970	−21 624	4 574	5 047	−3 518	6 103	−15 520
1989	92 389	116 987	−24 598	4 685	4 088	−4 578	4 195	−20 404
1990	102 036	120 653	−18 617	4 916	3 152	−4 897	3 171	−15 446
1991	103 704	113 823	−10 119	5 471	1 580	−1 332	5 719	−4 399

TRANSACTIONS IN UK EXTERNAL ASSETS AND LIABILITIES[1]

Year	Direct Investment		Portfolio Investment		Net Banking Trans-actions[2]	Official Reserves	Other Government Transactions	Other[3]	Net Transactions	Balancing Item
	UK Investment Overseas	Overseas Investment in UK	UK Investment Overseas	Overseas Investment in UK						
	9	10	11	12	13	14	15	16	17	18
1980	-4867	4355	-3310	1431	1385	-291	-423	-1953	-3940	917
1981	-6005	2932	-4467	257	-659	2419	-113	-1801	-7436	530
1982	-4091	3027	-7565	-11	3855	1421	248	598	-2519	-2130
1983	-5417	3386	-7350	1701	2850	607	-1062	724	-4562	797
1984	-6033	-181	-9759	1288	10431	908	-783	-3636	-7766	5955
1985	-8456	3865	-16755	9671	7419	-1758	-706	2639	-4082	1204
1986	-12038	4987	-22095	11785	10449	-2891	-331	2900	-7234	7047
1987	-19215	8478	7201	19210	2173	-12012	1033	-1059	5810	-1651
1988	-20880	10236	-8600	14387	14703	-2761	-60	2620	9645	5875
1989	-21521	17145	-31283	13239	16855	5440	1244	11796	12916	7488
1990	-8909	19031	-12052	5034	7924	-79	-519	3290	13722	1724
1991	-9805	11968	-29081	19499	8989	-2662	-3011	12923	8820	-4421

Sources: ET(AS), 1991; ET, April 1992.
Notes:
[1] All items listed represent a positive flow if not otherwise indicated; for transactions in assets and liabilities a positive flow represents an increase in UK assets (decrease in liabilities). The relationship between columns is as follows: Col 3 = Col 1 − Col 2; Col 7 = Cols 4 + 5 + 6; Col 8 = Col 3 + Col 7; Col 17 = Cols 9 + 10 + 11 + 12 + 13 + 14 + 15 + 16; Col 18 = (with sign reversed) Col 8 + Col 17.

[2] Borrowing from, less lending to, overseas residents by UK banks.

[3] Borrowing from, less lending to, overseas residents by UK residents other than banks and government.

TABLE A-8

PRODUCTION IN INDUSTRY, 1980–91 (Index Numbers, 1985 = 100)

	1980	1981	1982	1983	1984	1985	1986	1987	1988	1989	1990	1991
Energy	83.3	86.4	91.6	96.8	88.8	100.0	105.0	103.9	99.3	89.6	89.0	92.3
Manufacturing												
Food, drink and tobacco	99.0	97.3	98.8	99.5	100.5	100.0	101.3	103.2	105.1	105.1	105.5	105.5
Chemicals and man-made fibres	84.0	83.5	83.7	90.9	96.7	100.0	101.8	109.0	114.2	119.4	118.3	121.8
Metals	88.7	94.1	91.5	94.2	92.9	100.0	100.3	108.6	122.3	124.7	121.3	110.3
Engineering and allied inds.	96.2	88.3	89.3	92.6	96.5	100.0	100.2	103.7	112.3	119.9	119.7	110.0
Building materials	105.7	94.2	96.1	96.8	100.4	100.0	101.3	106.8	117.3	120.1	113. 4	103.1
Textiles, clothing	98.1	91.0	89.6	92.6	96.1	100.0	100.7	103.7	102.0	98.3	95.9	87.7
Other manufacturing	101.0	94.1	91.7	93.6	98.4	100.0	104.5	115.0	126.6	132.3	133.2	126.4
Total Manufacturing	96.7	91.0	91.2	93.8	97.4	100.0	101.3	106.6	114.1	118.9	118.4	112.2
Consumer goods	96.5	93.1	92.6	95.3	98.1	100.0	101.2	106.4	112.0	114.5	114.0	109.7
Investment goods	97.0	88.6	89.6	91.8	95.2	100.0	100.6	103.0	111.1	120.4	121.4	114.4
Intermediate goods	88.8	88.1	90.0	95.5	93.2	100.0	103.6	106.4	107.9	104.2	103.1	101.6

Source: NIER, February 1992; MDS, April 1992. The headings are those of the 1985 Standard Industrial Classification (SIC).

Table A-9
GDP BY INDUSTRY[1]

	1980		1985		1990	
	£m	%	£m	%	£m	%
Agriculture, forestry & fishing	4 247	2.1	5 725	1.9	7 102	1.5
Energy & water supply	19 416	9.7	32 696	10.7	24 334	5.1
Manufacturing	53 588	26.8	73 432	23.9	106 995	22.4
Construction	12 269	6.1	17 904	5.8	36 085	7.6
Distribution, hotels & catering: repairs	25 929	12.9	40 839	13.3	70 151	14.7
Transport & communication	14 584	7.3	21 725	7.1	34 031	7.1
Banking, finance, insurance, business services and leasing	14 782[2]	7.4	29 729[2]	9.7	60 520[2]	12.7
Ownership of dwellings	12 147	6.1	18 175	5.9	30 719	6.4
Public administration, national defence and compulsory social security	14 547	7.3	21 466	7	31 524	6.6
Education and health services	18 023	9	26 567	8.7	45 143	9.5
Other services	10 710	5.3	18 602	6.1	30 983	6.5
GDP at factor cost (income definition)	200 242		306 860		477 587	

Source: BB, 1991.
Notes:
[1] The contribution of each industry to GDP before providing for depreciation but after providing for stock appreciation. Percentages may not add to 100 due to rounding.
[2] After deducting the adjustment for financial services.

TABLE A-10

REGIONAL UNEMPLOYMENT RATES (%), 1980–91

	1980	1981	1982	1983	1984	1985	1986	1987	1988	1989	1990	1991
South East	3.1	5.5	6.7	7.5	7.8	8.0	8.2	7.1	5.4	3.9	4.0	6.9
East Anglia	3.8	6.3	7.4	8.0	7.9	8.0	8.1	6.8	5.2	3.6	3.7	5.8
South West	4.5	6.8	7.8	8.7	9.0	9.3	9.5	8.2	6.2	4.5	4.4	7.2
East Midlands	4.5	7.4	8.4	9.5	9.8	9.9	9.9	9.0	7.1	5.4	5.1	7.3
West Midlands	5.5	10.0	11.9	12.9	12.7	12.7	12.6	11.1	8.9	6.6	6.0	8.4
Yorkshire and Humberside	5.3	8.9	10.4	11.4	11.7	12.0	12.4	11.3	9.3	7.4	6.7	8.6
North West	6.5	10.2	12.1	13.4	13.6	13.8	13.9	12.7	10.4	8.5	7.7	9.4
North	8.0	11.8	13.3	14.6	15.3	15.4	15.2	14.0	11.9	9.9	8.7	10.2
Scotland	7.0	9.9	11.3	12.3	12.6	12.9	13.3	13.0	11.3	9.3	8.1	8.8
Wales	6.9	10.5	12.1	12.9	13.2	13.8	13.9	12.5	9.8	7.3	6.6	8.7
Northern Ireland	9.4	12.7	14.4	15.5	15.9	16.1	17.6	17.6	15.6	14.6	13.4	13.9
United Kingdom	5.1	8.1	9.5	10.5	10.7	10.9	11.1	10.0	8.1	6.3	5.8	8.1

Sources: Unemployment Statistics – seasonally adjusted series, *EG*, Historical Supplement No. 1, April 1989; *EG* April 1992.
Note: The unemployment rate is the number of unemployed claimants aged 18 and over expressed as a percentage of the estimated workforce (employed employees and unemployed claimants + self-employed + HM Forces).

Index

small firms, 106, 327
Small Firms Loan Guarantee Scheme, 271,
    327
Small Firms Merit Award for Research and
    Technology (SMART), 289
Small Firms Service, 331
Smith, A., 337
Smith, P., 41n
'Social Chapter,' 360–364
'Social Charter,' 361
'Social Contract', 62–63
Social Fund, 348
social security, 346–348
social security benefits, 121, 346–349
Social Security, Department of, 348
Society of Shuttlemakers, 351
Soete, L., 206n
South Africa, 200
Soviet Union, the end of, 234
Spain:
    capital movements in EC, 208
    entry to EC, 169
    and ERM, 174
    hours worked, 306
    and VAT, 140
Spanos, A., 18n
Special Drawing Rights (SDRs), 97, 153,
    228–229
special development areas, 134
State Earnings Related Pension Scheme
    (SERPS), 131
steel industry:
    nationalization, 270
    privatization, 270
    strikes, 356
sterilization, 159, 190
sterling: (see also exchange rate)
    appreciation, 187, 189, 207
    denominated bonds, 86
    denominated UK trade, 149
    deposits in foreign banks, 90
    depreciation, 187
    ECU exchange rate, 196
    EER, 177–178
    and EMS and ERM, 174–175, 189–200
      passim
    floating, 161, 164, 172–173, 227
    interbank market, 85
    investments, 86
    management of, 158, 189
    money market, 85, 95–97
    1967 devaluation, 161, 163
    as a 'petrocurrency', 186–188 *passim*
Stevens, M., 351
Stewart, M. J., 38n, 62n
Stiglitz, J. E., 214n
Stock Exchange: (*see also* London as an
    international financial centre)
    Dublin and Cork, 106

    and eurobonds, 108
    listing, 106
    and 1986 reforms, 108–111
    and restrictive practices 268
    and technical progress, 109
    and investment trusts, 114
    and unlisted securities, 106
Stock Exchange Automated Quotations
    (SEAQ), 110
Stock Exchange Takeover Code, 267
stock-adjustment principle, 20–23,
stockbrokers and jobbers, 106–110 *passim*
stocks:
    appreciation adjustment, 6
    business cycles and, 12
    and stockbuilding, 23–25
Stolper, W. F., 209n
Strikes, 38, 62, 354–357
subsidiarity, 361
Sugden, R., 254n
Sumner, M. T., 18n, 47n, 53n
superannuation funds, 104 (*see also* pension
    funds)
Supply Estimates, 125, 126
Swann, D., 291
Sweden, employment policy, 333

'tap stock', 106
tarriffs, 210–213
Taylor, J., 326, 343
taxation:
    allowances, 129–130
    balance of payments and, 58
    and budgets, 125–129
    budget deficits and, 59, 60, 61
    capital gains tax (CGT), 135
    capital transfer tax (CTT), 136–137
    community charge, 142
    corporation tax, 132–134
    council tax, 142–144
    customs duties, 139–140
    Customs and Excise, 125
    demand management and, 58, 72–73
    depreciation, 133–134
    and development areas, 134
    on employment,58
    estate duty, 136
    and EC, 138–139, 144–147
    excise duties, 139–140
    exemptions from VAT, 138
    and exports, 138–140 *passim*
    and imports, 138–140 *passim*
    income tax, 128–132
    inflation and, 66, 129
    inheritance tax, 55, 135–137
    Inland Revenue, 125
    input tax, 137
    local taxes, 140–144
    marginal rates, 131, 132–3